D1571223

Dewey's Logical Theory

THE VANDERBILT LIBRARY OF AMERICAN
PHILOSOPHY offers interpretive perspectives on the
historical roots of American philosophy and on present
innovative developments in American thought, including
studies of values, naturalism, social philosophy, cultural
criticism, and applied ethics.

Series Editors
Herman J. Saatkamp, Jr., General Editor
(Indiana University Purdue University Indianapolis)
Cornelis de Waal, Associate Editor
(Indiana University Purdue University Indianapolis)

Editorial Advisory Board
Kwame Anthony Appiah (Harvard)
Larry Hickman (Southern Illinois University)
John Lachs (Vanderbilt)
John J. McDermott (Texas A&M)
Joel Porte (Cornell)
Hilary Putnam (Harvard)
Ruth Anna Putnam (Wellesley)
Beth J. Singer (Brooklyn College)
John J. Stuhr (Pennsylvania State)

Dewey's Logical Theory

New Studies and Interpretations

Edited by
F. Thomas Burke,
D. Micah Hester,
and Robert B. Talisse

Foreword by
Larry A. Hickman

Vanderbilt University Press
Nashville

McConnell Library Radford University

© 2002 Vanderbilt University Press
All rights reserved
First Edition 2002

This book is printed on acid-free paper.
Manufactured in the United States of America

Library of Congress Cataloging-in-Publication Data

Dewey's logical theory : new studies and interpretations /
edited by F. Thomas Burke, D. Micah Hester, and Robert B.
Talisse ; foreword by Larry Hickman.
    p. cm. — (The Vanderbilt library of American philosophy)
Includes bibliographical references and index.
    ISBN 0-8265-1368-9 (cloth : alk. paper)
    ISBN 0-8265-1394-8 (pbk. : alk. paper)
1. Dewey, John, 1859–1952—Logic. I. Burke, F. Thomas, 1950–
II. Hester, D. Micah. III. Talisse, Robert B. IV. Series.
B945.D44 D496 2002
160'.92—dc21

                                         2001005614

Contents

**Part III
Values and Social Inquiry   237**

Foreword

There is probably no better measure of the resurgence of interest in John Dewey's version of pragmatism than the book you now hold in your hand. Even as recently as a decade ago, it hardly seemed possible that a volume of thirteen original essays—fourteen, counting the excellent introduction—could be dedicated to his work on logic. The issue of commercial viability aside, there simply did not appear to be enough expertise or interest among a sufficient number of Dewey scholars to produce such a collection.

With the exception of the ideas he put forth in *Knowing and the Known*, which was published in 1949 as a result of his collaboration with Arthur F. Bentley, Dewey's essays and books on logic have perhaps elicited less understanding and provided more occasion for offense than any other area of his thought. Apart from some remarkable exceptions, which include studies by H. S. Thayer, Gail Kennedy, Ralph Sleeper, and Thomas Burke, responses to Dewey's instrumentalist logic have tended to range from studied indifference, to wincing incomprehension, to unvarnished hostility. Along the way there has also been a fair amount of damning with faint praise.

The response of fellow pragmatist Charles Sanders Peirce to Dewey's 1903 *Studies in Logical Theory* provides an interesting case in point. In an acerbic letter dated June 9, 1904, Peirce accused Dewey of having yielded to a "debauch of loose reasoning." As if that were not enough to clarify his position, he then went on to intimate that Dewey's moral fiber had been weakened by having lived in Chicago for too long—that is, that he had lost his sense of dyads such as true and false, right and wrong. To his great credit, however, the normally pugnacious Peirce appears to have had second thoughts about posting his incendiary remarks. There is evidence that his letter is a draft of one that he never mailed.

Dewey's 1916 *Essays in Experimental Logic* was greeted with charges that he had mangled not only the history of logic but its present as well. In an essay published in the *Journal of Philosophy, Psychology, and Scientific Meth-

ods, for example, Daniel Sommer Robinson issued a sharp response to chapter 14, "Logic of Judgments of Practice." He charged Dewey with having misunderstood the logical works of both Aristotle and Hegel, having embraced a version of psychologism, and, even worse, having engaged in a "loose use of the term *judgment*." The term *loose* seems to have been a favorite among Dewey's critics.

In his own now-famous review of the 1916 *Essays*, Bertrand Russell raised the stakes to a level that could hardly be surpassed. After a brief complaint that philosophical discussions had become too "eristic," or polemical, he continued by asserting that "what he [Dewey] calls 'logic' does not seem to me to be a part of logic at all; I should call it part of psychology." Apparently afraid that his readers might have missed his point, he added that "in the sense in which I use the word, there is hardly any 'logic' in the book." Given the reputation of psychologism among the adherents of Russell's logicist program, this was, of course, tantamount to charging that Dewey had exhibited loose reasoning.

Dewey's ideas fared little better in the hands of those who attempted to respond to his 1938 *Logic: The Theory of Inquiry*. May Broadbeck, for example, writing in the *Journal of Philosophy*, was determined to expose what she termed "Dewey's empiricist orthodoxy" by demonstrating that his views were covertly Hegelian and thus "fundamentally rationalistic." Then, rising to a kind of critical crescendo, she charged Dewey with holding that laws of nature are "'analytic' in the full Kantian sense of the word." Ernest Nagel, writing the introduction to the critical edition of the 1938 *Logic* some years later, may have had Broadbeck's remarks in mind when he argued that "no analytic proposition, in the contemporary technical sense, would be tested in the way frequently proposed by Dewey for his universals" (LW12:xviii).

Given the long line of interpretive essays such as the ones I have just described, in which the main points of Dewey's innovative treatment of logic have for the most part been either misunderstood or ignored, the material presented in this volume reflects a kind of sea change in Dewey studies. It is not so much that these essays are uniformly positive or uncritical, for they are certainly not that. Their importance lies rather in the fact that serious scholarship on Dewey's logic, building on the solid advances won over the years by Thayer, Kennedy, Sleeper, Burke, and others, seems finally to have reached a critical mass. Perhaps even more important, when taken together these essays establish an important way-marker along a road that Dewey hoped his students would follow. They seek to push Dewey's ideas forward: to work out the consequences of his logic—his theory of inquiry—for a living philosophy.

In his introduction to the critical edition of *Logic: The Theory of Inquiry*, Ernest Nagel proposed that Dewey had looked upon his logical theory "as a hypothesis, the detailed confirmation of which would have to be supplied by others in the future" (LW12:x). The publication of this volume provides evidence that the future that Dewey envisioned, and hoped for, has now arrived.

—Larry A. Hickman

Editors' Introduction

Dewey's First and Last Love

In 1938, John Dewey completed the mammoth volume *Logic: The Theory of Inquiry*, which some would consider the "crowning work" of his career (e.g., Edman 1938, 5). Although Dewey had published dozens of articles in the philosophy of logic, some of the most important of which were assembled in the 1916 *Essays in Experimental Logic*, the *Logic* of 1938 features a unity of expression and fullness of vision lacking in his earlier treatments. In many ways, the *Logic* marks the consummation of Dewey's lifelong occupation with logical theory, confessedly his "first and last love."[1]

The product of the effort of "over forty years" (LW12:5), Dewey's *Logic* is a systematic and comprehensive exposition of his experimentalist philosophy. Accordingly, one finds within its pages discussions of standard logical themes as well as treatments of topics in epistemology, metaphysics, the philosophy of science, the philosophy of language, the philosophy of history, the philosophy of law, and social philosophy. The scope and depth of its ambitions combined with the notoriously taxing style characteristic of Dewey's writing make the *Logic* a difficult and at times exhausting treatise. It consequently enjoys the curious distinction of being at once among the most highly regarded of Dewey's mature works and the least commonly studied.

Despite the challenges it presents, Dewey's *Logic* merits close attention. In fact, one could plausibly argue that the theory of inquiry developed in the book constitutes the fulcrum of Dewey's philosophy as a whole. A rejection of traditional ways of philosophizing and the problems to which they give rise and a subsequent effort to "reconstruct" philosophy lie at the heart of Dewey's project, evidenced as early as his four essays in *Studies in Logical Theory* (1903). Dewey contends that our inherited philosophical traditions arose out of and have failed to advance beyond assumptions and habits of a prescientific worldview. Principal among these presuppositions is a "spectator theory of knowledge," a view according to which knowledge is the passive beholding by an extranatural or "internal" mind of a complete and fixed "external" world. This makes knowledge a mystery insofar as it presumes that the knower and the known belong to two distinct metaphysical realms which in some inexplicable way must come together in the act of knowing. This predicament consequently gives rise to all of the textbook "problems of philosophy": the problem of skepticism, the problem of the external world, the mind-body problem, the problem of other minds, the problem of induction, and so forth.

Dewey's response to these problems, prominent in his work as early as the 1890s, is well known. He contends that many of the concerns central to traditional philosophy should be regarded not as problems in a strict sense but rather as "puzzles" arising from the vocabulary and presuppositions of philosophy itself (1925, LW1:17). Dewey would recommend that we "not solve" these puzzles but rather that we "get over them" (1909, MW4:14). We need a new, reconstructed conceptual vocabulary, which we may obtain by subjecting traditional assumptions and categories to philosophical criticism informed by a scientific worldview. The insight driving Dewey's reconstructive program is that the spectator theory of knowledge is untenable in the light of the successes of modern science. As even the most cursory examination will show, scientific inquiry is premised on the idea that knowing and acting are intimately related. The practice of pursuing knowledge by means of deliberate experimentation, a mode of directed and controlled action, constitutes a rejection of the spectator conception. On the scientific model, a knower as such is an agent within the world that is known, not a ghostly beholder of an antecedent and alien Reality.

Dewey's reconstruction of philosophy therefore stands the traditional conception of the relation of philosophy to natural science on its head. Previous thinkers have taken the job of philosophy to be that of grounding or justifying the practices and results of science, treating philosophical inquiry as if it were logically and epistemically prior to science. Dewey, by contrast, contends that philosophy must begin with the methods of scientific inquiry, deriving its content and modeling its own practices upon them. Hence, his reconstructed philosophy is fundamentally an experimentalist philosophy.

The project of developing such a position requires, therefore, a careful examination of methods employed in the sciences, with regard to both their successes and their failures. From this examination, a more general pattern of inquiry may be developed that would account not only for procedures employed by natural scientists but also for conceptual methods and means employed in a variety of investigatory contexts—from the physical and social sciences to commonplace inquiries into everyday matters. As part of this project, the relation of formal logical and mathematical systems to experimental inquiry must be explicated, though this does not exhaust the subject matter of a theory of inquiry. Rather, the resulting general theory must be pertinent and applicable to the full range of philosophical subject matters, including problems of explicit moral, political, and social significance.

This complex undertaking is the mission of logical theory, which Dewey appropriately defines as an inquiry into inquiry (1938, LW12:28). Accordingly, logic is the linchpin of his experimentalism. Although his *Essays in Experimental Logic* and other logical essays of the 1920s and 1930s begin to make explicit Dewey's reconstructive project, his *Logic: The Theory of Inquiry* records his most comprehensive inquiry into inquiry. It is therefore not only an essential text in the Deweyan corpus but an integral contribution to pragmatic experimentalism in general.

An Outline of Dewey's Logical Theory

The following essays address a variety of concerns regarding Dewey's logical theory. As each of these essays presumes some degree of familiarity with the general contours of Dewey's theory of inquiry, it would be appropriate to set out a general overview of that theory.

While much of the following overview draws on the 1938 *Logic*, the basic outlines of Dewey's logical theory can be traced to articles dating back to the 1890s, his *Studies in Logical Theory* (1903), and his *Essays in Experimental Logic* (1916b). In particular, much of this earlier work challenges both idealist and realist conceptions of experience and the implications those conceptions have on logical theory.[2] In Dewey's view, traditional logical theory is marked by a recurring controversy regarding the "ultimate subject matter" of logic (1938, LW12:9). What, after all, do the standard logical operators and relations—*if-then, or, and, not, is, iff, some, all, none*, etc.—designate? Rationalist and idealist logicians have argued that principles governing such operators and the relations they signify epitomize fixed and necessary "laws of thought" which are discoverable a priori through rational intuition. Empirically minded philosophers understandably have looked with suspicion upon rationalist appeals to any such faculty of "intuition" that perceives or grasps superempirical logical principles. Accordingly, empiricists have endeavored to develop a logical theory based solely upon experience. On the standard empiricist model, the logical relations to which the logical operators refer are inductive generalizations drawn from sense-experiences and thus are known a posteriori.

Despite disagreements concerning the ultimate subject matter of logic, rationalists and empiricists alike subscribe to a spectator theory of knowledge where acts of knowing and the contents and forms of knowledge are separated. Both schools accept as a fundamental premise the view that the mind stands apart from the proposed source of logical principles. On a rationalist view, logical principles belong to a separate metaphysical realm that is intuited by the mind from a distance. According to empiricists, logical principles are formed by the mind and then overlaid upon sense-experience. Neither view is acceptable.

> To take what is discovered to be reliable evidence within a more complex *situation* as if it were given absolutely and in isolation, or apart from a particular historic situs and context, is the fallacy of empiricism as a logical theory. To regard the thought-forms of conception, judgment, and inference as qualifications of "pure thought apart from any differences in objects," instead of as successive dispositions in the progressive organization of the material (or objects), is the fallacy of rationalism. (Dewey 1903, MW2:347)

The persistent failure of both of these schools of thought calls for a radical response. For Dewey the solution lies in developing a fundamentally new conception of *experience*.

Unlike traditional empiricisms that presuppose a particularistic and sensationalistic psychology, Dewey begins from a Darwinian premise of interaction. On this view, experience is "an affair of the intercourse of a living being with its physical and social environment" (1917, MW10:6) and thus "an affair primarily of doing" (1920, MW12:129). Experience then is not a matter of a mind being passively affected by objects, nor a matter of a mind receiving and filtering sensory data from an external world. It is rather an *exchange*, a *transaction*, between an organism and the physical and social factors within its environment: "When we experience something, we act upon it, we do something with it; then we suffer or undergo the consequences. We do something to the thing and then it does something to us in return" (1916a, MW9:146).

Dewey's placement of experience in the interactions and transactions between an organism and its environment is further augmented with the recognition of a stabilization propensity characteristic of living beings. Experience is episodic, punctuated by occasions of disturbance and resolution, of imbalance and regained composure. Thus experience is not only transactional. It also has force and direction, impelled by an innate drive of the living being to maintain its own *well*-being. In short, experience is an activity in and by which an organism maintains integration with its environment.

The story does not stop there, of course, since there is also the issue of the role of reflection and rationality in human experience. But it is only a small step from Dewey's characterization of experience to the doubt-belief picture of *inquiry* that he adopted from Charles Peirce. Dewey is able to characterize inquiry as a particular kind of experience in which deliberate experimentation and reflection may be a controlling factor in the resolution of doubt and in problem solving more generally. Namely, "Inquiry is the controlled or directed transformation of an indeterminate situation into one that is so determinate in its constituent distinctions and relations as to convert the elements of the original situation into a unified whole" (1938, LW12:108; entire passage originally in italics). This characterization of inquiry is couched in Dewey's own technical vocabulary, and therefore requires some unpacking.

Consider first the idea of a "situation." A situation is both a context and a subject matter for inquiry. We "never experience nor form judgments about objects and events in isolation," but always within the context of a "field in which observation of this or that object or event occurs" (LW12:72–73). The term *environment* tends to connote physical as well as social surroundings, but this is not what Dewey means by a situation. What stimulates inquiry is not just an environment as such but rather a field of organism-environment interaction, particularly an instance of breakdown or disturbance in organism-environment transactions. Dewey introduces the idea of a "situation," the "contextual whole" of an "environing experienced world" (LW12:72), as that to which an inquiry is addressed, arising initially as a kind of disturbance that requires attention. Such a situation, as a stimulus to inquiry, will initially be indeterminate not just in its origins but in possible consequences inherent in how the inquiring agent deals with it.

It should be emphasized that Dewey understands an environment to be composed of both physical and social conditions. Within the environment in which we presently act there are ordinary physical objects such as tables and chairs and books, ordinary physical conditions such as the temperature and atmospheric pressure, as well as certain social factors: laws, customs, traditions, institutions, and social relations of many sorts. The interactions and transactions that initiate and constitute experience may touch on any of these environmental factors. This point applies all the more to inquiry. Social communication and coordination of shared activities is often an integral part of instituting and implementing effective methods of inquiry, particularly in cases where the stimulus to inquiry, an indeterminate situation, is social in nature.

Note, further, that while Dewey elaborated Peirce's doubt-belief picture of inquiry within the framework of his own theory of experience, he also adapted certain ideas from William James's theory of experience, particularly certain aspects of James's radical empiricism (cf. Dewey 1934, LW10:123–25). Dewey is insistent that, as a subject matter of inquiry, a situation is given (taken) all at once as a qualitative whole. This is not difficult to comprehend if, following James (1909/1978, 172–73; 1912/1976), we acknowledge that relations, not just things related, may be empirically immediate. In such a view there is no limit in principle to how complex empirically immediate "givens" may be. In particular, situations, involving both physical and social relations, may be quite complex, though they are immediately "had" as qualitative wholes (1930, LW5:246–47). This is not to say that everything pertinent to a given situation will be immediately present. But situations as such—the situation of women in contemporary culture, the problem of AIDS, the conflict in Kosovo, etc.—will have a whole individual presence for anyone for whom they are indeed concrete situations.

A situation, then, is both the qualitative context and the background in which processes of inquiry are played out in order to transform that very situation. When a situation is indeterminate, it is "uncertain, unsettled, disturbed" (1938, LW12:109). An indeterminate situation is one that sets a problem for the inquirer. Thus inquiry is a process by which a living being deliberately confronts and deals with an indeterminate situation, a process by which it transforms an indeterminate situation into one that is no longer indeterminate. Inquiry, as pursued by *thinking* creatures, involves reflection, deliberation, and the use of conceptual tools, but it is not just a mental process insofar as it is a type of directed action aimed at resolving a problematic situation.

So how does all this bear on logical theory? For Dewey, the project of logical theory is to develop an empirically robust account of norms and guiding principles that distinguish better and worse methods of inquiry as they are employed and evaluated in actual inquiries. In a passage that is more prospective than explanatory, Dewey asserts that "all logical forms (with their characteristic properties) arise within the operation of inquiry and are concerned with control of inquiry so that it may yield warranted assertions" (1938, LW12:11). With experience and inquiry cast as above, we can begin to understand what it means to say that logical forms arise within experience rather than being imposed on it from transcendent sources—though this requires some explanation.

As a study of generic features of inquiry, logical theory is largely concerned with the function of language and conceptual systems in such resolution processes. On the basis of erroneous metaphysical and epistemological background assumptions, modern logic has focused too narrowly on formal properties of linguistic grammars and deductive argument forms. What Dewey requires of logic is that it frame such concerns explicitly within a broader theory of inquiry which incorporates and assimilates inductive and abductive inference as conjoint complements of deductive inference.

Consider, for instance, the common logical notion of a "proposition." Dewey's "instrumentalist" view of propositions as tentative proposals will not seem so peculiar as many critics have maintained when it is kept in mind that he is concerned not just with deductive argument forms and their formal validity or invalidity. He is equally concerned with processes and principles of abductive hypothesis formation and their inductive "validation" by means of careful experimental design and skillful use of refined techniques of measurement and observation. Contemporary philosophy of science has essentially incorporated all of the key aspects of Dewey's instrumentalism in its recognition that theories, as systems of propositions, are formulated and judged as workable models that advance (or fail to advance) the purposes of scientific investigation. This notion is now (still) usually couched within the unworkable constraints of modern epistemology, but instrumentalism as Dewey initially conceived of it was nothing else but a view of what propositions and theories are as tools of inquiry. As such, it is their function to clarify (to make determinate) facts of the matter at hand, whatever the problem may be, and to articulate an appropriate and workable interpretation of such facts in light of standing conceptual categories. The latter are, of course, subject to modification if and when new problems arise to which existing conceptual systems are apparently inadequate. The history of science provides ample evidence of the conjoint development and evolution of the conceptual schemes, experimental methods, and instrumentational devices and techniques of observation and measurement which supply the contents and forms of the propositions it uses.

Logic as the theory of inquiry encompasses all of these concerns as they evolve both within single inquiries and in the course of ongoing inquiry. In a given inquiry, the twofold function of propositions—to articulate facts and to interpret them theoretically—is aimed at an eventual formulation and assertion of a *judgment* as a conclusion that will withstand any subsequent critique. Insofar as the terms of a theory are ultimately framed in operational terms, this renders judgment practical and thus assertible as a formulation of what to do in the given situation in light of determined facts. This clearly applies to everyday practical situations and to issues that are decidedly ethical or moral in character. But it also applies to problems in the sciences and in mathematics, where determining "what to do" is more a matter of deciding which competing theories or research programs to *go* with, that is, which are on the right track, which should receive research funds, etc.

Dewey's notion of *warranted assertibility*, which many have mistaken to be a theory of truth, applies not to propositions as such but rather to judgments in their office as conclusions of inquiry. Some judgments will indeed be adequate as responses to a given situation, as formulations of what resolves the given problem, while others will be inadequate. To discover criteria of warranted assertibility, insofar as this can be done generally, is thus a major goal of logical theory. Such an enterprise is not trivial insofar as criteria of warranted assertibility must be discovered and sanctioned in the very process of using them. This has everything to do with understanding the changing ways in which propositions are formulated and operationally instituted to transform given situations. The history of science as well provides ample evidence of how new methods of inquiry and thus new criteria of warranted assertibility have arisen in the ongoing refinement and elaboration of scientific inquiry, providing ample evidence of how logic itself has evolved, from ancient times to the present day. Logic in this sense is no less normative than it is usually taken to be, though it is an evolving experimental enterprise concerned with more than just good and bad deductive argument forms. Logic as a science will be concerned with discovering and validating those methods of inquiry which distinguish better inquiries from worse, particularly with an eye on what promises to work in the long run, not just in the here and now.

Logic is empirical and experimental insofar as it is addressed to actual inquiries, not to mere abstractions. It is rational insofar as it is concerned with methods and principles of inquiry that promise to have relevance and efficacy in the continuation of inquiry in the long run. From this perspective we should expect that the value of contemporary mathematical logic, statistics, probability theory, linguistics, computer science, and the cognitive sciences at large will be as evident as ever, though these disciplines have so far developed in a piecemeal way against a background of erroneous conceptions of the nature of logic.

Contents of This Volume

The essays in the present volume are organized into three topical groups. We will forego the standard duty of providing the reader with synopses of the essays and attempt instead to place the issues addressed in the volume within the context of broader philosophical themes.

The volume begins with a number of essays addressing concerns regarding the possibility of a strictly experimentalist logic. Experimentalism, insofar as it is also a kind of naturalism, would reject traditional appeals to transcendental and superempirical foundations for formal logic. That is, Dewey is committed to a metaphysics that rejects a traditional source and ground for formal logical properties and relations such as apriority, necessity, identity, possibility, entailment, and validity. Logical theory on this view is instead experimental, empirical, like any good scientific theory. However, it is unclear that one can establish on a strictly experimentalist basis normative claims about how one *ought* to infer, deduce, hypothesize, and inquire. If a strictly naturalist metaphysics can generate only a *descriptive* account of how we in fact inquire, then it cannot yield a *prescriptive* theory of how inquiry is *properly* conducted. To invoke Peirce's worry, a merely descriptive logical theory can provide nothing more than a "natural history" of thought.

By Dewey's own admission, a solely descriptive account of inquiry is inadequate. Logical theory as an inquiry into inquiry must involve a descriptive *and* a normative aspect. It must not only provide "an organized and tested descriptive account of the way in which thought actually goes on" but also prescriptions "by which future thinking shall take advantage of the operations that lead to success and avoid those which result in failure" (1920, MW12:157). If there is to be a viable experimentalist logic, then it must be shown that an empirical study of the ways in which we do inquire can give rise to a theory of how we *ought* to inquire.

Consequently, the pragmatist tradition has generated a number of attempts to reconcile the formal requirements of traditional logical theory with a naturalistic metaphysics. Tom Alexander's contribution engages the crucial exercise of tracing the development of Dewey's logical thinking from its idealist beginnings to its experimentalist culmination. Also focusing on Dewey's earlier work, Jennifer Welchman examines the theoretical underpinnings of Dewey's conceptions of moral inquiry and of practical judgment more generally. The last three essays in part 1 compare and contrast Dewey's theory with the thought of other prominent pragmatist logicians. In Vincent Colapietro's essay, Dewey is brought into critical dialogue with his pragmatist predecessor, Charles Peirce. Sandra Rosenthal and John Shook facilitate similar encounters between Dewey and his successors in logic, C. I. Lewis and W. V. Quine. The result of these conversations is a tighter grasp on the specifics of Dewey's theory and those of his interlocutors, as well as a deepened sense of the difficulties and challenges inherent within the project of constructing a naturalistic logical theory.

Dewey saw his 1938 *Logic* as both his most comprehensive treatment of logical theory and yet as "introductory" and in need of further development (LW12:5). There is accordingly more work to be done in articulating an experimentalist theory of logic. It is the business of the essays collected in part 2 to further the experimentalist program laid out in Dewey's *Logic: The Theory of Inquiry*.

Insofar as Dewey's experimental logic is a new *kind* of logical theory, it confronts the obvious difficulties stemming from the immanent conservatism and aversion to the novel that is characteristic of any long-standing intellectual tradition. What is the relation of an experimentalist logic to traditional logic? What advantages does an experimentalist approach have over these standard approaches? Scholars working within a Deweyan paradigm must not only direct their efforts to an internal clarification of the philosophical aspects of Dewey's logical theory, they must also endeavor to establish a working relation with contemporary developments and techniques in formal logic.

As indicated earlier, a central contention of an experimentalist logic is that logical forms at once "accrue" (LW12:29) to subject matter within the process of inquiry, "originate" in inquiry, and "control" inquiry (LW12:11). This conception of the nature of logical forms allows Dewey to avoid the transcendentalism of rationalist logical theory and the particularism and sensationalism of the traditional empiricist theories. However, even sympathetic commentators such as Ernest Nagel (1986) have found Dewey's account perplexing: How can logical forms both originate in inquiry and control inquiry?

Dewey's account of the generation of logical forms within inquiry is the principal focus of the essays by Hans Seigfried and Jayne Tristan, while Tom Burke and Douglas Browning address concerns regarding what may generally be thought of as the status of Dewey's theory. More specifically, Seigfried carefully evaluates Dewey's 1938 discussion of logical forms as evolving conditions that all inquiries must satisfy. Tristan looks at the fundamental role of measurement (broadly conceived) in the origin and nature of logical forms. Burke attempts to integrate the novelties of Deweyan experimentalism with current developments in mathematical logical and natural language semantics—arguing not that Dewey's theory of inquiry can be "formalized" but that contemporary formal techniques may nevertheless be incorporated into Dewey's logical theory. Browning is concerned more fundamentally with examining the very idea—and possibility—of inquiring into inquiry in ways that do not beg important questions. A second essay by Burke evaluates Goodman's new riddle of induction in light of Dewey's theory of predication.

The concept of *continuity* pervades Dewey's work in all its aspects. Central to Dewey's logical theory, then, is the idea that there is a general pattern of inquiry that may be extracted from the natural sciences and applied (hopefully with success) to any indeterminate situation. As situations are contextual wholes composed not only of physical and biological factors but of moral and social factors as well, there are situations that are indeterminate in such ways as to constitute *moral, social,* and *political* problems. Hence, an identification and consistent systematization of the pattern of inquiry does not exhaust the aim of an experimentalist logical theory. One must also show *how* this pattern is applicable to actual problems, including problems of *value.*

At this suggestion, some will brandish the traditional philosophical saws concerning the metaphysical and epistemological distinctions between fact and value, "is" and "ought," description and prescription. These dualisms have pushed philosophers to adopt either a subjectivist theory of evaluative language, namely, a view which reduces evaluative claims to descriptive claims about the speaker's psychological attitudes—or else an intuitionist view, in which evaluative expressions allegedly refer to non-natural properties apprehended by a private mental faculty. Maintaining that there is a *continuity* between scientific and value inquiry, the experimentalist must reject both of these options.

The essays in part 3 address Dewey's attempts to reconstruct value theory according to an experimental theory of inquiry. John Capps and Michael Eldridge evaluate the theory through examinations of its practice. Capps looks at how Dewey's theory measures up against actual present-day AIDS research, as well as its implications for the ever-recurrent creationism/evolutionism debate. Eldridge looks instead at a case of social inquiry in which Dewey himself took part, painting a not entirely flattering picture of Dewey as a political problem solver. The volume closes with John Stuhr's critical assessment of the theory of inquiry proposed in Dewey's *Logic,* posing several challenging questions concerning Dewey's inadequate acknowledgment of the impact of social conditions on inquiry (and thus the theory of inquiry).

It is safe to say that there is presently a resurgence of interest in the thought of John Dewey. Recent years have seen an impressive number of important studies of various elements of Dewey's philosophical vision. Despite this swell of scholarship, Dewey's logical theory has received less attention than it deserves. As a collection of essays devoted specifically to Dewey's theory of inquiry, *Dewey's Logical Theory: New Studies and Interpretations* will hopefully encourage future clarification, revision, and debate.

Method of Citation

The complete works of John Dewey are available in a critical edition of thirty-seven volumes published by Southern Illinois University Press. As they are standard in Dewey scholarship, all citations to Dewey's works will be keyed to these volumes. There is a controversy, however, concerning the proper method of citation. The dominant convention among Dewey scholars is to include a parenthetical indication of the volume and page number in the critical edition. As the critical edition is divided into three chronological periods—the *Early Works* (5 vols.), the *Middle Works* (15 vols.), and the *Later Works* (17 vols.)—a standard citation reading (LW12:109) would indicate page 109 of the twelfth volume of the *Later Works*. Whereas this method of citation is simple and convenient for Dewey scholars who work with the critical editions, it lacks some of the virtues of the more generally employed author/date style of citation. In particular, the convention among Dewey scholars gives no indication of the *title* or *date* of the work from which a quote is drawn. Thus, as individual volumes in the critical editions typically contain several essays, articles, reviews, and lectures, this often leaves the specific identity of the source text a mystery.

Wanting to make the present volume accessible to a wide audience, we have elected to revise slightly the conventional method in a way that is more compatible with a standard author/date citation style. We believe this composite style will make for readable citations that convey useful information without too much distraction. With the author/date style, citations usually specify the author and the date of the publication cited, followed by page numbers where appropriate. Citations are included in parentheses when the citation is indeed parenthetical in nature, but otherwise they are given without parentheses. If the author of the citation is already clear from the context, then just a date and page number(s) are given. If both the author and date of the publication are obvious from the context, then just page numbers are given. References to Dewey's publications follow this same pattern except that page numbers are replaced by a conventional critical-edition citation.

All of this should apply as well to Peirce's works, where the convention among Peirce scholars is to cite volumes and *paragraph* numbers in Peirce's *Collected Papers* (CP). So "CP4:156" would denote paragraph 156 in volume 4 of the *Collected Papers*. As the latter multivolume collection is not chronologically ordered, we make no concerted attempt to identify the date of Peirce's various writings but simply use the standard "CP" style of citation.

Acknowledgments

The editors have incurred a number of professional and personal debts in the preparation of this volume, some of which they would here like to try to repay. The idea for a volume of essays assessing Dewey's logical theory grew out of a series of conversations with persons who were originally invited to contribute essays to accompany a scholarly reprint of Dewey's 1916 *Essays in Experimental Logic* (Southern Illinois University Press, 2002). The resulting volume of essays eventually took on a broader life of its own. Nevertheless, our thanks are extended to those who encouraged the project in its early stages, especially Tom Alexander, Mike Eldridge, Larry Hickman, John McDermott, and H. S. Thayer.

Notes

1. Dewey to Albert C. Barnes, 30 November 1934, Ratner/Dewey papers. Cited in the Textual Apparatus of the 1938 *Logic* (LW12:537).
2. Readers interested in the chronology of these ideas should consult Ralph Sleeper's *The Necessity of Pragmatism* (1986/2001). Sleeper's study is the most comprehensive and arguably the best available critical summary and evaluation of Dewey's views on logic and their development from the 1890s until his death in 1952.

Works Cited

Dewey, John, ed. 1903. *Studies in Logical Theory*. Chicago: University of Chicago Press. University of Chicago Decennial Publications, 2d ser., vol. 11. Dewey's contributions reprinted in Dewey 1916b, 75–182, and in MW2:293–375.

———. 1909. The Influence of Darwin on Philosophy. *Popular Science Monthly* 75:90–98. Originally published with the title "Darwin's Influence upon Philosophy." Revised and reprinted in Dewey 1910, 1–19, with the title "The Influence of Darwinism on Philosophy." Reprinted in MW4:1–14.

———. 1910. *The Influence of Darwin on Philosophy, and Other Essays in Contemporary Thought*. New York: Henry Holt. Essays reprinted separately in EW5, MW1,3,4,6.

———. 1916a. *Democracy and Education*. New York: Macmillan. Reprinted in MW9.

———. 1916b. *Essays in Experimental Logic*. Chicago: University of Chicago Press. Essays reprinted separately in MW1,2,4,6,8,10.

———. 1917. The Need for a Recovery of Philosophy. In *Creative Intelligence: Essays in the Pragmatic Attitude*, 3–69. New York: Henry Holt. Reprinted in MW10:3–48.

———. 1920. *Reconstruction in Philosophy*. New York: Henry Holt. Reprinted in MW12:77–204, including a new introduction to 1948 reprint (Boston: Beacon Press), 256–77.

xxiv					*Editors' Introduction*

———. 1925. *Experience and Nature*. Chicago: Open Court. Reprinted in LW1.

———. 1930. Qualitative Thought. *Symposium* 1:5–32. Reprinted in Dewey 1931, 93–116, and in LW5:243–62.

———. 1931. *Philosophy and Civilization*. New York: Minton, Balch.

———. 1934. *Art as Experience*. New York: Henry Holt. Reprinted in LW10.

———. 1938. *Logic: The Theory of Inquiry*. New York: Henry Holt. Reprinted in LW12.

Edman, Irwin. 1938. Review of *Logic: The Theory of Inquiry,* by John Dewey. *New York Herald Tribune Books,* 11 December, 5.

James, William. 1907. *Pragmatism: A New Name for Some Old Ways of Thinking*. New York: Longmans, Green. Reprinted in the series Works of William James (Cambridge: Harvard University Press, 1975). Reprinted with James 1909 in *Pragmatism and the Meaning of Truth* , with an introduction by A. J. Ayer (Cambridge: Harvard University Press, 1978).

———. 1909. *The Meaning of Truth*. New York: Longmans, Green. Reprinted in the series Works of William James (Cambridge: Harvard University Press, 1975). Reprinted with James 1907 in *Pragmatism and the Meaning of Truth* , with an introduction by A. J. Ayer (Cambridge: Harvard University Press, 1978).

———. 1912. *Essays in Radical Empiricism*. New York: Longmans, Green. Posthumous, ed. R. B. Perry. Reprinted in the series Works of William James (Cambridge: Harvard University Press, 1976).

Nagel, Ernest. 1986. Introduction to Dewey's *Logic: The Theory of Inquiry*. In *Dewey 1938, LW12:ix–xxvii*.

Peirce, Charles Sanders. 1867–1914. Collected Papers of Charles Sanders Peirce (CP). Cambridge: Harvard University Press (1931–1958). Vols. 1–6 edited by Charles Hartshorne and Paul Weiss; vols. 7–8 edited by Arthur W. Burks. Publication of items in this edition are indicated by CP followed by volume and paragraph numbers.

Sleeper, Ralph William. 1986. *The Necessity of Pragmatism*. New Haven: Yale University Press. Reprinted with an introduction by Tom Burke (Urbana: University of Illinois Press, 2001).

Dewey's Logical Theory

Part I

Situations, Experience, and Knowing

1

The Aesthetics of Reality: The Development of Dewey's Ecological Theory of Experience

Thomas Alexander

The Transcendence of Epistemology

The period between Dewey's emergence as a major philosophical voice and his becoming the leading figure in the movement that became known as "pragmatism" is not well understood. That it was something of a mystery to Dewey himself is evident by the prominence it has in his intellectual autobiography, "From Absolutism to Experimentalism" (1930). In 1887, with the publication of his *Psychology*, Dewey, rather than Royce, could well have been called the crown prince of American idealism. In 1903, with the appearance of *Studies in Logical Theory*,[1] Dewey was recognized as the head of the Chicago School, which was understood as presenting a platform of radical, "dynamic" idealism that was taking an affirmative, indeed enthusiastic, approach to contemporary sciences, unlike the defensive theologically driven idealism dominant in Germany and England and represented in America by Royce, among others. Yet Dewey had already been strangely silent on the topic of "idealism" for some time. He left Chicago in 1904, hotly resigning his position in the controversy over his wife's dismissal from heading the Laboratory School. By 1905 he was at Columbia, and that was the year his article "The Postulate of Immediate Empiricism" appeared. I believe this article is one of the most radical and revolutionary pieces Dewey wrote, though it is also far from being a clear, accessible statement of the nature or implications of those crucial ideas that indicate a sea change in Dewey's philosophy. It quite explicitly is a response to James's articles on radical empiricism, which had begun to appear in 1903, though the relationship of radical empiricism to pragmatism was still nebulous. It was a decade later that the collection of articles known as *Essays in Experimental Logic* (1916) appeared, containing in its lengthy introduction perhaps the most sophisticated explanation to date of Dewey's theory of experience. And it would be another decade before the appearance of Dewey's most systematic exploration of the idea in *Experience and Nature* (1925).

As one looks at the developmental dynamics of Dewey's early period, there seem to be a variety of issues that demand his attention: ethics, logic, psychology, pedagogy, and so on. It is less clear whether there was a basic, underlying issue that drove Dewey from one formulation of his thought to the next. If one looks, however, at the trajectory of his thought, especially from the *Psychology* (1887b) to the introduction of *Essays in Experimental Logic* (and beyond to *Experience and Nature*), the importance of Dewey's "Postulate of Immediate Empiricism" becomes evident, summing up not only his discontent with idealism but also realism and anticipating the most profound issues that would characterize Dewey's radical, revolutionary mature philosophy. I maintain that this involves a major transformation of a commitment of the Western tradition from its very inception in the pre-Socratic period on the correlation of the object of knowledge with the nature of reality. Though articulated by Parmenides, it is perhaps most clearly exhibited in Plato's famous "Divided Line" (*Republic*, 509d–511e) with its gradations of the diverse cognitive powers of the soul on one side and their appropriate cognitive objects, ontologically graded, on the other.

Dewey's radical shift is to question this equation. Knowing for him becomes merely one aspect of the ways in which reality manifests itself, a contextualized and mediating way, but certainly not final or ultimate. Rather, experience in its precognitive and postcognitive forms indicates a qualitatively rich and aesthetically diversified field of meaning, conscious and unconscious, that supports and renders intelligible the cognitive enterprise itself. This is one reason why Dewey's own thought is poorly described by the term *instrumentalism*, which refers specifically to the theory of inquiry, of knowing. Dewey had difficulty in finding a fitting name for his complete philosophy of experience. The list of terms introducing the subject in the revised first chapter of *Experience and Nature*, "naturalistic empiricism" and "naturalistic humanism," left Dewey unsatisfied, so that by 1938, in *Logic: The Theory of Inquiry,* he used the phrase "cultural naturalism" (LW12:28). Dewey's frustrations reflected both the depth of his insight and the inability of his opponents—as well as many of his followers—to grasp the nature of his revolution, an inability echoed in the work of many neopragmatists, who still held on to the correlation of natural objects and the objects of knowledge, of metaphysics and epistemology. It was one of Dewey's major claims that while nature manifests itself in a variety of ways, in one sense it exhibits itself best in its fullest and most complex actualizations, which for Dewey were expressed in the artistic-aesthetic mode of experience that is the subject of *Art as Experience* (1934).

The purpose of this essay is to sketch out some of the major steps that led Dewey to his radical break with this fundamental commitment of the Western tradition. It asks that we look at Dewey's philosophy as setting the stage for a more developed exploration of the idea of an ontology of environed or ecologically situated being, an "eco-ontology," to use my own term. In this way, then, the introduction to *Essays in Experimental Logic* has a crucial place in the Deweyan corpus, not only in its resolutions of the tensions that had driven Dewey's philosophical development from the arms of idealism, or in its anticipations of the position laid out in *Experience and Nature*, but in terms of being an "introduction" to one of the most forceful statements of Dewey's instrumentalism. Questions of inquiry must be contextualized within the fundamentally noncognitive enterprise of experience. Attempts, moreover, to read Dewey as somehow contributing to "epistemology" must be questioned. To understand Dewey's revolution is to grasp fully that what has occupied the role of "an epistemology of *knowledge*" in the West for Dewey must be replaced with the nature of an aesthetics of *learning*.

The outcome of understanding this revolution is highly significant. The world of the twenty-first century is one that will face the double problem of confronting an emerging global civilization that is already significantly engaged in the process of environmental degradation of the planet and the widespread destruction of biodiversity. A philosophy that engages us in ways of environmentally and ecologically conceptualizing our interactions with the world and which is oriented toward an aesthetically deep, ongoing experience of life is one that may help us negotiate successfully the daunting challenges ahead.

Dewey's Chicago Years

As the University of Chicago emerged from the marshes in 1892, it was clear that President Harper intended to make three departments the center jewels in the crown: Semitics, classics, and philosophy. Rockefeller was funneling millions of dollars into the project, as were Chicagoans. Harper needed builders of departments, and he could afford them. He would have Paul Shorey in Greek and James Henry Breasted in Egyptology along with a large portion of Yale's Department of Semitic Languages. But who for philosophy? He sent feelers out to "established, solidly respectable men" like George Herbert Palmer of Harvard (Rucker 1969, 11). William James discreetly suggested his old friend, Charles Sanders Peirce. Harper was cautious—Wasn't there some "problem" with Peirce back at Hopkins years ago? Harper decided to write Palmer. Palmer was shocked: "I am astonished at James's recommendation of Peirce," he gasped; after admitting that he "had no personal acquaintance with Peirce," Palmer went on to "advise" Harper to make "careful inquiries" into the reports of Peirce's "broken and dissolute character." "I am sure it is suspicions of this sort which have prevented his appointment here, and I suppose the same causes procured his dismissal from Johns Hopkins" (Rucker 1969, 10; Brent 1993). Peirce, in fact, was not "safe"—the fundamental flaw in his character revealed itself to his fellow Victorians, as Joseph Brent has shown, in actually daring to marry his mistress after finally getting a divorce from his estranged wife.[2] Though the theme of this essay is Dewey, we might pause for a moment to reflect on the very different department Peirce might have built. Whatever its character, I doubt there would have been a laboratory school.

It was then that James Tufts suggested a young professor at Michigan, John Dewey, who, said Tufts, "is a man of a religious nature, is a church member and believes in working with churches" (Rucker 1969, 10). The comment, true at the time, was about to become dramatically inaccurate—such are the vagaries of academic appointments! As Robert Westbrook has pointed out, when Dewey left the church in moving from Ann Arbor to Chicago, he never affiliated with any other denomination again (Westbrook 1991, 79). The offer was made and accepted, and Dewey's remarkable decade in Chicago began.

When Dewey arrived, he was recognized as one of the foremost exponents of absolute idealism in the United States. George Sylvester Morris, Dewey's mentor, had died in 1889, and Royce had only published two philosophical books, *The Religious Aspect of Philosophy* in 1885 and *The Spirit of Modern Philosophy* in 1892. Dewey also was the author of two books, a study of Leibniz (1888) and the *Psychology*, a sophisticated attempt to wed empirical psychology with idealist metaphysics, while junking Hegel's cumbersome a priori dialectic. He had published an impressive monograph in ethics, *Outlines of a Critical Theory of Ethics* (1891). This work astutely critiqued the classical panorama of ethical theories and restlessly argued for a dynamic character-based ethics of self-realization. In 1894, it had just been superseded by Dewey's first and much more radical, if schematic, analysis of moral psychology, *The Study of Ethics: A Syllabus*, which advocated what Dewey briefly dubbed "experimental idealism" (1894a, EW4:264).[3]

When he left the University of Chicago in 1904, he was no longer a contender with Royce as the leading defender of absolute idealism. Dewey had been strangely moot on the whole question of idealism. In fact, there had been pointed criticisms of Green, Bosanquet, Lötze, and Royce, but these could still be interpreted as family squabbles. Now he was the recognized leader of educational psychology; his own contributions to the science not only were aligned with James's functional empiricism but stood on a par with it and, in fact, had advanced it on certain key points, especially in such breakthrough pieces as "The Theory of Emotions" (1894b) and "The Reflex Arc Concept in Psychology" (1896). Though Dewey continued to give important lectures on moral psychology, his major books and monographs dealt with education—*Interest in Relation to Training of the Will* (1899a), *The School and Society* (1899b), and *The Child and the Curriculum* (1902a). More and more Dewey had been absorbed in the problem of knowledge viewed in terms of an active process of inquiry rather than an elaborate epistemological system of elements and laws providing a background for justifying beliefs. In his contributions to the *Studies in Logical Theory* (1903), Dewey had trained his guns on the sprawling system of Herman Lötze as a case study exemplifying the futility of metaphysical epistemology. Dewey was now so insistent upon treating logic in terms of a functional or genetic process that an exasperated Charles Sanders Peirce savagely reviewed the book. Unlike the British logicians, whose work Peirce said "may be expected to lead to results of high value for the positive sciences," Dewey's work must be classified with that of the German logicians, like Husserl, which makes truth "a matter of linguistic expression" rather than a "matter of fact." "The Chicago school or group are manifestly in radical opposition to the exact logicians, and are not making any studies which anybody in his senses can expect, directly or indirectly, in any considerable degree, to influence twentieth-century science." Indeed, the new century would see the dominion of a mathematical logic utterly contemptuous of "psychological questions" and "the genetic fallacy." Peirce (CP8:190–91) added that though Dewey claimed to be opposed to the German school, "had he not put so much emphasis upon it, we should hardly have deemed the point of difference so important." Peirce found the whole thesis perplexing: "He seems to regard what he calls 'logic' as a natural history of thought." Exactly so.

Years later, when Dewey (1930, LW5:154) roughly sketched out his intellectual autobiography, he referred to this period as one of "drifting" away from Hegelianism, though—a point that is often missed here—remaining deeply impressed by *Hegel*, if not by his followers. Indeed, looking back, we can see in this period Dewey moving in some ways closer to the concrete "spirit" of Hegel's own philosophy and away from the more dualistic renditions of T. H. Green and the other British idealists, as well as those of

George Sylvester Morris and Josiah Royce. Dewey adds a tantalizing detail in the quasi-autobiography for the *Library of Living Philosophers* volume devoted to him: "There was a period extending into my early years at Chicago when, in connection with a seminar in Hegel's *Logic* I tried reinterpreting his categories in terms of 'readjustment' and 'reconstruction.' Gradually I came to realize that what the principles actually stood for could be better understood and stated when completely emancipated from Hegelian garb" (Schilpp 1939, 18).[4] A common interpretation of what happened during Dewey's Chicago years is that as he became dissatisfied with religion, even liberal Christianity, and more engaged in experimental work, he went through an antimetaphysical period. Upon arriving at Columbia and falling under the influence of people like Woodbridge, Bush, and Montague, Dewey once again began to tinker with metaphysics, with the culmination appearing some twenty years later (1925) in *Experience and Nature*, a book that can pretty much stand as the antithesis of Dewey's old *Psychology* of 1887. Though there is some truth to this assessment (Dewey has sharp words about metaphysics in his letters of the period), I would like to raise three issues concerning it. First, such a view really does not answer for us *why* Dewey became disappointed with "experimental idealism," for such a doctrine could have worked very well as a theoretical underpinning to Dewey's psychological and political vision. Second, merely to label such a period of fundamental change "drifting" does little more than provide us an excuse for not looking for the details that culminated in what was a radical transformation. Worse, it provides ammunition to those critics of Dewey's mature philosophy who see it as a confused mish-mash of later naturalism and empiricism added on to an unchanged, early, fuzzy idealism that crops out here and there in such places as his metaphysics, aesthetics, ethics, and so on.[5] Finally, we are presented with the mysterious, pivotal essay of 1905, the year of Dewey's appointment to Columbia, "The Postulate of Immediate Empiricism." I believe this essay is one of the most crucial in Dewey's career because it formulates, albeit in a fumbling and annoyingly condensed manner, what I take to be the guiding insight of his mature philosophy: that reality is not synonymous with the object of knowledge. The range of experience and the realms of meaning and value extend far beyond the cognitive and, in fact, provide the supporting conditions within which inquiry makes sense. Such a thesis challenges the 2,500 years of Western philosophy stemming from Parmenides' identification of Being and the Known: "For it is the same thing, To-Be and To-Know."[6] Dewey's rejection of this is a *metaphysical* thesis, a profound one I believe, and it seems a strange bolt from the blue from someone who had "given up" metaphysics for educational psychology.

In the rest of this essay I will explore the development of Dewey's reconstruction of the thesis that knowledge is the measure of reality. My central claim is that by stressing the dynamic side of idealism while rejecting Hegel's dialectical logic for experimental psychology, Dewey was driven to contextualize the activity of knowing within a larger and richer view of experience. His work in educational psychology reinforced the importance of a theory of learning over the traditional philosophical emphasis upon "epistemology," the theory of knowledge. This is an insight we would do well to consider today. I will then look at the culmination of the transformation of Dewey's philosophical outlook in an article published just after his arrival at Columbia, "The Postulate of Immediate Empiricism." This piece not only exemplifies the sea change that had occurred during Dewey's Chicago period but also anticipates most of the major metaphysical developments of his later thought. After examining the argument presented in "The Postulate of Immediate Empiricism," I will try to show why I think it has radical implications even for today, especially for constructing a metaphysics that takes ecology seriously. I do not have the space here to discuss other intertwined threads contributing to the change in Dewey's philosophy during the Chicago years, such as his theory of ethical conduct and his theory of democratic life. But I will conclude by reflecting on the contemporary importance both of a theory of learning over epistemology and an ecological ontology over the ontology of perfection that has dominated Western philosophy.

The Absolute Goes to School

Justice can hardly be done here to the philosophical depth of Dewey's early period. The surprising thing is that while Dewey was an idealist, he was a remarkably original and powerful one. His early thought, in my view, far exceeds anything else done under the banner of idealism in this country until we get to John William Miller.[7] From his earliest writings it is evident that Dewey rebelled against anything that smacked of the abstract, formal, and lifeless. He had been drawn to idealism for the reason that it promised to be able to treat experience in all its richness and organic wholeness. British empiricism, with its atomic mental particles governed by mechanical "laws of association," and neo-Kantianism, with its Prussian bureaucracy of faculties automatically executing their judgments, never held any appeal for him. Thus he quickly adhered to the dynamic idealism of Hegel as filtered through the inspiring teachings of his beloved professor, George Sylvester Morris, and backed up by the liberal interpretation of Thomas

Hill Green. But the Hegel of the nineteenth century was the Hegel of
The Science of Logic (1812), not the *Phenomenology of Spirit* (1807). The West
was going through profound changes, social, political, and cultural, and
clutched at anything that seemed to discern order and reason at work, from
Swedenborgianism to dialectical materialism to social Darwinism. But for
Dewey, Hegel's dialectic presented yet another formalistic a priori system
removed in the end from the concrete in all but name. Even if Hegel's concepts moved in a ghostly ballet, it was no substitute for life. Dewey wanted
life.

Dewey had thus embraced only one side of Hegel and was casting about
for something to replace the very engine of Hegel's metaphysical dynamo.
He found this at Johns Hopkins in the teaching of G. Stanley Hall, one of
the first experimental psychologists in the United States. Psychology presented itself as the scientific study of individual consciousness. Idealism
presented itself as the claim that self-consciousness could establish that it
was the constituting origin and ground of everything else. Dewey put two
and two together: Psychology must be the science that gives us access to
ultimate reality. Only in his mid-twenties, Dewey, ever prolific, presented
the arguments for his "psychological idealism" from 1884 on, culminating
in his first original book, the *Psychology*.[8]

This book is one of the weirdest small masterpieces in the history of idealism. It rigorously presents itself as a textbook in psychology, appeals to
the latest empirical research coming from Germany, while holding down
the references to idealist metaphysicians to a discrete, well-hidden few.
Hegel is not mentioned, but the beginning is well laid out—every instance
of consciousness is also an instance of self-consciousness and thus of knowledge (Dewey 1887b, EW2:7–8). Ranging over the three cardinal faculties of
Knowing, Willing, and Feeling, with careful and often insightful discussions of memory, imagination, intellectual feeling, aesthetic perception, and
the formation of a moral identity, Dewey architectonically leads the reader
from the most immediate analyses of personal experience onward and up-
ward to the necessary postulate of Absolute self-consciousness as the underpinning Reality of everything. We are thus presented with the "scientific" conclusion:

> We find the unity of the psychical process already studied, and therefore
> their ultimate explanation, in the fact that man is a self; the essence of the
> self is the self-determining activity of the will; that this will is an objectify-
> ing activity; that, in objectifying itself, it renders itself universal. The result
> of this activity is *knowledge*. . . . The objective universal result is at one and

the same time existent in the medium of the individual's consciousness. This subjective activity is *feeling*. (EW 2:362)

Dewey concludes asserting that moral will is the realization that the real and the ideal *ought* to be one and the "Religious will is the realization that they are one because man is a self-determining power. It is the realization that a perfect will is reality" (EW2:362). Dewey flirts with heresy: Freedom is achieved "through the realization of the union of finite and the infinite Personality"—does God need us to be free just as we need Him? (EW2:362–63), and finishes off by listing all the "contradictions" that follow if this conclusion is rejected: Knowledge cannot be universal, only subjective; feeling can never be fully satisfied, for the ideal will never be real; and the will likewise will be frustrated and arbitrary, never becoming a rational desire. All psychical life is "the progressive realization by the will of its ideal self" achieved by the "idealization of the actual," ending in the insight that "real and ideal are one" and that "truth, happiness, and rightness are united in one Personality" (EW2: 363).

G. Stanley Hall, Dewey's former teacher, and William James had both had their work cited in support of this thesis; they were not pleased, Hall saying that it was like using geology to account for the six days of Creation, James merely clucking over how bloodless and abstract this ideal "Personality" seemed to be compared with real life.[9] What was remarkable for Dewey, even in this early work, was how well he integrated willing and feeling together with knowing. The aesthetic was no doormat to the temple of the Absolute, as it was for Hegel (with religion being the door and philosophy the edifice). But for our purposes, I want to note how well this book falls into the fundamental commitments of what might be termed "the ontology of Perfection," the legacy of the Greeks, the Medievals, and, in their own way, the Moderns. The basic claim is that Being is complete or perfect, needing nothing beyond itself to be. The fundamental access to this truth is through an act of intellectual insight. Being, as object, is realized in a timeless moment of knowing; Reason realizes its fullest power in achieving this insight. At the most fundamental level, Being is the known; the self is the knower, and both are mutually implicated, at the very least through a common ground, at most by being identified.[10] Thus Being is the object of contemplative insight, absolute knowledge, and apodictic insight is the essence of consciousness and the self. Being is self-identical, autonomous, atemporal. To the degree that the self is assimilated to its prime object, it, too, is self-identical, autonomous, and atemporal.[11] It is the Parmenidean turn of Western philosophy at work.

When the *Psychology* appeared in 1887, Dewey was not thirty; it would go through two revisions by 1891. But 1890 was the year marked by the publication of William James's *The Principles of Psychology*. Not only did this instantly eclipse any pretense Dewey's book could have as being the American answer to German or British psychology. It struck at the roots of the idealist philosophy itself and in the name of all that had committed Dewey to idealism in the first place: fidelity to the organic richness of experience and moving flow of life. The fundamental assumption was that for subject and object to be united in an act of knowledge (or self-knowledge, for idealism), some active synthesizing power was needed, be it the Form of the Good, the Active Intellect, God's Illumination, the Transcendental Ego, or the Absolute. James asked why experience needed "synthesizing" when it didn't come in pieces to begin with. Distinction and concepts emerged out of the ongoing process of life as functional refinements, useful in directing and responding to the course of the world. Life didn't need "saving" by reason to be made whole; all along it was "reason" that had depended on life. Dewey must have been stunned. His greatest effort in defense of the vitality of experience had to appear now as an elaborate, useless machinery. Dewey could, of course, have written a feisty defense of idealism and souped up his psychology. This is what Royce would have done and what, no doubt, Morris, Dewey's spiritual father, would have urged. But Morris had died the year before. In May 1891, Dewey wrote James, nominally to thank him for some kind remarks on Dewey's syllabus, *Outlines of a Critical Theory of Ethics*. The letter is candidly revealing about Dewey's own struggles:

> But unless a man is already living in the gospel and not under the law, as you express it, words thrown at him are idle wind. . . . The hope seems to be with the rising generation. . . . Many of my students, I find, are fairly hungering. They almost jump at any opportunity to get out from under the load and believe in their own lives. Pardon the confessional character of this note, but the man who has seen the point arouses the confessional attitude.

Dewey then added a postscript:

> I don't know that I told you that I have had a class of four graduates going through your psychology this year, and how much we have all enjoyed it. I'm sure you would be greatly gratified if you could see what a stimulus to mental freedom, as well as what a purveyor of methods and materials your book has been to us. (Perry 1935, 2:517)

Dewey had work to do.

During the course of his stay at Chicago, Dewey would tackle the problem of knowledge again and again. I cannot detail this progress, but three important milestones were reached with "The Superstition of Necessity" (1893), "The Theory of Emotions" and "The Reflex Arc Concept in Psychology." I can only summarize the central thesis of the first. "The Superstition of Necessity" analyzed the idea of necessary judgments, in terms of how they functioned in inquiry. They did not grant access to an a priori world of perfection; rather, they were moments or phases in which previously disconnected judgments were united into one new fact. Dewey still believes that gradually this will lead us toward the ultimate fact of the Absolute, but now the Absolute itself will lack "necessity." During this discussion, Dewey hits upon an entirely new conception of what the "object of knowledge" is: not a fixed "fact" out there waiting to be discovered, but a transformative focus in a broader field of inquiry, which "has its origin in the practical needs of our nature" (1893, EW4:24). Necessity and contingency get their meaning teleologically, i.e., functionally: "Necessary means *needed*; contingency means no longer required—because already enjoyed" (EW4:29). Logical necessity is simply practical, teleological necessity "read backward" (EW4:33). No wonder history had appeared so "necessary" to Hegel! No wonder his "science" could not predict the future! Wasn't it a Dane who pointed out that "we live forwards but understand backwards"? Dewey was trying to show *how* we could also *understand* forwards.[12]

While "The Theory of Emotion" and "The Reflex Arc Concept in Psychology" provided Dewey's basic models of affective, interactional developmental learning behavior, the *Studies in Logical Theory* carried out a sustained criticism of the whole "epistemological" approach to philosophy in favor of seeing experience in terms of its "natural history," that is, "ecology." From the start, Dewey is emphatic in refusing to privilege knowledge:

> Reflection busies itself alike with physical nature, the record of social achievement, and the endeavors of social aspiration. It is with reference to *such* affairs that thought is derivative; it is with reference to them that it intervenes or mediates. Taking some part of the universe of action, of affection, of social construction, under its special charge, and having busied itself therewith sufficiently to meet the special difficulty presented, thought releases that topic and enters into more direct experience. (1903 & 1916, MW2:299)

The antecedents of reflection and its consequents are not cognitive; they are what call thinking forth and into which it passes, and this, says Dewey, has great implications for "the relation of truth to reality" (MW2:298). "Thinking is a kind of activity which we perform at specific need, just as at other need we engage in other sorts of activity: as converse with a friend; draw a plan for a house; take a walk; eat a dinner; purchase a suit of clothes, etc." (MW2:299). The basis is laid for placing learning as more significant than knowing, of placing the process of growth above static insight, a method of discovery above a method of justification. The rest of the essays give poor Lötze a sockdolager from which he never recovered, but do not raise again the question of the relation of truth and reality. This would begin nearly nine years later, just after Dewey's move to Columbia.

The Postulate of Immediate Empiricism

As one of the first of Dewey's articles to appear after his arrival in New York, "The Postulate of Immediate Empiricism" may well have caused some colleagues to wonder whether they had made a mistake. Three eminent philosophers, including Columbia's Woodbridge, wrote sharp criticisms appearing in the newborn *Journal of Philosophy, Psychology, and Scientific Methods* where the article had been published, eliciting equally sharp responses from Dewey.[13] Dewey thought well enough of the article to include it in his 1910 anthology, *The Influence of Darwin on Philosophy*, though he added the disgruntled note stating he had been "unreasonably sanguine" that his careful description of empiricism at the beginning "would forfend misapprehension" (1905a, MW3:166). This, at least, would prepare Dewey for another forty years of critical misunderstanding regarding the central terms in his philosophy.

Dewey began his essay by firmly allying himself with "that vital but still unformed movement variously termed radical empiricism, pragmatism, humanism, functionalism" (MW3:158)—something he had not directly done so far. He proposed to state the fundamental but tacit presupposition that marked this movement off from any other, "a presupposition as to what experience is and means" (MW3:158). He wanted to reject any baggage imported into the sense of the term *experience* by associations with "sensationalistic empiricism" or transcendentalism (i.e., idealism), both of which "fall back on something which is defined in non-directly-experienced terms in order to justify that which is directly experienced" (MW3:158n. 2). Dewey presumably means such second order conceptual entities as Lockean ideas, "laws of association," manifolds, forms of intuition, transcendental egos,

Absolute Spirit, or whatnot. Dewey refers the reader to two places where such assumptions have been criticized, *The Studies in Logical Theory* and his two-part essay, "The Evolutionary Method as Applied to Morality" (1902b). Both approaches are driven, Dewey adds, by setting up "certain methodological checks and cues for attaining *certainty*" (1905a, MW3:159n. 2). The latter essay contrasted British empiricism with Dewey's appeal to experience; experience allowed for genetic or historical method, examining how ideas and value judgments arise from and function in practical situations. In the *Studies* Dewey had put it more bluntly: "It is not metaphysics, it is biology which enforces the idea that actual sensation is not only determined as an event in the world of events, but is an occurrence occurring at a certain period in the control and use of stimuli" (1903, MW2:244).

With these warnings in mind Dewey was prepared to introduce his radical postulate: "Immediate empiricism postulates that things—anything, everything, in the ordinary or non-technical use of the term 'thing'—are what they are experienced as" (1905a, MW3:158). Had Dewey wanted his readers to be reassured that radical empiricism or pragmatism amounted to little more than a return to Protagorean relativism, he could not have done better, except perhaps add an example that would confirm the fear, which is what he did. When a horse-trader, a timid family man, a jockey, and a zoologist look at a horse, he said, each one sees something different: a "good buy," a "safe ride," a "winner," or a specimen of "*equus* descended from *Eohippus*." He does not come right out and assert that there is no "horse in itself," but he does say that some of the accounts given by these different people will turn out to be "less real" than others, which will be judged to be "phenomenal." The same is true, adds Dewey, of "the psychologist's horse, the logician's horse, or the metaphysician's horse." "In each case," he says, "the nub of the question is, *what sort of experience* is denoted or indicated . . . so that we have a contrast not between *a* Reality, and various approximations to, or phenomenal representations of Reality, but between different reals of experience" (MW3:159). If we slip back into the mentalistic understanding of "experience," then Dewey would seem to be advocating a Berkeleyan world where God has dozed off.

Dewey tried to avoid such a reading in the next paragraph, but only seemed to get himself in deeper trouble. This postulate, he argued, is usually thought to be equivalent to saying that "things (or, ultimately, Reality or Being) are only and just what they are *known* to be or that things are, or Reality *is*, what it is for a conscious knower—whether the knower be conceived primarily as a perceiver or as a thinker being a further and secondary question." Dewey dismisses this as "the root paralogism of all idealisms" of whatever stripe and "if not the root of all philosophic evil, one of its main roots" (MW3:159–60)—and it would be hard to see, given this thesis, what doctrine in the history of the West did not automatically fall under this rubric. Even Hobbes would be classified as an "idealist" here. Dewey explains:

> By our postulate, things are what they are experienced to be; and, unless knowing is the sole and genuine form of experiencing, it is fallacious to say that Reality is just and exclusively what it is or would be for an all-competent all-knower; or even that it *is*, relatively and piecemeal, what it is to a finite and partial knower. Or, put more positively, knowing is one mode of experiencing, and the primary philosophical demand (from the standpoint of immediatism) is to find out *what* sort of an experience knowing is—or, concretely, how things are experienced when they are experienced *as* known things. (MW3:159–60)

This paragraph stands as a marvelous example of Dewey's classic involuted, stammering, murky style. He comments in "From Absolutism to Experimentalism" that when his early "schematic interest" was predominant, "writing was comparatively easy," but since then "thinking and writing have been hard work" (1930, LW5:151).[14]

The problem with the traditional assumption that Reality is what it appears to a knower is that it "leaves out of account what the knowledge standpoint itself is *experienced as*" (Dewey 1905a, MW3:160). When "the knowledge standpoint" is placed within its natural context, Dewey finds that it arises from a prereflective, qualitatively felt situation and passes into an aesthetic one, serving a mediating and transformative role between them. Dewey rejects the "grounding" knowledge upon a transcendental or dialectical analysis of the "possibility of knowledge"—the move that had inaugurated idealism and had led to the thesis that to be able to grasp its own conditions, the human mind had a self-transcending power to apprehend itself as the Absolute, the view Dewey had accepted at first. But when looked at as "experience," taken in Dewey's sense of "natural history," instead of knowledge "grounding" other types of experience, it is "grounded" by them—the process of knowing has its whence and its wither in events that are not instances of "knowing" at all.

The "root of most philosophic evil" had been to regard such experiences as either tacit instances of knowledge secretly employing a vast, hidden epistemological machinery or to dismiss noncognitive experience as irrelevant, deceptive, or meaningless with respect to the nature of Reality. In the first camp we might find as paradigmatic instances anyone who believes that any experience whatever stripe is also implicitly an instance of knowledge and forming cognitive judgments: the Stoics, Thomas Reid, Leibniz, Kant, Hegel, Husserl, Ryle, Sellars, Chisholm, Dennett. In the second camp we would find those who acknowledge that some experience is noncognitive but either utterly dismiss it as having ontological significance (for example, Descartes, Hume, Carnap, Stevenson, Rorty) or take its non-epistemic character as pointing toward degraded orders of Being (Plato, Aristotle, Plotinus, Augustine, Aquinas, Hegel, Peirce). The only tradition that seems to stand as an exception to the rule would be those thinkers who have implicitly accepted the argument that what is noncognitive is incomprehensible. Here we find what might be termed philosophers who advocate a "metaphysics of the will" in which the arbitrary ("free") nature of the will is asserted over against the authority of reason, thereby giving it creative access to Reality (Ockham, Fichte, Schopenhauer, Nietzsche, Kierkegaard, James, Sartre).

In his early period Dewey had followed the Hegelian approach of seeing all "phenomenal" or personal experience as fragmentary and incomplete instances implicated on the order of Reality in the infinite self-knowledge of the Absolute. However, in "The Postulate of Immediate Empiricism," Dewey followed the lead James had given in *The Principles of Psychology* of taking the phases of experience functionally and seeing how they operated together in the fulfillment of life activity. Knowing was in the service of life, not life in the service of knowing.

Dewey tried to illustrate this complex thought with a mundane example. When I am preoccupied and am startled by a noise, the noise is immediately imbued with the qualities of alarm. It is a frightful thing though it is not yet known. Upon discovering the cause to be the wind making the window shade tap, the fearsome quality is transformed into a sense of security and the situation, being resolved, contains within it an object which may truly be said to be "known," the shade, because a judgment about it has been made as a result of inquiry. The experience may fade off into a sense of mingled relief and humor, with a residual habit to check the window shade first should any similar noise be heard. The brute shock of alarm and the lingering amused relief are not instances of *knowing* because they are not, in themselves, inquiries guided by some method or plan of action. In Dewey's later terminology, they are "had" or "undergone." Instead of seeing them as involving tacit cognitive judgments, Dewey sees the phase of inquiry presupposing the noncognitive in order to make sense. Without the startling noise, no inquiry would have been initiated; without the sense of resolution or "closure" (as Dewey would call it), the inquiry would not have ended—there would have been no "object" which would have been the focus of a judgment. In the experience, there has been a process of transformation that integrated different aspects of experience so that sense or meaning was made. As Dewey rather awkwardly put it, "The experience has changed; that is, the thing experienced has changed—not that an unreality has given place to a reality, nor that some transcendental (unexperienced) Reality has changed, not that truth has changed, but just and only the concrete reality has changed" (1905a, MW3:160). In other words, the process is one of *learning* rather than *knowing*.

Dewey's whole thesis rides on the claim that neither the moment of fright nor the moment of relief after the identification of the cause has been made are *experienced as* moments of *knowing fright* or *knowing relief*. An experience of "knowing fear" would be to submit oneself to tests of courage or to undertake a psychological inquiry into what things cause fear under which circumstances. Likewise, "knowing relief" could range from simple personal techniques in dealing with frustration to studying conditions under which people tend to achieve satisfaction by responding to disturbing circumstances in an effective manner. Should anyone object that to have the feeling of fear or relief was also an instance of "knowing," Dewey's response is simply that this is not empirical but involves an hypothesis about experience, an hypothesis, moreover, that assumes its own truth in arguing for the thesis.

But we can still frame the obvious question: "Wasn't it *really* the window shade all along? The search didn't change *it*; what happened was that my confused state of mind was replaced by a well-justified belief." Isn't Dewey still caught in the Protagorean nightmare where "objects" out there change all the time as people perceive them? Dewey's analysis is still entirely from the viewpoint of the experiencing subject, not the objective world, and thus can still be criticized as exhibiting the "Hegelian Bacillus." Such is the case of the "realists" who responded to Dewey throughout his career, people like Woodbridge (in the case of this very essay), Lovejoy, and Santayana later on. What can Dewey say to this? I believe that it was Dewey's attempt to respond to this problem which led him to develop the naturalistic metaphysics that began to take shape with such essays as "Does Reality Possess Practical Character?" (1908), "The Subject-Matter of Metaphysical Inquiry" (1915), the important introduction to *Essays in Experimental Logic,* and on to *Experience and Nature.* Dewey had to frame a metaphysical outlook in which the whole idea of "objective reality" was exposed for the historical construct that it was and replaced with something other than Protagorean subjectivism or a metaphysical voluntarism. This was by no means an easy task (some would say: of course, since it is impossible).

The Essays in Experimental Logic

The introduction to Dewey's 1916 collection of articles dealing with logic, truth, meaning, and realism is over seventy pages long. Were it read together with Dewey's other famous article, "The Need for a Recovery of Philosophy" (1917), we would see the use of creative speculation in the former combined with trenchant criticism of the history of philosophy in the latter that characterizes *Experience and Nature*. Dewey had to try to formulate the general theory of experience that underlay his work from the early 1900s on; the most important element he notes immediately is the placing of logical functions "in their temporal context" (Dewey 1916, MW10:320). Dewey has rejected firmly and clearly any appeal to a transcendental condition for logical judgments and is fully conscious that any logic, no matter how formal, must ultimately be understood as embedded in temporality, which for Dewey means both contextually and transformationally.

A second key theme is the recognition that logic, so understood, is not a cognitive "foundation" for a fundamentally cognitive relationship between an "epistemic knower" and a "world" whose nature is likewise summed up in its status as a "known object." Knowledge—and so logic—exists within a noncognitive temporal framework, arising from experiences which are noncogitive and passing into experiences that also are noncognitive. However one may positively characterize the experience out of which inquiry arises, says Dewey, be it "social, affectional, technological, aesthetic, etc.," it "cannot be called a knowledge experience without doing violence to the term 'knowledge' and to experience" (MW10:320). The history of philosophy is filled with pervasive abuse of this key point, because when we *think* about experience, it takes on the quality of *thinking* and so appears naturally to the philosopher as primarily an affair of knowing. What is needed is to remember that knowing occurs within the qualitatively richer spectrum of life itself: "The intellectual element is set in a context which is non-cognitive, and which holds within it in suspense a vast complex of other qualities and things that in the experience itself are objects of esteem or aversion, of decision, of use, of suffering, of endeavor and revolt, not of knowledge" (MW10:322). Thus, the primary step in philosophical reflection for Dewey must be a firm and vivid remembrance by the philosopher of life itself, which also is a recognition of the temporality of experience and the functionality of distinctions that emerge from it—what Dewey will characterize in *Experience and Nature* as "the empirical denotative method."

The primary feature of this larger "non-reflectional" type of experience (as Dewey called it) is that in spite of the diversity and complexity it may have, all parts of it are "saturated with a pervasive quality" (MW10:322).

Indeed, if the word *thing* is taken in its Latin sense of *res* (or, in Greek, *pragma*), i.e., as "affair" or "event," we can understand how this quality takes on the salient trait: the qualitative character of a political campaign, a romance, or being sick (to give Dewey's examples). To see "things" in terms of being *res* also brings out the fact they are articulated wholes with focus and context: "brilliancy and obscurity, conspicuousness or apparency, and concealment or reserve, with a constant movement of redistribution" (Dewey 1916, MW10:323). The "axis" of the event remains, though what is in focus is changing, and this focus is consciousness. The term Dewey selects for this "immense and operative world of diverse and interacting elements" is "experience" (MW10:323). He argues that this term is preferable to words like *environment* or *world* precisely because it implies a "focus of immediate shining apparency" (MW10:324).

To root "logic" in a temporal, contextualized, experimental activity of inquiry means that this qualitative, noncognitive background must also be recognized and its conditioning presence acknowledged in the process of thinking. Looking back over the period in which the essays making up *Essays in Experimental Logic* were written, Dewey at last is able to articulate fairly clearly this radical view of experience which had been working itself out ever since, I think, his first shattering encounter with James's *The Principles of Psychology*. By 1916, Dewey was able to see just how deep a gulf separated his philosophy from the majority of other philosophical positions which maintained the crucial equation between reality and the object of knowledge. Dewey was still sanguine, however, that by spelling out his disagreement over this issue and putting forth his alternative situational view of experience, at least his critics would comprehend what he had done. Deep habits die hard, as Dewey would discover, and even after *Experience and Nature*, he would feel compelled to rewrite its first chapter and then return again and again to a long critical introduction that would remain an unfinished masterpiece at the time of his death.[15] It still remains perhaps the most significant—and unrecognized—contribution of Dewey's philosophy.

Dewey struggled the rest of his career to formulate an alternative outlook, one that was not only more faithful to experience as it is experienced, but one that could be the basis of enlightened, intelligent living, i.e., wisdom. His greatest effort in this direction, *Experience and Nature*, has been repeatedly misread and abused by generations of scholars from Santayana and Morris Cohen to Bernstein and Rorty as being infected with idealism because of its emphasis on the issue of experience and the processive, situational nature of knowing. At age ninety, a frustrated Dewey even toyed with junking the term *experience* for *culture*, as if that would do any good.

He and his odd friend Arthur Bentley tinkered on a fancy new terminology to get these ideas across, pedantic enough to be attractive even to the new wave of scientistic philosophy in the 1940s, but without success. Except, perhaps, one. The older term *natural history* had recently come to be replaced by another, *ecology*. In *Knowing and the Known*, Dewey and Bentley briefly appropriated it as an example of their broader term *transaction*. The "descriptive spade-work of the ecologies" has shown that environments evolve just as organisms do: "Ecology is full of illustrations of the interactional . . . and it is still fuller of illustrations of the transactional" (1949, LW16:117, 120). Rather than fighting the ghosts of idealism in Dewey's thought, we would do far better to see his work presenting the rudiments of an evolutionary metaphysics that replaces the Greek ideal-knower with that of a creative ecosystem in which change, plurality, possibility, and mutual interdependence replace the canonical concepts of substance, timelessness, logical identity, self-sufficiency, and completion. Such a position might be called "ecological emergentism" and its metaphysics in particular, "eco-ontology."

Conclusion

In this essay I have tried to sketch two sides of the revolution Dewey accomplished, the crucial years of which were spent at the University of Chicago. By abandoning the ontology of perfection and its presupposition of the privileged ideal-knower, Dewey at once created the possibility for replacing the traditional philosophical project of epistemology, analyzing how we know or upon what foundations knowledge is possible, with a theory of learning. It is, after all, learning in which imagination, not merely reason, transforms our past into a meaningful future. Learning allows us to adapt to new circumstances and communicate with those different from us rather than force us to defend the old and familiar and demand others adapt themselves to our ways of thinking. In its broader conceptions, Dewey points toward an ecological conception of metaphysics in which certain "generic traits" are used to keep the diverse areas of inquiry constantly in touch with each other, not allowing them to lapse into disconnected *Fachs*. Metaphysics thus becomes the intelligence of intelligence and provides the basis for intelligence applied to the most fulfilling ideals of human conduct, which Dewey calls "wisdom."

A contemporary Deweyan would point out how much the equation of reality with the object of knowledge still permeates our philosophical assumptions. We may have abandoned Plato's view of reality as constituted of ideal Forms along with Aristotle's conception of *ousia* as a formed individual, a member of known species. But we largely follow the early modern view of the real as a physical substance known through mathematical physics, and we still try to identify mental states with propositional attitudes. There is still the tacit assumption that the objective world in and of itself, apart from our experience, is essentially determinate and complete. There are formal laws governing fixed identities, and *that's it*. Dewey's philosophy offers us the opportunity to step back and question that assumption and perhaps adopt a more ecological approach to philosophical wisdom. The world of the twenty-first century has two central problems: preserving the planetary ecosystem and creating the basis for mutual understanding between diverse peoples in a world verging toward overpopulation. Given these looming concerns and the barrenness of contemporary philosophy, we might do worse than reconsider the advances begun by Dewey almost a century ago to formulate an ecological ontology and with it an ecological view of experience in which the aesthetic context of inquiry is acknowledged.

Notes

1. This work is a collection of writings by members of the Philosophy Department at the University of Chicago. Dewey edited the collection and contributed the first four essays.

2. See Brent 1993, especially 151–60. There were, of course, other factors—Peirce's arrogance, his carrying on a double career between Johns Hopkins and the Geodesic Survey, and the attack on his standing as a mathematician by a respected colleague in the field, Simon Newcomb.

3. Dewey's continuing struggles in this area can be examined in the three series of lectures on psychological ethics edited by Donald Koch (Dewey 1976, 1991, 1998). It would only be in 1908 that Dewey would, in collaboration with Tufts, publish the *Ethics*, the profound outcome of two decades of wrestling with the subject.

4. The essay "Biography of John Dewey" is attributed to "Dewey's daughters," with Jane Dewey appearing as editor. The words, however, are quoted as directly from Dewey in the text. Notes and stenographic typescripts of some of Dewey's lectures from this period exist, though it is still difficult to pinpoint the course or year when he makes this shift. A transcript from 1897 on Hegel's *Philosophy of Spirit* stays close to Hegel's own terminology, while notes taken by H. H. Bawden (no earlier than 1902) from a course Dewey taught on Hegel's logic beginning with the phrase: "Restating Hegel's meaning in psychology terms, he is asking here, What is initiative, momentum, [or] that process? ... Interpret bg [being], non-bg, & becoming in terms of focus & background [&] attention."

5. This problem has been explored, at least with respect to Dewey's metaphysics and aesthetics, in my book, Alexander 1987. But also see the studies by Rockefeller (1991) and Welchman (1995) for somewhat different analyses of Dewey's early development.

6. See Parmenides, DK 3 and 8—my translation.

7. I have undertaken a partial study of this period in my book, Alexander 1987. For Miller, see Tyman 1993.

8. Among the important articles indicating Dewey's earliest position are "The New Psychology" (1884), "The Psychological Standpoint" (1886a), "Psychology as Philosophic Method" (1886b), and "Knowledge as Idealization" (1887a).

9. See Dykhuizen 1973, 55.

10. In the *Republic*, Plato's analogy of the Sun makes it clear that the Soul as knower and the Forms as objects of *noesis* are caused and connected by The Form of the Good (508 f.). Aristotle's divine principle, the Unmoved Mover, is both knower and known without requiring any further transcendental ground. When Augustine collapses the hypostatic One of Plotinus (which is identified with Plato's Form of the Good) into the Christian God, the ultimate Being, the same move is accomplished. God is the self-caused all-knower eternally beholding the history of creation from beyond time.

11. This, of course, is one of the theses in the *Phaedo* and is found again in Aristotle's cloudy remarks on the active intellect and again in books X and XI of the *Confessions*.

12. James makes this reference to Kierkegaard in *Pragmatism* (1907). The Harvard critical edition cites Kierkegaard 1939, 127, sec. 465 as one of the possible sources (though obviously not in the 1938 translation). James may have heard it from Harold Hoffding.

13. See responses to this article (Dewey 1905a) by Bakewell (1905), Woodbridge (1905), and Bode (1905), as well as Dewey's subsequent responses (1905b–d).

14. Dewey actually makes a revealing insight: "My development has been controlled largely by a struggle between a native inclination toward the schematic and formally logical, and those incidents of personal experience that compelled me to take account of actual material. . . . Anyway, a case might be made out for the proposition that the emphasis upon the concrete, empirical, and practical in my later writings is . . . a reaction to what is more natural, and it served as a protest and protection against something in myself which, in the pressure and weight of actual experiences, I knew to be a weakness." (1930, LW5:150–51)

15. The various drafts of this Introduction were edited and organized by Joseph Ratner for the edition of *Experience and Nature* published in LW1:329–64. In it Dewey attempted to critique the whole Western philosophical tradition—an immense undertaking.

Works Cited

Alexander, Thomas M. 1987. *John Dewey's Theory of Art, Experience, and Nature: The Horizons of Feeling*. Albany: State University of New York Press.

Bakewell, Charles M. 1905. An Open Letter to Professor Dewey Concerning Immediate Empiricism. *Journal of Philosophy, Psychology, and Scientific Methods* 2:520–22. Reprinted in MW3:390–92.

Bernstein, Richard J., ed. 1960. *On Experience, Nature, and Freedom: Representative Selections by John Dewey*. New York: Bobbs-Merrill.

Bode, B. H. 1905. Cognitive Experience and Its Object. *Journal of Philosophy, Psychology, and Scientific Methods* 2:653–63. Reprinted in MW3:398–404.

Brent, Joseph. 1993. *Charles Sanders Peirce: A Life*. Bloomington: Indiana University Press.

Dewey, John. 1884. The New Psychology. *Andover Review* 2:278–89. Reprinted in EW1:48–60.

———. 1886a. The Psychological Standpoint. *Mind* 11:1–19. Reprinted in EW1:122–43.

———. 1886b. Psychology as Philosophic Method. *Mind* 11:153–73. Reprinted in EW1:144–67.

———. 1887a. Knowledge as Idealization. *Mind* 12:382–96. Reprinted in EW1:176–93.

———. 1887b. *Psychology*. New York: Harper and Brothers, Franklin Square. Reprinted in EW2.

———. 1888. *Leibniz's New Essays Concerning the Human Understanding*. Chicago: S. C. Griggs. Reprinted in EW1:251–435.

———. 1891. *Outline of a Critical Theory of Ethics*. Ann Arbor: Inland Press. Reprinted in EW3:237–388.

———. 1893. The Superstition of Necessity. *Monist* 3:362–79. Reprinted in EW4:19–36.

———. 1894a. *The Study of Ethics: A Syllabus*. Ann Arbor: Inland Press. Reprinted in EW4:221–364.

———. 1894b. The Theory of Emotions. *Psychological Review* 4:553–69. Reprinted in EW4.152–88.

———. 1895/1998. *Principles of Instrumental Logic: Dewey's Lectures in Ethics and Political Ethics, 1895–1896*. Edited by Donald Koch. Carbondale: Southern Illinois University Press.

———. 1896. The Reflex Arc Concept in Psychology. *Psychological Review* 3:357–70. Reprinted in Dewey 1931, 233–48, and in EW5:96–110.

———. 1898/1976. *Lectures on Psychological and Political Ethics, 1898*. Edited by Donald Koch. New York: Hafner Press.

———. 1899a. *Interest in Relation to the Training of the Will*. Chicago: University of Chicago Press. Reprinted in EW5:111–50.

———. 1899b. *The School and Society*. Chicago: University of Chicago Press. Reprinted in MW1:1–109.

———. 1900/1991. *Lectures on Ethics, 1900–1901.* Edited by Donald Koch. Carbondale: Southern Illinois University Press.

———. 1902a. *The Child and the Curriculum.* Chicago: University of Chicago Press. Reprinted in MW2:271–92.

———. 1902b. The Evolutionary Method as Applied to Morality. *Philosophical Review* 11:107–24, 353–71. Reprinted in MW2:3–38.

———, ed. 1903. *Studies in Logical Theory.* University of Chicago Decennial Publications, 2d ser., vol. 11. Chicago: University of Chicago Press. Dewey's contributions reprinted in Dewey 1916, 75–182, and in MW2:293–375.

———. 1905a. The Postulate of Immediate Empiricism. *Journal of Philosophy, Psychology, and Scientific Methods* 2:393–99. Reprinted in Dewey 1910, 226–41, and in MW3:158–67.

———. 1905b. Immediate Empiricism. *Journal of Philosophy, Psychology, and Scientific Methods* 2:597–99. Reprinted in MW3:168–70.

———. 1905c. The Knowledge Experience and Its Relationships. *Journal of Philosophy, Psychology, and Scientific Methods* 2: 652–57. Reprinted in MW3:171–77.

———. 1905d. The Knowledge Experience Again. *Journal of Philosophy, Psychology, and Scientific Methods* 2:707–11. Reprinted in MW3:178–83.

———. 1908. Does Reality Possess Practical Character? In *Essays, Philosophical and Psychological, in Honor of William James, Professor in Harvard University, by His Colleagues at Columbia University.* New York: Longmans, Green. Reprinted in Dewey 1931 as "The Practical Character of Reality," and in MW4:125–42.

———. 1910. *The Influence of Darwin on Philosophy, and Other Essays in Contemporary Thought.* New York: Henry Holt. Essays reprinted separately in EW1, MW1,3,4,6.

———. 1915. The Subject-Matter of Metaphysical Inquiry. *Journal of Philosophy, Psychology, and Scientific Methods* 12:337–45. Reprinted in MW8:3–13.

———. 1916. *Essays in Experimental Logic.* Chicago: University of Chicago Press. Essays reprinted separately in MW1,2,4,6,8,10.

———. 1917. The Need for a Recovery of Philosophy. In *Creative Intelligence: Essays in the Pragmatic Attitude,* 3–69. New York: Henry Holt. Reprinted in MW10:3–48.

———. 1925. *Experience and Nature.* Chicago: Open Court. Reprinted in LW1.

———. 1930. From Absolutism to Experimentalism. In *Contemporary American Philosophy,* ed. George P. Adams and William P. Montague, 13–27. New York: Macmillan. Reprinted in Bernstein 1960, 3–18, and in LW5:147–60.

———. 1931. *Philosophy and Civilization.* New York: Minton, Balch.

———. 1934. *Art as Experience.* New York: Henry Holt. Reprinted in LW10.

———. 1938. *Logic: The Theory of Inquiry.* New York: Henry Holt. Reprinted in LW12.

Dewey, John, and Arthur F. Bentley. 1949. *Knowing and the Known.* Boston: Beacon Press. Reprinted in R. Handy and E. C. Harwood, *Useful Procedures of Inquiry* (Great Barrington, MA: Behavioral Research Council, 1973), , 89–190, and in LW16:1–294.

Dewey, John, and James Hayden Tufts. 1908. *Ethics.* New York: Henry Holt. Reprinted in MW5.

Dykhuizen, George. 1973. *The Life and Mind of John Dewey.* Carbondale: Southern Illinois University Press.

Hegel, G. W. F. 1807/1977. *Phenomenology of Spirit*. Translated by A. V. Miller. Oxford: Oxford University Press.

———. 1812/1969. *The Science of Logic*. Translated by A. V. Miller. Highlands, N.J.: Humanities Press.

James, William. 1890. *The Principles of Psychology*. 2 vols. New York: Henry Holt. Reprinted in the series Works of William James (Cambridge: Harvard University Press, 1981).

———. 1907. *Pragmatism: A New Name for Some Old Ways of Thinking*. New York: Longmans, Green. Reprinted in *Pragmatism and Other Essays* (New York: Washington Square Press, 1963) and in the series Works of William James (Cambridge: Harvard University Press, 1975).

Kierkegaard, Søren. 1938. *The Journals of Søren Kierkegaard*. Edited and translated by Alexander Dru. London: Oxford University Press.

Peirce, Charles Sanders. 1867–1914. *Collected Papers of Charles Sanders Peirce*. Cambridge: Harvard University Press, 1931–58. Vols. 1–6 edited by Charles Hartshorne and Paul Weiss; vols. 7–8 edited by Arthur W. Burks. Publication of items in this edition are indicated by CP followed by volume and paragraph numbers.

Perry, Ralph Barton. 1935. *The Thought and Character of William James*. 2 vols. Boston: Little, Brown.

Rockefeller, Stephen. 1991. *John Dewey: Religious Faith and Democratic Humanism*. New York: Columbia University Press.

Royce, Josiah. 1885. *The Religious Aspects of Philosophy*. Boston: Houghton Mifflin.

———. 1892. *The Spirit of Modern Philosophy*. Boston: Houghton Mifflin.

Rucker, Darnell. 1969. *The Chicago Pragmatists*. New Haven: Yale University Press.

Schilpp, Paul Arthur, ed. 1939. *The Philosophy of John Dewey*. New York: Tudor Press.

Tyman, Stephen. 1993. *Descrying the Ideal*. Carbondale: Southern Illinois University Press.

Welchman, Jennifer. 1995. *Dewey's Ethical Thought*. Ithaca: Cornell University Press.

Westbrook, Robert B. 1991. *John Dewey and American Democracy*. Ithaca: Cornell University Press.

Woodbridge, F. J. E. 1905. Of What Sort Is Cognitive Experience? *Journal of Philosophy, Psychology, and Scientific Methods* 2:573–76. Reprinted in MW3:393–97.

2

Logic and Judgments of Practice

Jennifer Welchman

I

"The Logic of Judgments of Practice," first published in 1915 and then reprinted as the concluding essay of Dewey's 1916 *Essays in Experimental Logic*, has been recognized as an important statement of Dewey's developing naturalistic moral epistemology. It expands upon discussions to be found in earlier texts, such as "The Evolutionary Method as Applied to Morality" (1902), "The Logical Conditions of a Scientific Treatment of Morality" (1903), and the 1908 *Ethics* by Dewey and Tufts, and it clears the ground for later treatments of values and value judgments in *Reconstruction in Philosophy* (1920), *Human Nature and Conduct* (1922), and *The Quest for Certainty* (1929). Less widely recognized is its importance in the development of Dewey's pragmatic theory of logic. Commentators have found the paper instructive for its explication of Dewey's position on contemporary debates about valuation. But in 1916 Dewey was entering into those debates primarily in order to critique neorealist logic.

In a 1919 review of *Essays in Experimental Logic*, Bertrand Russell remarked that "in the sense in which I use the word, there is hardly any 'logic' in the book except the suggestion that judgments of practice yield a special form—a suggestion which belongs to logic in my sense, though I do not accept it as a valid one" (5–6). Had Russell thought through the implications of the essay to which he refers, he would have had to concede that most of the essays are devoted to logic. The question that "The Logic of Judgments of Practice" takes up is the adequacy of neorealist thinking about propositions, propositional forms, and propositional attitudes. Dewey not only criticizes neorealist notions about propositions as incomplete. He also argues that neorealists radically misunderstand what propositions and their constituents are. And since the positions taken in "The Logic of Judgments of Practice" are those to which the preceding essays point, *Essays in Experi-*

mental Logic is about what Russell himself would call the philosophy of logic.

This argument anticipates the view taken in *Logic: The Theory of Inquiry* (1938), namely, that "declarative propositions, whether of facts or of conceptions (principles and laws), are intermediary means or instruments (respectively material and procedural) of effecting that controlled transformation of subject-matter which is the end-in-view (and final goal) of all declarative affirmations and negations" (LW12:162). But the earlier essay is primarily critical rather than constructive. Dewey's objective is to challenge the neorealists' narrowing of logic from the study of inference to the study of implication. Because he believed that this faulty approach to logic was due largely to their commitment to realism and to a correspondence theory of truth, Dewey's essay is devoted more to critically dismantling the neorealist view of propositions (practical and scientific) and their verification than to construction and elucidation of a pragmatic alternative. Nevertheless, the essay clearly suggests the lines along which Dewey's construction would go. Thus it represents an important stage in the development of Dewey's distinctive theories of inference, implication, and propositional form. To understand the essay, the issues it addresses, and why Dewey addressed them as he did, we must first understand the contemporary debates to which it was directed.

II

Before 1916, the chief objections to Dewey's attempts to reconcile practical and scientific reasoning had come from idealists who argued that such attempts inevitably reduced principles and judgments of value and obligation to assertions about desires and the means and opportunities of their fulfillment. Consequently, in defense of his pragmatic approach to values, Dewey had sought to establish that an empirical approach was not inherently reductionist; that is, it need not reduce propositions about how we ought to act or what we ought to believe to propositions about how we do act or what we do believe. After all, Dewey argues, science is a practice, and like any other practice, it has its own rules, its own normative principles. It is in virtue of these that scientists determine how they ought to pursue their inquiries, what they may count as evidence, and what they are entitled to believe in specific situations. To say that practical reasoning operates in fundamentally the same way as scientific reasoning is not to say that moral philosophers can or should henceforth behave like descriptive anthropologists, cataloging human desires and the means of their satisfaction without passing any evaluative judgments upon them. On the contrary, moral philosophers should evaluate competing theories and beliefs about which ways of life and of interpersonal conduct really are desirable given what we know about human nature and the world. What will have to be "reduced" are the claims that moral philosophers can make about the scope of their results. Moral philosophers must recognize that the norms of moral inquiry are neither categorical nor unrevisable. The norms of scientific inquiry are hypothetical imperatives binding only on those who join the scientific community and share in its practices. So from a pragmatic perspective, the norms of moral inquiry and practice are likewise binding only on persons who commit themselves to a particular community and to sharing in their practices. Reliance upon particular moral judgments or norms is warranted only so long as it demonstrably serves the ends of community life and the practices that sustain and promote those ends.

But by 1916, neorealism had eclipsed idealism as the chief rival of pragmatism. Unlike the idealists, the new realists did not object to pragmatism or pragmatic ethics primarily on the ground that it would reduce values to facts. They did just the reverse. They objected to pragmatism precisely because pragmatists like Dewey did not reduce claims about values to claims about facts. British and American members of the new realist movement shared Dewey's belief that moral, aesthetic, and other practical propositions made genuine assertions about the world that were in principle confirmable by the sorts of observational methods used in physical science. But unlike Dewey, they took this to mean that moral and other value propositions had to be descriptive propositions whose truth was a matter of correspondence with a reality unmediated by subjective human attitudes or points of view. Thus to explain and defend his own position on the relation of practical and scientific reasoning in this new realist environment, Dewey had first to defend the legitimacy of his recognition of "practical judgment" as distinctive of evaluative reasoning and as central to the explication of practical inference. Only then could he go on to discuss the relation of practical propositions to the descriptive propositions used in scientific reasoning. This was the task of Dewey's "Logic of Judgments of Practice."

The positions to which Dewey responds in this essay are positions staked out in seminal works of some of the leading figures in the new realist movement. British realists G. E. Moore and Bertrand Russell and American neorealist R. B. Perry had each explicitly rejected the view that practical judgments involved a distinctive form of inference from nondescriptive propositions in their moral and epistemological works written before 1916, including Moore's *Principia Ethica* (1903a) and *Ethics* (1912), Russell's *Philosophical Essays* (1910) and his 1913 Lowell Lectures, published in 1914 as

Our Knowledge of the External World as a Field for Scientific Method in Philosophy, and Perry's article "The Definition of Value" (1914) and his contribution to *The New Realism* (1912).[1]

For example, Russell writes in the first of his *Philosophical Essays*:

> The study of Ethics is perhaps most commonly conceived as being concerned with the questions "What sort of actions ought men to perform?" and "What sort of actions ought men to avoid?" It is conceived, that is to say, as dealing with human conduct, and as deciding what is virtuous and what vicious among the kinds of conduct between which, in practice, people are called upon to choose. Owing to this view of the province of ethics, it is sometimes regarded as *the* practical study to which all others may be opposed as theoretical. . . . This view is . . . defective. It overlooks the fact that the object of ethics by its own account is to discover true propositions about virtuous and vicious conduct, and that these are just as much a part of truth as true propositions about oxygen or the multiplication table. (1910, 13)

Russell insists that philosophical ethics is "merely one among the sciences," a descriptive enterprise (1910, 14). Russell was following along lines Moore had laid out in *Principia Ethica*. Moore had insisted that "this question, how 'good' is to be defined, is the most fundamental question in all Ethics," because "it is impossible that, till the answer to this question be known, any one should know *what is the evidence* for any ethical judgment whatsoever" (1903a, 57). Moore insists, "The main object of Ethics, as a systematic science, is to give *correct* reasons for thinking that this or that is good" (1903a, 57–58). An essentially similar view underlies Moore's 1912 *Ethics*, in which he declares,

> Ethical philosophers have, in fact, been largely concerned, not with laying down rules to the effect that certain ways of acting are generally or always right, and others generally or always wrong, nor yet with giving lists of things which are good and others which are evil, but with trying to answer more general and fundamental questions such as the following. What, after all, is it that we mean to say of an action when we say that it is right or ought to be done? And what is it that we mean to say of a state of things that it is good or bad? Can we discover any general characteristic, which belongs in common to absolutely *all* right actions, no matter how different they may be in other respects? and which does not belong to any actions except those which are right? And can we similarly discover any characteristic which belongs in common to all "good" things, and which does not belong to any thing except what is a good? (1–2)

Their thinking ran roughly like this: If ethics is a science, then it must produce and operate on the basis of true or false propositions. And if ethical propositions are actually true or false, then they must be true or false in virtue of their correspondence to some real quality, property, or relation in the world. Moreover, these real qualities, properties, or relations must be in some respect independent of the person making judgments about them. Through the publication of Russell's *Philosophical Essays*, Moore and Russell were still agreed that the qualities about which ethics made true or false assertions and to which true assertions corresponded must be nonnatural properties supervening upon natural things, acts, and persons.

This analysis of values and of assertions about values was not widely accepted even by fellow neorealists. Perry rejected the view that value is an essentially mysterious, objective, nonnatural property inexplicably apprehended by human percipients. Perry writes, "I conclude that interest is not an immediate cognition of value qualities in its object, but is a mode of the organism, enacted, sensed, or possibly felt, and qualifying the object through being a response to it. To like or dislike an object is to create that object's value. To be aware that one likes or dislikes an object is to cognize that object's value" (1914, 153). Then as now, most self-declared epistemological and metaphysical realists were subjectivists in ethics, aesthetics, and value theory generally, basing their claim to realist status on the fact that after all, subjective psychological states *are* real constituents of the world. Thus they could hold, as Perry did, that "it is essential to realism to maintain that a property is independent of its being judged," and hold at the same time that what practical propositions are about are just subjective attitudes. Neorealism's view of properties was to be opposed to idealism, not subjectivism. Propositions about the values of things were to be interpreted as propositions about interests that motivate human action or about the extent to which particular policies, acts, and dispositions tend to satisfy given interests. While these are features of human consciousness and conscious behavior, their existence is independent of their being "judged" to exist by their possessors. And being independently real in this sense, they can be the subject of true or false reports. They can even be the subject of disagreements. Perry argues that what propositions asserting value assignments are really about is just the extent to which things are liked or enjoyed. These are assertions which can correspond or fail to correspond to reality and about which there can be cognitive disagreement because "superiority of a value founded on true presuppositions is quantitative: it signifies more of interest fulfillment and not value of a different and more fundamental order" (1914, 161). 'X is more valuable than Y' can be true because it can be the case that X satisfies more interests than Y. Thus moral or other value propositions are assertoric propositions and subject to the same sorts of truth conditions to which all other empirical assertions are subject.

This entails that the conclusions of "value judgments" must be expressible in ordinary propositional form, for they merely report states of affairs existing in the world. They do not express a peculiar form of immediate appreciative judgment or insight that would legitimate their being assigned a unique propositional form. On this, Perry is emphatic:

> I find this whole aspect of values confused through a careless use of the term "judgment." An act of liking, especially when it is reflective and mediated . . . is often spoken of as the "judgment of value." And it is commonly believed that we have to do here with a unique sort of judgment. But this belief is due to a lack of analysis. . . . If I consciously like the *Mona Lisa* on the conscious supposition that it is the work of Leonardo I may be said to judge twice. First I judge that I like the picture. There is nothing peculiar about this judgment. It is like the judgment that I see stars. . . . Second, I judge that Leonardo painted the picture. There is nothing peculiar about this judgment. . . . It is in all formal respects like my judgment that heat causes water to boil. . . . In addition to these two judgments my complex state of mind contains my liking of the picture. This is the central fact, but it is no more a judgment than my entering the Louvre to see the picture. . . . Mix these three things thoroughly and you have your normative or appreciative consciousness. (1914, 161)

Perry's analysis of the judgment that "the *Mona Lisa* is valuable because it was painted by Leonardo" clearly owes much to the theory of propositions and propositional attitudes that Russell was then developing. In this period, Russell held that propositions making meaningful assertions about particular things or events in the world were based upon "atomic propositions" that directly corresponded to sense data. These complex propositions were constructed from atomic propositions by means of the operators and quantifiers employed in mathematical logic (and, or, not, if-then, every, some). Thus any meaningful proposition about the value of the *Mona Lisa* must, on this account, be resolvable into simple propositions referring to the sensory properties associated with either the *Mona Lisa*, Leonardo, or attitudes experienced in response to them.

Russell recognized, of course, that propositions do not figure only in our assertions about the world. Propositions may themselves be the focus of attitudes: attitudes of hope, fear, uncertainty, or "belief." But Russell denied that propositional attitudes, including "belief," were themselves inferences or so implicated in inference as to come within the province of logic. He considered propositional attitudes and the processes by which they arise to be matters for psychological rather than logical investigation.[2]

One effect of this move was to introduce a sharp divide between logic, as the theory of "inference" in Russell's sense, and epistemology, as the science of knowledge generally—a division which did not always exist in nineteenth-century logical theory. When we engage in the inductive reasoning from which our conclusions about external things and events arise, we decide how much reliance to place on particular hypotheses given the evidence available to us. That is just to say we decide in what hypotheses *to believe* and to what extent we should do so. But since the processes by which we arrive at such conclusions are not forms of implication but incorporate claims about the rationality of belief, these processes are not strictly logical. They become the domain of a new field of study, lying somewhere between logic and psychology—namely, epistemology.

III

Dewey objected to the new distinction between logic on one hand and epistemology and its subdepartment, philosophy of science, on the other. And he objected to the conception of inference on which it was based. In the first section of "The Logic of Judgments of Practice," Dewey offers an argument that loosely parallels Moore's more famous "Refutation of Idealism" (1903b). Moore had argued that (Berkeleyan) idealism would be refuted if only one could find counterexamples in the form of mind-independent external objects, and then he offered his own hands as obvious counterexamples. Similarly Dewey refutes Russell's (and Perry's) view of propositions, that "the subject-matter of practical judgment *must* be reducible to the form *SP* or *mRn*" (Dewey 1915, MW8:14), by offering his own equally "obvious" counterexamples: "He had better consult a physician; it would not be advisable for you to invest in those bonds, the United States should either modify its Monroe Doctrine or else make more efficient military preparations; this is a good time to buy a house" (MW8:15). Russell had argued that "of the two parts of logic the first enumerates the different kinds and forms of propositions," and yet (Dewey insists) he "does not even mention [practical judgments] as a possible kind" (MW8:15). Russell's logic is thus flawed from the outset.

But counterexamples are only persuasive if we believe that they really are counterexamples. So Dewey follows up with an analysis of practical propositions and judgments to support his contention that they are not declarative assertions and thus are neither complex nor atomic Russellian propositions.

First, the truth conditions of the assertions at which practical judgments arrive are different from those of the propositions that Russell acknowledges. Descriptive propositions are true if they correspond with how things actually are. But a practical judgment holds that some X *may* be, *ought* to be, or *must* necessarily be held better, worse, wiser, kinder, or more or less valuable than some Y. Practical judgment arrives at assertions about relations between beliefs, facts, desires currently existing and those that may exist or might have existed at some other time. They do not simply report how things really are in the world at any given time. Nor consequently is it sufficient to verify the proposition simply to observe how things turn out.

Second, practical propositions do not describe states of affairs. They propose courses of action (sometimes purely mental) in response to the exigencies of a specific situation or type of situation. Both the situation and the options it permits feature in practical judgment and its products. Thus their conclusion must be indexed to specific situations for their meaning as well as for their verification, in ways that descriptive assertions need not be.

Third, Dewey points out, "A right or wrong *descriptive* judgment (a judgment confined to the given, whether temporal, spatial, or subsistent) does not affect its subject-matter: it does not help or hinder its development, for by hypothesis it has no development" (MW8:17). Both the propositions themselves and the evidence of their truth (the state of affairs to which they correspond) are presumed to be separate and independent. But practical propositions lack this sort of independence, since it is through adopting and acting upon a given proposition as warranted that the means of verifying it come to pass.

Fourth, Dewey claims "a practical proposition is binary" (MW8:17), in that it always makes two sorts of claims. One is a claim about the rationality of believing some course of action more or less desirable in a given circumstance. The other is a claim that the course of action proposed is possible (albeit only in some merely possible world to which a given judgment may be indexed). Thus courses of action, goals, or ideals that are absolutely unrealizable cannot be meaningfully asserted in the form of a practical judgment. Such propositions are not simply unverifiable; they are empty.

Fifth, practical propositions are necessarily hypothetical. An assertion that a given state of affairs exists or has certain characteristics is not hypothetical. Its truth does not depend upon the satisfaction of some prior condition. All that is necessary for it to be true that "There is a rose before me" is that there *is* a rose before me. For it to be true that "It would be better for me to believe that there is a rose before me," it is neither necessary nor sufficient that a rose be before me. That may not even be relevant.

Sixth, from all of the foregoing it follows that the truth of practical propositions can never be a matter of strict implication from true descriptive premises. Thus, unless we want to deny that inference is involved in practical judgments, we must conclude that inference involves more than implication.

Or rather, we should conclude that inference involves more than implication as Russell conceived it through 1919. Dewey's examples point indiscriminately to two quite distinct sorts of lacuna in Russell's account of inference. First, practical judgments involve what we now refer to as modal and deontic operators (necessarily, possibly, ought). Propositions containing such operators directly imply further propositions as necessary or possible by their connections to their premises, as C. I. Lewis would shortly be arguing in his 1918 *Survey of Symbolic Logic*. Thus Russell's conception of the nature of implication was (then) to that extent incomplete. But second, even if Russell's conception was adjusted accordingly, it would still be counterintuitive to limit inference to deduction and exclude experimental, inductive reasoning. Clearly, mathematical logic is sufficiently distinct from other forms of reasoning as to merit study in its own right. But it does not follow from this that we have any less reason to study other forms of inference or to include those other forms within the field of "logic."

Indeed, as Dewey points out, we should consider that "we may frame at least a hypothesis [*sic*] that all judgments of fact have reference to a determination of courses of action to be tried and to the discovery of means for their realization [so that] in the sense already explained all propositions which state discoveries or ascertainments, all categorical propositions, would be hypothetical, and their truth would coincide with their tested consequences effected by intelligent action" (1915, MW8:22). That is, we may view inductive inquiry as a prelogical or sublogical form of cognitive activity which so to speak prepares "material" in the form of propositions whose implications may then be studied by logic. Alternately, we may view empirical inquiry as the primary logical activity and inductive inference as the primary subject of logic. Since we use deduction to determine the implications of adopting various "rules" of procedure expressed in propositions, of granting that such and such may be true for the purposes of generating testable predictions or retrodictions, and so forth, the logic of implication would be studied as one of a number of instrumentally valuable procedures that empirical inquiry incorporates. This later view is the one for which Dewey would argue outright in *Logic: The Theory of Inquiry*. In "The Logic of Judgments of Practice," however, Dewey is only prepared to

argue for this conception of logic as an option at least as well worth purs-
ing as the realist alternative.

IV

Dewey anticipated the howls of protest his hypothesis was likely to produce. Four of the essay's five sections are devoted to replying to objections
such as: Is moral judgment then nothing but a form of practical judgment?
If so, why do moral realists believe they perceive moral and other value
objects to which their moral and nonmoral value judgments correspond?
Are scientific judgments practical judgments, and if so, what is the status
of the entities that scientists take to be real? How do we explain their error
in supposing that it is by correspondence to these real objects that their
theories are to be proved true or false? Section 2 deals with the first two
objections, while sections 3–5 deal with the remainder. I will not attempt to
cover these rather wide-ranging discussions fully. In what follows I will
focus only on the aspects that most directly connect with Dewey's analysis
of practical judgment.

In section 2, Dewey argues, like Perry before him, that "there is a deep-
seated ambiguity" in our use of terms like *good* that gives rise to a confusion of "the *experience* of a good and the *judgment* that something is a value
of a certain kind" (1915, MW8:23). It is this ambiguity which gives rise to
Moore's famous "open question" problem in *Principia Ethica*. Moore had
noted that if we say, "Pleasure is good," we can still meaningfully ask, "Is
pleasure good?" Moore had taken this to indicate that good does not *mean*
pleasure. Dewey would agree, of course, but would counter that Moore
had missed the more important point his open question highlights—that
we use *good*, as we use *value*, both as a *descriptive* and as an *evaluative* term.
"Pleasure is good" is true as a description just so long as the speaker who
is pleased finds her pleasure good. But she can still ask herself how this
experience ranks in comparison with alternatives open to her. When she
does, she no longer merely experiences enjoyment but also appraises it.

Dewey writes, "Contemporary discussion of values and valuation suffers from confusion of the two radically different attitudes—that of direct,
active, non-cognitive experience of goods and bads and that of valuation,
the latter being simply a mode of judgment like any other form of judgment. . . . 'To value' means two radically different things: to prize and ap-
praise; to esteem and estimate: to find good in the sense described above,
and to judge it to be good, to *know* it as good" (MW8:26). Pleasure may be
good, but I can still ask myself whether pleasure is what I ought to con-

sider 'good' in my current situation. Say I am at a party and I find myself by a plate of canapés that I nibble with pleasure as I talk with other guests. My enjoyment of them implies no evaluative judgment on my part. Suppose someone then remarks that canapés of that type are terribly fattening or contain *pâté de foie gras*, produced by means I consider unacceptably cruel. I will then be forced to evaluate my enjoyment, to rank it in comparison with other options. If I want to avoid appearing to condone cruelty to animals, I have a reason to conclude after all that abstaining from those canapés is *better* than partaking. Only when I arrive at a judgment of this sort does eating the canapés come to have a "value."

At first glance, Dewey's position might not seem significantly different from Perry's. Clearly Dewey's position is incompatible with Moore's, since Dewey holds that value judgments are practical judgments which are in part about noncognitive experiences of pain, pleasure, satisfaction, and so forth. But it may not be as immediately clear why it is incompatible with Perry's position or those of other subjectivist realists. Both Dewey and Perry are naturalists. Both assume a subjective basis for human evaluation, including moral evaluation. Nevertheless, there are important differences.

Recall that for Perry, a judgment such as 'the *Mona Lisa* is a particularly valuable painting because it was painted by Leonardo' describes the state of affairs that ensues upon the speaker's seeing or contemplating the *Mona Lisa:* satisfaction of her interest in visual representations plus satisfaction of her interest in perceiving or contemplating things connected with Leonardo. The proposition is true if and only if she actually experiences these satisfactions when she perceives or contemplates the painting. Dewey would object that this analysis is seriously incomplete.

First, it is not the case that 'the *Mona Lisa* is a particularly valuable painting because it was painted by Leonardo' simply reports a present or future state of affairs. On the contrary, it makes an assertion about the relative merit of one course of action (e.g., seeing, contemplating, preserving, investing in, setting fire to the *Mona Lisa*) versus others, given the constraints of her situation (e.g., her inability to see all the paintings in the Louvre on a given visit, to preserve or to buy all currently surviving Italian Renaissance paintings, or to make herself infamous by torching the Louvre's entire collection). As such, it clearly cannot be verified by simply putting the painting before the speaker's eye (or mind's eye) and measuring her emotional response. To know whether this inference is justifiable, we would have to know the circumstances of the speaker's situation, what alternatives are open to her, what beliefs she brings to it, as well as how she responds emotionally to interaction with this particular painting. Thus, whereas for Perry value judgments report facts, for Dewey "to judge value is to engage in instituting a determinate value where none is given" (MW8:35). Its verification depends in part on the practical consequences of its tentative adoption.

In sections 3–5, Dewey argues that the failings he has identified in realist analyses of practical propositions recur in realist analyses of factual propositions. These failings recur, he argues, because realists commit the same foundational errors in each case. First, realists fail to grasp that practical judgments are the rule rather than the exception. Second, realists systematically confuse experiences, such as enjoyments and sensations, with judgments made about them.

Taking the latter first, Dewey argues that the new realists mistakenly treat so-called primitive sense perceptions or "sense data" as a sort of "atomic fact" in the way we have seen Perry mistakenly treat the satisfaction of interests as basic units of "value." But as we have also seen, from Dewey's point of view, to say that a given experience has a particular value is to report a judgment about an experience. It is not to describe or report the event itself. Likewise, to assert that 'this is red' is to assert a judgment about an experience, not a description. The second error exacerbates the first. If we uncritically assume that true propositions are propositions that report how things are in the world independent of our attempts to know it, then our atomic facts are all, strictly speaking, false. For sense data are subjective experiences unique to the points of view of particular percipients at particular times. Our reward for adopting the realist point of view, Dewey argues, is an epistemological debacle from which realists have no escape.

But one might wonder, as indeed Russell himself wondered, how Dewey's pragmatic approach to sense perception would differ from his own. In his review of Dewey's *Essays in Experimental Logic*, Russell writes:

> Professor Dewey does not admit that we can be said to "know" what I call sense-data; according to him they simply occur. But this point, though he makes much of it, seems to me to make very little difference. . . . He admits . . . that perceptions are the source of our knowledge of the world, and that is enough for my purposes. I am quite willing to concede, for the sake of argument, that perceptions are not cases of cognition. . . . However that may be, Professor Dewey and I are at one in regarding perceptions as affording data; i.e., as giving the basis for our knowledge of the world. This is enough for the present; the question of the cognitive status of perceptions need not concern us. (1919, 23–24)

Russell had misstated and misunderstood the disagreement between himself and Dewey. Dewey does not agree with Russell that sense data are either the source of or a basis for our knowledge of the world that lies out-side our minds. For Dewey, the objects of sensory perception are the world. And as this world is of such immediate and practical concern to us, the primary object of our attempts to understand this world is not to describe it but to *manage* it. To manage it more effectively in a physical and emo-tional sense, we seek to manage it intellectually. Science is the practice of intellectual management of the sensory world.

Dewey remarks that "science is . . . such a specialized mode of practice that it does not appear to be a mode of practice at all" (1915, MW8:78) but simply a clearer vision or insight into how things are. Say, for example, we want to know more about cats. If a clearer vision or insight were all the advantage scientists had over ordinary individuals' investigations of cat behavior, anatomy, or environmental impact, they would achieve little more. Physical scientists, like the rest of us, obtain their knowledge of the world by manipulating objects, analyzing their relations to other things and events, and then generating empirically confirmable hypotheses which they attempt to verify. But sensory objects have no implications. "Cats have claws and teeth and fur," Dewey points out. "They do not have implica-tions. No physical thing has implications" (MW8:77).

The objects with which physical scientists have to deal then are not the cats of our experience, nor are they instances of an independent cat-reality outside and beyond human sensory experience. The "cat" about which sci-entific theories of behavior or anatomy are devised "may be called a pos-sible object or a hypothetical object" that does not "walk or bite or scratch." But because it is a construct of the qualities and relations we tentatively attribute to sensory cats, these conceptual cats do have implications for fu-ture experience that scientific investigation can develop into experimentally fruitful hypotheses.

Returning to the question of the relation of Dewey's pragmatic view of perception with Russell's realist account, we can see that for Russell the world of sense and the world of experimental science are rival descriptions of a third world whose actual qualities can never be determined. For Dewey, however, the world of sense is *the* world, and the world of experi-mental science is a world of hypothetical entities adopted for their value as intellectually manageable models of sensory objects. Dewey writes:

> There is then a great difference between the entities of science and the things of daily life. This may be fully acknowledged. But unless the admission is accompanied by an ignoring of the function of inference, it creates no prob-lem of reconciliation. . . . It generates no problem of the real and the appar-ent. The "real" or "true" objects of science are those which best fulfill the

demands of secure and fertile inference. To arrive at them is such a difficult operation, there are so many specious candidates clamoring for the office, that it is no wonder that when objects suitable for inference are constituted, they tend to impose themselves as *the* real objects. (MW8:78)

In a paraphrase of the Butlerian tag with which Moore had opened *Principia Ethica*, Dewey remarks that scientific objects are in a sense real, but "they are just the real objects which they are and not some other objects" (MW8:78).

Dewey certainly hoped and expected that his attack on Russell's account of propositions would be accepted as decisive. However, he did not imagine that his further arguments would be sufficient to establish to his readers' satisfaction that Russell's theory of logic mistook a subspecies of inference for its primary form. In his discussion of neorealist treatments of the problem of our knowledge of the external world, Dewey reminds the reader of his more modest goals: "My further remarks are not aimed at *proving* that the case accords with the hypothesis propounded, but are intended to procure hospitality for the hypothesis" (MW8:65) that a pragmatic theory of inference, containing mathematical logic as a subdivision, is not only conceivable but, if realized, would have at least as good a claim as Russell's to be considered a theory of "logic." It would be decades before Dewey would publish his attempt to make good on what in 1916 was merely a hypothesis. But the ongoing debate Dewey pursued with Russell and his neorealist colleagues in "The Logic of Judgments of Practice" and in succeeding essays helped shape the direction that Dewey's constructive efforts would eventually take. Thus it marks an important step in the development of Dewey's mature pragmatic theory, meriting closer study by historians of logic than it has so far received.

Acknowledgment

I would like to thank my colleague Bernard Linksy for helpful comments on this essay.

Notes

1. Perry 1914 was followed by Perry 1917, which is a reply to Dewey 1915.

2. When exactly Russell first used the term *propositional attitudes* in print is unclear; however, the term appears in his 1918–19 manuscript notes for his 1921 text, *The Analysis of Mind* (Russell 1986, 268). He comes very close at times in *The Philosophy of Logical Atomism* (e.g., Russell 1986, 200).

Works Cited

Dewey, John. 1902. The Evolutionary Method as Applied to Morality. *Philosophical Review* 11:107–24, 353–71. Reprinted in MW2:3–38.

———. 1903. The Logical Conditions of a Scientific Treatment of Morality. *Investigations Representing the Departments, Part II: Philosophy, Education.* University of Chicago Decennial Publications, 1st ser., vol. 3, 115–39. Chicago: University of Chicago Press. Reprinted in Dewey 1946, 211–49, and MW3:3–39.

———. 1915. The Logic of Judgments of Practice. *Journal of Philosophy, Psychology, and Scientific Methods* 12:505–23, 533–43. Reprinted in Dewey 1916, 335–442, and MW8:14–82.

———. 1916. *Essays in Experimental Logic.* Chicago: University of Chicago Press. Essays reprinted separately in MW1, 2, 4, 6, 8, 10.

———. 1920. *Reconstruction in Philosophy.* New York. Henry Holt. Reprinted with modifications 1948 by Beacon Press and in MW12.

———. 1922. *Human Nature and Conduct: An Introduction to Social Psychology.* New York: Henry Holt. Reprinted with modifications 1930 by Modern Library and in MW14.

———. 1929. *The Quest for Certainty.* New York: Minton, Balch. Reprinted in LW4.

———. 1938. *Logic: The Theory of Inquiry.* New York: Henry Holt. Reprinted in LW12.

———. 1946. *The Problems of Men.* New York: Philosophical Library.

Dewey, John, and James Hayden Tufts. 1908. *Ethics.* New York: Henry Holt. Reprinted in MW5.

Lewis, Clarence Irving. 1918. *A Survey of Symbolic Logic.* Berkeley: University of California Press.

Moore, G. E. 1903a. *Principia Ethica.* Cambridge: Cambridge University Press.

———. 1903b. The Refutation of Idealism. *Mind.* Reprinted in Moore 1959.

———. 1912. *Ethics.* London: Oxford University Press.

———. 1959. *Philosophical Studies.* Patterson, N.J.: Littlefield, Adams.

Morgenbesser, Sidney, ed. 1977. *Dewey and His Critics.* New York: Journal of Philosophy, Inc.

Perry, Ralph Barton. 1912. A Realistic Theory of Independence. *The New Realism: Cooperative Studies in Philosophy,* ed. E. B. Holt et al., 99–151. New York: Macmillan.

————. 1914. The Definition of Value. *Journal of Philosophy, Psychology, and Scientific Methods* 11:141–62.

————. 1917. Dewey and Urban on Value Judgments. *Journal of Philosophy, Psychology, and Scientific Methods* 14:169–81. Reprinted in Morgenbesser 1977, 586–98.

Russell, Bertrand. 1910. *Philosophical Essays*. London: George Allen and Unwin.

————. 1914. *Our Knowledge of the External World as a Field for Scientific Method in Philosophy*. Chicago: Open Court.

————. 1919. Professor Dewey's *Essays in Experimental Logic. Journal of Philosophy, Psychology, and Scientific Methods* 16:5–26. Reprinted in Russell 1986, 134–54, and Morgenbesser 1977, 231–52.

————. 1986. *The Collected Papers of Bertrand Russell, vol. 8: The Philosophy of Logical Atomism and Other Essays, 1914–19.* Edited by John G. Slater. London: George Allen and Unwin.

3

Experimental Logic:
Normative Theory or Natural History?

Vincent Colapietro

In 1903 John Dewey and seven of his associates at the University of Chicago brought out eleven essays under the title *Studies in Logical Theory*. Four of these essays were authored by Dewey himself. If one contrasts these four papers with Charles S. Peirce's own work in logic at this time—including the work sent by Peirce to Dewey, *A Syllabus of Certain Topics of Logic* (1903)—it is not evident that Dewey and Peirce were tilling the same soil. Furthermore, if one compares Dewey's 1903 approach to logic with other work in this field, it is hard to see how the leading logicians of the day would have found in these *Studies* much of immediate relevance to the central questions with which they were concerned. This should not be taken to imply anything regarding the quality of Dewey's work. It should be taken to imply that the character was such that the logicians of the time would not find there the tools to address *their* problems. The word *logical* in the title of this work might seem like a trivial matter, but for Peirce it was (in a certain sense) a vitally important topic.

In the year following the appearance of these *Studies*, the *Nation* (15 September 1904) published Peirce's review of this work.[1] At the time, Peirce was the leading logician in the United States, a figure about whom Ernst Schröder wrote to Paul Carus that, "however ungrateful [his] countrymen and contemporaries might prove, [Peirce's] fame would shine like that of Leibniz and Aristotle's into all the thousands of years to come" (quoted in Houser 1997, 4). However his stature is assessed by others, Peirce's own thoroughgoing identification with the pursuit of logical inquiries is unquestionable (Fisch 1986, 390). He characterized himself as "a life-long student of reasonings" (CP3:415) and went so far as to assert that, from the time he discovered logic at the age of twelve, he could never study anything at all except as an exercise in logic, in other words, as an opportunity to probe more deeply into the patterns of inference by which discoveries are made than he had been able to do thus far (Fisch 1986, 389). Peirce was trained in and committed to the minute accuracy characteristic of logical analysis (see, e.g., CP2:8–17), believing himself to be the first person since the Middle Ages to have devoted his life so completely to this discipline (MS 632; Fisch 1986, 390). Thus, by training and perhaps also temperament, he was suspicious of generalizations offered apart from such analysis. This view is pointedly expressed in his *Minute Logic,* a work written roughly at the same time as Dewey's contributions to *Studies*: "Broad generalization is glorious when it is the inevitable outpressed juice of painfully matured little details of knowledge; but when it is not that, it is a crude spirit inciting only broils between a hundred little dogmas, each most justly condemning all the others" (CP2:14). In his review of *Studies,* Peirce writes as a representative of logic as the discipline was historically constituted at that moment.

Even so, this review opens with Peirce proclaiming, "The volume of which Professor Dewey is the father forms a part of the University of Chicago's exhibit of an impressive decade's work, and is a worthy part of it, being the monument of what he has done in his own department" (CP8:188). For an appreciation of Peirce's evaluation of Dewey's work in "logic," however, we cannot limit ourselves to this public statement. In addition to the review in the *Nation,* there are several letters from Peirce to Dewey, two already published and thus easily available. Of these published missives, one was written before (date "1904 June 9") and the other after (circa 1905) the publication of his notice in the *Nation.*[2] The letters along with the review can be found in volume 8 of *The Collected Papers of Charles Sanders Peirce* (1931–58). But the review is also reprinted in its original form under its original title ("Logical Lights") in part 3 of *Charles Sanders Peirce: Contributions to the Nation* (1979).

There are also letters from Dewey to Peirce (cf. Dewey 1999). In one of these (January 11, 1904), Dewey writes to "Dear Mr. Peirce":

> I am taking very great pleasure in sending you a copy of the Logical Studies. It is a very poor return for all my indebtedness to you. . . . I wish very much we could have you here some time to deliver some lecture, and shall make a point to see if something can be done.

Apparently in response to this letter, though in one dated June 9, 1904, Peirce informs "My dear Prof. Dewey":

> I mean, if I can manage, to get some notice of the book of your Logical School into the *Nation.* But the editor fights very shy of the subject as I write about it or it is necessary to dilute or decorate it so that the result has not much

value for serious students. I will therefore write to express how your position appears as viewed from mine. I am struck with the literary tone of your
men, a sort of maturity which bespeaks the advantage of studying under
you & I thoroughly applaud your efforts to set them on their own legs. All
that is admirable & warms my heart. But I must say to you that your style of
reasoning about reasoning has, to my mind, the usual fault that when men
touch on this subject, they seem to think that no reasoning can be too loose,
that indeed there is a merit in such slipshod arguments as they themselves
would not dream of using in any other branch of science. You propose to
substitute for the Normative Science which in my judgment is the greatest
need of our age a 'Natural History' of thought or of experience. Far be it
from me to do anything to hinder a man's finding out whatever truth he is
on the way to finding out. But I do not think that anything like a natural
history can answer the terrible need that I see checking the awful waste of
thought, of time, of energy, going on, in consequence of men's not understanding the theory of inference.

Herein is to be found the heart of Peirce's reaction to Dewey's contributions to *Studies in Logical Theory*. Given the remark here about the slipshod arguments that Dewey allegedly allows himself and other remarks by
Peirce, including some public ones found in the 1904 review, it is not surprising that a defender of Dewey, like Larry Hickman, takes Peirce to have
"savaged the 1903 *Logic*" (Hickman 1986, 178). So Hickman asks, "What
was it that Peirce didn't like about Dewey's logic?" (178). He offers a detailed, informative, and helpful but (in some respects) distortive answer to
his own questions. Thus he provides a foil for my efforts in this essay. My
objective is not to pit my Peirce against Hickman's Dewey, nor even to pit
Dewey's Peirce against Hickman's (though this is closer to the center of
my goal). Rather, my aim is to think through an important statement of
Dewey's experimental logic in light of Peirce's reactions, with explicit and
detailed attention to the efforts of an important contemporary scholar
of classical American philosophy who has thought through Dewey's 1903
Studies in light of Peirce's critical response.

I

In "Why Peirce Didn't Like Dewey's Logic," Hickman proffers several hypotheses and marshals evidence in support of them to show just why Peirce
did not find Dewey's *Studies in Logical Theory* appealing. On this account,
Peirce's reservations and, indeed, antipathy show how flawed was his understanding of logic and how halting was his commitment to pragmatism.

Peirce is portrayed here as an apriorist (180–81, 183) and theoreticist.[3] Hickman alleges that "the test for inquiry is what is fated to be the case in a future community, and . . . the basis of such tests is *a priori*" (180–81). Hence, Peirce is not only an eschatologist (Hickman's word, 186) but also an apriorist (my term). Moreover, the key to understanding this aspect of Peirce's thought, Hickman contends, is the shotgun divorce between theory and practice, with the enraged father of the erstwhile bride Theoria forcing her to keep ever aloof from her lowly love. What seems to be especially galling to Hickman is the condescending manner in which this unabashed theoreticist speaks of practical endeavors ("Among the practical sciences are such things as 'pedagogics, gold-beating, etiquette, [and] pigeon-fancying'"). Whereas "Peirce here makes technology a kind of comic inferior science" (184), Dewey makes of inquiry itself and his logic (i.e., his theory of inquiry) *technologies*. Theory is for the instrumentalist Dewey not contaminated by being associated with technology. Rather it is best explained in terms of tools, instruments, scaffoldings, blueprints, etc. In short, Dewey appreciates precisely what Peirce disparages; moreover, he brings together what Peirce tears asunder.

However, it is difficult for me to recognize much of Peirce in Hickman's portrait. For Peirce is not, even in his logic, the apriorist alleged by Hickman. Nor is he the sort of theoreticist who warrants the ire of anyone who appreciates the skill and intelligence exhibited by, say, an expert carpenter or gardener. Perhaps it is not irrelevant to recall here one of Peirce's own comments on carpentry. One will be able to see that the target of disparagement is not practice but theory. Peirce states: "For the most part, theories do little or nothing for everyday business. Nobody fit to be at large would recommend a carpenter who had to put up a pigsty or an ordinary cottage to make an engineer's statical diagram of the structure. In particular applications of theories would be worse than worse where they would interfere with the operation of trained instincts" (CP2:3). Abstract, formal theory is rarely useful and often worse than useless to the naturally talented and properly trained craftsperson. Those modes of deliberation which are intimately connected with carrying out tasks constitutive of a practice are, of course, extremely valuable. But such deliberations are better named just that, not theory. The principal motivation for Peirce's apparently theoreticist stance is, then, the protection of practice as an undertaking with a character and integrity of its own, including the practice of theory!

On the one side, abstract formal theory rarely has direct applicability to our quotidian affairs. The indirect application of theoretical insights can be immensely valuable, whereas their direct imposition is characteristically harmful (see, e.g., CP2:3). The severe training of our inferential powers obtained through actual engagement in a particular practice (e.g., carpentry or chemistry), including the examples, suggestions, and criticisms offered by those expert in this practice, provides skilled practitioners with a *logica docens* as well as *logica utens* (in this case, "an instinctive *theory* of reasoning" as well as an embodied approach to reasoning). Experimental results rather than arbitrary dicta or abstract principles are the principal factor in this severe training. Often in minute detail and always to the governing purpose, our efforts are checked, corrected and guided by the results consequent upon those efforts. What grows up under such training is rarely aided by going before the bar of theory. For the inability of craftspersons to offer a verbal account of how they carry out their tasks (whenever there is such inability) might cause us to miss the eloquence of their physical execution. So, at least, Peirce argues.

On the other side, the sort of sustained, disciplined, and yet playful attention requisite for our *practices of inquiry* needs to be cultivated for its own sake, without too frequent demands made to show its relevance or utility (Peirce 1898, 113–14). Such demands are distractions here. Like every other kind, our practices of inquiry have an integrity of their own.[4] This means that their *extrinsic* instrumentality (their value as tools for practices and purposes other than those of the practitioners who, through their efforts, achievements, and above all unresolved problems, give definitive shape to their particular practice) is, at most, of secondary concern. Their intrinsic instrumentality is one with their heuristic function, their function as tools by which investigation is aided.

There are texts in which Peirce separates theory from practice, but properly understood he is distinguishing one array of experimental practices from another. He is not contrasting contemplation and experimentation. Nor is he identifying theory with a priori reasoning and practice with blind custom or unreflective engagement.

This needs to be stressed in opposition to Hickman's depiction of Peirce's theory of inquiry. Let me make explicit the relevance of "Why Peirce Didn't Like Dewey's Logic" to this volume. In 1916, two years after Peirce's death, Dewey's contributions to these *Studies* were incorporated in *Essays in Experimental Logic*. So the logic against which Peirce was pitting himself was, in part, these *Essays*. Thus Hickman's account of Peirce's antipathy toward Dewey's logic applies to the central chapters (2–5) of *Essays in Experimental Logic*. Especially since Dewey himself was keenly aware that *"Peirce wrote as a logician* and James as a humanist" (1925a, LW2:10; emphasis added), it seems proper to consider what Peirce, precisely in his role as logician, wrote about Dewey when *he* wrote as a logician in the *Studies* of 1903.

As already indicated, what Hickman argues in this paper is informative,

in certain respects just but in other respects unjust. In order to work toward rounding out the picture of the relationship between Peirce and
Dewey concerning logic, it would be useful to write a complementary essay: "Why Peirce Should Have Liked Dewey's Logic Better than He Did." I
intend my contribution to this volume to be a sketch of that essay. This
endeavor is not likely to make either Peirceans or Deweyans happy. Even
so, it may provide helpful suggestions for attaining a more nuanced understanding of the affinities as well as differences between Peirce and Dewey.
Beyond this, such an undertaking provides an opportunity to touch upon
an important philosophical question at the very heart of classical American
pragmatism. This problem is that of normativity. More fully, it concerns
the origin, status, and function of norms in human inquiry and indeed in
other human practices.

There is no need to purchase either Dewey's naturalistic account of
norms or an explicit understanding of this account at the expense of Peirce's
own naturalistic account. Contra Thomas Goudge, Peirce's philosophical
psyche did not harbor two warring temperaments, two irreconcilable per-
sonalities. He was not, at once, a naturalist and transcendentalist; rather,
he was a naturalist of a somewhat peculiar sort, but a naturalist nonetheless. As Josiah Royce noted, contrast is the mother of clearness. But there
are so many normative transcendentalists in the philosophical firmament
that it is unnecessary to fashion Peirce into one in order to contrast his allegedly transcendental "pragmaticism" with Dewey's truly consistent naturalism. Peirce is no champion of "apart thought"[5] even if his own philosophical tutelage in Kantian philosophy disposed him to use expressions
suggestive of that commitment and, moreover, disposes interpreters to
overlook his decisive break with transcendental philosophy.

For this reason, Peirce should have liked Dewey's logic better than he
did, at least a little better. Dewey was offering not so much a rival logic as
a complementary part of what Peirce himself sketched, to wit, a comprehensive account of our heuristic practices in which the theory of biological
evolution, the history of experimental investigations, and the forms of reliable inference (to name but three main strands) are woven together into a
single fabric. Whether he should have liked it *as a contribution to logic* is
another matter, not at all incidental or insignificant.

II

In contemplating this task, however, a ghost appears before me, trying to
bar my path down this road. Since our topic is at least in part Dewey's

logical theory, it seems especially appropriate to introduce this specter, since this presence is the internalized voice of one who was arguably the most astute student of Dewey's philosophy of logic in the past several decades. Let me introduce him by way of recollecting a philosophical exchange with him when he possessed more tangible form.

The title of Dewey's most significant contribution to logical theory, *Logic: The Theory of Inquiry*, goes far beyond his *Essays in Experimental Logic* (and thus *Studies in Logical Theory*, the book to which Peirce was reacting). But the *Logic* of 1938 is continuous with the *Essays* of 1916 and, indeed, the *Studies* of 1903. It is also a work in which Dewey acknowledged that Peirce "was the first writer on logic to make inquiry and its methods the primary and ultimate source of logical subject-matter" (quoted in Hickman 1986, 187). But just this tendency on Dewey's part makes Hickman and the companionable antagonist of my ghostly interlocutor reach for a sufficiently bracing qualification, lest Peirceans assume too deep affinity with their Deweyan siblings or, better, cousins! Hence, Hickman concludes "Why Peirce Didn't Like Dewey's Logic" by asserting, immediately after quoting the above passage from *Logic: The Theory of Inquiry*, "This is true as far as it goes, and as a description of logic it certainly applies to Dewey's own instrumental, that is, technological one. But it leaves out some of the elements that Peirce thought were essential to his own theory of inquiry" (elements to be identified in due course) (187).

The arresting specter of Ralph Sleeper is still a formidable boxing-master (cf. CP5:12), as his recollected and merely imagined objections still carry a hard punch. In a letter written to me on April 5, 1988, Sleeper struck this blow:

> Dewey remained loyal to Peirce's 'pragmatism' long after Peirce himself abandoned it by making the transcendental move into 'pragmaticism.' I suppose that, in my book [1986] for all the folks [read: all *you* folks, for I was clearly intended in this reference] who want to paper over the split between Dewey and Peirce, it is that they do so at the cost of making pragmatism irrelevant to what has been going on in mainstream logic since 1903, just as Richard Rorty would make it irrelevant to what has been going on in mainstream metaphysics.

So once again, here I am apparently trying to paper over a crucial difference between Peirce and Dewey. What justifies this persistence? In part, it is Sleeper's own admission and error (though note, *not* an admission of error on his part, but only of exaggeration). His admission of hyperbole was a response to a criticism of mine:

I do *not* want to paper over this split. . . . I think that you exaggerate the
difference. . . . From my perspective, you make too much out of Peirce's review of *Studies in Logical Theory* (CP8:188–90) and the two letters from Peirce
to Dewey in this same volume of the *Collected Papers* (CP8:239–44); also you
make too little of Dewey's sense of indebtedness to Peirce's work in logic.
(April 10, 1988)

Ralph replied, "You are, of course, right to say that I exaggerated the
Dewey-Peirce split. I did so on purpose!" (April 17, 1988). The context of
this admission is important. In the letter to which Ralph was responding
here, I tried to take him to task for his claim in *The Necessity of Pragmatism*
that "at no time did Peirce describe logic as a theory of inquiry" (1986, 49).
In my letter of April 10, 1988, I cited chapter and verse to show that this
claim is erroneous. In the face of these citations, Ralph nonetheless held his
ground:

> I did not know of the Peirce text where he calls logic a "theory of inquiry."
> It makes clear from that text, however, that he is thinking of logic as *norma-
> tive of inquiry* and not, in good Deweyan fashion, as having been *derived* from
> inquiry. So the split is there, all the same. . . . [Moreover] you should under-
> stand that it was my purpose in *Necessity* to show that Dewey quite radi-
> cally reconstructs Peirce. It would take another book to show how much he
> gets from Peirce, for . . . it is a very great deal. In the book that I wrote it was
> important for me to show how great the difference between Dewey's *con-
> ception of philosophy* is from both Peirce's and James's. (See my subtitle!) Even
> Dewey seems to want to paper over their differences when he can find a
> way, as he surely does in the 1938 *Logic!* But that is exactly what I find an-
> noying about most accounts of Dewey's work, *including his own!*

So even if Peirce *did* characterize his own logic as a theory of inquiry, what
he meant when he did so was quite different from what Dewey meant when
he did so! From Ralph's perspective, then, the crux of the matter is that, for
Peirce, logic is a purely formal discipline ("apart thought") having thereby
the transcendental authority to impose norms on inquiry whereas logic is
for Dewey a truly experimental affair wherein the norms used to guide inquiry are derived from the practice of inquiry itself. That the same characterization of logic can be found in both Peirce and Dewey does not mean
that they shared substantively the same conception of this discipline or discourse; indeed, the terminological commonality masks a substantive disagreement. This was, at any rate, the view Ralph vigorously defended.

I offer my thesis in opposition to this viewpoint. This thesis is quite simple. The differences between Peirce and Dewey regarding the nature of logic are not nearly as fundamental as either Peirce himself or Deweyans tend to suppose. There *are* differences, and these are not to be papered over. But they cannot be mapped by counterpoising Peirce's allegedly transcendental logic against Dewey's undeniably naturalistic logic. More generally, not every attempt to identify and highlight crucial affinities ought to be greeted with the dismissive trope of covering over what ought, in honesty, to be acknowledged. But my interest in this thesis is not so much exegetical as philosophical. Moreover, it is broader than logic, for it concerns norms, ideals, and procedures of every imaginable type. What is at stake here is a compelling articulation of a truly pragmatic account of logical and other norms. Whether such an account is best found in Peirce or Dewey—in both equally, or partly—is, in the end, of secondary importance. Can pragmatism offer an adequate account of logical norms? What does it mean to offer such an account in this context? These questions are of primary significance.

Like Hickman, Sleeper makes a transcendentalist of Peirce.[6] He sees the father of pragmatism as an advocate not only of fixed forms but also of transcendental norms (see, e.g., 1986, 47) secured and employed in an a priori manner. But Peirce was actually other and better than either Sleeper or Hickman suppose, precisely on the points with which they are inclined to mark his difference from Dewey. Peirce espoused an ontology of *evolving* forms and a logic of *immanent* norms. Thought is of the nature of signs; in turn, any sign exhibits at least a rudimentary form of life. As such, the genesis and transformation of signs in the course of experience are, for certain purposes, crucial foci of semeiotic (i.e., logical) attention. In order to offer a comprehensive account of the norms governing our reasoning practices, some form of genealogy is required. In order to exhibit these norms as norms in their regulative function within human inquiry, it may be legitimate to abstract them from the actual (or imagined) course of their historical emergence and to study them in their own right. Such abstraction and study does *not* mean that their analysis is ultimately dissociable from their genesis and evolution (cf. Hickman 1986, 181). Rather, it means that, proximately and provisionally, these abstracted forms in their multifarious formal relationships are a legitimate object of scientific investigation. A philosophy of logic would be incomplete without considering the origin, status, and function of these forms. But logic as logicians conceive this discipline would be impossible without sustained, systematic investigation of these forms and their relationships.

III

In one of his reviews of Peirce's *Collected Papers,* Dewey observed that "Peirce lived when the idea of evolution was uppermost in the mind of his generation. He applied it everywhere" (1937, LW11:482–83). Indeed, Peirce truly did apply the idea of evolution *everywhere,* including logic. But for various, deep, and complex reasons, he was tentative toward the adequacy of Darwinism when taken alone (i.e., apart from other principles of explanation). He was a thoroughgoing evolutionist but only a halfhearted Darwinian. Peirce firmly believed that an evolutionary account of scientific intelligence, of the form of intelligence capable of learning from experience (CP2:227) and, in some cases, even of learning how to learn more effectively, is not only possible but desirable. Moreover, he himself offered such an account in a variety of contexts, including some of his efforts to frame his more technical work in logical theory. So his utterly sharp opposition between logic pursued as a normative science and logic envisioned from the perspective of its evolution (of how reasoning about reasoning evolved out of the acritical inferences of embodied agents implicated in perilous circumstances) seems, given his own work, misplaced. However, it is likely that Peirce would say to me in this connection what Ralph Sleeper said in another: "You are right—I have exaggerated the split, but I did so on purpose! For otherwise the most pressing need of the present age was likely to be eclipsed by a discussion of less important topics, misleadingly treated under the rubric of logic." Whatever justice there is in this imagined response to me, there is an injustice in Peirce's actual response to Dewey.

What Peirce almost totally missed in his review and in his letters to Dewey is the extent to which Dewey's genetic logic *is* a normative logic. More accurately, it is a descriptive account of logic as a normative discipline. Peirce was contesting not the intrinsic validity of such an account but only its comparative value (i.e., it answers a far less important need than that of providing a normative account of our inferential practices in which our processes and practices of reasoning are broken down into their simplest steps). But Peirce should have taken greater pains to mark this distinction himself.

What Hickman astonishingly overlooks is the extent to which Peirce's own logic *is* genetic. Hickman stresses that Dewey "specifically identified genesis with analysis, and history with validity" (1986, 181). Moreover, he suggests, "The reconstruction of the normative element of inquiry allowed Dewey to establish a naturalistic connection between . . . the 'narrow' sense of logic . . . and its 'wider' sense" (182). But then he fails to note that Peirce draws an analogous distinction. For Peirce no less than for Dewey, it is necessary to "work back and forth between the larger and narrower fields" (Dewey 1916, 103; Hickman 1986, 182). What is most relevant here, however, is that the reconstruction of the normative element in logical theory is in effect an acknowledgment of normativity.

Peirce's logic is itself genetic, since it takes seriously the need to trace the forms of thought to their genesis and transformations in our experience. Consider, for example, Peirce's letter of application for a chair in physics at Johns Hopkins University. In a letter to Daniel Coit Gilman, the president of that university, Peirce indicated that his knowledge of physics was obtained primarily in conjunction with his study of logic. He went on to explain that "the data for the generalizations of logic are the special methods of the different sciences"; "to penetrate these methods the logician has to study various sciences rather profoundly" (Houser 1997, 1–2). Peirce was not only a historian of science and logic, before either field was clearly established; he was also a historian of these fields in his capacity as a logician. The history of logic and, more fundamentally, of our more or less "instinctual" processes of drawing inferences is relevant to an adequate understanding of logical theory. Even the *physiology* of reasoning has a proper place within logic proper (see, e.g., CP3:154ff.). The formal validity of inferential patterns (or sequences) can be abstracted from the historical practices and certainly the physiological processes in which these patterns have been operative and to which they are applicable. There is, accordingly, a point to pushing logic in a formally mathematical direction, as long as one does not lose sight of the purpose in doing so.

Both Peirce and Dewey hold that, in almost every age, the logic implicit in the actual methods of successful inquirers outstrips the explicit comprehension, let alone the symbolic formalizations, of logical investigators who presumably are concerned with exhibiting the highest forms of investigative procedure. In other words, our practices of inquiry outstrip our theory of inquiry. Indeed, part of their mission was to help logic get up to speed, to shorten the distance here. In this regard, Peirce writes:

It may seem strange that the dilemma is not mentioned in a single medieval logic. It first appears in the *De Dialectica* of Rudolph Agricola [or some other Renaissance author]. But it should surprise nobody that the most characteristic form of demonstrative reasoning of those ages is left unnoticed in their logical treatises. The best of such works, at all epochs, though they reflect in some measure contemporary modes of thought, have always been considerably behind their times. For the methods of thinking that are living activities in men are not objects of reflective consciousness. They baffle the student [including the student of logic], because they are a part of himself.

"Of thine eye, I am eye-beam," says Emerson's sphynx. The methods of thinking men consciously admire [and logicians formally analyze] are different from, and often, in some respects, inferior to those they actually employ. (CP3:404)

What is Dewey's experimental *logic* but a concerted effort to transform traditional logic into a discipline more attuned to the actual procedures of *experimental* science? But, as he so explicitly acknowledged, Peirce anticipated and to some extent guided him in this endeavor. A theory of inquiry can only result from an inquiry into inquiry. In turn, such an inquiry must take as its proper subject the most successful procedures of such historically accredited disciplines as physics, chemistry, and biology. As already noted, Peirce was not only a logician but also a philosopher and historian *of* logic. His work on the history of logic, including his painstaking attention to the working methods of the successful sciences, was not extraneous to his work *in* logic, comprehensively conceived.

Why then would Peirce have missed the kinship between his own efforts as a logician and those of Dewey in this same capacity? Part of the answer to this question is that, from his perspective, Dewey's treatment of logic was excessively descriptive, even if it provided a description of how norms emerge and function *as norms*. Another part is that the historical contextualization of the *constitutive* distinctions of a logical outlook can be stressed in such a way as to undermine the authority or inescapability of these distinctions, however they are named (e.g., warranted versus unwarranted assertability, rather than truth versus falsity). In "The Relationship of Thought and Its Subject-Matter" (1903b), Dewey contends, "Working terms, terms which as working are flexible and historic, relative and methodological, are transformed [by the epistemological and transcendental logician] into absolute, fixed, and predetermined properties of being" (1903b, MW2:306). But however fluid and variable are the distinctions between truth and falsity, validity and invalidity, any adequate formulation of logical theory should provide us with the methodological resources (more simply, the tools) by which to mark effectively these telling differences. *That* logic should provide such tools is nowhere denied by Dewey in his *Studies*, even if not adequately emphasized. *What* precisely these tools are and, moreover *how* they are to be acquired and applied are left excessively vague. Peirce could not have missed Dewey's repeated insistence that the reflective viewpoint concerns not how thought happens to occur but how thinking ought to be conducted (see, e.g., 1903a, MW2:325–25). But, then, Deweyans ought not to miss the significance of what Peirce felt was missing in the logic (*Studies*) of 1903.

One reason why Peirce might have failed to appreciate the normative cast of Dewey's experimental logic is that Dewey's essays in *Studies in Logical Theory* are not so much theoretical as metatheoretical: They are a critical examination of logical theories that are themselves highly theoretical. But certainly Dewey is not here solely or primarily responsible for Peirce's misreading. Hickman suggests that Peirce's dismissive attitude toward Dewey's experimental logic might be illuminated by considering that Peirce felt slighted by the absence of any reference to him in *Studies in Logical Theory:* Given his assessment of his own stature as a logician (cf. Houser 1997), could Peirce "then fail to have been offended that Dewey nowhere mentioned him in his essays? James and Royce are there, as are Lotze and Mill. Peirce's remark in the second letter [to Dewey, dated 1905] that in going after Lotze he had picked 'small game' may reflect some such sentiment" (1986, 179).

The plot thickens if the context is thickened. So let us fill in several important details here. Recall that, less than a decade before, Dewey had secured a position at the University of Chicago, where Peirce was two years earlier considered but rejected primarily on the basis of a letter from George Herbert Palmer to William Rainey Harper, the president of that university (Dykhuizen 1973, 77; Brent 1998, 220). Peirce's remark to Dewey about the city of Chicago (the city "hasn't the reputation of being a moral place; but I should think that the effect of living there upon a man like you would be to make you feel all the more the necessity for Dyadic distinctions,—Right and Wrong, Truth and Falsity" (CP8:240), thus all the more need to stress the *normative* character of logical theory) may also reflect other sentiments, not the least being resentment. Also recall that Dewey was one of Peirce's students in logic at Johns Hopkins University (Dykhuizen 1973, Brent 1998). And further recall that in 1883 (at the very time of Dewey's matriculation at Johns Hopkins), Peirce brought out with a number of his students (though Dewey was not among them) a volume entitled *Studies in Logic by Members of the Johns Hopkins University* (Brent 1998, 128). The character and indeed the very title of this work bear an unmistakable similarity to the work put together by Dewey and *his* students exactly twenty years later.

We also know that Dewey was not drawn to Peirce as a teacher. Early in his time at Johns Hopkins, Dewey wrote to H. A. P. Torrey, one of his teachers at the University of Vermont: "I am not taking the course in Logic." He explained: "The course is very mathematical, & by Logic, Mr. Peirce means only an account of the methods of the physical sciences, put in mathematical form as far as possible. It's more of a scientific, than philosophical course. In fact I think Mr. Peirce don't [*sic*] think there is any Phil. outside the generalizations of physical science" (found in the Dewey correspondence on CD-ROM, 1882.10.05 [00415]). The next year, however, Dewey did take Peirce's course in logic. In a letter to W. T. Harris, he reported, "Mr. Peirce lectures on Logic, but the lectures appeal more strongly to the mathematical students than to the philosophical" (1882.10.05 [00415]). Did Peirce entirely miss the attitude of this student toward the lectures in logic about which other students were excited? There were a number of mathematically inclined students *in philosophy* who were drawn to Peirce. The young Dewey stood in such marked contrast to these students that Peirce would have sensed that this student was not buying what he was selling. Indeed, we can reasonably surmise that, in turn, Peirce was not overly impressed with Dewey as a student of logic. Is it irresponsible speculation to suppose such an understandable defensive reaction on Peirce's part, especially when we know how defensive he could be in other contexts?

What makes this especially poignant is that, still animated by his abiding hope to win a hearing for his technical work in logical theory, Peirce could not have helped but feel threatened by what he supposed would happen if Dewey's approach were to become widespread. This can be gleaned from Peirce's second letter to Dewey. He is responding to a letter in which Dewey praised him for an article in the *Monist*: "Your letter . . . gave me keen pleasure,—all the more so because I was somewhat surprised to learn you found so much good in what I said. For your Studies in Logical Theory certainly forbids all such researches as those which I have been absorbed in for the last eighteen years" (CP8:243). From Peirce's perspective, this is the most serious charge one logician could level against another. It is, however, not certain that the charge is fair.

If it is true that Peirce had already traveled down the path being explored by Dewey, then why did Peirce not recognize the terrain as one he had previously visited and explored? If Peirce's own logic was truly genetic, why did he so strenuously resist Dewey's genetic logic and, more specifically, the explicit attempt to offer a "natural history" of logical thinking? Though partly answered above, this question presses for a fuller answer. An important part of the answer concerns just how persnickety Peirce was about strict adherence to the technical terms of scientific discourse: These technical terms should be used *only* in strict accord with their established usage. In another context, he wrote to James, chastising him for using the word *experience* to designate the undifferentiated, primordial *that* which James called "pure experience": "It is downright bad morals to misuse words, for it prevents philosophy from becoming a science" (CP8:301). In his first letters to Dewey (June 9, 1904), Peirce took pains to explain what "natural history" means in the decisive context of scientific discourse. He observed, "You propose to substitute for the Normative Science which in my judgment is the greatest need of our age a 'Natural History' of thought and of experience. Far be it from me to do anything to hinder a man's finding out whatever kind of truth he is on the way to finding out" (CP8:239). He might have written: Far be it from me to block the road of another's inquiry, even if the unwitting effect of this other inquirer is to bar the path of my own investigations!

So a genetic account in a broad sense is one thing. Such an account presuming to cover the entirety of logic is another. And the use of "natural history" as an appropriate designation of such a genetic account is yet a third thing. While Peirce would grant the legitimacy of offering a genetic account in a broad sense of the logical forms upon which our heuristic practices utterly depend, he would contest that logic in all of its branches must be cast into a genetic form. Moreover, he would fight against using "natural history" as the most apt term to designate those treatments of logic in which the historical evolution of logical forms is quite legitimately addressed.

What's in a name? It is not so much that one's own discipline by any other name would smell as sweet. Nor even that another's discipline by the name more properly belonging to one's own quite different discipline would smell foul. What, then, is in a name? Perhaps power, including the power to determine who counts as a practitioner of a discipline.[7] So what falls within the scope of logic carries implications for *who* falls within the class of logicians!

Peirce is acutely aware that what is at stake is nothing less than how his beloved discipline of logic is to be defined. The politics of naming is, within numerous contexts, a matter of importance. To name the act of naming *political* is to throw in bold relief the likely stakes involved in this act. In determining what counts as logic, one in effect also determines *who* counts as a logician. It is therefore not insignificant that Peirce concludes his review of Dewey's *Studies* by implicitly identifying the politics of naming as the basis of his reservations regarding what at the outset he called "an impressive decade's work": "If calling the new natural history by the name 'logic' (a suspicious beginning) is to be a way of prejudging [or begging] the question of whether or not there be a logic which is not a mere natural history, inasmuch as it would pronounce one proceeding of thought to be sound and valid and another to be otherwise, then we should regard this appropriation of that name to be itself fresh confirmation of our opinion of the urgent need of such a normative science at this day" (CP8:190).

Does anything justify this territorial claim (a claim in effect of the form "Hands off!") issued by the lifelong logician to this perceived upstart? Dewey's *Logic* of 1938 is more truly a logic than his *Studies* of 1903 or even that of 1916.[8] But, then, it is also the articulation of his experimental logic most closely allied to the spirit of Peirce's semeiotic investigations. Granted that what's in a name can be power, including the power of excommunication, considerations of who possesses the legitimate power (i.e., the least contestable authority) to institute or alter the names by which disciplines are designated become pertinent. The ethics of terminology is inevitably linked to a politics of discourse. In turn, this politics is played out at various levels, including that of labels.

The *life* of any inquiry is primarily in the questions posed and pursued by those devoted to a *line* of inquiry (cf. H. W. B. Joseph's *Introduction to Logic* [1906], quoted in Dewey 1938, LW12:97). This is as true of logic as anything else. The question of logic, then, is best addressed by considering the questions most profitably investigated under that rubric. This does not mean that questions falling outside the scope of logic are unimportant or less important than those falling inside this scope. It simply means a more or less strict division of intellectual labor in the interest of sustaining an intense level of critical attention on what inquirers hope to be tractable problems.

Let me consider briefly one sort of problem apparently banished from logic by instrumentalism. Does the instrumentalist depiction of declarative propositions and other logical matters as heuristic tools truly carry the implication that Dewey and, following him, Hickman, declare? In *Logic: The Theory of Inquiry,* Dewey explains that, from an instrumentalist perspective, declarative propositions "are intermediary means or instruments . . . of effecting that controlled transformation of subject-matter which is the end-in-view (and final goal) of all declarative affirmations and negations. . . . The point at issue concerns not their being but their function and interpretation" (1938, LW12:162; cf. Hickman 1986, 185). Hickman stresses that "Dewey cautions that a discussion of the 'being' of such instruments [as propositions] is irrelevant to logic, that is, to inquiry into inquiry" (1986, 185). But is it? Is it not relevant to an inquiry into inquiry to ascertain the complex, subtle nature of the tools upon which we depend in order to open and explore fields of inquiry? Does this even square with Dewey's own practice? Does it square with what he preaches (cf. Sleeper 1986, 5)? It is not only the case that language is a tool; it is also the case that tools constitute a language, in some respects a more adequate language than either our natural languages or our artificial formal ones. Dewey himself is quite explicit about this: "Tools constitute a language which is in more compelling connection with things of nature than are words" (1938, LW12:99). The syntax of their operation "provides a model for the scheme of ordered knowledge more exacting than that of spoken and written language" (LW12:99).

On one hand, we not only can but should abstract from certain kinds of questions regarding the being of the tools used by investigators. Are propositions mental entities? Are they entities having a subsistence apart from the operations in which they are employed? Etc. On the other hand, it is ultimately not possible or even desirable to abstract from the semeiotic character of our heuristic tools—not if tools constitute a language, in which case their very being is semeiotic (their being as tools is their function as signs and aids to the use of other signs). Dewey no less than Peirce saw the need to provide an explicit and systematic account of the manifold, interrelated signs upon which inquirers depend. Can Hickman dismiss such works of Dewey as *Knowing and the Known* with the same insouciance as does Richard Rorty? It would certainly be ironic if a move effective in opening the road of inquiry into inquiry all too quickly resulted in closing off certain paths (e.g., an investigation into the "being" of the tools of inquiry, when "being" is not conceived as a transexperiential subject-matter but rather a regional ontology calling for phenomenological description).

Semeiotic is the destiny of logical inquiry in any narrower sense. Our reasonings about reasoning are destined to transform themselves into a theory of signs. A functional ontology *is*, to the unprejudiced philosopher, an ontology.[9] For such an ontology, things *are* what they reveal themselves to be in their operations and functions, not in this or that insular context, but in the entire range of their complex entanglements. Hence to institute an invidious contrast between the *being* and the *function* of, say, a proposition is not so much to free oneself from ontology as to engender an illusion. For the most part, Dewey knew better. As Sleeper has pointed out, "Dewey argues a deeper-rooted theory of the instrument, one that links the *reality* of the instrument with the reality of the object" (1986, 65; emphases added).

IV

Within the context of this discussion, it seems plausible to suggest that, whereas Peirce took the pressing need of his own time to be the formal elaboration of a normative logic, Dewey took it to be providing a naturalistic account of our logical (and other) norms. But this should not be taken to mean either that Peirce eschewed naturalism or that Dewey eschewed normativity. This can perhaps be best seen in reference to the status of inference.

What we cannot get behind or underneath are illative processes. These are, in a certain respect, irreducible facts: They have to be taken on their own terms, as relations of a relatively unique character. As Dewey notes, "A student of the history of man finds that history is composed of beliefs, institutions, and customs which are inexplicable without acts of inference. This fact of inference is as much a datum—a hard fact—for logical theory as any sensory quality whatsoever. It is something men [and women] do as they walk, chew, or jump. It is just a brute empirically observable event" (1916, 420). A spoken word is a physical sound as much as any other audible event. It is, as such, a qualitatively unique occurrence. But utterly unique events could never function as signs, for iterability is of the essence of signs and this potentiality concerns the ways, however qualitatively or existentially unlike one thing is from another, that distinct events or objects can perform similar or equivalent functions. Existential objects and sequences of events have an immediate character as they exist or occur in themselves (what Peirce would call the firstness of secondness); but in their mediating functions, these objects and sequences display distinctive, observable, and thus describable traits, *due to their function as signs* (i.e., due to their work within patterns of inquiry). Natural objects and events functioning mediately are, at once, more and less than they immediately are: *more,* because they are by virtue of their mediating operations taken up in fields of involvement other than the one in which they actually occur, here and now; *less,* because the respect or aspect that allows them to be carried over into these other fields of operation is but one or, at most, a handful of qualities or properties (e.g., the audible difference between two sounds, such as *pit* and *bit*). The firstness of secondness (things in the immediacy of their actuality) needs to be set in contrast to the secondness of thirdness (signs in the process of *actually* doing their distinctive work). Signs so regarded allow us to envision thirds as thirds, the thirdness of thirdness itself. But signs can be regarded in this way only by a flight of fancy taking off from the actuality of the flights by which thought wings from one position to another (i.e., from the actuality of inference). There is no thirdness without secondness (CP5:434, 436), no thought without some form of embodiment (CP4:6); in short, no purely "formal, apart thought" (Dewey 1891, EW3:138).

If our life is truly a life of signs, these signs are first and foremost instruments of inference, the means by which we infer a position from our suppositions. In ordinary life these suppositions are ordinarily more than that. They are the unquestioned beliefs of our habituated selves. In any event, we cannot help but begin with inference as it is exhibited throughout nature and operative within our experience. Inference is a process encountered and enacted by human beings in their everyday involvements and every other context; as such it *is* experienced and *can be* observed. In brief, the illative relation is a natural process. Though it occurs in nature, it can generate the means by which we can not only transcend virtually any given, natural situation (at least in imagination) but also can even imagine the transcendence of nature *in toto*. The extent to which such transcendence is illusory should not deflect attention from the inherent power of this natural process to generate such powerful illusions. But inference always provides the means by which illusions and errors, trivial or grand, can be detected and corrected.

But consider Peirce's suggestion that "a decapitated frog almost reasons" (CP6:286).[10] This seems to imply a rather robust form of *naturalized* logic! In some respects and in some contexts, this undeniably natural process is transformable into a historical practice, wherein a sequence of inferences comes to alter the character of inference itself. But many philosophers and logicians will resist this naturalistic way of conceiving inference. For them, the norms of inquiry are first derived on a transcendental plane and *then* applied to a temporal continuum. But Peirce's logic is *not* normative of inquiry in that sense. It is normative of inquiry in the way that experience might be turned upon itself, to enhance, intensify, and direct more effectively its own course (cf. Dewey 1934, LW10:41). This is as true of our intellectual[11] as of our aesthetic experience. When Dewey writes in *Art as Experience* of turning experience back upon itself, his statements concern more than the aesthetic dimension of experience or the artistic form of execution. Experience can be turned back upon itself for the intelligent direction of its own course as well as for aesthetic intensification of its own qualities. Regarding our logical (and other) norms, empirical naturalism makes a twofold claim. First, "we can account for the origins of our most stable reliable norms of inquiry without postulating any source other than experience" (Sleeper 1986, 51). Second, we can account for experience in this very capacity as a process *in* and *of* nature (Dewey 1925b, LW1:11). Experience, naturalistically conceived, provides a sufficient explanation of human norms in all of their guises.

"For home rule may be found in the unwritten efficacious constitution of experience" (1906, MW3:87). In Peirce's language, this unwritten constitution is the *logica utens:* Its unwritten character does not ordinarily limit its remarkable efficacy. An explicit formal codification of the operative principles in our *logica utens* might nonetheless serve certain purposes of theoretical inquiry better than does leaving these principles implicit and thus unexamined. That is, logic—for Peirce no less than for Dewey—is normative of inquiry in the sense that the norms always already inherent in experience itself might be explicated and formalized to such a degree that they go beyond what has been, to date, the actual range of their experiential authority. The abstractable forms of rational procedure are, in their germinal form, abstracted forms. In turn, these abstracted forms are in their most immediate guise embedded forms implicit in the complex interactions of natural beings with one another and with themselves. Logical norms are ultimately derivable from the successful execution of controllable processes. The justification of these norms directs us primarily not to their origin in our actual experience but to their applicability to an unimaginably comprehensive range of possible experience. For the pragmatists, outcomes count for more than origins, fruits are more valuable than roots—though roots are valuable for their indispensable contribution to the delicate process of producing edible and thus sustaining fruit. If logical theory does take the form of natural history, it does so only in the service of fulfilling itself as an art (Dewey 1906, MW3:99). That art is at bottom the means by which our manifold experiences of ignorance, error, and deception (including self-deception) are squarely confronted.

For Peirce, logic is at bottom an ethics of intelligence (see, e.g., CP8:240). The incredibly complex and purely formal aids by which such an ethics often carries out its deliberations regarding what ought to be done (including what inference ought to be drawn, for inferring *is* a form of doing) should not block from our view the distinctive character of logical inquiry. Whatever its aids and instruments, logical reflection is a *deliberative* process. The norms by which it guides itself can be traced to those inherent in experience, as these have been elaborated and transformed by what may be called the mathematical imagination. Unquestionably, these norms outstrip the actualities of our experience. But, then, our experience is insistently suggestive of its own transcendence and transformation, especially when the frequently tyrannical pressures of immediate need and the excessively severe discipline of immutable traditions are thrown off.

The issue of "apart thought," not useless inquiry (see Hickman 1986, 181), is the crucial one here. The article in the *Monist* apparently prompting Dewey to write Peirce makes it clear that the only forms of thought or anything else with which we have any dealings are always embodied and embedded forms (CP5:436). What Dewey liked in Peirce's 1905 essay on pragmaticism ("What Pragmatism Is," EP2:300–324) should have given Peirce not so much surprise as pause: Perhaps he misinterpreted the implication of Dewey's repeated emphasis on logical theory assuming a genetic form. The concluding sentences of his second letter to Dewey, however, suggest a way of rapprochement: "What you had a right to say [in your *Studies in Logical Theory*] was that for certain logical problems the entire development of cognition and along with it that of its object become pertinent, and therefore should be taken into account. What you do say is that no inquiry for which this development is not permitted should be permitted" (CP8:244). What Peirce himself might have realized was that his own efforts to frame a theory of logic, in both the broad sense of an inquiry coextensive with the general study of signs and in the narrow sense of an explicitly normative discipline in which formal procedures for assessing the force or reliability of inferential patterns are established, could be greatly assisted by Dewey's own efforts in this direction.

Logic is at bottom a theory of inquiry for which the successful practices of quite diverse communities are of abiding relevance. This implies that logic is a theory of inquiry for which the tangled histories of various inquiries are of invaluable pertinence. To insist that a responsible account of these tangled histories can be a "natural history"[12] only in a certain sense of this term, and further to insist that even the most responsible form of a natural history of our exemplary heuristic practices encompasses only part of logic, does not require one to disparage or dismiss the importance of framing logical theory in this genetic manner. From Peirce's perspective, the earnest, deferential but distant, unengaged student of twenty years earlier should not, after all, be allowed to redefine the field to which Peirce had devoted his entire life, in such a way that the elder logician would in effect be exiled from his homeland. John Dewey was too genial and generous a philosopher to repay his debt to Peirce's pragmatism by banishing this logician from the realm of logic. He was, however, too fundamentally committed to the radical reform of our social institutions, including such historically instituted disciplines as logic, to allow a knot of specialists to act like a caste of priests.

The logic of experience is discoverable within the history of experience itself. Experience is always an incipient, inchoate experiment in which the organism itself is, to some degree, on trial. The blind gropings of a vulnerable organism, especially if it is in effect a unique representative of an organic form that has proven itself over the course of centuries, are always more than blind gropings. The evolution of species is itself, in certain respects, an instance of learning (Burks 1997). It is inference writ large, so large as to be difficult to see. The history of experience is one of ceaseless striving and countless failures. It is inscribed in the very physiology of those beings who undertake and undergo experience. These inscriptions primarily take the form of habits, inherited as well as acquired.

While there is a pressing, immanent need within the course of experience to make warranted assertions, to draw reliable inferences, etc., there is no necessity to look beyond experience to secure the means for making such assertions, drawing such inferences, etc. The field within which unwarranted assertions are made and unreliable inferences are drawn is also, however, the one wherein the motives and materials for crafting the tools to detect and correct these mistakes are available.

If anything is indigenous to experience, it is the unimaginably vast array of errors, confusions, illusions, and deceptions to which humans are prey. "There is something humorous," Dewey wryly notes, "about the discussion of the problem of error as if it were a rare or exceptional thing—an anomaly—when the barest glance at human history shows that mistakes have been the rule, and that truth lies at the bottom of a well" (1915, MW8:72). The omnipresence of inference entails the presence of fallibility at every significant juncture of our mental lives. Every step is shadowed by the possibility of a misstep (cf. Colapietro 1997). Dewey no less than Peirce lived in the unblinking awareness of our ineradicable fallibility. Peirce no less than Dewey lived with the abiding hope that even though the methodological *tools* needed to detect and correct our inevitable errors are, at present, never entirely adequate to the task, they can be made ever more so. Both were, at bottom, fallibilists. An experimental logic is the working faith of a pragmatic fallibilist who, in a visceral way and at a muscular (if not neuronal) level, knows the significance of failure *consequent upon trial*— and trial *tempered by failure*. It is a faith at once modest and bold: modest in the uncompromising acknowledgment of its own finitude and fallibility; bold in its practical confidence to be able to craft the necessary tools for its most adventurous undertakings.

Dewey claimed, "Peirce will always remain a philosopher's philosopher. His ideas will reach the general public only through the mediations and translations of others" (1937, LW11:480). The tradition of pragmatism is not so much a series of misunderstandings, beginning with James's mistranslation of Peirce's ideas (Perry 1935) as it is an extended argument about (among other topics) the meaning of *practice* and its cognates (see, e.g., Dewey 1908).[13] Peirce's felt distance from Dewey's relatively early formulation of his logical theory would need to be highlighted, in a fuller account than I am able to provide here, as much as Dewey's also keenly felt sense of his indebtedness to Peirce's writings. The tradition of pragmatism *is* an argument about the meaning of practice and other matters. I have no doubts or illusions about this. The disagreements *within* this tradition can be expressed in vitriolic tones and with dismissive intent. But, upon a historically inflected and philosophically nuanced reading, Peirce's severe reservations about Dewey's experimental logic are not expressed in such tones or with such intent. Given his increasingly marginal position within the intellectual life of the United States during the first decade of the twentieth century, it is best to see these reservations as acts of self-defense: Peirce was trying to secure a place for himself within the discourse of logic, a discourse he feared was becoming usurped by literary men keen to do battle with theologically inclined philosophers but not scientifically animated ones.

Without question, that is unfair to Dewey. It is, however, how matters may have looked to Peirce from his perspective on the periphery. Though unjustifiable (especially in retrospect), this viewpoint was not entirely unreasonable. The editor of the *Nation* was willing to publish Peirce's review of Dewey's *Studies*, but only if Peirce would avoid the technicalities and the formalizations any logician would take to be of the essence of logic. Of even more stinging relevance, Dewey was in the position to bring out his views on logic, in the form of a book, whereas Peirce was not, despite repeated attempts and the strenuous interventions of such influential figures as William James. Is it fair, let alone charitable, to begrudge the aging Peirce his growing sense of futility? After all, he staked his very existence on logic as much as on anything else. Peirce was fighting *for* the future of logic and also for his own desperate chance to win a public hearing for technical work having limited appeal. He was fighting *with* one whom he respected and, seemingly, liked. But, then, the fight was about logic, a discipline in which Peirce staked nothing less than his identity. Lest I be misunderstood here, let me stress that none of this *justifies* Peirce in his failures to appreciate the value of Dewey's contribution to logic or, at least, a metatheoretical discourse about logical theory (a discourse on which Peirce spilled more than a few bottles of ink). The pressing need for Peirce was not for a discourse so far removed from the directly normative questions of how to differentiate warranted from unwarranted assertions, reliable from unreliable inferences, etc., nor for a detailed refutation of a minor contributor to logical theory who would, in time, become even more negligible. Was he so wrong in this? Might not Dewey's efforts have been better expended on more significant figures in logical theory (the book on *Logic* by Lotze to which Dewey is responding in the 1903 *Studies* is a translation into English made in 1888 or earlier) and less theoretical matters?

"Apart thought" both reflects and reinforces what might be called *life apart*—our natural, mortal life divided against itself, wherein this life is set in marked and invidious contrast to another life. Thus near the conclusion of his introduction to *Essays in Experimental Logic*, Dewey states:

> God only knows how many of the sufferings of life are due to the belief that the natural scene and operations of our life are lacking in ideal import, and to the consequent tendency to flee for the lacking ideal factors to some other world inhabited exclusively by ideals. (1916, MW10:364)

For Dewey, one of the most pressing needs of our time is for philosophy and other disciplines to provide whatever aid they can to make "it clear to a troubled humanity that ideals are continuous with natural events, that they but represent their possibilities, and that recognized possibilities form methods for a conduct which may realize them in fact" (1916, MW10:364-65). Peirce uses the term *monasticism* to designate apart life (life divided against itself in such a way that we purchase another life with the coin of this life). It amounts to "sleepwalking in this world with no eye nor heart except for the other" (CP1:673). These two pragmatists would, with their naturalistic account of our most authoritative norms and indeed with various other doctrines, arouse us from our somnolent lives.

For Dewey, "theory is with respect to all other modes of practice the most practical of all things, and the more impartial and impersonal it is, the more truly practical it is" (1915, MW8:82). For Peirce, the *heuristic* life (the life devoted to inquiry for its own sake) is different in character from either the *practical* or the *artistic* life (CP1:43). But this is not so much a difference that always and univocally makes a difference. It is a difference that *can* make a difference in *various* ways. Consequently, it is for the most part misleading simply to pit Peirce the theoreticist against Dewey the instrumentalist and then to run several other stigmatizing contrasts together under these rubrics (i.e., contrasts designed to stigmatize Peirce): Peirce the transcendentalist versus Dewey the naturalist, Peirce the apriorist versus Dewey the experimentalist, Peirce the eschatologist versus Dewey the historical actor implicated in everyday affairs for whom both recollections of the past and considerations of the future are tools for the direction, illumination, and intensification of the present (1922, MW14; Colapietro, 1998b).[14] Perhaps Dewey's translations of Peirce are more faithful to that philosopher's philosopher than many of Dewey's own advocates appreciate. For me at any rate, some of the points where the thought of Charles Peirce and that of John Dewey intersect are ones worthy of not only critical attention but also cultural celebration. For this partial but significant consensus reached by thinkers who truly *are* quite different from one another in various important ways is the kind of achievement that underwrites their shared ideal of cooperative inquiry and, beyond this, Dewey's singular ideal of democratic deliberation.

Notes

1. Cf. Peirce 1979. It is worthwhile to note that William James also wrote a review of *Studies in Logical Theory*. This brief notice appeared under the title "The Chicago School" (1904). See Dykhuizen 1973, 84–85.

2. It is not certain whether all of these letters were actually sent by Peirce to Dewey. This raises interesting questions regarding how much stock is to be placed in the views expressed therein.

3. I have borrowed this term from Frederick Crews but am using it in a sense quite different from the one that he assigns to this neologism. In "The Grand Academy of Theory" he contends that "today we are surrounded by *theoreticism*—frank recourse to unsubstantiated theory, not just as a tool of investigation but as anti-empirical knowledge in its own right" (1986, 164). I am using the term to designate the position of anyone who divorces theory from practice and, then, elevates theory to a higher plane than practice.

4. "Can any man with a soul deny that the development of pure science is the great end of the arts? Not indeed for the individual man. He uses them, as [he] uses the deer … and just as … I am burning great logs in a fireplace. But we are barbarians to treat the deer and the forest trees in that fashion. They have ends of their own, not related to my individual stomach or skin. So, too, man looks upon the arts from his selfish point of view. But they, too, like the beasts and the trees, are living organisms, none the less for being parasitic to man's mind; and their manifest internal destiny is to grow into pure sciences" (Peirce 1898, 119; also in EP2:39).

5. Dewey uses this expression (more fully, "formal, apart thought") in a very early essay (1891, EW3:138), quoted and used by Ralph Sleeper (1986) to designate a principal target of a thoroughly naturalistic approach to normative structures and relations (what might otherwise be called a transcendentalist position).

6. Despite their opposition to Rorty on so many other fronts, Sleeper and Hickman are comrades in arms with him on this one (see, e.g., Rorty 1982, 160–61).

7. In the actual rhetoric of professional philosophers, consider how such judgments as "That is not philosophy!" function ideologically. The ideological dimension of any discursive practice pertains to the relationship between discourse (Who is entitled to speak? In what context? In what manner? Etc.) and the structures of power actually in place.

8. Sleeper contends that "the 1903 *Studies* are just the beginning of Dewey's development of what he called the 'logic of experience,' a development that would not be brought to completion until his 1938 *Logic: The Theory of Inquiry*" (1986, 5).

9. Dewey, in response to Ernest Nagel, in a text Larry Hickman himself quotes, asserts: "I do not think that logic can be divorced from ontology" (1930, LW5:203; Hickman 1986, 183). So it is puzzling why Hickman contrasted function with being in such a way as to imply that ontology is avoidable (1986, 185). Certain kinds of questions about the being of, say, propositions *are* avoidable. But the *being* of the instruments upon which we rely and, moreover, the relation between the strictly

logical character of our various symbolizations and the natural world (LW5:203) are legitimate questions for a naturalistic logic.

10. The example Peirce appears to have in mind is that of a decapitated frog instinctively wiping acid from its leg. For he goes on to write: "The habit that is in his cerebellum serves as a major premiss. The excitation of a drop of acid is his minor premiss. All that is of any value in the operation of ratiocination is there, except only one thing. What he lacks is the power of preparatory meditation" (CP6:286). In the absence of such power there is no possibility of there being a self-controlled inference; and in the absence of this possibility there is not, properly speaking, any instance of reasoning. There is, however, the pattern of an inference exhibited in the behavior of the frog.

11. In *The Quest for Certainty,* Dewey offers helpful definitions of the mental and the intellectual. He observes: "Many definitions of mind and thinking have been given." Then he suggests: "I know of but one that goes to the heart of the matter:—response to the doubtful as such" (1929, LW4:179). He goes on to define the intellectual as a species of the mental: "The intellectual phase of mental action is identical with an indirect mode of response, one whose purpose is to locate the nature of the trouble and form an idea of how it may be dealt with—so that operations may be directed in view of an intended solution. Take any incident of experience you choose . . . and it has or has not intellectual, cognitive quality according as there is deliberate endeavor to deal with the indeterminate so as to dispose of it, to settle it" (LW4:180–81).

12. "Nor does [Peirce's view regarding logic] lead us into the divarication of those who know no other logic than a 'Natural History' of thought. As to this remark, I pray you, that 'Natural History' is the term applied to the descriptive sciences of nature, that is to say, to sciences which describe different kinds of objects and classify them as well as they can while they still remain ignorant of their essences and of the ultimate agencies of their production, etc." (CP4:8).

13. In one text, Peirce explains: "By 'practical' I mean apt to affect conduct; and by conduct, voluntary action that is self-controlled, i.e., controlled by adequate deliberation" (CP8:322).

14. Dewey no less than Peirce supposes that even judgments regarding the past refer us, in a certain sense, to the future. He certainly does insist that humans "face the future, but for the sake of the present, not the future" (LW12:238). But a living sense of an open future, a sense structuring our activities in the present, does not make anyone an eschatologist. The ideal of the long run is invoked to contextualize our activities in the meantime, in the living present in its dynamic mediation between a constitutive heritage and nonetheless an open future.

Works Cited

Brent, Joseph. 1998. *Charles Sanders Peirce: A Life.* Rev. ed. Bloomington: Indiana University Press.

Burks, Arthur W. 1997. Logic, Learning, and Creativity in Evolution. In *Studies in the Logic of Charles Sanders Peirce*, ed. Nathan Houser, Don Roberts, and James Van Evra, 497–534. Bloomington: Indiana University Press.

Colapietro, Vincent. 1997. The Dynamical Object and the Deliberative Subject. In *The Rule of Reason: The Philosophy of Charles S. Peirce*, ed. Jacqueline Brunning and Paul Forster, 262–88. Toronto: University of Toronto Press.

———. 1998a. Transforming Philosophy into a Science: A Debilitating Chimera or a Realizable Desideratum? *American Catholic Philosophical Quarterly* 72 (2):245–78.

———. 1998b. Entangling Alliances and Critical Traditions: Reclaiming the Possibilities of Critique. *Journal of Speculative Philosophy* 12 (2):114–33.

Crews, Frederick. 1986. *Skeptical Engagements*. New York: Oxford University Press.

Dewey, John. 1891. The Present Position of Logical Theory. *Monist* 2:1–17. Reprinted in EW3:125–41.

———, ed. 1903a. *Studies in Logical Theory*. University of Chicago Decennial Publications, 2d ser., vol. 11. Chicago: University of Chicago Press. Dewey's contributions reprinted in Dewey 1916, 75–182, and in MW2:293–375

———. 1903b. The Relationship of Thought and Its Subject-Matter. First published as "Thought and Its Subject-Matter: The General Problem of Logical Theory" in Dewey 1903a. Reprinted in Dewey 1916, 75–102, and MW2:298–315.

———. 1906. Beliefs and Existences (Beliefs and Realities). *Philosophical Review* 15:113–19. Reprinted in *The Influence of Darwin on Philosophy*, 169–97 (New York: Henry Holt, 1910). Also reprinted in MW3:83–100.

———. 1908. What Pragmatism Means by Practical. *Journal of Philosophy, Psychology, and Scientific Methods* 5:85–99, with the title "What Does Pragmatism Mean by Practical?" Reprinted in Dewey 1916, 303–29, and MW8:98–115.

———. 1915. The Logic of the Judgments of Practice. *Journal of Philosophy, Psychology, and Scientific Methods* 12:505–23, 533–43. Reprinted in Dewey 1916, 335–442, and MW8:14-82.

———. 1916. *Essays in Experimental Logic*. Chicago: University of Chicago Press. Essays reprinted separately in MW1, 2, 4, 6, 8, 10.

———. 1922. *Human Nature and Conduct*. New York: Henry Holt. Reprinted in MW14.

———. 1925a. The Development of American Philosophy. *Studies in the History of Ideas* 2:353–77. Reprinted in LW2:3–21.

———. 1925b. *Experience and Nature*. Chicago: Open Court. Reprinted in LW1.

———. 1929. *The Quest for Certainty*. New York: Minton, Balch. Reprinted in LW4.

———. 1930. The Applicability of Logic to Existence. *Journal of Philosophy* 27:174–79. Reprinted in LW5:203–9.

———. 1934. *Art as Experience*. New York: Henry Holt. Reprinted in LW10.

———. 1935. The Founder of Pragmatism (A Review of *The Collected Papers of Charles Sanders Peirce*, vol. 5). *New Republic* 81:338–39. Reprinted in LW11:421–24.

———. 1937. Charles Sanders Peirce (A Review of *The Collected Papers of Charles Sanders Peirce*, vols. 1–6). *New Republic* 89:415–16. Reprinted in LW11:479–84.

———. 1938. *Logic: The Theory of Inquiry*. New York: Henry Holt. Reprinted in LW12.

———. 1999. *The Correspondence of John Dewey*, vol. 1 (1871–1918). Edited by Larry Hickman. Charlottesville: InteLex Corporation.

Dykhuizen, George. 1973. *The Life and Mind of John Dewey*. Carbondale: Southern Illinois University Press.

Fisch, Max H. 1986. *Peirce, Semeiotic, and Pragmatism*. Ed. Kenneth L. Ketner and Christian J. W. Kloesel. Bloomington: Indiana University Press.

Goudge, Thomas. 1950. *The Thought of C. S. Peirce*. Toronto: University of Toronto Press.

Haack, Susan. 1993. Peirce and Logicism: Notes Toward an Exposition. *Transactions of the Charles S. Peirce Society* 29 (1):33–56.

———. 1997. The First Rule of Reason. In *The Rule of Reason: The Philosophy of Charles S. Peirce*, ed. Jacqueline Brunning and Paul Forster, 241–61. Toronto: University of Toronto Press.

Hickman, Larry. 1986. Why Peirce Didn't Like Dewey's Logic. *Southwest Philosophy Review* 3:178–89.

———. 1992. *John Dewey's Pragmatic Technology*. Bloomington: Indiana University Press.

Hintikka, Jaakko. 1997. The Place of C. S. Peirce in the History of Logical Theory. In *The Rule of Reason: The Philosophy of Charles S. Peirce*, ed. Jacqueline Brunning and Paul Forster, 13–33. Toronto: University of Toronto Press.

Houser, Nathan. 1993. On 'Peirce and Logicism': A Response to Haack. *Transactions of the Charles S. Peirce Society* 29 (1):57–67.

———. 1997. Introduction to *Studies in the Logic of Charles Sanders Peirce*, ed. Nathan Houser, Don Roberts, and James Van Evra, 1–22. Bloomington: Indiana University Press.

Hull, Kathleen. 1994. Why Hanker after Logic? *Transactions of the Charles S. Peirce Society* 30 (2):271–95.

James, William. 1904. The Chicago School. *Psychological Bulletin* 1:1–5.

———. 1977. *The Writings of William James: A Comprehensive Edition*. Edited by John J. McDermott. Chicago: University of Chicago Press.

Joseph, H. W. B. 1906. *An Introduction to Logic*. Oxford: Oxford University Press.

Levi, Issac. 1997. Inference and Logic According to Peirce. In *The Rule of Reason: The Philosophy of Charles S. Peirce*, ed. Jacqueline Brunning and Paul Forster, 34–56. Toronto: University of Toronto Press.

Peirce, C. S. 1898 [1992]. *Reasoning and the Logic of Things*. Edited by Kenneth Laine Ketner. Cambridge: Harvard University Press.

———. 1903. *A Syllabus of Certain Topics of Logic*. Boston: Alfred Mudge and Son.

———. 1931–58. *Collected Papers of Charles Sanders Peirce*. Vols. 1–6 edited by Charles Hartshorne and Paul Weiss; vols. 7–8 edited by Arthur W. Burks. Cambridge: Belknap Press of Harvard University Press. Cited as CP.

———. 1978. *Charles Sanders Peirce: Contributions to the Nation*, vol. 2 (1894–1900). Edited by Kenneth Laine Ketner and James Edward Cook. Lubbock: Texas Tech Press.

———. 1979. *Charles Sanders Peirce: Contributions to the Nation*, vol. 3 (1901–8). Edited by Kenneth Laine Ketner and James Edward Cook. Lubbock: Texas Tech Press.

———. 1998. *The Essential Peirce,* vol. 2 (1893–1913). Edited by the Peirce Edition Project. Bloomington: Indiana University Press. Cited as EP2.

Perry, Ralph Barton. 1935. *The Thought and Character of William James.* 2 vols. Boston: Little, Brown.

Piatt, Donald A. 1939. Dewey's Logical Theory. In *The Philosophy of John Dewey,* ed. Paul Arthur Schilpp, 105–34. New York: Tudor.

Rorty, Richard. 1982. *Consequences of Pragmatism.* Minneapolis: University of Minnesota Press.

Russell, Bertrand. 1939. Dewey's New *Logic.* In *The Philosophy of John Dewey,* ed. Paul Arthur Schilpp, 137–56. New York: Tudor.

Sleeper, Ralph W. 1986. *The Necessity of Pragmatism: John Dewey's Conception of Philosophy.* New Haven: Yale University Press.

———. 1988. Private correspondence to author.

4

The Logical Reconstruction of Experience: Dewey and Lewis

Sandra B. Rosenthal

In his review article on Dewey's logic, C. I. Lewis focuses his "brief comment" on the conception which he considers to be pivotal for Dewey's "logic and for his point of view in general," and which he believes to be both correct and important: "the conception, namely, that meaning and action are essentially connected" (Lewis 1939, 572). As he elaborates on this view, Lewis notes that its distinctiveness, which renders it incompatible with most views, lies in the recognition that the cognitive or meaning situation cannot be bifurcated into the activity of the knower, on the one hand, and a preformed object, which is contemplated on the other. "Meanings themselves serve to frame the situations of action into which they enter, and exercise an operational force upon what they serve to formulate" (572). As a result, the reality known cannot be characterized as "antecedent" to the activity of knowing, nor can the knower be portrayed as a disinterested "spectator" of a ready-made world (572). Here Lewis has indeed encapsulated a conception that is central to Dewey's entire logical reconstruction of experience, and Lewis can express this conception and its general implications so well because it is at the same time an expression of his own position. It is some of the implications of this shared view that this essay will explore.

Such an endeavor may strike some as strange, since there is a general perception that the interests of Lewis are far removed from those of Dewey, concerned as the former is with abstract logical systems, the a priori element in knowledge, and a general approach to issues that is viewed as narrowly epistemic. The epistemology to which Dewey objects, however, is one to which Lewis objects as well, for it will be seen that they both reject all remnants of Cartesian philosophy and the resultant epistemology that begins with a subject-object split, which illicitly detaches itself from the "external world" and then tries to prove its existence, attempting to put together again that which it never should have torn asunder. They both espouse a rich and fundamental epistemological focus on existence that opens meanings to the fullness and richness of their epistemic depth at the ground level of lived experience. At this level, the examination of the prereflective epistemic substrate for knowledge is inextricably intertwined with an explication of the structure and process of the being of the knower. Ontology and epistemology thus become two distinct perspectives from which reflection gets at the same fundamental features of existence. Just how deeply this epistemic-ontological unity is rooted in our concrete mode of being in the world can be seen by turning to the understanding of logic offered by Dewey and Lewis. It will be seen that this understanding involves a reconstruction of the relation of meaning and action, knowledge and practice, and the nature of our ontological embeddedness in the world and our mode of access to it.

Dewey's interest in logic can be broadly characterized as an interest in the logic of experience. And his pursuit of this broad interest both emanates from and reinforces his view that knowing the world is not a detached apprehension of the way things are but an active resolution of problematic situations. Knowing and doing are intimately interconnected. Through the data of immediate experience we discern indications of possible creative resolutions of problematic contexts, and in experimenting with various possibilities we arrive at a course of action directed by the creative integration of the data and tested by its success in resolving the initiating problem. This instrumentalism or experimental methodology, which is at once theoretical, practical, and ontologically embedded is the concrete process within which are developed the very logical laws and forms that are selectively isolated from the contexts which gave rise to them and, in becoming formalized, provide the norms for ongoing inquiry. As he summarizes the scope of experimental method, "In all this, there is no difference of kind between the methods of science and those of the plain man" (Dewey 1903, MW2:305).

As Dewey notes of its rootedness in human behavior, logic is a naturalistic theory. "The primary postulate of a naturalistic theory of logic is continuity of the lower (less complex) and the higher (more complex) activities and forms." Continuity, in turn, "excludes complete rupture on one side and mere repetition of identities on the other; it precludes reduction of the 'higher' to the 'lower' just as it precludes complete breaks and gaps" (1938, LW12:30). There is, according to Dewey, an adjustment of means to consequences in the activities of human beings in the ordinary or "natural" processes of living. In the course of time the intent is so generalized that inquiry is freed from limitation to special circumstances. Thus, concerning the basic "patterns" of human thought, Dewey writes, "Rationality as an abstract conception is precisely the generalized idea of the means-consequence relation as such" (LW12:17). The serial relations of logic are rooted in the conditions of life itself; they are "prefigured in organic life" (LW12:385). Or, as he states analogously of mathematical distinctions and relations, "They fit nature because they are derived from natural conditions" (1916, MW10:355).

Dewey can deny a fixed difference between logic and the methodology of scientific and practical inquiry, for all are rooted ultimately in the purposive, experimental interaction of organism and environment. Any inquiry develops in its own ongoing course the logical standards and forms to which further inquiry must submit. Further, inquiry, in its emergence in the context of basic human response to situations, may generate problems in its own development, and thus logic becomes autonomous in solving the problems necessary for its own advancements (1938, LW12:17ff.). And, as Dewey states, the greatest freedom is permitted, or rather encouraged, in laying down postulates—a freedom subject only to the condition that they be rigorously fruitful of implied consequences (LW12:18).

The implication relation and the principle of consistency in which it is rooted are the fundamental tools for the explication of creatively generated meaning relations, whether at the level of abstract logical systems or at the level of concrete perceptual awareness, and these principal tools by which meanings are logically related are themselves rooted in the anticipatory structure of human activity. Indeed, it is precisely the if-then implication relation rooted in the temporal spread of anticipatory experience and incorporated in the dispositional generation of forms which diverse symbolic systems are attempting to capture in getting at the "truth" of implication.

Nature, for Dewey, is intelligible in that it can be made intelligent through the organizing, ordering activity of concrete inquiry. His emphatic separation of logic from ontology is not a rejection of our epistemic-ontological embeddedness in nature but rather the rejection of the ontological reification of logical forms, which for Dewey are not ontological ultimates but tools by which we render reality intelligible and suitable to our needs. Logical forms emerge from concrete human behavior and are used to render intelligible the natural world in which we are embedded. As he makes this point from the opposite direction, "Existence in general must be such as to be capable of taking on logical form, and existences in particular must be capable of taking on differential logical forms. But the operations which constitute controlled inquiry are necessary in order to give actuality to these capacities or potentialities" (1938, LW12:387).

This position can be further pursued from another direction by turning to Lewis's concern with abstract symbolic systems; in tracing the pragmatic element in logic to its very roots, Lewis "descends" to the point from which Dewey begins his own logical "ascent" to the understanding of abstract symbolic systems. Indeed, it is precisely the experiential roots of the foundation of logic which Lewis is attempting to articulate and explicate by beginning with abstract logical systems and the problems they engender, and from there working down to the conditions of their possibility in the interactions of anticipatory human activity within a universe which reveals itself within the contours of such activity.

Lewis spent many years in the study of logic, disturbed mainly by two sorts of problems.[1] The first set of problems arose from the paradoxes of the extensional logic of *Principia Mathematica* (Russell and Whitehead 1910) and led Lewis to the development of the system of strict implication in symbolic logic. The second set of problems, arising from the possibility of an alternative to the logic of material implication, led to his interest in the existence, within the field of symbolic logic, of alternative logics such as many-valued logics and "queer logics." He recognized from the start of his logical investigations the more general scope into which he would be drawn and thus set his plans "to argue from exactly determined facts of the behavior of symbolic systems to conclusions of more general problems" (1930, 34).

Lewis holds that all propositions of logic are truths of intension, including the logic of material implication which claims to be based on relations of extension and the corresponding denotational truth values. Real denotational truth has reference to the empirical, while no part of pure logic is concerned with the question of empirical truth. Any abstract system of logic has intensional meaning through the systematic interrelation of its terms. The logical rules have meaning in terms of the operations that the logical rules prescribe. The logical meaning of truth values, then, just like all other logical meaning, is pure or intrasystematic intension and is not dependent upon a locus within experience. This general view of the nature of logical truth lends support, according to Lewis, to his own theory of strict implication, which purports to analyze the intensional categories forming the basis of the validity of ordinary inference. However, like any logic, it is itself circular.

Thus, Lewis is led to his second task, that of understanding the criteria for deciding which possible logistic systems, among various options, contain the principles which state the truth about valid inference. Two points become clear to him. First, internal consistency is not sufficient to determine a truth which is independent of initial logical assumptions. Second, every process of reasoning within a logical system itself contains an extra-logical element, for anything presented as a conclusion is selected from an indefinite number of valid inferences that can possibly be drawn. The guiding fact in both cases is purpose or interest. Thus, Lewis is led to the position that the inferences chosen to be made within a logical system, as well as the original choice of a logical system, answer to criteria best called pragmatic. We choose that which works in answering our interests and needs. Lewis holds that "some logic is true and some logical principles necessary" (1929, 210). When he makes this claim, however, he has in mind not formal truth but rather extralogical truth, truth determined by workability within the ongoing course of experience. The further assertion that some logical principles are necessary must be seen in the light of his own claim that the "stamp of mind's creation . . . is not inevitability but exactly its opposite, the absence of compulsion and the presence of at least conceivable alternatives" (1929, 213). Some principles of formal logical systems are "necessary," only in the sense that *if* we are to express the structure of valid ordinary inference, *then* certain formal principles are required to accomplish this work.

Lewis pushes the issue to a more fundamental level in attempting to understand the foundation of valid ordinary inference. Logical relationships represent implications of our accepted definitions in accordance with consistent thinking. And if the law of noncontradiction is the ultimate ground of the validity of logical principles themselves, then what is its own ground of validity?[2] As the canon of deductive inference, Lewis grounds logic, and logical laws such as that of excluded middle and the very necessity of consistency itself, in his pragmatism, which reaches down into the very core of his thought.

Humans are basically acting beings. As he summarizes, "Practical consistency cannot be reduced to or defined in terms of merely logical consistency. But logical consistency can be considered as simply one species of practical consistency" (1969, 122). Meanings that mind entertains, the logic that explicates such meanings, and mind itself emerge from behavioral responses to the environment in which humans find themselves. Our ways of behaving toward the world around us, which are made explicit in our accepted logic, are those ways of behaving which have lasted because they work. The final ground of the validity of the principle of consistency, as well as the validity of ordinary inference which explicates our meanings in accordance with the principle of consistency, is rooted in a "pragmatic imperative" (Lewis 1957, 101).

The basis of this "pragmatic imperative" to be consistent is held by Lewis to be a "datum of human nature." However, this does not reduce to the "merely psychological," for, as he notes, we do act and think inconsistently. Psychologically, it may even be easier and more natural to do so. Pragmatically, it is imperative that we overcome this tendency if thought and action themselves are not to be stultified.[3] The final ground for the imperative of consistency, as well as for the possibility of acting inconsistently, lies ultimately in the nature of experience as inherently anticipatory.

The principle of consistency upon which the "if-then" of ordinary inference is based in following through the implications of decision making, and to which some formal logics correctly apply while others do not, is a pragmatic imperative which must be adhered to if thought and action are not to be rendered ineffectual. The nature of logical necessity arises from the experiential necessity of inference. As Dewey makes this point, the practical character of necessity is teleological, and as such the nature of certitude is hypothetical. "If I am to reach an end, certain means must be used" (Dewey 1893, EW4:30), and "logical necessity rests upon such teleological necessity" (EW4:33).

It can be seen, then, that for Lewis and Dewey alike, logic does not imply ontological commitments as absolute referents of logical principles; it does not involve an ontology of substances or relationships resulting from the illicit reifications of a spectator theory of knowledge; it does not correspond either to abstract metaphysical structure or to empirical structures independent of human activity; it does not stem from necessary structures of mind. Nor, however, is it rooted in contingent factual activity or in psychological facts, least of all in linguistic or symbolic conventions. Rather, any logic is grounded in the temporal structure of the human way of being and knowing which provides the ontological conditions of possibility for both consistent and inconsistent behavior, which allows for the self-obligating choosing of possibilities within the context of an experienced world of possible involvements reflecting both our creative activity and our embeddedness in a reality not of our making. Such a grounding of logic reveals the way in which we are ontologically committed in the very ability to ask about and to think through the issues of abstract logical systems and the philosophic problems they engender.

One of the most distinctive and most crucial aspects of the positions of both Dewey and Lewis is the understanding of experience as having the character of an interaction or transaction between organism and environment. Experience is that rich ongoing transactional unity between organism and environment, and only within the context of meanings which reflect such an interactional unity does what is given emerge for conscious awareness. Such a transactional unity is more than a postulate of abstract thought, for it has epistemic or phenomenological dimensions. That which intrudes itself inexplicably into experience is not bare "datum"; rather, it evidences itself as the over-againstness of a thick world "there" for our activity. And if experience is an interactional unity of our responses and the ontologically real, then the nature of experience reflects both the responses we bring and the pervasive textures of that independent reality or surrounding natural environment. In such an interactional unity both poles are manifest: the ontological otherness onto which experience opens, and the active organism within whose purposive activity it emerges.

What appears within experience is also the appearance of the independently real; there is no ontological gap between appearance and reality. Further, it is at the same time "to me" to whom it appears and reflects my intentional or interactional link with the externally real. What appears within experience, then, opens in one direction toward the structures of the independently real and in the other direction toward the structures of our mode of grasping the independently real. Or, in other terms, what appears within experience is a function of both in interaction and thus "mirrors" neither exactly, though it reflects characteristics of each. The pervasive textures of experience, which are exemplified in every experience, are at the same time indications of the pervasive textures of the independent universe which, in every experience, gives itself for our responses and which provides the touchstone for the workability of our meanings. There is an elusive coerciveness at the basis of our selectivity in organizing experience that cannot be selected, or at least not at will, but rather must be acknowledged by any selective organization that is to be workable.

It is precisely a failure to recognize this interactional "reflecting" and, as a result, to substitute for it a mirroring either of the ontologically real alone or of our selective activity alone, which leads to the self-defeating alternatives of traditional realism or idealism, realism or antirealism, foundationalism or antifoundationalism, objectivism or relativism. As Lewis captures the import of this interactional unity: "It may be that between a sufficiently critical idealism and a sufficiently critical realism there are no issues save false issues which arise from the insidious fallacies of a copy theory of knowledge" (1929, 194).

Dewey's own rejection of these alternatives and his frustration at being pushed into idealism by his critics is succinctly captured in one of his letters to James, where he stresses that his "instrumental theory of knowledge is clearly self-contradictory unless there are independent existences of which ideas take account and for the transformation of which they function. . . . I have repeated *ad nauseam* that there are existences prior to and subsequent to cognitive states and purposes, and that the whole meaning of the latter is the way they intervene in the control and revaluation of the independent existence."[4] Indeed, throughout his logical considerations Dewey presents a running attack on both idealism and what he calls analytic, presentative, and epistemological realisms. His objection to all of these realisms are variations on one theme, his objection to the "ubiquity of the knowledge relation" held by all of these spectator theories of knowledge, which involves the confusion between mediated and nonmediated knowledge (see esp. Dewey 1911).

This move beyond the alternatives of idealism or traditional realism is mirrored in Lewis's emphatic rejection of the set of alternatives that have shaped philosophy since Descartes, namely, "(1) knowledge is not relative to the mind, or (2) the content of knowledge is not the real, or (3) the real is dependent on mind" (Lewis 1929, 154). Realists accept our knowledge of an independent reality by rejecting the view that knowledge is relative to the mind. Idealism, accepting the relativity of knowledge to the mind, accepts the unqualified dependence of reality on mind. Kant and phenomenalists in general, in accepting the relativity of knowledge to the mind as well as the dependence of the phenomenal object on the mind, accept the conclusion that we cannot know the real in itself (Lewis 1929).[5] Lewis holds at once that the content of knowledge is the ontologically real, that the ontologically real has an independence from mind, and yet that the content of knowledge is partially dependent upon the knowing mind. As he well indicates, insistence on rejecting one or the other of the above alternatives stems from a failure to once and for all reject the presuppositions of a spectator theory of knowledge.

The role of dispositional meaning in transforming the processive universe into a context of meaningfully structured objects[6] is evinced in Dewey's assertion that "structure is constancy of means, of things used for consequences, not of things taken by themselves absolutely" (1925, LW1:64–65). Further, the "isolation of structure from the changes whose stable ordering it is, renders it mysterious—something that is metaphysical in the popular sense of the word, a kind of ghostly queerness" (LW1:65).[7] Lewis makes a similar point in comparing worldly facts to a landscape: "A landscape is a terrain, but a terrain as seeable by an eye. And a fact is a state of affairs, but a state of affairs as knowable by a mind" (Lewis 1968, 660).

For Dewey and Lewis alike, the structures of objectivities grasped by the knowing mind do not reach a reality more ultimate than the temporally extended anticipatory interactions of concrete experience. Rather, there is a lived-through grasp of our openness onto a temporally developing universe as the very foundation for the emergence of meaningful structure within experience.[8] The failure to recognize the radical reconstruction of experience offered by Dewey's position leads to criticisms not only that he ultimately falls into either idealism or traditional realism but also that he cannot reconcile his discussions of process and physical objects and that he anthropomorphizes the universe in general. The failure to understand Lewis's similar radical reconstruction of experience leads to persistent interpretations of his position as one of sense data phenomenalism, a position which he emphatically denied (see Lewis 1946, 1968).

Given what has been so far developed regarding a shared reconstruction of the logic of experience, the ensuing discussion will focus on Lewis's explicit development of an a priori element in knowledge and on Dewey's own statements, which indicate a fundamental rapport with Lewis on this point. Dewey's polemic against the quest for certainty is, of course, the cornerstone of his philosophy. However, while rejecting all traditional vehicles of a priori certitudes, there pervades Dewey's philosophy a pragmatic conception of an a priori element in knowledge which converges with Lewis's own development of the pragmatic a priori. Indeed, the above reconstruction of experience leads directly to a shared reconstruction of the nature of the analytic-synthetic distinction and the nature and function of the a priori element in knowledge, a reconstruction clearly offered by Lewis and incipient in Dewey's writings.

Logic reveals pragmatic criteria of choice of initial postulates or rules. And if the logical system is to adequately express and further the methods of empirical inquiry, it must contain an implicational ordering among consequences that is ultimately rooted in the context of purposive human activity. A priori truth, which runs throughout and makes possible all knowledge according to Lewis, is explicitly modeled after such logical systems. For Lewis, an a priori truth is a definition or rule (1929, 320ff) that determines the way experience will be organized or interpreted. Such a definition or rule is legislative (1929, 240), for "We know in advance that any experience which does not conform to our principle will not be veridical because the principle states the criteria of reality of that type" (1929, 225). The necessity of the a priori, then, lies in its character as legislative act, for the alternative is not its falsity but merely its abandonment in favor of some other. To claim it is false is senseless, indeed, literally so.

Thus, a priori truth arises from the concept alone. This happens, according to Lewis, in two ways. First, there is a type of truth, best represented in pure mathematics, which results from the explication of concepts in the abstract with no reference to any sort of application to experience. Second, the concept in its application within experience exhibits principles for interpreting, for distinguishing, relating, and classifying, "and hence the criteria of reality of any sort."[9] In this second way, the principles or rules and their implied consequences are pragmatically justified not by their fruitfulness in generating abstract symbolic consequences but by their fruitfulness in organizing the welter of experiences into a meaningful system of objects or facts. They accomplish this by legislating the criteria according to which types of objects or facts may emerge within experience.

However, though the relation between meanings is statable apart from any particular instance of fact, the meanings are built up in the light of past experience and chosen for pragmatic reasons. A priori truth as legislative emerges within the context of purposive attitudes of interpretation drawn from the context of past experience. As Lewis summarizes this point, "What is *a priori* is prior to experience in almost the same sense that purpose is. Purposes are not dictated by the content of the given; they are our own. Yet purposes must take their shape and have their realization in terms of experience. . . . In somewhat the same fashion what is *a priori* and of the mind is prior" to present experience "yet in another sense not altogether independent of experience in general" (1929, 24).

The regulative aspect of the a priori, as well as its emergence within the ongoing course of experience, is expressed in Dewey's claim that "a postulate as a rule of action is thus neither arbitrary nor externally a priori. It is not the former because it issues from the relation of means to the end to be reached. It is not the latter, because it is not imposed upon inquiry from without but is acknowledgment of that to which the undertaking of inquiry commits us" (1938, LW12:25). However, such a postulate or rule of action "is empirically and temporally *a priori* in the same sense in which the law of contracts is a rule regulating in advance the making of certain kinds of business engagements. While it is derived from what is involved in inquiries that have been successful in the past, it imposes a condition to be satisfied in future inquiries" (LW12:25).

Such an a priori element within experience, exemplified for Dewey in the postulational aspect of logic as the theory of inquiry (LW12:26), is to be found running throughout all of experience, for as he observes, "*a priori* character is no exclusive function of thought. Every biological function, every motor attitude, every vital impulse as the carrying vehicle of experience is thus *a priori*ty regulative in prospective reference; what we call apperception, expectation, anticipation, desire, demand, choice, are pregnant with this constitutive and reorganizing power" (1906, MW3:136). It is this a priority regulative feature rooted in activity which "makes possible the subject-matter of perception not as a material cut out from an instantaneous field, but a material that designates the effects of our possible actions" (1912, MW7:13). Indeed, insofar as thought does exercise this a priority regulative aspect, "it is because thought is itself still a vital function" (1906, MW3:136). Similarly, though Lewis develops his understanding of the nature of the a priori through work in logic, he holds that such a priori criteria as meanings entertained in advance can be considered in terms of incipient behavior or behavior attitudes (Lewis 1946, 144). As he emphasizes the point, such a link with activity is never broken, for cognition itself is "a vital function, continuous with animal behavior and with habit" (1946, 19–20). As Dewey well observes, that the practical character involved in this as well as in features of experience such as meanings and facts "may be overlooked or denied is due to the organic way in which practical import is incarnate in them" (Dewey 1907, MW4:90).

The legislative aspect active at all levels of grasping the world in which we live leads Dewey to distinguish two main categories of propositions: (i) existential, referring directly to actual conditions as determined by experimental observations, and (ii) ideational or conceptual, consisting of interrelated meanings which are nonexistential in content or direct reference but which are applicable to existence through the operations they represent as possibilities (1938, LW12:283–84). Such propositions express necessary relations because they express the implications of our own meanings as legislative acts. These conceptual meanings represent possibilities for resolution of problematic or potentially problematic situations, and the characters or qualities they contain are necessarily interrelated, belonging to a single conception because of their function in our dispositional modes of response. In this way Dewey's understanding of definition accounts both for its "necessary function in the redintegration of experience" (1903, MW2:336) and for the fact that the terms of a definition are logically grounded rather than arbitrary.

And as Dewey elaborates the "important positive logical principle involved" in such a view, all propositions of existential import are "a matter of the execution of delimiting *analytic operations of observation*. . . . The operations of observation executed are, however, controlled by conceptions or ideational considerations which define the conditions to be satisfied . . . in *descriptive determination of kinds*" (1938, LW12:242, italics added). Thus, for Dewey and Lewis alike, the a priori element in knowledge that regulates in advance the possibility of the emergence within experience of certain kinds of facts or objects is rooted in human behavior as partially constitutive of the environment in which it operates. Further, the line between the a priori and the a posteriori corresponds with the division between the analytic and the synthetic, the conceptual and the empirical.

Although the previous discussion should clearly indicate that Lewis's understanding of meaning and of analyticity cuts beneath the level of linguistic conventionalism, the continuing assimilation of his position to the framework of linguistic analysis perhaps demands a more explicit focus on this aspect of his position before turning to further similarities with Dewey. Analytic truths, for Lewis, state relations between sense meanings and not merely between linguistic meanings. The claim that the a priori is coextensive with the analytic but dependent on linguistic conventions fails, according to Lewis, to justify the epistemic function of the a priori. Contrary to this conventionalist view, the analyticity of the linguistic meaning is determined by the fixed intensional relationships of sense meanings.[10] To separate linguistic meaning from the sense meaning it conveys is to engage in a process of abstraction, for these two aspects are supplementary, not alternative, and "separable by abstraction rather than separated" (1946, 133). The abstraction of language from the sense meaning it expresses can serve a useful function for some purposes of analysis, but Lewis considers it disastrous for philosophical theory when one makes the distinction absolute and posits linguistic meaning as the focal point for investigations.

Lewis's focus on sense meaning, however, is in large part responsible for another popular interpretation of his position that distances him from Dewey, for he is viewed as putting forth a phenomenalistic reductionism that views meanings as reducible to the sense data out of which they are built.[11] But, though meaning is derivative from the sensuous, and though meanings themselves can be termed sensuous insofar as they refer to experience, yet meaning even in its sensory aspect cannot be reduced to the content of experience. The difference can perhaps best be clarified by stating that for Lewis the sensuous aspect of meaning provides, literally, the "sense" or principle or form by which humans interpret and organize the sensory aspect of experience. Meaning incorporates a response which, as an interpretive principle, enters into the very character of what is grasped, and thus the meaning of anything is irreducible to any data as existing apart from the character of the response. It is only within the context of such an interpretive principle that the sensory comes to awareness.

Lewis points out that there is a generally unnoticed complexity to sense meaning. He introduces the schema in describing a sense meaning as a rule and an imagined result (1946, 134). An implicit sense meaning is a disposition or habit by which humans interact with the environment, while an explicit sense meaning is a precise "inspectable" schema or criterion in mind by which one grasps the presence of that to which a particular type of response is appropriate in order to gain a certain type of result.[12] As specifying types, the schema with its possible aspects is general as opposed to the particulars grasped by it.

For Lewis, the relation of a dispositional rule to that which it generates can best be indicated by the model of a "mathematical rule generating a number series" (1946, 110). Such a mathematical rule cannot be reduced to the number series, nor can it be constructed out of the series, for it is necessary to the formation of the series. Further, like a mathematical rule, such a dispositional rule of generation cannot be separated from that which it generates, for that which is generated represents an aspect of the relational structure of that which generates it. In understanding the relational structure of that which is generated, we understand to that extent the rule which generates it. Similarly, the disposition or basis of meaning cannot be inspected exhaustively, but it is inspectable in any aspect. Such a "living meaning" is inspectable in any aspect through its possible particular applications, but can never be exhaustively examined, since it can never be reduced to any series of such applications. What follows from this is that though a meaning is never fully inspected, it is inspectable in any aspect. The fundamental concept of Lewis's notion of analyticity, then, is not synonymy but rather containment.

Dewey's own clear focus on meaning in terms of behavior can be briefly encapsulated in his claim that "language is made up of physical existences; sounds, or marks on paper. . . . But these do not operate or function as mere physical things when they are media of communication. They operate in virtue of their representative capacity or meaning" (1938, LW12:52). Such meaning is rooted in behavior, and if this fact is not recognized, warns Dewey, "the intrinsic connection of language with community of action is then forgotten" (LW12:54). Yet neither Dewey nor Lewis denies the inextricable connection of linguistic meaning and meaning as behavioral response. Thus Dewey holds that the question as to whether meaning-relations in discourse arise before or after significance-connections in existence "is rhetorical"; it "cannot be settled." Rather, the question serves "to indicate that in any case ability to treat things as signs would not go far did not symbols enable us to mark and retain just the qualities of things which are the ground of inference" (LW12:61).

In turning to the grounding of linguistic meaning in action, Dewey's understanding of the concept emerges in a way that grounds, as for Lewis, the legislative analyticity of the a priori. Like Lewis, Dewey understands the purposive activity constitutive of the concept in terms of a disposition or habit generative of schematic rules for the structuring of experience. Dewey holds that the concept is a mode or form of construction or a method of action (Dewey 1891, EW3:144). As such, it is dispositional in nature and general rather than particular, while any given instance, actual or as a mental existence, is particular (EW3:144). Just as a disposition cannot be reduced to any indefinite series of actions, or as a mathematical rule cannot be reduced to the generation of any indefinite series of numbers, so the concept "has an ideality which cannot be reduced to sense contents" (EW3:144) or to particular activities, though it "is grasped only in and through the activity which constitutes it" and to which it gives rise (EW3:144). As a rule for the generation of types of experiences, a concept cannot be reduced to the content of any experience, imagined or actual, for the concept "contains not less but more than the percept. . . . It is true that certain features are excluded. But this dropping out of certain features is not what gives rise to the concept. On the contrary, it is on the basis of the concept, the principle of construction, that certain features are omitted. Nay they are more than omitted." As he clarifies this, they are not just omitted: "They are positively eliminated. They are declared to be irrelevant" (EW3:144).[13] For Dewey as for Lewis, the move to the concrete involves the "filling up" of the schema (Dewey 1893, EW4:31).

Dewey's entire discussion in terms of concepts and percepts can be misleading. There is no percept independent of dispositional modes of behavior that provide the structure of experience, and thus the distinction between the concept and the percept is "not fixed but movable" (1891, EW3:145). If one starts from the individual, "we call it percept," whereas if one starts from the principle, "we call it concept" (EW3:145) or, as Dewey clarifies this interrelationship, perception is surcharged with ideal factors (1906, MW3:138). Thus he can claim that perception is "the operation of constituting a stimulus" (1912, MW7:19). The amount of such "saturating intellectual material" varies with the complexity and maturity of the acting agent and is "carried by affectional and intentional contexts" of varying degrees (1912, MW7:19). Further, there is no level of awareness so rudimentary as not to be "surcharged" with the structural possibilities implicit in dispositional modes of behavior. "Even the most rudimentary conscious experience contains within itself the element of suggestion or expectation," and thus "the object of conscious experience even with an infant is homogeneous with the world of the adult" (1915, MW8:95). Such a structure of knowing extends from the realm of the infant to the most abstract and systematic of scientific reflections. "Modern science did not begin with discovery of any new kind of inference. It began with the recognition of the need of different data if inference is to proceed safely" (MW8:95).

If that which a meaning generates or contains is too frequently inapplicable, our meaning may alter through the formation of new habits that creatively fixate inductively accumulated experiences in new ways. But what we then have is a new meaning, or a new rule of generation of conditions of verification, which now necessarily contains at least partially different schematic possibilities. Although the same words may be used, the meanings attached to them are different (see, e.g., Lewis 1929, 235). Meaning is fundamentally a relational system not among words but rather among schematic possibilities contained in our dispositional tendencies as ways of acting toward a situation.[14] A meaning does not literally change. A meaning is replaced by another meaning, each of which is a logically distinct genera-tive rule. If the rootedness of analyticity in the structure of meaning is ig-nored in favor of language, then indeed the analytic-synthetic distinction will seem inoperative, and the a priori–a posteriori distinction will seem to be a functional one only, a characterization given continually to Lewis's distinction as well as to that of Dewey.

However, the same word can both house and hide an accepted change of meaning. Lewis's distinction between the intensional and the extensional "all" is instructive here (1946, 434). The a priori proposition and the em-pirical generalization are usually indistinguishable by their form. Both are universal in intent and are normally expressed by an "all" proposition or by one in which the "all" though unexpressed is obviously understood. The difference between these two is one between the intensional and extensional "all." The first expresses in the predicate something logically contained in the subject; the subject concept implies the predicate concept. The second states a factual connection of two classes of objects which are not related intensionally. Dewey makes a similar point, noting that the intensional "all" of meaning relationships implies a necessary relation, while the extensional "all" of empirical claims provide a high degree of probability at best (1938, LW12:283–84).[15] Although the denotation of the subject term in each case may in fact be the same, its meaning in the two cases is different, for in the first case, the meanings contained in the predicate terms are included in the possibilities of experience necessarily contained in the meaning of the subject term.

A similar distinction can be made between an intensional and an exten-sional "if-then." Dewey notes that if-then claims are systematically ambigu-ous in their meaning. Sometimes they refer to the existential and sometimes to the ideational (1938, LW12:255–56). Existential propositions, as discussed earlier, refer directly to actual conditions as determined by experimental observation, while ideational or conceptual propositions consist of interre-lated meanings that are nonexistential in content in direct reference but which are applicable to existence through the operations they represent as possibilities (LW12:238–84). Thus, if-then claims sometimes refer to exis-tential circumstances and sometimes to a logical relation among meanings. Likewise, Lewis makes a distinction between the conceptual or ideational if-then, which involves logical necessity, and the existential if-then, which can involve only probability relations.[16]

Thus, though one may carelessly speak of "the same" proposition serv-ing now in one capacity, now in the other, what is involved is not the same proposition but rather two different propositions having the same sentential expression. What is determined by our attitudes of response is not the function of one proposition but rather the choice between two propositions: the one eternally analytic and eternally valid if ever valid—though perhaps not always a useful tool for prescribing what will count as an instance of a kind—and the other eternally synthetic and subject to the verdict of experience. Thus, what is functionally determined is not whether a "given proposition" is analytic or synthetic; a specific proposition is either analytic or synthetic and is eternally that which it is. What is determined functionally is which of two propositions, the same only in their sentential expression, is to be entertained. The two propositions are, indeed, often difficult to distinguish, for the terms are identical. But as the meaning of the subject term in one case is a logically distinct and different meaning from the meaning of the subject term in another case, what is involved is the choice between two logically and epistemologically distinct propositions. Thus, though analytic relationships are determined by us in the light of pragmatic considerations and are often determined prereflectively, yet the analytic and the synthetic proposition are different in kind.

For both Lewis and Dewey, then, concepts are a priori rules, rooted in dispositional tendencies, which legislate ways in which experience can be interpreted, and a priori truths explicate the implicational relations contained within and among them. Genetically, these rules arise through the cumulative effect of past experience and the creative synthesis[17] or fixation, within the ongoing course of experience, of dispositionally organized relationships among possible experiences. But at any point in the experiential process, the dispositional meaning logically contains all that it has creatively synthesized or "fixated" or, conversely, all that it now has the power or potential to generate.

This relatedness to experience leads to the objection that structures so rich in empirical meaning can arise neither through induction, nor definition, nor linguistic stipulation, and hence require a synthetic aspect. However, the "fixation" of meaning structures corresponds to none of these alternatives. They arise through the creative "fixation" of a set of relationships unified by habit as a rule of organization of the related experiences and our possible responses to them. The fixation intended corresponds most closely to the creative process which Peirce calls abduction, though what are here fixed by such creative activity or abductive processes are not empirical hypotheses asserting the applicability of meanings to experience but rather the very structure of the meanings themselves. And habit, as creatively structuring, always brings a "more than" to the organization of past experience.

The meanings embodied in our conceptual schemes are built up in the light of past experience. They are drawn from the empirical situation, although the relation between the meanings is statable apart from any particular instances of fact. The origin of our analytic structures, then, is empirical, pragmatic, functional. This genesis of meanings from the context of experience is in no way analogous to the logical reducibility of meanings to experience. Meaning qua created structure contains no truth claim as to applicability in experience. Although for pragmatic reasons we must create or fixate meanings with workable applications in the ongoing course of experience, a meaning itself is a deductive system applying to a hypothetical state of affairs, the implications of which we can know because we create it. Thus the genesis of an a priori structure involves a creative synthesis, but its structural nature, which is rooted in the absoluteness of relationships grounded in sense meanings, is analytic.

Such intensionally grounded analytic relationships emerging from purposive activity pervade all levels of experience, from the most rudimentary expectations of prereflective experience to sophisticated scientific knowledge and the development of abstract formal systems. Important meaning structures may be difficult to capture by tracing which concepts are included in which in an explicit articulation of a relationship. But explicit articulation of the analysis of a concept is ultimately an attempt to capture what has been implicitly operative in the structure of our purposive activity, a structure that contains the schematic forms of its applicability.

The claims implicit in such conceptual interrelationships cannot be reduced to the contents of experience or to empirical generalizations about relationships within experience. They are legislative for what types of objects or facts can conceivably emerge within experience to provide the basis for empirical generalizations about facts and objects. Further, they are legislative for the very possibility of the emergence of anything within experience. And though a priori legislative for future experience and containing analytic, intensionally grounded relationships, their justification is ultimately pragmatic or functional. If the contours of realities of various types which they delimit do not adequately work in capturing the indeterminate richness of experience, then they will be replaced by logically distinct and new meanings.[18]

For Dewey and Lewis alike, then, the a priori element in experience, which regulates in advance the possibility of the emergence within experience of facts and objects, is rooted in the concreteness of purposive human behavior, and it arises from, is made possible by, and is replaceable or alterable within the finite temporal structure of such behavior. Further, while it emerges through a behaviorally operative creative synthesis, it contains within its structure the conditions for its applicability in the ongoing course of experience. This containment houses within its very structure a reference to the sensible, and thus the features of its relational structure can be apprehended within sensible experience. This a priori element operative in human behavior makes possible a perspectival grasp of an independent processive universe. In so doing, it provides the vehicle by which we render determinate within our environment the inherent indeterminacy of a universe in process with its indefinite richness of possibilities and potentialities.

The pragmatic a priori operative in the philosophies of Dewey and Lewis in an important sense undercuts some of the contemporary debates about the nature of analytic truths as articulated in explicit claims. More significantly, it changes as well the very nature of the analytic-synthetic debate, casting each of the "opposing alternatives" in a new, fruitful, and complimentary light. It carries the analytic-synthetic distinction beyond the conventionalism of language, beyond the functionalism of decisions of usage, and beyond the distinction between logic and knowledge about the world. It founds the absoluteness of the analyticity of an a priori which coerces the mind within any system but which can be nonetheless exchanged for another system, and which is linked to experience by the method of experimentation, for it founds an a priori analyticity that both arises from the concretely rich matrix of experience and is justified by the intelligibility it introduces into experience.

This broadly based pragmatic reformulation of the a priori by Dewey and Lewis alike is inextricably woven into their shared logical reconstruction of experience. This reconstruction is one in which action is a mode of understanding and transforming the world and in which our primary openness onto the world is presentation not to a cognitive subject or an objectifying consciousness but to purposive active beings in interactive contexts within an ontologically "thick" universe. This interactive unity at the heart of experience, at once practical, ontological, and epistemic, undercuts a long philosophic tradition of false dilemmas and self-defeating alternatives.

Notes

1. The following problems are most concisely summarized in Lewis 1930.

2. Asher Moore (1968) argues that the principle of noncontradiction is synthetic a priori in Lewis's position, and he shows with startling clarity various far-reaching implications that wreak havoc with Lewis's position concerning logical relationships.

3. "A decision without intent to adhere to it would not be a genuine decision. But one who should adopt the decision 'Disregard consistency,' would be deciding

to disregard his decision as soon as made. And, adherence to that decision would require that it be promptly disregarded" (Lewis 1957, 100–101).

4. Letter from Dewey to James, March 21, 1909. Reprinted in Dewey 1999, 1909.03.21, Perry 1935, 2:532, and Schneider 1963, 473.

5. Although Kant is considered the beginning of "the rejection of the spectator," he himself was not immune to some of its presuppositions, for Kant, in attempting to justify the absoluteness of the Newtonian or Modern Worldview in some sense, was still caught up in the problematics emerging from the absolutizing of scientific content based on an inadequate understanding of scientific method.

6. The way in which the logical reconstruction of experience involves, for Dewey and Lewis alike, a process view of reality lies beyond the scope of this essay but is developed in Rosenthal 1986. Here the concern is only to point out that a reality of process and the experience of objects is not incompatible, for meanings transform a processive reality into "stable" objects of knowledge.

7. Richard Rorty attempts to interpret reality in Dewey's philosophy as a Kantian unknowable (see Rorty 1982, 84–85). On the contrary, reality, in its various aspects, may be known or unknown at any particular time, but it is eminently knowable and is what becomes known.

8. As Ralph Sleeper succinctly puts the point, "Reality is always in process and is not fixed in character, which means that judgment is efficacious in the reconstruction and transformation of the real" (1986, 63).

9. As Lewis points out, "This is most clearly evident in the case of those basic concepts, determining major classes of the real, which may be called categories, though in less important ways it holds true of concepts in general (1929, 230). For Lewis, the difference between a concept and a category is one of degree, not of kind. For example, one would speak of the category "physical object" but of the concept "chair." A category is more deeply embedded within our interpretive attitudes.

10. For Lewis, "Meaning cannot be literally put into words or exhibited by exhibiting words and the relations of words" (1946, 140).

11. This phenomenalistic interpretation can be seen throughout Schilpp 1968.

12. Although Lewis usually speaks of sense meaning as a precise, explicit schema, yet sense meaning is, for Lewis, intensional or conceptual meaning, and this he frequently identifies as a disposition or habit. He clarifies this dual aspect of sense meaning when he observes that "A sense meaning *when precise and explicit,* is a schema" (1946, 134, italics added).

13. The title of Dewey's essay can be superficially misleading. Concepts "arise from percepts" in the sense that an explicit conceptual awareness requires an abstracting out of perceptual experience of that which we have previously, though unreflectively, put into it.

14. Thus, Peirce holds that a self-contradictory proposition is not meaningless; it means too much (CP2:352).

15. It has been held that this former type of proposition involves a kind of knowledge that eludes experimental method and thus reveals Dewey as inconsistent. In fact, this type of proposition reflects experimental method in its genesis from the

matrix of experience, in the establishment of its usefulness in terms of workability in experience, and in its role in guiding activity.

16. However, these if-then probability relations become logically incorporated with the structure of meanings as implying probable consequences of possible kinds of activities. See Lewis 1946.

17. Peirce's use of the term *abduction* is more appropriate here.

18. Although the meanings change, words used to designate them may remain the same.

Works Cited

Dewey, John. 1891. How Do Concepts Arise from Percepts? *Public-School Journal* 11:128–30. Reprinted in EW3:142–46.

———. 1893. The Superstition of Necessity. *Monist* 3:362–79. Reprinted in EW4:19–36.

———. 1903. *Studies in Logical Theory.* University of Chicago Decennial Publications, 2d ser., vol. 11. Chicago: University of Chicago Press.

———. 1906. Experience and Objective Idealism. *Philosophical Review* 15:465–81. Reprinted in Dewey 1910, 198–225, and MW3:128–44.

———. 1907. The Control of Idea by Facts. *Journal of Philosophy, Psychology, and Scientific Methods* 4:197–203, 253–59, 309–19. Reprinted in Dewey 1916, 230–49, and MW4:78–90.

———. 1910. *The Influence of Darwin on Philosophy, and Other Essays in Contemporary Thought.* New York: Henry Holt. Essays reprinted separately in EW1, MW1, 3, 4, 6.

———. 1911. Brief Studies in Realism. *Journal of Philosophy, Psychology, and Scientific Methods* 8:393–400, 546–54. Reprinted in Dewey 1916, 250–80, and MW6:103–22.

———. 1912. Perception and Organic Action. *Journal of Philosophy, Psychology, and Scientific Methods* 9: 645–68. Reprinted in MW7:3–30.

———. 1915. The Existence of the World as a Logical Problem. *Philosophical Review*, 24:357–70 (with the title "The Existence of the World as a Problem"). Reprinted in Dewey 1916, 281–302, and MW8:83–97.

———. 1916. *Essays in Experimental Logic.* Chicago: University of Chicago Press. Essays reprinted separately in MW1, 2, 4, 6, 8, 10.

———. 1925. *Experience and Nature.* Chicago: Open Court. Reprinted in LW1.

———. 1938. *Logic: The Theory of Inquiry.* New York: Henry Holt. Reprinted in LW12.

———. 1999. *The Correspondence of John Dewey,* vol. 1, 1871–1918. Intelex. CD-ROM.

———, ed. 1903. *Studies in Logical Theory.* University of Chicago Decennial Publications, 2d ser., vol. 11. Chicago: University of Chicago Press. Dewey's contributions reprinted in Dewey 1916, 75–182, and in MW2:293–375.

Lewis, Clarence Irving. 1929. *Mind and World Order.* New York: Charles Scribner. Reprinted with corrections in 1956 by Dover.

———. 1930. Logic and Pragmatism. In *Contemporary American Philosophy,* ed. G. P.

Adams and W. P. Montague, 2:31–50. New York: Humanities Press. Reprinted in Lewis 1970, 3–19.

———. 1939. Meaning and Action. *Journal of Philosophy, Psychology, and Scientific Methods* 36, 21:572–76. Reprinted in *Dewey and His Critics*, ed. Sidney Morgenbesser, 556–60 (New York: Journal of Philosophy, Inc., 1997).

———. 1946. *An Analysis of Knowledge and Valuation.* La Salle, Ill.: Open Court.

———. 1957. *Our Social Inheritance.* Bloomington: Indiana University Press.

———. 1968. Replies to My Critics. Schilpp 1968, 653–76.

———. 1969. *Values and Imperatives: Studies in Ethics.* Edited by John Lang. Stanford: Stanford University Press.

———. 1970. *Collected Papers of Clarence Irving Lewis.* Edited by John D. Goheen and John L. Mothershead Jr. Stanford: Stanford University Press.

Moore, Asher. 1968. *Lewis's Theory of the A Priori.* Schilpp 1968, 155–99.

Peirce, Charles Sanders. 1867–1914. *Collected Papers of Charles Sanders Peirce.* Cambridge: Harvard University Press (1931–58). Vols. 1–6 edited by Charles Hartshorne and Paul Weiss; vols. 7–8 edited by Arthur W. Burks. Cited as CP.

Perry, Ralph Barton. 1935. *The Thought and Character of William James.* 2 vols. Boston: Little, Brown, 1935.

Rorty, Richard. 1982. *Consequences of Pragmatism.* Minneapolis: University of Minnesota Press.

Rosenthal, Sandra. 1986. *Speculative Pragmatism.* Amherst: University of Massachusetts Press.

Russell, B. and A. N. Whitehead. 1910. *Principia Mathematica,* vol. 1. Cambridge: Cambridge University Press.

Schilpp, Paul A., ed. 1968. *The Philosophy of C. I. Lewis.* LaSalle, Ill.: Open Court.

Schneider, Herbert. 1963. *A History of American Philosophy.* 2d ed. New York: Columbia University Press.

Sleeper, Ralph William. 1986. *The Necessity of Pragmatism.* New Haven: Yale University Press.

5

Dewey and Quine on the Logic of What There Is

John R. Shook

> I espouse a more thorough pragmatism.
>
> (W. V. O. Quine 1980, 46)

Standing apart from much of twentieth-century Anglo-American philosophy, both John Dewey and W. V. Quine hold that logic is a discipline relevant to the question of what exists. Logic is relevant to questions of existence, they agree, only because it is an integral component of an empirical-scientific understanding of the world, not some sort of non-empirical and rationalistic high road to existence. They have a common devotion to science and its fallibilism, they reject the correspondence theory of truth and epistemic foundationalism, and their naturalism opposes any "first philosophy" of metaphysical rationalism. Philosophers who have preferred to use logic rather than empirical science to decide questions of ultimate existence claim in effect that "logic is the science of what there is." Dewey and Quine would reverse this slogan, instead claiming that "science is the logic of what there is." And to those philosophers who would prefer to withhold logic from any relevance to existence, Dewey and Quine would argue that logic properly understood is indeed an important component of empirical science. The logic of scientific inquiry has a central, although indirect, bearing on deciding questions of existence.

Should Quine have a secure place in the pantheon of American pragmatists, as a worthy successor to the spirit of Dewey's philosophy? Possibly, but what cannot be ignored is the fact that Quine reaches many conclusions that Dewey expressly denied. This essay is concerned with two major disagreements between Quine and Dewey over scientific method and knowledge. First, Quine's philosophy argues that objects of scientific knowledge are never within human experience but always beyond experience. Dewey's philosophy instead finds objects of knowledge to be within human experience. Second, Quine holds that scientific practice demands a realistic construal of unobservable theoretical entities postulated by successful theories. Dewey's understanding of science precludes such a realist demand, as unobservable theoretical entities have only a hypothetically pragmatic meaning.

The ultimate cause of these disagreements, I propose, is the order of the dependencies among various aspects of their respective views. Quine's philosophy offers a rationalistic scientism, a naturalized epistemology, an empiricism, and a pragmatism, in that order. Dewey's philosophy, in contrast, offers a metaphysical empiricism, a naturalism, a functionalist epistemology, and a pragmatic realism. These two philosophies, despite having several fundamental agreements, advance two very different pragmatic logics of what there is.

Logic and Normative Epistemology

An examination of their differences on scientific method should proceed from a summary of their agreements on logic and epistemology. For many years Quine allowed the promise of evolutionary epistemology and cognitive psychology to support his contested claim that his epistemology would naturally be normative. More recently, Quine's sparse comments on his vision of the normativity of epistemology have taken a somewhat different direction. If we take Quine's two characteristic claims together, that pragmatic norms are among the subject-matter of epistemology, and that epistemology is a scientific enterprise, then Quine seems to be saying that the study of pragmatic norms is a component of science. There is more to science, after all, besides the postulated entities of theories. There must be pragmatic strategies to deal with occasions demanding either novel theorizing or theory adjustment. These strategies are not "given" to us, but rather historically and culturally situated as fallible and revisable. In *Pursuit of Truth* Quine distinguishes theoretical epistemology from normative epistemology while defending the normativity of his epistemology against critics.

> But they are wrong in protesting that the normative element, so characteristic of epistemology, goes by the board. Insofar as theoretical epistemology gets naturalized into a chapter of theoretical science, so normative epistemology gets naturalized into a chapter of engineering: the technology of anticipating sensory stimulation. (1992, 19)

Since Quine characterizes science as the theoretical effort to anticipate sensory stimulation, normative epistemology is the engineering technology that recommends and tests ways of improving the scientific method. Quine and Ullian's *The Web of Belief* (1978) offers just this sort of understanding of the strategic, pragmatic side of science. The philosophical effort to understand the logic of proper scientific method, to grasp exactly why theory alteration or creation is needed, and to formulate methods of regulating theory alteration and creation, is Quine's notion of the technology of normative epistemology. This philosophical activity is a necessary component of the scientific process. Pragmatic norms are formulated by normative epistemology, not by theoretical epistemology.

Quine has closely approached the spirit of Dewey's own understanding of the role of philosophy in scientific method. Dewey's functionalist epistemology is aptly described as an inquiry into the technology of knowing. Not only is science an aspect of technology, and not the reverse, but the very processes of science can be best understood as technologies. Technology is the intelligent fashioning of tools for useful purposes. According to Dewey, our habits of inference are no less human-made tools than are hammers or telescopes.[1] Such a view supports Quine's controversial claim that even logical principles are in principle revisable should theoretical success demand it.

> It can hardly be denied that there are habits of inference and that they may be formulated as rules or principles. If there are such habits as are necessary to conduct every successful inferential inquiry, then the formulations that express them will be logical principles of all inquiries. . . . They are formulations of ways of treating subject-matter that have been found to be so determinative of sound conclusions in the past that they are taken to regulate further inquiry until definite grounds are found for questioning them. While they are derived from examination of methods previously used in their connection with the kind of conclusion they have produced, they are *operationally a priori* with respect to further inquiry. (Dewey 1938, LW12:21)

The intelligent control and improvement of habits of inference constitute the subject-matter of logic proper as the inquiry into inquiry. In Dewey's philosophy, the field called logic is therefore just epistemology: the technology of the methodology of inquiry, aiming in particular at understanding and refining the processes of scientific inquiry. Quine's isolated reference to normative epistemology as a technology is fortuitous, but not coincidental. Dewey and Quine fundamentally agree on the nature and function of normative epistemology in a way that few other philosophers do. Their commitment to a naturalistic and empiricist notion of science, combined with a repudiation of any metaphysical theories of experience, belief, knowledge, truth, and reality, compels both philosophers to locate all epistemic inquiry inside science itself. Both Dewey and Quine agree that logic/epistemology is an essential component of the science of what there is. Their disagreement rests rather on what each philosopher takes to be the materials available for the project of epistemology.

Quine's Scientism

Quine's attempted solution to many difficulties for logical positivism involves the elimination of the analytic/synthetic distinction.[2] Quine's holism exposes analytic propositions as just firmly held synthetic propositions functioning at the heart of scientific theories. The essence of scientific method according to Quine is basically Popper's falsificationist hypothetico-deductive method. Observation sentences are deduced from theories and compared against the evidence of actual experience. The observed evidence is never capable of verifying or even warranting any theory, because any number of theories can predict the same evidence (as the undetermination or "Duhem-Quine" thesis appears to imply). The evidence can only falsify theories, requiring scientists to alter theories or create new theories. The combination of holism and the hypothetico-deductive method together imply that no single theoretical proposition can be put on trial by evidence, since only an entire theory, including its deeply imbedded logic, is capable of supplying the premises for a deduction to a concluding observation sentence.

Like the positivists, Quine believes that a theory has scientific meaning only if it can be put on trial by empirical evidence. He suitably adapts the positivist tenet that the meaning of a scientific proposition lies in its truth-conditions by reformulating this tenet in light of holism. Since only whole theories are testable, only entire theories can properly said to be fully meaningful. Quine concludes that the meaning of a theory lies in its testability conditions, which are the sum of all predictions the theory can make. Quine's philosophy thus completely replaces the Kantian triad of analytic a priori, synthetic a priori, and synthetic a posteriori propositions with a single kind of intellectually meaningful entity: the scientific theory. Logic cannot be demarcated from science or assimilated to metaphysics, since it shares in meaning only insofar as it is scientific. Rationalistic metaphysics collapses because there are no genuinely a priori propositions. Phenomenalistic or positivistic metaphysics collapses because there are no foundationally true empirical propositions. All such metaphysical propositions simply fail to have scientific meaning and hence cannot refer to anything. Without ontological competition, the ontology of empirical science remains standing as the only measure of what exists. This is the significance of referring to Quine's philosophy as a form of "scientism."[3] This scientism has important consequences for the proper understanding of the nature of experience, and for the question of the reality of postulated scientific objects.

On the nature of experience, Quine finds that his scientism is eminently compatible and supportive of empiricism, provided that empiricism is purged of metaphysical and positivistic debts. Older traditions of empiricism have foundered when tempted to metaphysically guarantee the validity of scientific knowledge. With the possibility of metaphysics eliminated, the epistemological attempt to explain human knowledge cannot appeal to the a priori or the sense-datum. Instead, the epistemologist must take for granted current scientific practice and knowledge, to weave together a story about the growth of human knowledge using only causal relations among known scientific objects.

> This human subject is accorded a certain experimentally controlled input—certain patterns of irradiation in assorted frequencies, for instance—and in the fullness of time the subject delivers as output a description of the three-dimensional external world and its history. The relation between the meager input and the torrential output is a relation that we are prompted to study for somewhat the same reasons that always prompted epistemology; namely, in order to see how evidence relates to theory, and in what ways one's theory of nature transcends any available evidence. (Quine 1969, 82–83)

Quine's empiricism is therefore a consequence, and not a presupposition, of naturalized epistemology. Bereft of any mental entities, sense-data, or a priori propositions, the naturalized theory of knowledge will understand experience as physical, amenable to objective scientific inquiry. Naturalized ontology implies naturalized epistemology which in turn implies naturalized experience. At every turn the possibility of metaphysics has been erased by science: metaphysics can be neither a description of physical reality, an account of mental knowing processes, nor a portrait of phenomenal experience.

When Quine considers how discussion of scientific methodology may be conducted, he only allows scientists to ask whether theories successfully predict observed phenomena, to compare theories on their features that permit such prediction, and to contrast new theories with old theories using scales of "conservatism," "simplicity," and other pragmatic norms. No questioning of the existence of entities that theories postulate is permitted on a meta-theoretical level, since Quine holds that only the acceptance of a theory enables one to ask and answer such questions in a meaningful way. Truth, like knowledge, is a denizen of scientific commitment, not metaphysics. But also, no questioning of the existence of entities that theories postulate is permitted on the theoretical level, according to Quine, because while doing science the existence of theoretical entities must be taken for granted. Therefore, since there is no meaningful metaphysical standpoint from which to make ontological commitments or debate truth, and since the only standpoint remaining is one of scientific commitment, we must be realists about postulated entities of currently accepted scientific theories. At the meta-theoretical level, we must be ontological relativists and pragmatists.

> We can improve our conceptual scheme, our philosophy, bit by bit while continuing to depend on it for support; but we cannot detach ourselves from it and compare it objectively with an unconceptualized reality. Hence it is meaningless, I suggest, to inquire into the absolute correctness of a conceptual scheme as a mirror of reality. Our standard for appraising basic changes of conceptual scheme must be, not a realistic standard of correspondence to reality, but a pragmatic standard. (Quine 1980, 79)

However, this appeal to pragmatic standards does not mean that Quine is offering a pragmatic theory of truth. While doing science one does not use pragmatic standards, and while using pragmatic standards one cannot make assertions about what does or does not exist.

Quine's unyielding stance on the real existence of theoretical entities has caused much consternation. Critics have had understandable difficulty reconciling this stance of scientism with two of Quine's other firm tenets: his scientific idealism, which states that scientific entities are created, not discovered, by the human imagination, and his fallibilism, which states that theories can never be taken to be absolutely true since they are underdetermined by any amount of evidence. Their reconciliation is mediated by Quine's realism, grounded by the absence of any alternative metaphysical source of knowledge.[4] Comparing his own philosophy with other pragmatists who were not realists concerning theoretical entities, Quine states that his scientific fallibilism and idealism are quite compatible with realism.

For naturalistic philosophers such as I, on the other hand, physical objects are real, right down to the most hypothetical of particles, though this recognition of them is subject, like all science, to correction. I can hold this ontological line of naïve and unregenerate realism, and at the same time I can hail man as largely the author rather than discoverer of truth. (1981, 33–34)

Fallibilism would seem to undermine this "global" realism by denying the absolute truth of any theory. Without the possibility of finding a true theory, how could any theory be interpreted realistically? Quine rejects the metaphysical path to realism taken by the correspondence theory of truth, understanding "truth" only in the Tarskian deflationary sense (see 1992, 79–86). Fallibilism would also seem to undermine global realism by implying relativism; namely, if any theory suffers from competition from other empirically equivalent theories, how could it be thought that a theory's entities are more likely to exist? Quine rejects theoretical relativism by arguing that it is either self-refuting or tantamount to making a knowledge claim from a metaphysical perspective. If theoretical relativism is itself a scientific claim, this claim cannot be both absolutely correct and only relatively correct. If theoretical relativism is not a scientific claim, it must be a metaphysical judgment from a perspective that attempts to contrast reality as it really is with the portraits of reality generated by all theories. But no such perspective can actually be taken; all knowledge claims are made from within one theory or another. Quine is very careful to point out that his scientific fallibilism cannot be equated with theoretical relativism.

Consider then Quine's idealistic stance on the creation of theoretical entities. Such idealism would seem to preclude global realism, since there could be no guarantee available to us (metaphysics aside) that a product of human theorizing might really exist. But Quine infers from the collapse of metaphysics just the opposite conclusion, that we as theorizers have no choice but to view nature as containing the entities postulated by our current theories. Keeping in mind Quine's stance on the nature of experience and the reality of postulated entities, the meaning of the term *theory* takes on heightened significance. In Quine's philosophy, *theory* refers not just to those judgments pertaining to unobservable entities (like quarks or the force of gravity) in the usual sense of *unobservable*. *Theory* instead refers to the entire collection of meaningful judgments about nature, which also includes ordinary observation statements about "medium-sized" physical objects. Quine declines an invitation to use the functional distinction between these two kinds of judgments to erect an ontological distinction, because his epistemology cannot distinguish between them. Both kinds are just scientific propositions that accordingly must answer to the evidence of sensory stimulations. This epistemological stance implies that neither kind of judgment enjoys any special status over the other. If they have an equivalent privilege to make claims about reality, the ontological status of the entities referred to must also be the same. Put simply, if we want to be realists about houses and trees, we must also be realists about molecules and gravity. For Quine, all four things are theoretical entities, postulated by current theories, and judgments about all four things go beyond the available evidence of the senses.

Dewey's Empiricism

Dewey, like Quine, rejected rationalistic metaphysics and the two dogmas of logical positivism early in his own career. However, this did not bring him to Quine's scientism. His intellectual path from idealism to naturalistic pragmatism did not start out from neo-Kantianism, but from the absolute idealism of Hegel. The story of this evolution is too long to tell here,[5] but four central tenets of this idealism were retained in Dewey's later philosophy.

First, there can be no appeal to trans-experiential realities in scientific or philosophical explanation. The actualities and possibilities of human experience exhaust all matters of meaningful discussion. This opposes transcendentalism, which attempts to survey and discuss realities alleged to be forever beyond the reach of human experience. There are two categories of transcendentalism that especially earned Dewey's scorn: a philosophy asserting the bare thing-in-itself (e.g., Locke's or Kant's) and a philosophy asserting the existence of scientifically knowable yet transcendent objects. Dewey objected to the first category of transcendentalism largely on the grounds that it offers an empty conception. Quine's philosophy falls under the second category, since its notion of scientific knowledge demands that the object of knowledge exists beyond the range of human experience. We have seen how Quine's elimination of metaphysics led him to suppose that science alone can decide on what exists. But only his determined application of scientism to the notion of experience itself, as just a matter of bodily reactions to physical excitations, would account for his conclusion that human experience is a small, delimited realm beyond which lies all the other objects of scientific knowledge (like tables and stars). Dewey, in rejecting a physicalist psychology of experience, instead locates objects of knowledge within human experience.

Second, following from the rejection of the dualism implied by transcendentalism, Dewey's philosophy refuses to conceive of experience as necessarily subjective. Subjective idealism cannot be formulated or defended without the notion of some sort of reality forever beyond what is privately available to a mind. Dewey argued that the only nonsubjective view of experience available is to find that experience is a mixture of the public and the private. If the private can only exist in contrast to the public, both kinds of experience must be available for those who can grasp the distinction. But this should be understood as a functional distinction arising within the totality of human experience itself, and not as a metaphysical distinction grounded on the problematic notion of the thing-in-itself. Publicly available experience can also be termed "social" or "cultural" experience, and not surprisingly Dewey's philosophy pays far more attention to it than private experience. Where epistemology is concerned with the object of knowledge, this object exists within social experience.

Third, when knowledge is achieved, the known object is a creation of the knowing process, generated out of the problem-solving methods of scientific inquiry. Dewey's functionalist epistemology agrees with Quine's philosophy that known objects are created by humans and that knowledge claims are scientific judgments. Our creation of known objects should answer the false supposition that known objects really lie beyond the bounds of human experience.

Fourth, Dewey did not believe that an ontology should only consist of actual and possible objects of knowledge. It was the mistake of a rationalistic absolute idealism, and of all rationalistic metaphysics, to declare that reality consists solely of known realities, or worse, solely of a priori conceptual categories that permit knowledge. Relatively little of human experience consists of known things, and even if this portion is growing, it could never be expected to engulf all experience. While the meanings of things are considerably enhanced when they are transformed into known objects, the meaning of an object is far broader than just the meaning established by knowing it.

This metaphysical view that things are what they are experienced to be, and not only what they are known to be, is Dewey's "immediate empiricism." Dewey thus denied that only known objects possessed meaning, and unlike Quine, he never thought that linguistic reference only held between known objects and utterances. Therefore, ontology is not the exclusive preserve of science, and successful reference is not limited to scientific propositions. Dewey's mature philosophy retained the term *metaphysics* to cover empirical inquiry into traits common across all experience and hence across all of the multifarious modes of knowing as well. Not all accurate descriptions of the traits of experience are scientific propositions. There are also "denotative" judgments, descriptions of traits of things that are not designed to be held up to the scrutiny of science. Put another way, such traits denotatively described are not possible objects of knowledge.[6]

Dewey's alternative to rationalistic metaphysics is a pluralistic empiricism roomy enough for anything and everything of human experience, from the social to the private and from the known to the unknown. This empiricist metaphysics countenances the known things provided by science, of course. It also respects the doubtful experiences of things that provide the problematic material necessitating scientific inquiry, and the consummatory experiences signaling the successful resolution of inquiry resulting in the production of knowledge. Dewey's empiricism is naturalistic, but empiricism is the proper starting point for understanding his philosophy. The all-important difference between a naturalistic empiricism (Quine) and an empiricist naturalism (Dewey) is whether one's ontology consists solely of scientifically known or knowable objects. From Dewey's perspective, Quine's scientism and naturalistic empiricism is just as perniciously rationalistic as is traditional metaphysics. It cannot embrace the width and breadth of all human experience, and hence fails to locate the justification for the very existence of science within this expansive context.

Dewey's empiricism is no cousin to the subjectivist phenomenalism so rightly derided by Quine. Unlike a phenomenalistic attempt to make provision for a category of privileged judgments by postulating private mental states, Dewey's concept of experience is not characterized by privilege or privacy. Quine says, "Any subjective talk of mental events proceeds necessarily in terms that are acquired and understood through their associations, direct or indirect, with the socially observable behavior of physical objects" (1960, 264). Dewey agrees:

> The realm of meanings, of mind, is at home, securely located and anchored in an empirically observable order of existence. And this order stands in genetic continuity with physical and vital phenomena, being, indeed, these phenomena taken up into and incorporated within a wider scope of associated interactions. We do not have to read the mental back into the antecedent physical, much less resort to the desperate measure of making it so all-inclusive that the physical is treated as a disguised and illusory "appearance" of the mental. The social affords us an observable instance of a "realm of mind" objective to an individual, by entering into which as a participating member organic activities are transformed into acts having a mental quality. (1928, LW3:50)

Beyond this agreement on the failure of phenomenalism, Dewey and Quine have quite different views of the nature of experience. Their common use of the "social" as primary over talk of "private" mental states can obscure Dewey's rejection of Quine's physicalist empiricism. The "social" for Quine means the "scientifically objective," and his conception of experience is solely a matter of sensory impacts. Thus experience for Quine can never be of physical objects, or alternatively stated, observed physical objects cannot be in experience but only capable of causing experience. On Dewey's conception of experience, observed physical objects are within experience, since there is nowhere else for them to be when they are observed. Thus Quine's elimination of phenomenalism does not imply a victory for his scientism, since Dewey's immediate empiricism stands as a viable third alternative.

There is another aspect to Quine's preference for scientism that should be mentioned here. Quine believes that only his scientism can defuse the challenge of skepticism, on two fronts: the Cartesian skepticism raised by dualistic metaphysics, and the naturalistic skepticism raised by questioning the ability of sense experience to supply knowledge of the natural world. Dualism evaporates with the demise of rationalistic metaphysics. Naturalistic skepticism offers a scientific hypothesis, grounded by a measure of scientific knowledge. It is this kind of skepticism which plays on the same field as Quine's own philosophy, and the question it raises is answerable by science itself. It thus earns Quine's respect as a coherent position, but not as a plausible position, because he contends that its scientific plausibility is very low. Dewey's empiricism similarly defuses Cartesian dualism and presents no threat of skepticism over and above the usual admission of the fallibility of all science. Quine's scientism enjoys no advantage over Dewey's empiricism in its ability to resist skepticism. Indeed, both may be classified as closely related forms of Pyrrhonist skepticism.[7] To summarize, Quine's deflation of rationalistic metaphysics does not eliminate all metaphysics and cannot eliminate Dewey's immediate empiricism in particular.

Dewey's empiricism is the foundation of a different approach to naturalism. While mental entities are likewise absent from his philosophy, physical objects are not automatically granted exclusive dominion. For Dewey, naturalism should not be confused with physicalism or materialism (see Dewey et al. 1945). Hence Dewey's agreement that all knowledge has its origin in experience cannot share in Quine's physicalist interpretation. Dewey reserves the metaphysically empirical right to speak of experience in a much broader sense than Quine, as Dewey does not conceive experience to be spatially and temporally limited to the activities of the nervous system. Rather, Dewey describes experience as continuous with and penetrating deeply into nature. Put another way, experience is wherever both the experienced thing and the experiencer are. Quine's physicalist conception of experience would instead locate an experience of an object in the stimulation of retinas and other sensory membranes and perhaps further along into the nervous system. Quine's philosophy avoids idealism because of the claim that all reality is physical. Dewey's philosophy avoids idealism because experience is not taken to be in some non-natural realm and because experience is identical with only those regions of nature having experiencers as foci.

Dewey's metaphysical empiricism only declares that science and philosophy are not permitted to postulate anything permanently beyond the range of experience in its effort to explain experience or any features or events within experience. Rejecting transcendentalism is not sufficient; to be naturalistic, Dewey's empiricism must not collapse into idealism either. Such a collapse is prevented by the distinction in Dewey's philosophy between the transcendent entity and the independent entity. Unlike the transcendent entity, which by definition never comes into the range of experience, the permitted independent entity can naturally come into and pass out of the range of human experience. Nature extends beyond experience at any given moment, because Dewey does not mean to assert that experience exhausts reality.

It is important at this stage to forestall a typical objection made by many realists: That Dewey's distinction between the "transcendent" object, which is forever beyond experience, and the "independent" object, which must at least reside within experience occasionally, is a distinction without a real difference. If the object can drift in and out of experience unchanged, then the object possesses an existence entirely independent of human experience. Such complete independence makes its forays into human experience irrelevant to its actual nature, and thus the object would remain what it is regardless of whether it ever came into human experience at all. Thus, a realistic view of the object is by default a transcendentalist view, and Dewey's protest against transcendentalism reveals a bias toward idealism by assuming that experience must supply the object's reality. Dewey's reply is simple. It is the transcendental realist, not Dewey, who imports an assumption that we can know with certainty that an object retains its experienced qualities and traits when it is not in human experience. Our experience of most objects encourages us to believe that this is the case, but this can only be a fallible belief. Transcendental realism is unnecessary and indemonstrable, and Dewey's immediate empiricism is sufficient to guard against outright idealism.[8]

There is a third kind of "object" besides the transcendental and independent objects. This is the "postulated" but unobservable object that is postulated by many scientific theories. Dewey's philosophy recognizes, against narrow positivism, that the sciences should be permitted to postulate transcendent entities that permit scientific explanation of experienced events. However, Dewey refuses to take a realistic attitude toward such "objects," while Quine encourages realism here. Dewey's naturalistic understanding of experience is the ontological claim, against dualism, that experience refers to a special kind of natural event involving a transaction between an organism and its environment. Accordingly, his naturalism is not limited to what is scientifically "objective," and it is concerned with far more than just linguistic behavior. Dewey considered the unit of meaning to be the act: a goal-directed interaction with the environment. On this immediate empiricist view, such interactions reveal to us the experienced traits of things. Dewey's rejection of scientism implies that objects as they are known do not exhaust our experience of them. Conversely, we experience things in a variety of meaningful ways besides through knowing them. This does not mean that Dewey has abandoned naturalism. His empiricism holds that there are many things in human experience that are not actual or possible objects of scientific knowledge.

Quine has argued powerfully that the only type of knowledge is scientific knowledge of natural objects. But this stance has no bearing on whether all of human experience must be scientifically conceived solely in terms of physical and knowable objects. To assume so, as Quine does, simply begs the question of whether a legitimate description of experience must be capable of being scientifically valid. Dewey denies this view, holding that we can legitimately describe actual and real features of the world regardless of whether such descriptions could ever stand up to scientific scrutiny. Dewey's denotative method is not a matter of nature causing knowledge in us, since it is we who selectively attend to features of the world that may or may not meet the standards of knowledge. Immediate empiricism points out that if such features cannot withstand scientific scrutiny, they do not lapse into nonexistence or illusion; they remain real features of the world. Dewey's philosophy, to repeat, does not permit objects of present or future scientific knowledge to exhaust reality.

A Pragmatic Philosophy of Science

Dewey's functionalist epistemology finds that some kinds of propositions of scientific theories should not be construed realistically. A thorough examination of Dewey's logic of propositions is inappropriate here.[9] To contrast clearly Dewey's philosophy of science with Quine's, it is sufficient to notice that Dewey's logical theory permits him to distinguish three senses of "theoretical" which are too often conflated or ignored. The notion that experience is "theory-laden" has been popular since the demise of naive realism in the early decades of the twentieth century. While Quine did much to eliminate confusions about this notion, he did not go far enough. A major obstacle to further progress is the requirement, laid down by Quine's naturalized epistemology, that all objects of knowledge lie beyond human experience. This requirement, Dewey argued, not only generates as much mystery as any old-fashioned transcendentalism but also is inconsistent with actual scientific practice.

While a theory is supposed to permit a "seeing," as befits the Greek meaning of *theoria*, the question of exactly what is seen remains vague. One prominent answer is that a theory permits an intellectual seeing of an entity that cannot be seen by ordinary human senses. This answer is not very precise and covers a lot of territory; both Democritus's atoms and Plato's Forms are theoretical in this sense. But it is a very common answer given by nineteenth- and twentieth-century scientists and philosophers. For example, the concept of an "electron" is taken to be a theoretical means of "seeing" what cannot ordinarily be sensed. Those ignorant of atomic theory cannot intellectually "see" electrons.

A second prominent answer is that a theory permits an intellectual seeing of an observable thing in a new way. For example, the concept of a "voltage meter" is a theoretical means of "seeing" an object in a way unavailable to those not yet initiated into the theory of electrons. Those ignorant of atomic theory cannot intellectually see a voltage meter. This convoluted talk of "intellectually seeing a voltage meter" is generated by the fact that an electrician can see a voltage meter while my toddler cannot, although both can look at that same physical object. A voltage meter is, in the second sense of "theory," a theoretical object that is observable to trained observers. Now, Quine would also call a voltage meter a theoretical object, but Quine uses only the first sense of *theory*, not the second sense. By a theoretical entity Quine always refers to a *transcendent* entity postulated by a theory, existing beyond the sensory evidence of everyone's experience. The second sense of *theory* permits discussion of a *transformed* object created by a theory, existing within the experience of those trained in the theory. The transformed entity is an independent but not transcendent entity, since it can be experienced, yet it is experienced as the sort of thing that exists whether or not it is experienced. Dewey's functionalist epistemology has room for both propositions about transcendent entities and propositions about transformed entities. To make the connection between propositions and observations a bit clearer at this stage, we can notice that many kinds of scientific observations are made possible through transformative propositions, which may be assisted by transcendent propositions.

Dewey often uses astronomical examples. When an astronomer observes a star, this star is observed as being many light-years distant. The transformative proposition would be, for example, "Polaris is 300 light-years away." No one ignorant of modern astronomy would observe the star in this manner. A child, for example, could at best observe the star as *very* far away. The astronomer observes a more extensively known star than does a child, thanks to scientific training that includes the transformative proposition that stars are many light-years distant. Stars can be transformed into objects of knowledge within experience due to the science of astronomy. Astronomical science also includes the transcendent proposition that photons of light travel through space at a definite rate. This proposition is transcendent because it concerns "photons," which by definition are not observable, although their alleged effects on the retina are. This transcendental proposition, when conjoined with other transcendental propositions about the expansion of the universe and a measurement of a star's red-shift, can permit an astronomical calculation of a star's distance.

Transcendent postulated entities have four characteristics very different from transformed objects according to Dewey's functionalist epistemology: They can never be observed; they are only hypothetical entities; their meaning as hypothetical is exhausted by their definitions; and they are imaginative creations of theories that are not only fallible but underdetermined by any amount of practical success. Transcendent postulated entities have these characteristics because their meaning consists entirely of their role in "universal" and "hypothetical" propositions of scientific law.

Scientific laws concerning transcendent postulated entities are universal and hypothetical propositions in Dewey's terminology if and when such statements employ terms in a purely formal way, placing them in relations so that they mutually contribute to each other's definitions. Some scientific laws are not universal but "generic" in nature. Generic propositions make reference to traits of observed things (e.g., "metals are shiny"). They originate in series of specific observed cases, and therefore they can be shown to have exceptions through further observation. It is consistent with the function of generic propositions that they can be falsified by possible future observation. This is not the case for universal propositions, which cannot be falsified by further observation. This is not merely because, as Quine would have it, they are deeply imbedded in scientific theories and hence cannot be held individually accountable to observation. Universal propositions are not answerable to observations because they do not make existential claims in the first place. The proposition that "mammals are vertebrates" would not be falsified on the discovery of some mammal-like organism lacking a spine, since this proposition currently functions in biology in such a way that biologists would simply deny that this organism is a mammal because it lacks a spine. Nor would this proposition be falsified if all mammals were to become extinct. Its function can be captured in the rephrasing: "If a thing is a mammal, then it has a spine." That is why Dewey refers to universal propositions as hypothetical and nonexistential propositions, since they function in science regardless of their descriptive (in)accuracy or whether their terms actually refer to anything at all.[10]

Universal hypothetical propositions are science's equivalent of analytic a priori propositions, since their truth is grounded not in experience but in the relations between the employed terms. For example, when an elementary physics text declares that electrons have a charge of –1, it does not mean to say that all of the electrons observed so far have turned out to have a charge of –1. Rather, the text is explaining how science introduces a definition of an electron: "If a thing is an electron, then it has a charge of –1." A more advanced text may instead state that an electron has a charge of -1.602×10^{-19} coulombs. This is not intended to correct the elementary text, since the two propositions have somewhat different theoretical functions. The former suffices for electronics, while the latter is used in atomic physics. Still, neither proposition is based only on observations of electrons, and neither can be falsified by such observations. The proposition that an electron has a charge of -1.602×10^{-19} coulombs only shares *grammatical form* with a statement like "an adult male black bear has a weight of 750 pounds." However, a proposition's *genuine function* in a scientific theory may be obscured by its surface grammatical form. Since scientific theories are used to guide inferences toward predictions, it is instead best to examine how a proposition is actually used in inferences by scientists.

As physicists have already noted, the scientific theory of electrons cannot distinguish one electron from another, since no electron could possibly have any feature other than exactly what every other electron must also have according to the scientific laws regarding electrons. For all we know, there really is only one electron, and it is nearly everywhere at once! Well, Dewey's functionalist analysis of transcendent postulated entities shows that there is no need to suppose that science actually declares that even one electron exists. Science's inability to individuate transcendent postulated entities is not a shortcoming to be remedied. This is only a confirmation that propositions about such things are nonexistential and hypothetical in meaning. Another way to make the same point is to point out that the foundations of chemistry rest on the absolute interchangeability of all electrons, for if any deviated from the strict definition or had additional influential features, the laws of chemistry would be threatened.

Where scientific practice alters its use of a proposition, its meaning necessarily changes as well. Universal hypothetical propositions are particularly vulnerable to scientific progress, since theoretical revolutions dramatically alter the meanings of key terms and abolish many others. A realistic stance toward terms in universal hypothetical propositions creates interminable confusion. For example, it can be asked whether the older versions of a theory permitted successful reference to entities that have been retained, with dramatically altered meaning, in current theory. Could J. J. Thomson, the discoverer of the electron, have actually been referring to electrons, since his notion of an electron shares so few common features with what we today call "electrons"? Puzzles of this sort have been exploited by global relativists eager to pursue the bizarre repercussions of theory "incommensurability."

The confusions evaporate when it is admitted that the meaning of *electron* has never been existential in import and hence cannot be captured by a realist's correspondence notion of reference. As a postulated entity, the meaning of *electron* is subject to theoretical advancement, and hence no universal proposition is "true" in the sense that no one must perpetually admit its existential validity. A pragmatic understanding of universal propositions discerns both their aloofness from actual observation and their vulnerability to theoretical progress. They are necessarily true but can also be abandoned. They earn allegiance only through their participation in successful theories. Allegiance ends when scientists alter the meanings of terms or simply drop the use of certain terms altogether. The term *phlogiston* notoriously shifted in meaning many times in the theory's brief history before being abandoned. The proposition, "metallic phlogiston has negative weight," for example, remains an analytic proposition, since anyone who comprehends the meanings of the terms must accept its truth. This proposition cannot be falsified by any observation, since metallic phlogiston by definition cannot be observed. But all this is quite consistent with the fact that no one accepts phlogiston theory today, since accepting the truth of this sort of universal hypothetical proposition does not entail any commitment to the existence of phlogiston. Only a philosopher devoted to the incorrect notion that the meaning of a term rests exclusively on its ability to semantically refer to an actually existing thing would deny this consistency. Quine has surely done a great deal to show how reference is relative to a community of language-users, as another of Quine's attacks on analyticity shows. He questions rightly whether a radical translator could learn the analytic propositions of a foreign language from only empirical evidence. But analytic propositions are not learned by observation and ostension. That process can only instruct one in generic propositions. Analytic propositions are grounded on a community's decision to elevate generic propositions to analytic propositions and to use them in inferences accordingly. Access to such community decisions comes from joining the community; there is obviously no objective "fact of the matter" about the meaning of analytic propositions independent of community participation.

So long as a proposition is directly or indirectly answerable to experience, it cannot be a priori in any sense. But only by using the further assumption that all a priori propositions would be analytic, and vice versa, could Quine conclude that there are no genuinely analytic propositions. But that is false: Not all analytic propositions are a priori. A universal hypothetical proposition is instead an analytic a posteriori proposition, in the sense that it loses scientific allegiance when the theory in which it is imbedded is abandoned in a scientific revolution. Readers will recall that a universal hypothetical proposition was also categorized as an analytic a priori proposition, in the sense that it is not falsifiable by any observation. The notions of the "analytic" and "a priori" are indeed too vague, as Quine argues. In Dewey's philosophy of science, universal hypothetical propositions are analytic, nonexistential, nonfalsifiable, and abandonable propositions. They can also be termed "operationally a priori" because their immunity from testing is provisional while the community relies on them during inquiry. In contrast, generic propositions are synthetic, existential, falsifiable, and abandonable propositions.

To complete the contrast between Quine's and Dewey's philosophies of science, there is a third answer to the question of what a theory allows us to see. A theory, in a third sense of "seeing," can permit an intellectual seeing of an object that could possibly be observed by mechanically aided senses. Astronomers use propositions such as "A sunspot observed through a telescope is a cool surface area created by a strong magnetic field inhibiting the sun's convective forces." Geologists postulate tectonic fault lines lying miles underground to explain earthquakes. An example of a geological transformative proposition is "A fault line lies deep underground beneath Los Angeles." To give a different sort of example, the concept of an "atom" has recently expanded beyond its original transcendent meaning, because new technologies have allowed us to observe individual atoms using an electron microscope. Thanks to atomic theory and this instrument, a trained observer can indirectly observe an individual atom. The concept of an atom now has additional meaning provided by atomic theory in this third sense, because atomic theory permits an intellectual seeing of a mechanically observable thing by a trained observer. Many scientific theories have undergone this expansion thanks to technology.

Dewey's functionalist epistemology would recognize a proposition about a mechanically observable object as just a kind of transformative proposition, since the combination of theory and mechanical instrumentation transforms the trained observer's experience into one that includes observing the object. Furthermore, there cannot be a principled ontological distinction between the referents of propositions about ordinarily observable objects and referents of propositions about mechanically observable objects, because our sensory systems are themselves natural instruments of seeing, hearing, etc. And just like mechanical instruments, our natural sensory systems can be adjusted and trained to improve sensitivity and accuracy. Quine's philosophy of science does not recognize this third sense of "theory" either, since such objects of knowledge do not fall within observational experience. This contributes to his very strange claim that science asserts the existence of sets and numbers in the same manner and for the same reasons that it asserts the existence of germs and molecules. This bizarre claim contradicts the evident fact that scientists attempt to observe and track the properties of only the second kind of entities.[11] Transformative propositions, in Dewey's philosophy of science, are synthetic, existential, falsifiable, and abandonable propositions. They refer to objects that can possibly be experienced in ways other than by theoretically knowing them.

Quine's scientistic failure to distinguish between transcendent propositions and transformative propositions ensnares his philosophy in the difficulties surrounding the logical relations between theories and evidence. Critics like Davidson are right to complain that Quine's philosophy of science still requires an absolute theory/evidence separation, in order to keep the scheme of theoretical propositions safely at a logical distance from the content of unadulterated experience.[12] This lingering Kantian formalism, along with Quine's passion for forcing scientific theories into the Procrustean bed of extensionalist set theory and logic, condemns his philosophy as just another rationalism.[13] One of the characteristic traits of a rationalistic philosophy is its view that knowledge is the only relationship that we can have with the known object. And indeed, Quine's philosophy asserts that we cannot have any relationship with objects of scientific knowledge save through our intellectually knowing them by means of adopting a scientific theory. This scientific rationalism, by holding that theories consist only of transcendent propositions, is a profound departure from the spirit of Dewey's pragmatism.

Dewey adhered to an antirationalistic empiricism that sees theory and content only as aspects of experience. It is quite unnecessary to hold that our experience of the natural world is entirely a construct of theory in the transcendental sense, once it is realized that theory in the transformative sense is a quite natural and unavoidable component of much of, but not all of, human experience. This is the true meaning of the oft-claimed but little understood point that observation is theory-laden. However, not all experiences are observations of known objects. Dewey's immediate empiricism makes it evident that we can have, and necessarily must have, a wide variety of ways of experiencing objective physical things other than by knowing them. This empirical denotative method permits meaningful and legitimate claims to be made about traits of all kinds of experiences. The denotative method breaks down the barren Quinean notion that a genuinely meaningful theory must have independently specifiable testability conditions. Through denoting characteristic traits of various modes of experience, meaningful discussion of inquiry is possible, without having to justify reflections upon inquiry with more inquiry and so on. The denotative method, for example, permits functional epistemology to examine the wider context of the process of inquiry and the functional role of theories in experience. Quine does emphatically say that our experience of the world is thoroughly infused with theory, but his rationalistic scientism prevents him from following this notion to its proper destination in the metaphysics of immediate empiricism.

Quine's failure to distinguish between transcendent propositions and transformative propositions thus prematurely forces him toward the position that science must take a realistic attitude toward theoretically transcendent entities. If all theoretical entities are transcendent, then Quine is forced into the limited options of global phenomenalistic relativism or global realism: either we cannot claim that any physical objects beyond experience exist, or we must claim that all objects posited by our best theories exist in addition to experience. Dewey's recognition of transformed objects resolves this dilemma by offering a third option: Our ontology should include, in addition to all things ordinarily experienced, those transformed objects experienced thanks to our most pragmatically warranted theories.[14] Dewey's empiricist metaphysics and rejection of rationalism demand that we respect all experiences of things as real in the contexts in which they are found. This "pragmatic realism" is the pluralistic consequence of immediate empiricism and functionalist epistemology. Pragmatic realism defeats the phenomenalism of a philosopher like Bas van Fraassen, whose "constructive empiricism" does not recognize the transformative roles of theory and mechanical instruments.[15] A pragmatic realist notion of contextualized knowledge also surmounts the arguments of thoroughgoing relativists like

Goodman and Feyerabend by removing any need to suppose that "different worlds" are ontologically created by divergent theories.

Pragmatic realism agrees with Quine that the fallibility of our theories does not entail any sort of antirealistic relativism, but disagrees with Quine's position that the only alternative to such global relativism is global realism. Known objects are quite real, in the contexts in which they are known, just as anything is real in its own context. To speak of "knowledge in a context" does not sneak relativism in through the back door. The refusal of pragmatic realism to grant absolute existence, independent of inquiry, to known objects is simply a manifestation of its foundation in metaphysical empiricism. Dewey agreed with Quine that global relativism is a metaphysically inconsistent contrivance. At any rate, Quine could not object to the contextualization of knowledge, as it is his own position as well.[16] The dispute under scrutiny here is Dewey's denial and Quine's affirmation that transcendent entities can be known.

Pragmatic realism and its realistic stance toward known objects is quite consistent with an attitude of antirealism toward transcendent theoretical entities. Known objects are capable of being experienced (e.g., manipulated, altered, and controlled) in a respectably objective manner. Transcendent entities, on the other hand, are only hypothetical and imaginative creations of theories that are not only fallible but underdetermined by any amount of practical success. Now, Quine does not dispute this, but only his scientific rationalism compels his allegiance to global realism. Dewey's metaphysical empiricism instead established an expansive territory of pragmatic realism between the extremes of phenomenalism and global realism. Standing firmly on this pragmatic ground and liberated from the rationalist strictures of scientism, Dewey's functionalist epistemology rightly interprets the transcendent propositions of science as only logical instruments, lacking existential import, but operating in such a way as to orchestrate the process of scientific inquiry. Like any instrument, they are altered or replaced as the progress of science demands by the procedures of pragmatic epistemology: the technology of scientific methodology.

Dewey's functionalist epistemology and pragmatic realism can successfully defuse a recently favored argument for global scientific realism. According to this argument, the fact that the history of science is replete with observations of previously theoretical entities, such as atoms or distant planets, lends great support to the notion that scientists should construe their theories realistically. However, this argument conflates transcendent propositions with *transformative* propositions about instrumentally observable objects. These propositions have very different functional roles in the logic of scientific inquiry, as explained above. Many scientific theories have indeed formulated transformative propositions on the basis of originally transcendent propositions, and then those transformative propositions, together with the invention of required experimental tools, have led to the discernment of previously unobserved objects. Thus the realistic stance taken by pragmatic realism toward transformative objects cannot be carried over to any realistic understanding of transcendent entities.

Functional epistemology is also capable of explaining why many theories never formulate transformative propositions, insofar as these theories' transcendent entities could never be modulated into transformative objects. Prominent examples would include theories about forces or space-time curvatures. There is an important difference between a commitment to understanding the world in light of hypothesized transcendent entities, and believing that scientists could empirically discern such entities if only an appropriate observational apparatus could be invented. A commitment to a theory and its transcendent propositions is not equivalent to a belief that a theory's transcendent propositions more or less accurately describe actually existing entities.

Conclusion

Quine's philosophy offers a rationalistic scientism, a naturalized epistemology, an empiricism, and a pragmatism, in that order. His philosophy of science thus cannot recognize the crucial distinction between transformative propositions and transcendent propositions. His scientific rationalism, while recognizing logic as the technology of scientific method, badly deforms this logic by misconstruing actual scientific methodology and the role of experience in it. Quine's logic of what there is can be classified as pragmatic only in the most marginal of senses and at best is perhaps only more pragmatic than Carnap's philosophy.[17]

What is far worse for Quine's philosophy than a paucity of pragmatism is the collapse of his scientific rationalism as the sole measure of what exists. His scientific rationalism is the only support for his physicalism, which in turn is the sole support of both his project of naturalized epistemology and his infamous doctrine of the indeterminacy of translation. And upon the fate of these rests the fate of much of the rest of his philosophy. Ironically, several aspects of Quine's system more congenial to Dewey's pragmatism could alleviate these difficulties. I have particularly in mind the fact that Quine has repeatedly expressed a fondness for the behavioral approach to meaning because of its naturalistic basis.[18] Yet Quine never pursued the idea that language and theory are far better understood in terms of the purposive behavior of humans interacting together with a world of useful objects.[19] A behavioral approach, considering the undeniable plurality of human activities and purposes, would champion the sort of metaphysical and discourse pluralism inaugurated by classical pragmatism.[20]

Dewey's philosophy espouses a more thorough pragmatism by offering a metaphysical empiricism, a naturalism, a functionalist epistemology, and a pragmatic realism, in that order. By providing an empirical context for known objects, inquiry (as a process yielding knowledge) can be studied naturalistically as the production of solutions to problematic situations. Functionalist epistemology is Dewey's logic of inquiry. Since the meaning of propositions is not merely a matter of semantic reference, functionalism is able to discriminate the logical significance of transcendent propositions from transformative propositions. Pragmatic realism, the conjunction of immediate empiricism and a realistic yet fallible attitude toward known objects, offers a pluralistic ontological alternative to the stark extremes of global relativistic phenomenalism and global realism.

Acknowledgments

This paper has benefited from helpful suggestions from Tom Burke, Robert Talisse, Micah Hester, Frank Ryan, Jody Azzouni, and Peter Hare. I am also grateful to the discussion participants at two readings of versions of this chapter, with the Society for the Advancement of American Philosophy and the philosophy department at Oklahoma State University.

Notes

1. An excellent discussion of knowledge as a technological artifact is found in Hickman 1990.

2. The reader is referred to two discussions of Quine and Carnap by Richard Creath (1990) and Neil Tennant (1993). On the evolution of Carnap's thought, see Richardson (1998).

3. The term "physicalism" is inappropriate as a label here, since Quine's philosophy countenances any entities required by scientific theories, such as those of logic and mathematics. The label of "naturalism" is also problematic, as Susan Haack (1993) explains. Where carefully defined, as attempted here, the label of "scientism" should carry sufficient meaning despite the fact that Quine rarely uses it.

4. Two helpful discussions of this issue are Hookway 1988, 203–220, and Hylton 1994.

5. That story is told in my work, Shook 2000.

6. Dewey announced his version of empiricism in his essay, "The Postulate of Immediate Empiricism" (1905, MW3:158–167). An explicit restatement of his position on empiricism, primary experience and known objects, and the denotative method, is found in *Experience and Nature,* particularly the first chapter written for the revised edition (1925, LW1:10–41).

7. Pyrrhonism has been understood in at least two opposed ways: as a refusal to have any beliefs, or only the effort to suspend belief concerning other philosophical schools' dogmatic standards of knowledge. I side with the latter interpretation, convinced by Fogelin 1994. Fogelin's "neo-Pyrrhonist" participates in the fallible practices of making and improving on knowledge claims, but disdains the "quest for certainty," as Dewey phrased it.

8. Dewey's complaints against transcendental realism are numerous. See Dewey 1911.

9. See Burke 1994. My terminology in what follows is not Dewey's or Burke's, but it may better convey Dewey's intentions for the limited purposes of this essay.

10. The more significant portions of Dewey's *Logic* (1938) for this discussion are LW12:300–307, 374–82.

11. Jody Azzouni (1997) has called attention to this peculiarity of Quine's philosophy.

12. For a survey of the Quine-Davidson dispute see Picardi 1994.

13. See Harold N. Lee's protest (1998) against Quine's logicist ontology. Quine's reply is characteristically oblivious to the perspective of a broader empiricism from which Lee speaks.

14. Rom Harré (1986) has formulated a sophisticated philosophy of science largely agreeing with this ontological outlook, similarly basing his approach on a three-fold distinction between propositions about ordinarily observable objects, instrumentally observable objects, and objects impossible to ever observe. Harré appears to be insensitive to the transformative power of theories on experience, however.

15. See Van Fraassen 1980. However, critics of Van Fraassen are legion. A good discussion of realism and instrumentation congenial to pragmatic realism is Ian Hacking's, "Do We See Through a Microscope?" (1985).

16. John Capps (1996) explores in detail the fertile notion that professed naturalists like Quine should be contextualists on knowledge along with Dewey.

17. Leemon B. McHenry (1995) also reaches this conclusion.

18. For example, Quine applauds the pragmatic notion of "behaviorist semantics" in "The Pragmatists' Place in Empiricism," (35–37). Quine singles out Dewey to praise his "behavioral view of meaning" in "Ontological Relativity" (1969, 26–29).

19. Quine's fixation on the role of sensory stimuli has disturbed many critics, but the complaints of his friends are most telling. Dagfinn Føllesdal (1975) argues

that belief and meaning are generated by social behavior. Donald Davidson (1984) has also emphasized how the public sociality of language is a better starting point than the particularity and individuality of one's sensations.

20. Two contemporary pragmatists, Huw Price (1992) and Robert Almeder (1997), have lamented the divergence of Quine's naturalism from an empiricist pluralism.

Works Cited

Almeder, Robert. 1997. Carnap and Quine on Empiricism. *History of Philosophy Quarterly* 14:349–64.

Azzouni, Jody. 1997. Thick Epistemic Access: Distinguishing the Mathematical from the Empirical. *Journal of Philosophy* 94:472–84.

Burke, Tom. 1994. *Dewey's New Logic: A Reply to Russell*. Chicago: University of Chicago Press.

Capps, John. Dewey, Quine, and Pragmatic Naturalized Epistemology. *Transactions of the Charles S. Peirce Society* 32:634–67.

Creath, Richard. 1990. Carnap, Quine, and the Rejection of Intuition. In *Perspectives on Quine*, ed. Robert B. Barrett and Roger F. Gibson, 55–66. Oxford: Blackwell.

Davidson, Donald. 1986. On the Very Idea of a Conceptual Scheme. In *Truth and Interpretation*, ed. Ernest LePore, 183–98. Oxford: Oxford University Press.

Dewey, John. 1905. The Postulate of Immediate Empiricism. *Journal of Philosophy, Psychology, and Scientific Methods* 2:393–99. Reprinted in Dewey 1910, 226–41, and in MW3:158–67.

———. 1910. *The Influence of Darwin on Philosophy, and Other Essays in Contemporary Thought*. New York: Henry Holt. Essays reprinted separately in EW1, MW1, 3, 4, 6.

———. 1911. Brief Studies in Realism. *Journal of Philosophy, Psychology, and Scientific Methods* 8:393–400, 546–54. Reprinted in Dewey 1916, 250–80 and MW6:103–22.

———. 1916. *Essays in Experimental Logic*. Chicago: University of Chicago Press. Essays reprinted separately in MW1, 2, 4, 6, 8, 10.

———. 1925. *Experience and Nature*. Chicago: Open Court. Reprinted in LW1.

———. 1928. The Inclusive Philosophic Idea. *Monist* 38:161–77. Reprinted in LW3:41–54.

———. 1938. *Logic: The Theory of Inquiry*. New York: Henry Holt. Reprinted in LW12.

Dewey, John, Sidney Hook, and Ernest Nagel. 1945. Are Naturalists Materialists? *Journal of Philosophy* 42:515–30. Reprinted in LW15:109–26.

Fogelin, Robert J. 1994. *Pyrrhonian Reflections on Knowledge and Justification*. Oxford: Oxford University Press.

Føllesdal, Dagfinn. 1975. Meaning and Experience. In *Mind and Language*, ed. Samuel Guttenplan, 25–44. Oxford: Clarendon Press.

Haack, Susan. 1993. The Two Faces of Quine's Naturalism. *Synthese* 94:335–56.

Hacking, Ian. 1985. Do We See Through a Microscope? In *Images of Science: Essays on Realism and Empiricism, with a Reply from Bas C. van Fraassen,* ed. Paul M. Churchland and Clifford A. Hooker, 132–52. Chicago: University of Chicago Press.

Hahn, Lewis E., and Paul A. Schilpp, eds. 1998. *The Philosophy of W. V. Quine.* Chicago: Open Court.

Harré, Rom. 1986. *Varieties of Realism: A Rationale for the Natural Sciences.* Oxford: Blackwell.

Hickman, Larry. 1990. *John Dewey's Pragmatic Technology.* Bloomington: Indiana University Press.

Hookway, Christopher. 1988. *Quine: Language, Experience, and Reality.* Stanford: Stanford University Press.

Hylton, Peter. 1994. Quine's Naturalism. In *Philosophical Naturalism,* ed. Peter French, Theodore Uehling, and Howard Wettstein, 261–82. Notre Dame, Ind.: University of Notre Dame Press.

Lee, Harold N. 1998. Discourse and Event: The Logician and Reality. Hahn and Schilpp 1998, 295–314.

McHenry, Leemon B. 1995. Quine's Pragmatic Ontology. *Journal of Speculative Philosophy* 9:147–58.

Picardi, Eva. 1994. Davidson and Quine on Observation Sentences. In *Language, Mind, and Epistemology: On Donald Davidson's Philosophy,* ed. Gerhard Preyer, Frank Siebelt, and Alexander Ulfig, 97–116. Dordrecht: Kluwer.

Price, Huw. 1992. Metaphysical Pluralism. *Journal of Philosophy* 89:387–409.

Quine, W. V. O. 1960. *Word and Object.* Cambridge: MIT Press.

———. 1969. *Ontological Relativity and Other Essays.* New York: Columbia University Press.

———. 1980. *From a Logical Point of View.* 2d ed. Cambridge: Harvard University Press.

———. 1981. The Pragmatists' Place in Empiricism. In *Pragmatism: Its Sources and Prospects,* ed. Robert J. Mulvaney and Philip M. Zeltner. Columbia: University of South Carolina Press.

———. 1992. *Pursuit of Truth.* Rev. ed. Cambridge: Harvard University Press.

Quine, W. V. O., and J. S. Ullian. 1978. *The Web of Belief.* 2d ed. New York: Random House.

Richardson, Alan W. 1998. *Carnap's Construction of the World: The Aufbau and the Emergence of Logical Empiricism.* Cambridge: Cambridge University Press.

Shook, John R. 2000. *Dewey's Empirical Theory of Knowledge and Reality.* Nashville: Vanderbilt University Press.

Tennant, Neil. 1993. Carnap and Quine. In *Logic, Language, and the Structure of Scientific Theories,* ed. Wesley Salmon and Gereon Wolters, 305–44. Pittsburgh: University of Pittsburgh Press.

van Fraassen, Bas C. 1980. *The Scientific Image.* Oxford: Clarendon Press.

Part II

Logical Theory and Forms

6

Prospects for Mathematizing
Dewey's Logical Theory

Tom Burke

This essay discusses ways in which contemporary mathematical logic may be reconciled with John Dewey's logical theory. Standard formal techniques drawn from dynamic modal logic, situation theory, fuzzy set theory and fuzzy logic, generative grammar, generalized quantifier theory, category theory, lambda calculi, game theoretic semantics, network exchange theory, etc., are accommodated within a framework consistent with Dewey's *Logic: The Theory of Inquiry* (1938). This essay outlines many of the basic features of Dewey's logical theory, working in a top-down fashion through various technical notions pertaining to existential and ideational aspects of inquiry, from contextual notions of *situations* and *ideologies*, to primitive operational and empirical notions of *modes of action* and particular *qualities*. The aim here is to display the scope of Dewey's logical theory and thus establish a framework relative to which details may be explored without losing sight of their larger significance.

Dewey's Perspective on Logic

> [T]he insistent theme of the [1938] *Logic* is that an adequate system of symbolization is contingent on both a better theory of language than was then available to philosophical logicians and a better theory of the materials to be symbolized. . . . His *Logic* is dedicated, Dewey says in the preface, to the conviction that the general principles of language which he will set forth "will enable a more complete and consistent set of symbolizations than now exists to be made." (Sleeper 1986/2001, 135–36)

This essay takes these remarks at face value. Matters have progressed such that we may begin to propose strategies for reconciling Dewey's philosophy of logic with contemporary mathematical logic and natural language semantics—not necessarily because linguists and logicians are now working with better theories of language or better theories of the ontological commitments of mathematical logic but because more sophisticated systems of "symbolization" have been developed which more easily accommodate the kind of logical theory that Dewey presented.

Dewey's 1938 *Logic* casts logic as a scientific inquiry into general features of inquiry itself, with the aim of determining normative principles that distinguish better and worse methods of inquiry. Can this view of logic accommodate formal techniques and principles of contemporary mathematical logic? Specifically, how do we position such technical concerns within Dewey's theory of inquiry? How do we link them to the operational and empirical foundations of that theory? Can this be done without compromising Dewey's conceptions of inquiry and experience? Contemporary mathematical logic is more technically sophisticated than anything Dewey was in a position to consider in his day. But if he was right about what logic is and what inquiry is, then these technical developments should fall within the scope of his logical theory.

Reconciling Dewey's view of logic with contemporary mathematical logic will not be straightforward insofar as Dewey imposed various stringent constraints on logic as a science. In particular, to say that logical theory should be fundamentally oriented to operational and empirical concerns is not to say that it should be oriented exclusively to inductive inference. But it means that human conceptual schemes and linguistic capabilities are based ultimately on our abilities to act in the world, individually and collectively, and to note and interpret the results of those actions. Natural language semantics and issues regarding "logical form," deductive or otherwise, would then depend on operational and empirical matters as much as they do on sentential truth-functions or a set-theoretic semantics for names, predicate symbols, variables, and quantifiers. The objects, properties, and relations in the world of things we typically observe, talk about, and have knowledge of would be products of interactions and transactions that are made possible because of our operational and empirical capabilities. If formal semantic theories are to explicitly accommodate this transactional character of experience, language, thought, and knowledge, then we have to start with a set of basic notions that are often regarded as extralogical—namely, notions of agents' operational abilities and of their capacities to register the results of such actions. Only on that basis should we introduce notions of things, entities, objects, occasions, space-time points, events, or whatever else may belong to domains of discourse, have properties, stand in relations to one another, or otherwise characterize possible or actual states of affairs. This requires an integrated type of operationalism and empiricism affecting every aspect of logic as a science.

While this essay outlines some ways to incorporate mathematical techniques into Dewey's theory of inquiry based on such operational, empirical foundations, the most glaring omission will be the details, both mathematical and philosophical. An extensive and highly commendable philosophical critique of Dewey's logical theory can be found in Sleeper's *Necessity of Pragmatism* (1986). The more modest aim here is simply to survey in a cursory way the range of mathematical techniques that may be brought to bear just to begin to cover all of the features of that theory. Hence the coverage will be broad but not as deep as it ultimately must be.

It is important to stress that inquiry on the whole is not explicable in terms of any one formal system or computational paradigm, and yet various formalisms can be used to characterize its numerous aspects. We only have to show how these various formalisms cohere within a single theory of inquiry. I will try to outline certain minimal requirements in this regard, hopefully without precluding finer developments. The result should be viewed as a body of tools, principles, methods, etc., for modeling various aspects of inquiry, to be applied and tested in any concrete inquiry. This is intended to underwrite modeling methods that any problem-solver might use to survey and control the resolution of a given problem domain in the course of thinking about the problem at hand.

Dewey's notion that inquiry is a clarification and transformation of some concrete problematic *situation* (1938, chap. 6) is presupposed here. This pattern of inquiry is essentially the basic pattern of experience—a redirection of life activities—except that it also involves deliberate observation and experimentation guided by theoretical reflection. Inquiry is a type of concrete experience that involves experimentally applied thinking. Of special interest here is the notion that inquiry involves the correlative development and manipulation of both *existential* and *ideational* contents:

> Inquiry is progressive and cumulative. Propositions are the instruments by which provisional conclusions of preparatory inquiries are summed up, recorded and retained for subsequent uses. In this way they function as effective means, material and procedural, in the conduct of inquiry, till the latter institutes subject-matter so unified in significance as to be warrantably assertible. It follows (1) that there is no such thing as an isolated proposition; or, positively stated, that propositions stand in ordered relations to one another; and (2) that there are two main types of such order, one referring to the factual or existential material which determines the final subject of judgment, the other referring to the ideational material, the conceptual

meanings, which determine the predicate of final judgment. In the words of ordinary use, there are the propositions having the relation which constitutes *inference,* and the propositions having the serial relation which constitutes reasoning or *discourse.* (LW12:310; see also 1942, LW15:37–38)

How and to what extent might contemporary logical theory help to explicate these two types of ordered relations among propositions? The following discussion falls into three parts designed to answer this question. We will first look at some aspects of "the factual or existential material which determines the final subject of judgment." This is followed by a look at "the ideational material, the conceptual meanings, which determine the predicate of final judgment." Finally, these will be considered in conjunction with one another as conjugate aspects of inquiry.

Existential Aspects of Inquiry

For Dewey, logic is more than just a study of principles of reasoning. Historically, logic is rooted in studies of language and reasoning. But an account of good reasoning requires more than just a logic of linguistic representations (Neisser 1976; Gibson 1979; Searle 1980; Putnam 1983; Brooks 1990; Gärdenfors 1990; McClamrock 1995). More attention must be given to experimentation, observation, perception, and bare phenomenal aspects of experience. A treatment of these existential aspects of inquiry should begin by examining the nature of the concrete *situations* that undergo transformation in inquiry and in reference to which the existential subject of judgment is determined.

Situations

First, we must distinguish concrete situations in our actual experience from abstract representations of situations in a theory of inquiry (where we are now thinking of an inquiry as a deliberately controlled transformation of a situation). Representations of situations will be referred to as *situation-types.* Situations themselves, as immediately given qualitative wholes, are concrete individual realities (Dewey 1929, 1930, 1938). The existential subject matter of inquiry occurs within some concrete situation—which is not a simple atomic sense datum and not a holistic sense of the entire universe, but something that is potentially complex and yet which is immediately sensed or felt or otherwise *had.* A situation is not a formal construction. But situation-types, as representations of situations, are means for stepping back and referring to situations abstractly as changing but structured entities that function as contextual factors in inquiry. A logician's task (in part) would be to formally model *types* of situations, where the transformation of a concrete situation would be a matter of changing the type of situation that it is.

There are various ways to model situation-types. Following Barwise and Etchemendy 1989 or Fenstad et al. 1987, a situation might be represented as a partial "possible world." The course that an inquiry takes could be represented formally as a sequence of transitions, starting from a partial and comparatively uninformative situation-type and moving in the direction of a more complete and determinate situation-type. As one option, a formal model of inquiry in this sense could involve a structure (S,R,V)—along the lines of a model for a dynamic logic (Fischer and Ladner 1979; Groenendijk and Stokhof 1990, 1991; Harel 1984)—consisting of a collection S of possible situation-types, a binary accessibility relation R mapping out possible transitions among those situation-types, and a valuation function V specifying (partially) what is or is not the case in each situation-type. Inquiries would be modeled as sequences of state transitions in this space, with special regard for those sequences of transitions that move from indeterminate (partial) situation-types to determinate (less partial) ones.

We need not rule out this sort of model if it is feasible in specific cases, but it is not the best way to think about inquiry as Dewey described it. It does not embody enough detail to reflect the internal dynamics of situations in themselves. Minimally, we should acknowledge the internal dynamics of situations, independent of inquiry as such, in order to characterize stages of inquiry (particularly initial and final ones) as domains of activity and not just as static arrays of existential data.

Another shortcoming of this "partial worlds" picture of situations is that it presupposes a fixed *grammar* of potential facts on which a structure (S,R,V) is defined. We want to allow that the transformation of a situation may involve not only modifications of facts with respect to a given grammar of potential facts but also modifications of this grammar itself. Hence generally we cannot presuppose any such semantic structure (S,R,V) as a given space in which inquiry moves, insofar as we cannot presuppose any one grammar of potential facts on which that structure would be defined, as if this grammar could be fixed independently of the given inquiry.

We may address both of these concerns simultaneously—the dynamicity of situations, and the malleability of grammars of potential facts—if we model a situation not as a single partial world but as a dynamic structure (W,C,A), or better, *as a class or family of such structures*. Each such structure—a *situation-type*—would be (minimally, as a first approximation) a collection W of possible states of affairs, where these are viewed as collections or systems of potential facts (as specified by an assignment function A). A collection C of binary reachability relations (connections) would be defined on the collection W, typically in terms of certain state-change functions. With a single situation-type as the simplest case, an inquiry could be represented as a process of modifying an indeterminate and insufficiently informative *initial* situation-type $S' = (W', C', A')$. This process allegedly should move toward a determinate and more fully informative *final* situation-type $S'' = (W'', C'', A'')$. This presents inquiry not as a process of moving through a fixed state space but rather as a process of successively transforming features or parameters of an initial state space S'—a matter of altering such a space toward a more preferable configuration.

Still, there is not much here to indicate what would distinguish an indeterminate from a determinate situation. The notion of indeterminacy is in fact multifaceted. Concepts of partiality, partial functions, partial models, partial worlds, etc., suggest one kind of indeterminacy (Barwise 1989; Fenstad 1996). Probability theory also comes to mind as a way of handling some types of indeterminacy. But fuzzy set theory (Black 1937; Zadeh 1965; Dubois and Prade 1980; Klir and Folger 1988; Yager and Filev 1994; Bandemer and Gottwald 1995; Klir and Yuan 1995) is perhaps better-equipped to characterize indeterminacy of situation-types. For instance, a subject of inquiry may be modeled as a *fuzzy* class of situation-types (W, C, A), where membership in this class is not a crisp yes/no matter but rather a matter of degree. Moreover, we may treat the sets W, the relations in C, etc., in situation-types as fuzzy sets and relations. Applications of fuzzy modeling to real-world engineering problems indicate that the final determinacy that should characterize acceptable conclusions of inquiry would not be a matter of eradicating fuzziness but rather of finding suitable levels of fuzziness that best accommodate the problem at hand, in a world that inevitably evades constraints imposed by crisp models. Crisp models may well be typical of early stages of inquiry where issues are established in only a preliminary fashion. Hence we would expect a positive correlation between increased determinacy and more explicit and more precisely modeled fuzziness, at least in regard to situation-types.

If this is the case, then fuzzy set theory would have a key role to play in explicating existential aspects of inquiry. But before such details can be profitably explored, we need to continue to lay out details of the overall pattern of inquiry in both its existential and ideational aspects. At this point we have the nice feature that any given situation-type is potentially dynamic, given that we can allow some kind of movement among states of affairs within that situation-type. Second, a single overarching superstructure of situation-types or states of affairs is not necessary, nor do we presuppose a single grammatical infrastructure of potential facts on which any such superstructure might be built, not even within a single inquiry. This can accommodate an account of inquiry (including scientific inquiry) with robust perspectival and pluralistic features. Of course, in adopting this latter way of modeling subjects of judgment as classes of situation-types (W,C,A), we must be able to make sense of several notions employed in this sort of structure. In particular, what is meant by a *state of affairs* (namely, an element of W) and, more fundamentally, what is meant by a *potential fact* (namely, an element in the domain of an assignment function A)?

Potential Facts

Situations are or support domains of both actual and potential facts (or factual potentials). As Dewey would put it, facts *signify* other facts. Remote facts may be inferred from present facts (smoke signifies a possible fire, rain is suggested by dark clouds, etc.) by virtue of established *involvements* among potential facts (1938, chaps. 2–3). Grammars of potential facts should be able to convey the range of such potentials when such involvements are at all systematic.

We presuppose no single grammar of potential facts from one situation-type to the next, although we do so for each situation-type (W,C,A). So we should be able to say something in general about what would constitute a well-defined grammar of potential facts. A systematic development of a typical grammar of potential facts would not be appropriate without first considering some general constraints on what is meant by a "potential fact."

In particular, it should be noted that the *testability* of potential facts can account for some of the dynamic character of situation-types, if not the mechanism for transforming situations as well. To speak of a correspondence between factual propositions and the facts they are about is fairly straightforward if we maintain Dewey's distinction between primary and reflective experience. Propositional formulations of potential facts in reflective experience must in some way draw on and in turn be applicable to the exigencies of primary experience. The operational and empirical foundations of Dewey's account of kinds, objects, and various types of propositions as building blocks for such grammars play a key role in making sense of this notion of the testability of potential facts (1929, 1938; see below). The "facts of the matter" in a given inquiry range over potential facts (singular or general) which may or may not be actualized in primary experience. (For example, it is an astrophysical fact that one could kick a football a very long way on the surface of Pluto, but no one has actually done it.)

Thus we must allow that actual facts typically occur not singularly but within systems of involvements among potential facts, all of which constitute facts of the matter at hand.

Moreover, we have to allow that facts of the matter in a given inquiry are subject to change in the course of inquiry. A grammar of potential facts, by its very nature, is a step removed from concrete practical considerations as they arise in actual inquiries. In actual inquiries, the existences that constitute present objects having properties and standing in relations among themselves will be products of actual implementations of activities and sensitivities involved in the direct engagements of primary experience. Nothing is more concrete in our experience than these direct engagements, but neither is there anything absolutely fixed about these engagements. The basic operational abilities and empirical sensitivities that constitute the nuts and bolts of these direct engagements are themselves mutable and as such permit (for better or worse) a good deal of flexibility in what the facts of the matter may be. Propositional formulations of potential facts are only as reliable as are the methods by which they can be tested against conditions imposed by primary experience. And the facts themselves are only as reliably determinate as are the routines and attunements that constitute the direct engagements of primary experience.

In chapter 15 of the 1938 *Logic*, Dewey outlines several basic sorts of existential propositions suitable for formulating potential facts in a given inquiry. Among the more immediate potential facts will be those concerning individual demonstrable "objects" having particular "qualities" (*This is yellow*; *That is running*; etc.) formulated as "particular propositions." Potential facts may also concern singular objects of various "kinds" (*This is a lemon*; *That is a tiger*; etc.) formulated as "singular propositions." Polyadic kinds would allow for singular facts about relations among things (*This is bluer than that*; *This is between that and the other*; etc.). And then there are general existential facts concerning relations among kinds (*Tigers are animals*; *Lemons are yellow*; etc.) formulated as "generic propositions."

Examples in English or any other natural language are misleading guides in distinguishing these various types of potential facts. If nothing else, the semantic efficiency of natural languages allows that single words (like *yellow* or *running*) may refer (at least) to qualities or kinds. Herein lies the value of unambiguous mathematical grammars for logic-theoretic purposes. We cannot explore such details without first presenting a number of other technical considerations. But clearly we must allow for grammatical complexities that go beyond a simple predicate calculus insofar as the latter would not acknowledge the distinction between qualities and kinds as two different sorts of properties and relations. Likewise, kinds may be not just nominal (as in *This is a blaze; This is a fire*) but verbal (*This is blazing; This is burning*), adjectival (as in *This is ablaze; This is afire*), adverbial (*This is blazingly hot*), adpositional (*This is on fire*), and so forth. For that matter, we should be able to countenance not just literal potential facts but also metaphors and similes (*Juliet is the sun; The news hit like dynamite*, etc.).

One strategy would be to appropriate grammatical formalisms like X-bar theory and theta theory (Chomsky 1981, 1995) to piece together grammars of potential facts in ways that are not specific to any one spoken language or representational medium. Kinds may be regarded as (proto-) lexical items in a generative grammar, and hence not just as properties or relations as countenanced by an extensionally interpreted predicate calculus. (Extensional quantificational logic would at best have a secondary status in characterizing so-called logical forms of linguistic expressions.)

More specifically, propositions of any sort will have both unarticulated and articulated features. In saying *This is sour* (to express a singular proposition), what is explicitly articulated are the three words in a certain order appropriate for English. What is crucial to understanding this as an utterance of a singular proposition is that (1) it has that function in some given inquiry, and (2) it is uttered in some stage of that inquiry in which the respective situation has been more or less squared away as possibly being of some (in)determinate type (W,C,A). More specifically (3) this utterance characterizes one or more states of affairs w in W. And (4) we should keep our options open and allow that its content and use may draw on still other contextual factors not yet considered (Dewey 1931a). Most of this crucial content of the proposition is not actually articulated, so any technical jargon we develop would have to distinguish those features which are articulated and those which are not. Thus we would have to recognize that existential propositions have the basic form

Unarticulated features $\models$ Articulated features

(where the "$\models$" symbol may be read as "supports"). Specifically, articulated features will include what is actually uttered, expressed, when the proposition is stated in English or in some such language (in Dewey's broad sense, where we should not be limited to verbal or even linear languages). Unarticulated features will include existential contextual factors that must in some way be grasped in order to understand the import of what is articulated. The task of "model theory" is precisely to surmise what shapes and forms these unarticulated features may take.

Whatever is articulable in this sense should be expressible in some natural language. Any grammar we use to represent this aspect of propositions should be suitable for *any* natural language. Without getting into details that distinguish different natural languages or that account for the many exceptions and qualifications that naturally arise, we could employ a formalism like Chomsky's X-bar theory as a first approximation of the linguistic facts. The *articulated* features of an existential proposition might respect the following compositional rules:

(A) Sentence → NounPhrase VerbPhrase
(B) XPhrase → (Determiner) X-bar YPhrase*
(C) X-bar → X ZPhrase*

where X, Y, and Z may be Noun, Pronoun, Verb, Adjective, Adverb, Preposition, Conjunction, etc. Clause (A) specifies the grammatical form of a basic expression-type SENT. Clause (B) specifies the grammatical form of expression-types NP, VP, AdjP, AdvP, PP, etc. Clause (C) specifies the grammatical form of basic expression-types N, V, Prep, Adj, Adv, etc. The asterisk in (B) and (C) indicates that this element may occur zero or more times in succession (not all repetitions having to be of the same expression-type). The determiner in (B) is optional—allowing terms like *all, some, the, a* or *an, many, few*, etc., as explored in generalized quantifier theory (Barwise and Cooper 1981; Gärdenfors 1987). To accommodate Dewey's theory of existential propositions, we add the provision that the basic *lexical* terms for expression-types X, Y, and Z will denote qualities or kinds or else will be demonstrative terms like *this, that, it*, etc.

It is not clear that this kind of grammar will apply to anything besides linear languages (as in oral speech or linear writing), but at least it should serve as a preliminary illustration of what is possible here. To pursue these suggestions further, we will first need to address Dewey's conceptions of *qualities* and *kinds*, insofar as these constitute the basic lexicon for grammars of potential facts. And before we can do that in sufficient detail, we should back up and say something about *states of affairs* and also outline the *ideational* aspects of inquiry.

States of Affairs

The standard notion of a "possible world" is difficult to accommodate here, given the associated metaphysical baggage. But we can introduce the more modest notion of a *state of affairs* to play a similar role in characterizing some modal features of potential facts. The structure of a situation-type (W,C,A) will depend on compositional details of a basic grammar Φ of potential facts, as outlined above. We cannot supply details here without looking at specific examples (for various possibilities, see Fischer and Ladner 1979; Groenendijk and Stokhof 1990, 1991; Harel 1984). But the set W will be some collection of states of affairs, and the function $A : \Phi \rightarrow 2^W$ will associate basic potential facts with various states of affairs in W.

In characterizing a grammar Φ, we should acknowledge a third sort of basic term, designating not just kinds and qualities but also what Dewey refers to as *ways of acting* or *modes of being*. I will refer to the latter simply as *abilities*—denoting basic abilities of the agent(s) engaged in a given inquiry. This provides a basis for a multimodal dynamic logic. Abilities (whether engrained as habits or newly developed on the run) may be implemented or otherwise executed so as to yield qualitative results (listening yields sounds, looking yields sights, running yields motions, hammering yields focused pressures, polling yields tangible data, questioning yields answers, posturing yields counterpostures, etc.). The possible execution of an ability to yield a qualitative result will be referred to as a *program* (a manner of behavior, a mode of conduct, a plan of execution). Any given inquiry will rest upon certain basic abilities, taken for granted as such, which may in turn be composed or combined in various simple or complex, standard or innovative ways to yield a repertoire Π of possible programs.

For a given situation-type (W,C,A), the function $C : \Pi \rightarrow 2^{W \times W}$ will specify ways in which states of affairs are mutually accessible, for example, through modifications of their respective potential facts (by means of updates, additions, deletions, changes of polarities, etc., effected by executing some program or other). The means by which such modifications are made will determine modal operators that extend and refine the array of determiners in the grammar Φ. Capacities to test basic propositions in Φ will in turn extend the array of programs in Π.

States of affairs, formally speaking, are in some ways like possible worlds, but they need not correspond to maximal collections of compatible potential facts, especially if we want to acknowledge indeterminate if not inconsistent arrays of facts. Principles of fuzzy set theory and fuzzy logic explain how such inconsistencies are possible without a complete breakdown in the management of information—where a potential fact and its negation may both be assigned some degree of membership in one and the same state of affairs (Dubois and Prade 1980; Yager and Filev 1994). A major goal of inquiry is to eventually achieve appropriate degrees of consistency and coherence that initially may not characterize many potential states of affairs.

We need not think of a state of affairs as being temporally instantaneous or internally static. A state of affairs is characterized by an array of contemporaneous facts, possibly involving temporal durations—e.g., where a certain regular process is occurring: *It is raining; The landscape viewed through the train window is passing by; The casserole is now baking; Flight 123 is in holding pattern ABC*. This is a matter of perspective on the problem at hand, a matter of choosing an appropriate level of analysis. The weather, a cross-country train trip, or the preparation of a meal may be resolved into various changes of state in numerous ways, but rarely (it would seem) will it be practical to do so in terms of instantaneous temporal instants. Rather, states of affairs will be empirically distinguishable stages of activity in a dynamic system (W,C,A) where changes of state wholly within such a system are only a way of maintaining a dynamic status quo insofar as the given situation is of that respective type.

Various social factors can be acknowledged at this point. If we have grounds for thinking of communities as inquiring agents (a company, a scientific community, a government agency, a family, a team, etc.), then we should be able to talk about abilities, potential facts, and states of affairs as formal constructs distributed over communities of individuals. This would require that individual persons or agents be given some appropriate ontic status as interrelated nodes in the distributed primary and reflective experience of a community as a whole.

One likely tool for modeling social structures at this level of analysis is "network exchange theory," or the theory of directed graphs (digraphs) applied to social organizations (Harary, Norman, and Cartwright 1965; Willer and Anderson 1981; Knoke and Kuklinksi 1982; Markovsky et al. 1993; Willer, Lovaglia, and Markovsky 1997; Willer and Skvoretz 1997a, 1997b; Willer 1987, 1999). There need not be just one way to apply these techniques within Dewey's theory of inquiry. But one option is to use digraph networks to model specific social-structural relations (lines of exchange, communication, authority, kinship, sentiment, sanctions, etc.) among "actors" (people, social or organizational positions, etc.) whose joint efforts and interactions serve to constitute singular abilities—abilities that presumably could not be characterized any other way. I cannot lift a piano up the stairs, but several of us acting in unison can. Football teams, teams of lawyers, teams of engineers and scientists, etc., will have abilities which team members, alone or taken as a mere set, will not have.

Social structures built into a treatment of basic abilities (for a given situation) would, of course, affect higher-level structural details. In particular, this would affect how states of affairs are modeled, with connections specified on grounds other than standard (state-change, or otherwise nondescript) accessibility relations. Socially based relations could account for certain common linguistic practices that would otherwise escape customary methods of semantic analysis. The function C in a given situation-type (W,C,A) would have to be augmented in some way that accommodates these kinds of connections. For instance, as part of the bricks and mortar that help to form states of affairs and to determine their mutual connectedness, we may consider social *status* or *power relations* as determinants of various deontic modalities (e.g., exploiting ideas developed by Gärdenfors and Winter 1995). What one may or must do in various circumstances may thus depend more on social relations and less on merely alethic possibilities and necessities. Somewhat less perspicuously, Brandom (1994) considers the role of discursive *commitments* and *entitlements* (obligations and permissions, duties and rights) in conferring semantic contents on many linguistic social practices. Such relations are ripe for the sort of treatment provided by network exchange theory.

All of this is compatible, of course, with the social-psychological underpinnings of Dewey's (and Mead's) conceptions of consciousness and "selves" (Dewey 1925, 1938; Mead 1934, 1956). The issue there is not just a matter of accounting for linguistic practices but for the emergence of human individuality (selfhood and even our ability to *think*) from deeper primordial social origins. The theory of directed graphs may afford ways to make such conceptions more precise if not empirically testable.

In any case, with regard to existential aspects of inquiry: If the present treatment of states of affairs is to be feasible, we need a principled account of *qualities, abilities, kinds,* and *objects* as building blocks for grammars of potential facts. To do this properly, we should next consider some ideational aspects of inquiry, to explore key elements of the discussion that have been passed over too quickly. This will help to clarify how kinds are not just constructs within individual heads but may be ecologically and socially distributed.

Ideational Aspects of Inquiry

In response to a particular problem, inquiry has two main concerns: to determine what the facts of the matter are, and to determine what is to be done about them (Dewey 1938, LW12:112–118, 121, 300). Facts of the matter (actual and potential) constitute the existential aspects of inquiry (providing the subject of judgment), while ideational aspects of inquiry (generating the predicate of judgment) are constituted by methods or plans of action. Dewey identifies ideas as plans of action, thus espousing a kind of operationalism in which ideas designate possible ways of acting, possible modes of being, abilities to act or be in specific ways, etc. (LW12:289, 350,

516): "Ideas are operational in that they instigate and direct further operations of observation; they are proposals and plans for acting upon existing conditions to bring new facts to light and to organize all the selected facts into a coherent whole" (LW12:116).

Insofar as ideas are embodied in symbols, one may "have an idea" and yet not be concerned with performing any respective action(s). We consider (look at) ideas only as they are embodied in physical symbols. "Without some kind of symbol no idea" (LW12:114). Thought, silent or overtly expressed, requires a medium of symbols. Thus physical symbols in their office as embodiments of ideas ultimately stand for *possible* modes of action. This cannot account for the whole range of linguistic contents and practices, but it is key to understanding the specifically ideational aspects of inquiry. Reflection upon ideational aspects of a problem constitutes a significant portion of our abstract discourse in a given inquiry, including (but not limited to) mathematical discourse (1938, chap. 20). Moreover, reflection upon factual matters does not in itself constitute, much less exhaust, the ideational aspects of inquiry. Nevertheless, reflection upon factual matters is only possible by virtue of the conjugate development of existential and ideational factors in relation to each other. Hence, in discussing reflective experience, we should consider some elements of experience that are specifically ideational in nature.

As denoting possible modes of action, ideas are termed *universals* by Dewey in virtue of their abstract function in inquiry. Possible ways of acting or modes of being, as terms which are functionally universal, are nevertheless rooted in basic animal abilities tempered by distinctively human cultural forces. Dewey's characterization of ideas as abilities or possible modes of action is rooted in a natural history of biological and sociocultural developments. He discusses such genetic matters in the opening chapters of his 1938 *Logic* as necessary background for his logical theory. As specimen inquirers we have abilities to act in certain ways, where such abilities are often secured and stabilized as habits ready for implementation as appropriate conditions arise. Many of these habits (customs, taboos, manners, principles of social etiquette, including modes of speech and other linguistic abilities) are socially distributed and culturally transmitted from one generation to the next. From an anthropological perspective, human culture is wholly and inextricably embedded in nature, and thus is part of nature, in which case a naturalistic methodology should be entirely adequate for logical theory. We are born into a community, inheriting physically engrained abilities that have grown up over eons of evolutionary development. Some of these abilities pertain to basic animal needs (procreating, eating, breathing, locomoting, stalking or fleeing); and some are more recent developments (speaking, thinking, living with histories that span generations). Our "social" nature is rooted in our animal origins, as sexual creatures but also as creatures capable of engaging in a variety of coordinated shared activities—child rearing, hunting, farming, commerce. Some of the engrained abilities with which individuals are born presuppose a social matrix in which these abilities may properly unfold (e.g., our inherited ability to learn and use languages now takes for granted participation in a preexisting community of adept language users), just as other abilities presuppose some proper physical and biological matrix for their proper development (e.g., our ability to walk takes for granted the continued existence of solid ground in a more or less constant gravitational field). Many of the abilities our species has taken eons to "learn" have only to be triggered and activated in the individual growing infant, and our collective learning continues in and through our ongoing transactions among ourselves and with the world at large. Thus universals are regarded here as wholly natural in their origins and in their continuing development.

While genetic considerations are crucial to understanding the functional nature of universals in inquiry, our primary concern here is with their function in inquiry. Our abilities may function as universals insofar as they are possibly relevant and thus available for use in virtually any situation. Such abilities embody ideational aspects of inquiry insofar as a specimen inquirer has the capacity to consider different options regarding how to act under given conditions, rather than simply being driven mechanically by established habits. Existential conditions will support certain suggestions as to possible options, and these suggestions take on the status of "ideas" when developed symbolically in relation with other symbols (Dewey 1938, LW12:58, 113, 275, 300, 350). We will not go into how our capacity to forestall instinctive reactions and to consider possibilities in the abstract has naturally come about, though Mead's evolutionary social psychology contains the basic outlines of such a story (1934, 1956; see Dewey 1931b, 1931d, 1936, 1938; see also Taylor 1995). Rather, we are interested in examining how contemporary mathematical logic is consistent with this ability-based conception of ideas and their function as universals in inquiry.

The first point to make is that ideas do not arise in isolation but rather in systematic "constellations of related meanings" (Dewey 1938, LW12:55–59, 82, 116, 312). Contemporary mathematical logic can help to articulate details of this possible systematicity of ideas. But to make this work, to explain how frameworks of ideas are brought to bear in specific inquiries, we need to introduce two technical notions—the notion of an *ideology* and the notion of a *worldview*—basically to impose these notions on Dewey's logical theory, since he does not often use these terms himself.

Ideologies and Worldviews

Inquiry is an existential process of transforming a situation, seeking a satisfactory resolution of a given problem. We want to consider possible systems of ideas that may play a role in guiding and constraining such transformations. An inquiry may involve competing systems of ideas. These systems may fail to be satisfactorily systematic, or they may fail singularly or together to address the problem at hand, or they may tend to conflict with one another in determining what is most appropriate for the given existential situation. The primary question here concerns what it means to say that a system of ideas is indeed *systematic*.

Traditional conceptions of scientific inquiry acknowledge experimental versus theoretical aspects of science. With regard to inquiry more generally, scientific or otherwise, the notion of a *theory* is not rich enough to characterize the ideational aspects of inquiry. To facilitate a discussion of these aspects of inquiry, we will need to introduce some terminology that Dewey does not regularly use but that helps to properly square away the sorts of things he wants to build into a treatment of ideational aspects of inquiry. As with situations and situation-types, we will need to distinguish systems of universals from representations of systems of universals (where the transformation of a situation through inquiry is largely guided by the development and application of one or more systems of ideas that are functionally universal in character). I will refer to actual systems of universals in the broadest sense as *ideologies*. Representations of ideologies will be referred to as *ideology-types*. A logician's task would be (in part) to formally model "types" of ideologies, where the use and development of an ideology in a given inquiry will often involve changes in the type of ideology employed.

The term *ideology* should be taken in neither a laudatory nor a pejorative manner. An ideologue is a person who makes decisions and otherwise acts primarily if not blindly on the basis of some tenaciously favored ideology. But ideologies, for better or worse, are just ideational contexts, constituted by systems of ideas (universals), where ideas are understood to be not just representational or explanatory but directly instrumental in laying out programs of action in or with respect to possible situations. The fact that universals are social and cultural in their origins and constitution speaks in favor of employing the term *ideology* here in the sense intended. But this term should not carry only the limited meaning given to it in social and political philosophy. In the present view any inquiry, political or otherwise, is ideological insofar as ideas are employed (well or badly) in that inquiry.

The notion of an ideology is introduced here only to allow reference to abstract contexts in which systems of ideas are couched.

To accommodate the pluralistic nature of ideational aspects of inquiry, we cannot assume that an ideology can always be represented by a single theory. If we think of theories as systems of definitions and hypotheses and everything that follows from them by given derivation rules, then many of our ideas arise in "constellations" that could not properly be called theories at all. Before we can say what a theory is, we need a more general construct, analogous to a state of affairs in a situation-type. This will be termed a *worldview*. A worldview will accommodate possibly numerous theories, and an ideology-type will consist of a class of systematically related worldviews. We want to acknowledge that in any inquiry we bring to bear different families of worldviews (in varying degrees of salience or relevance). These families will be distinguished by various systematic relations among their constituent worldviews and by what systems of abstract hypotheses obtain in each worldview.

More precisely, we want to think of the predicate of judgment as couched not just within a single worldview but within a possibly fuzzy class or family of ideology-types. An ideology-type can be modeled by a triple (V,R,T), where V is a (possibly fuzzy) set of worldviews. If Λ is a grammar for a language of abstract hypotheses (see below), the (possibly fuzzy) function $T : \Lambda \to 2^V$ will constitute a set of *ontologies* associating basic hypotheses and their constituent terms (universals, modes of being) with various worldviews.

If we acknowledge various ways of operating with universals (e.g., introducing or removing terms, definitions, or axioms; redefining old terms or constructing new ones; specifying or changing principles of argumentation or rules of proof; calculations and derivations; proving theorems or producing arguments analogous to existential test-programs, etc.), then these operations may be composed or combined in simple or complex, standard or innovative ways to yield a repertoire Γ of possible forms of reasoning or discourse. In a given ideology-type (V,R,T), the (possibly fuzzy) function $R : \Gamma \to 2^{V \times V}$ will specify ways in which worldviews are mutually accessible through transitions in discourse, e.g., by these methods of reasoning.

A *theory*, then, will be a more or less coherent set of definitions, axioms, or basic hypotheses and implications thereof, holding within a given worldview, possibly shared across many worldviews. A given worldview may countenance several competing theories, not all mutually consistent. Moreover, there will be no assurance nor requirement that theories will be *existentially applicable* or even developed with regard to possible existential reference (in mathematics, for instance, in contrast with theories in other sciences where existential applicability often both spurs and constrains their development).

But now, if we adopt this way of modeling predicates as classes of ideology-types (V,R,T), we must be more precise about what we mean by *abstract hypotheses* and grammars thereof.

Universals and Abstract Hypotheses

The same natural language that is used in inquiry to discuss concrete matters of fact should also accommodate abstract discourse. Hence the generative grammar (A)–(C) that was outlined earlier should accommodate both abstract discourse and existential subject matters. In particular, mathematicians do much of their work informally, although the nature of their work, whether formally or informally presented, allows a kind of rigor that is not typical of one's dealings with most existential matters.

Later we will look at how existential and ideational factors in inquiry may be woven together. Here we will focus on universal propositions in a more abstract sense, unconstrained by any particular existential reference. Again, we want to say that universal propositions (propositions whose terms are universals) will have both unarticulated and articulated features. If an utterance of *Seven plus five is twelve* functions as the utterance of a universal proposition relative to some given inquiry, then it will occur in some stage of that inquiry relative to an ideology of some type (V,R,T), and it will characterize some worldview v in V. Generally, abstract universal propositions have the basic form

Unarticulated features $\Vdash$ Articulated features

(where the "$\Vdash$" symbol will be read as "yields"). Specifically, the articulated features of a universal proposition will be what is actually expressed when the proposition is stated in some natural language, whereas unarticulated features will include ideological contextual factors that must be shared or otherwise grasped in order to understand the import of what is articulated.

The articulated features of such a proposition should respect compositional rules for the given natural language (as outlined in the discussion of potential facts), along with certain other constraints. Namely, the basic lexical terms for its expression-types will designate universals or compositions of universals. The main "verb" (like *is*) in an atomic universal statement will designate a reduction relation or an abstract identity relation (not that there is just one such identity relation). Complex universal propositions will trace implications and equivalences entailed by the postulation or stipulation of such relations. Universal propositions will be *definitional* in character, ideal and very likely contrary to fact, as opposed to existentially descriptive (Dewey 1938, LW12:259–60, 270–71, 300–303, 404–5).

A universal term, as part of a symbol system, is an abstraction representing an ability (a possible way of acting or a mode of being). Various existing mathematical formalisms can be employed to explain how such abilities may be systematically composed or otherwise related. For instance, a lambda calculus (Barendregt 1984; Hindley and Seldin 1986; Stansifer 1995) could describe how complex abilities may be composed systematically out of simpler abilities. But a lambda calculus is just one sort of Cartesian closed category. The type of systematization of universals that Dewey discusses in the 1938 *Logic* (chaps. 16–20) thus could be cast more rigorously in category-theoretic terms (Arbib and Manes 1975; Rydeheard and Burstall 1988; Barr and Wells 1990; Pierce 1991). Pure category theory as a going concern in mathematics is clearly not beholding to Dewey's logical theory. But it can play a role in clarifying what Dewey had to say about ideational aspects of inquiry, specifically with regard to systems of universals. Indeed, the history of the lambda calculus if not category theory more generally goes back at least to the 1930s (Church and Rosser 1936; Church 1941; Eilenberg and MacLane 1942, 1945); so it is not inconceivable that similar hearsay ideas influenced Dewey's thinking while writing the 1938 *Logic*.

One sort of system of universals would be a typed lambda calculus with universal terms (ability terms) serving as basic types. Following Barr and Wells (1990, 150), there would be types and terms in such a system, where to each term there corresponds a type, according to stipulations such as the following:

1. Variables: For each type A, there is a countable set of terms x^A of type A, called *variables* of type A (such that a variable is an abstract possibility of a certain type).
2. Morphisms (or functions): If A and B are types, there is a morphism type $[A \rightarrow B]$.
3. Application: If a is of type A and f is of type $[A \rightarrow B]$, then there is a term $(f\,a)$ of type B.
4. Abstraction: If x^A is a variable of type A and b is a term of type B, then there is a term $\lambda x^A.b$ of type $[A \rightarrow B]$.

In all of these clauses, a *type* might correspond to an *ability*, elementary or complex, and a *term* would be a symbol constructed according to guidelines stipulated by such clauses.

In addition to types and terms, the theory of lambda calculi includes a treatment of formulas. For example, terms may be equivalent on the grounds of certain *conversion* rules (Barr and Wells 1990, 151; Barendregt 1984, chap. 2). Trivially, we will want to say that $(\lambda x^A.b\ a) = b[x^A := a]$ (where "$b[x^A := a]$" is just b but with all free occurrences of x^A in b replaced by a). This and other rules will allow substitutivity of equivalent terms, will guarantee that this equivalence relation is indeed an equivalence relation, and so forth. Likewise, there will be various unidirectional *reduction* rules allowing a sort of formula where convertibility of two terms may entail reducibility of the two to a common term, etc. Various stepwise reduction rules will give rise to a number of equality and congruence relations. Details may be found in the references cited. Stansifer 1995 (233 ff.) shows how basic features of computation (choice, numbers, iteration, etc.) and thus basic elements of logic and arithmetic may be constructed within this simple sort of formal system. These results indicate how rich this kind of formalism is, generally considered to be a possible foundation for mathematics (Barendregt 1984, vii; Rydeheard and Burstall 1988, 38). This sort of formalism makes possible a rigorous treatment of Dewey's conception of "abstract hypotheses," as sketched in chapters 16–20 of the 1938 *Logic*, particularly with regard to "formal relations of completely abstract subject-matters, in which transformation as abstract possibility takes the form of transform*ability* in the abstract" (394).

Clearly this sort of formalism fits the strictures of a generative grammar for a natural language as outlined earlier. Identity and reduction relations will provide the basic verbs in such a grammar, and terms will serve as nouns.

A *theory* in this kind of framework will be a consistent extension of a lambda calculus that is closed under its respective modes of transformability. Such a theory is obtained from a set of abstract hypotheses by adding them as axioms to the axioms and rules of the lambda calculus (Barendregt 1984, chap. 4). A given worldview in a given ideology-type will correspond to a class of (possibly incompatible) alternative theories, each of which is based on its own category of universals. Thus a worldview will correspond to some space of categories, each constituting a system of universals in Dewey's sense, and each supporting the systematic formulation of abstract hypotheses. Hence if Λ is a grammar for a language based on a lexicon of universal terms, the function $T : \Lambda \rightarrow 2^V$ in a respective ideology

(*V*,*R*,*T*) will constitute a set of *ontologies* associating basic hypotheses and their constituent terms with various worldviews in *V*.

So far we have not adequately emphasized the relevance of fuzzy set theory and fuzzy logic to ideological features of inquiry. The present account should accommodate fuzzy ideology-types (*V*,*R*,*T*), worldviews *V*, accessibility relations *R*, ontologies *T*, etc. As well, the basic systems of universals that populate these various structures may be formulated in terms of fuzzy categories (Dubois and Prade 1980, 120–22). An account of the possible systematicity of ideas need not be so crisp and rigid as the previous illustration of a typed lambda calculus may suggest. With regard to ideational aspects of inquiry in general, we may echo an important point made earlier with regard to existential aspects of inquiry. The increased determinacy that should characterize acceptable conclusions of inquiry would not be a matter of eradicating fuzziness but rather of finding suitable levels of fuzziness that best accommodate the problem at hand, in a world that inevitably evades constraints imposed by rigid ideologies. Crisp ideologies may well be typical of early stages of inquiry where issues are established in only a preliminary fashion. Hence we should expect a positive correlation between increased determinacy and more explicit and more precisely specified fuzziness, at least in regard to ideology-types. If this is the case, then fuzzy set theory would have a key role to play in explicating ideational aspects of inquiry.

The sort of systematicity of ideas outlined above (fuzzy or not) suggests a rather abstract manner of discourse—one that is characteristic of mathematics, mathematically sophisticated sciences, and other types of inquiry in which abstract discourse plays a key role. This is a descriptive matter, not a normative one. One measure of the coherence of a system of ideas would be the degree to which such ideas lend themselves to some such systematic composition and transformation—by means of lambda calculi or through category-theoretic means more generally. Systematic coherence in this sense and to this degree is not always to be expected, as illustrated apparently by many social and political problems we face on a regular basis. If and when systematic coherence of ideas is expedient or advantageous, category theory simply provides ideal standards. The science of logic will have performed an important service simply by describing some standards in this regard.

Beyond standards of coherence, the question of the existential applicability and productivity of abstract discourse is another matter. We must acknowledge that systems of ideas independent of existential reference do not constitute the only conceptual materials that are developed and employed in inquiry.

In the chapters preceding [chap. 20], we have been concerned with the relation of meanings and propositions in discourse where discourse is conducted in reference to some final existential applicability. In discourse of this type application is suspended or held in abeyance but relationship to application is not eliminated in respect to the content of the conceptions. When, however, discourse is conducted exclusively with reference to satisfaction of its own logical conditions, or, as we say, for its own sake, the subject-matter is not only non-existential in immediate reference but is itself formed on the ground of freedom from existential reference of even the most indirect, delayed and ulterior kind. It is then mathematical. The subject-matter is completely abstract and formal because of its complete freedom from the conditions imposed upon conceptual material which is framed with reference to final existential application. Complete freedom and complete abstractness are here synonymous terms. (Dewey 1938, LW12:393)

An illustration from physics would be helpful here. Physicists have found that abstract group theory, for example, would be useful in developing a theory of quarks. So they have *applied* group theory, a bit of preexisting mathematics that had been developed without regard to quarks or any other particular application outside of mathematics itself. If these same physicists were to find that the existing mathematics were inadequate in some way to accommodate such applications, they might pause to study group theory as such, not with reference to specific models in quark theory, but nevertheless so that they may eventually develop such applications with a more thorough understanding of the mathematics involved. The historical relation between Newtonian mechanics and differential calculus is perhaps a more familiar example of this sort of intimate connection between concrete and abstract developments of systems of ideas.

Notice also the robust ontological relativity entailed by the conception of "universals" employed here. For example, a study of ideal gases may proceed in various ways. We may take ideas like pressure, volume, and temperature as operational primitives; or we may employ ideas from statistical mechanics applied to the molecular constitution of gases. Neither system of ideas is once and for all more "right" or "realistic," though the one is allegedly reducible to the other. Either may be more appropriate than the other in different existential contexts.

Another topic to address here concerns possible applications of network exchange theory (see above) to ideational aspects of inquiry. The first thing to note is that any category is essentially a graph (Rydeheard and Burstall 1988, 37, 79). In a different sense, digraphs (the basic modeling tools of network exchange theory) constitute a specific category (Pierce 1991, 51–52;

Rydeheard and Burstall 1988, 40–41). These are trivial points in themselves, though they become more interesting when we consider their ramifications for a treatment of social factors in a theory of inquiry. This means that there is literally no extra formal work involved in rigorously accommodating social factors in a treatment of basic ideational aspects of inquiry. Methods by which complex abilities are systematically composed out of simpler abilities may just as well include digraph constructions designed to accommodate social networks.

The second thing to note, from an entirely different perspective, is that network exchange theory may provide a useful way to model relationships among different *ideology-types*, that is, if and when it is possible to treat whole ideologies as points or nodes in a network (social or otherwise). In this case points would represent positions characterized by different ideologies, and edges would denote which relationships among these ideologies are appropriate for a given analysis (to handle modes of transaction, communication, authority, alliance or conflict, kinship, etc.). Other technical methods we have covered here deal specifically with formal features internal to singular ideologies, whereas network exchange theory provides a way to formalize a treatment of relations *among* ideologies, e.g., within a class of ideologies that constitute a predicate of judgment. Similar methods could be used, of course, to treat existential relations within a class of situation-types that constitute a subject of judgment.

Existential and Ideational Factors Integrated

We come then to the question of how existential and ideational aspects of inquiry may systematically work together in a given inquiry, where immediate situations and standing ideologies together supply the full context of inquiry. This question is at the heart of Dewey's conception of *judgment*, as an assertible conclusion of inquiry, whose *subject* is existential in content and whose *predicate* is ideational in content (together asserting what the facts of the case are and what if anything is to be done about them). Judgments should thus reflect an integration of existential and ideational aspects of inquiry (Dewey 1934, LW10:263–64). Both existential and ideational propositions should be articulable in and by means of a common natural language, but this may guarantee only a sort of schizophrenia if we do not have classes of terms which in themselves integrate existential and ideational aspects of experience in a fairly robust manner. This is where Dewey's conception of *kinds* comes into its own.

Kinds and Objects

We could develop an *extensional* account of kinds in standard ways by (a) treating them as functions from tuples of objects to truth values; or (b) introducing contextual factors and treating them as functions from states of affairs and tuples of objects to truth values; or (c) perhaps even more broadly, treating them as functions from situation-types, states of affairs, and tuples of objects to truth values. Any such extensional account will not be inconsistent with what we want to say about kinds in general. But approaches (b) and (c) presuppose a superstructure of states of affairs if not situation-types, whereas we want an account of kinds whose operational and empirical basis allows them to contribute content to any number of inquiries independently of fixing such contextual parameters ahead of time.

Any of these extensional accounts of kinds would also require reference to domains of *objects*. Presumably an inquiry will involve domains of objects. But in principle, an inquirer may bring or project various taxonomies of kinds into a given inquiry prior to establishing that there is anything in the given situation to start with which satisfies the specifications of any of those kinds. Where experimental activities are a predominant factor in the progress of inquiry, an inquirer will be able to extend or constrict or otherwise modify the domains of things that satisfy such specifications. Hence one or more "domains of discourse" will be determined *in the course of* inquiry, not fixed full-blown prior to the process of inquiry. Domains of objects relevant to a given inquiry may thus change without altering one's taxonomy of kinds in that inquiry.

Conversely, inquiry may lead to the discovery or invention of new kinds of things, or modifications of given kinds, by virtue of exposure to new objects or to old objects considered in new ways. This may be due not to changes in how we carve up domains of objects into relevant extensions but rather to changes in how we interact with and think about those objects—due, for instance, to advances in instrumentation as well as in theoretical and experimental methods. Consider the way that physicists have proposed and refined one model of the hydrogen atom after another, each different from the others in various ways, but all presumably with the same intended extension. Something else besides extensionality is at work here to distinguish, for example, a Bohr kind of hydrogen atom from a Schrödinger kind of hydrogen atom.

Thus an extensional characterization of kinds may be a sort of post hoc characterization, suitable in certain circumstances. But whenever and to whatever extent it is feasible, an extensional treatment of kinds will provide a one-sided perspective on some logical machinery that should otherwise be constructed on other grounds, essentially independent of any particular infrastructure of objects or superstructure of states of affairs and situation-types.

In the face of difficulties presented by extensional possible-worlds semantics, Barwise and Etchemendy (1989, 237) suggest that we could take kinds and things as primitives (presumably in an open-ended sense, rather than fix a basic set of them once and for all) and then *define* possible worlds in terms of the grammatical machinery we can construct on that basis. This is in contrast, for example, to positing possible worlds as primitives and defining propositions as sets of possible worlds. We are following a similar bottom-up strategy here. But our approach is more radical in that worlds (that is, states of affairs), kinds, and things are to be rectified if not defined in terms of a still more elementary set of primitives—namely, in terms of a given agent's operational abilities or skills, and possible qualitative outcomes of exercising such abilities.

The notion of *kinds* is a pivotal notion in this regard. Kinds will be determined not with respect to some superstructure of possible worlds or a universal domain of rigidly designatable objects, but in terms of the operational abilities and skills of living agents (see esp. Dewey 1929; see also Hickman 1990; Kennedy 1970; Sleeper 1986). If anything is absolutely primitive in Dewey's logical theory, it would be living agents and their various ways of operating in the world and among themselves. Attunements to *kinds*, as well-behaved systematic associations of such abilities and the qualitative events to which these abilities provide access, are the means by which a live agent finds structure and meaning in the world—the means by which anything for that creature is experiencable. These attunements will, of course, vary from agent to agent, though we all exist in one and the same world, insofar as different agents reside in and make up different parts of the world, insofar as skills vary from agent to agent and insofar as any given agent's skills tend to change in various ways as the world at large changes.

An Ecological Theory of Objects

If kinds are well-behaved systematic associations of operational abilities and possible differential traits (qualitative events) accessible to living agents, then actual *objects*—from coffee cups to clouds, from Julius Caesar's hairdo to Bugs Bunny's ears—should be regarded as actual or potential concrete instantiations of kinds, capable of evidencing characteristic traits resulting from respective systematic activities. As such, objects may serve as generic prototypes for various kinds, familiar or novel.

Objects that persist in our ongoing experience embody a continuity and concreteness that allows them to be incorporated as parts or aspects of our own abilities. As Dewey says in *Essays in Experimental Logic* (1916, MW8:87–88), this calls for a redefinition of the nature of an *object* not as "a substance in which attributes inhere" (as a subject of predicates) but as "a constant correlation of variations of qualities." Our capabilities to manipulate and negotiate our way through terrestrial environments are attuned to these constancies. The gravitational pull of the Earth provides a simple illustration of the "ecological" character of our operational constitution. That our shin and thigh bones remain rigid while we walk is as much an integral part of our walking abilities as is the fact that the gravitational pull of the Earth is always present to facilitate such activities. Similar points can be made with respect to breathable air, ambient light, drinkable water, edible food, manageable weather conditions, etc. That such objects exist and persist in our experience has everything to do with the evolving determination of our operational and empirical capabilities.

An ecological conception of objects does not bode well for AI projects that restrict the hardware and software of an AI system to the workings of CPUs, ROMs, and RAMs. An ecological view is more in line with the embedded and distributed behavioral approach to AI taken by Brooks (1990), or with Gibson's ecological psychology and his conception of direct perception (1979)—versus common approaches in the cognitive sciences that identify intelligence with internal computational capacities (Fodor and Pylyshyn 1981; Turvey and Shaw 1981). A careful study of the mushware and software that embodies our operational abilities should show them to be irreducibly distributed across what we might otherwise distinguish as an organism versus its environment, considered in both biological and cultural terms (Dewey 1922; 1934, chaps. 1–4; 1938, chaps. 2–3). Various functions of human physiology can be identified and productively studied in isolation (What are livers? spleens? lungs? muscles? What do they do, and how do they do it?). But this kind of study ultimately leads to viewing ourselves as inextricably embedded in larger ecological settings that constitute what these functional units are and how they do what they do.

This principle becomes especially salient when considering Dewey's characterization of *objects* and *kinds* as constituents of potential facts. Actual objects—as entities in a grammar of potential facts—should be regarded as ecologically constituted insofar as the abilities in terms of which they might be rectified are themselves ecologically constituted. Where kinds are embodiments of attunements to objects in general ways, objects are possible singular instances of experience in which such attunements may be exercised and on the basis of which such attunements are established in the first place.

Likewise it may be emphasized again that we want to include skills or abilities which may be socially distributed (as a special case of the ecological constitution of abilities). The possibility that primitive abilities may be socially shared or constituted—not just as held in common but as irreducibly distributed across several or many individuals (teams, companies, armies, governments, etc.)—permits the introduction of concrete social parameters into logical analysis in a fundamental way, accommodating social aspects of inquiry and experience at the most primitive levels of logical analysis, rather than having to rely only on higher-level applications of individualistic cognitivist conceptions of logic to language and discourse.

To give a principled account, then, of kinds and objects as systematic associations of our skills or abilities, we need a sort of logical formalism that accommodates and incorporates both operational and empirical aspects of our ecological constitution as living creatures.

Ability-based Empirical Logics

We can build a logical apparatus—what I will call an *ability-based empirical logic* (ABEL)—that is consistent with the ecological constraints outlined above. This ground-level logic will allow us to properly characterize kinds as systematic associations of operationally accessible differential traits.

First, we must distinguish ability-based empirical logics from the grammars of facts that serve to constitute states of affairs and situation-types. These are two distinct sorts of "logics" at different levels of organization of our experience. Grammars of facts are rather high-level constructions, whereas ability-based empirical logics are at the bottom level of analysis exercised in an inquiry. These fundamental logics are determined in their details by the operational abilities and empirical sensitivities that one brings to that inquiry. This distinction among formal structural levels is only a functional distinction, but it is crucial, nonetheless. In broadest terms there may be no true "bottom" to the depths of possible analysis, but practically speaking, one usually goes only so far in plumbing these depths. Certain abilities and possible events will function (tentatively, stipulatively) as bottom-level abilities and events. This is practically expedient if not unavoidable, and is not problematic as long as the stipulation of logical primitives remains flexible (subject to modification as circumstances change) and as long as we do not mistake analytical primitivity for some sort of absolute ontological primitivity.

To construct an ability-based empirical logic, we start by presupposing a body of basic skills or abilities and the types of phenomenal (sensible, determinable, registrable) events that these skills are capable of producing.

Practical issues normally associated with measurement and instrumentation are thus introduced right at the start. There is, of course, little chance that we can once and for all from an armchair perspective solve practical problems inherent in securing accuracy and reliability (precision, lack of bias, etc.) in the employment of such abilities. But we require two things to begin with. First, the class of possible outcomes of a given operational ability should be specifically determined. Which of these outcomes will be obtained in any given instance may be unpredictable. But an outcome once obtained should be immediately identifiable as such. Second, the operational abilities by means of which such outcomes are randomly obtained should under suitable conditions be routinely and repeatably executable.

To construct a logic on this basis, given some repertoire of basic abilities, we should allow recursive constructions of complex abilities, e.g., along category-theoretic lines outlined earlier. Similarly, we should allow for recursive constructions of complex phenomenal events, not as symbols but as potential empirical "traits" that may characterize possible objects (see below). Third, we may define basic *variables* with reference to such abilities and events, simple or complex. Variables in this nonprimitive sense will range only over possible events accessible by utilizing such abilities. Each ability, simple or complex, will generate a class of variables (indexed in some way appropriate to their particular use), so that we have an array of variables sorted according to available abilities. A variable in this kind of logic is not just a primitive (empty, meaningless) placeholder. Rather, it signifies the possibility of some sort of operationally accessible empirical event. Variables in this sense thus embody a kind of operational content.

With this foundation in place, the rest of an ABEL construction should be fairly standard. If we introduce certain primitive relations—an identity relation, if nothing else, justified by a principle of radical empiricism (James 1912, Dewey 1905) which renders certain relations immediately accessible—then we are able to accommodate elementary empirical statements along with standard truth-functional connectives, to generate truth-functional ability-based empirical logics. Richer logics (quantificational, modal, etc.) can be constructed in more or less standard ways as well, with respective proof systems and canonical models.

Hintikka's "independence-friendly" branching-quantifier logic (1996) is especially well suited to developing some of the formal details at this level of analysis with a *game-theoretic semantics* for the usual connectives and quantifiers (see also Hilpinen 1983). One feature that Dewey would add to Hintikka's rules for semantical games (1996, 25–26) is a particular elaboration of the rule for atomic formulas—acknowledging that certain types of actions must be executed to verify or falsify (accept or reject) a given atomic formula as an endpoint of a semantic game. The semantical game rules for connectives and quantifiers do not specify such actions. Something more than just these rules is needed to articulate how atomic sentences are verified or falsified—something on which the system of game rules as a whole depends if it is not just built on sand. Atomic ABEL formulas may have the form "$p(t_1,...,t_n)$" for some predicate symbol "p" and terms "t_i" (including variables "v", event-types "e", or functional combinations of terms "$f(t_1,...,t_m)$"). For example, in an ABEL involving simple arithmetic operations, a simple closed formula like "$Id(2+2,4)$" or "$2+2=4$" would ultimately be interpreted in terms of prespecified actions (abilities) capable of yielding event-types such as "2" or "4" or "2+2." A perusal of an atomic formula should thus allow one to discern what would have to be *done* to verify or falsify that formula. This explicit reference to abilities and to their empirical outcomes in the "form" of the formula itself is just what an ABEL is designed to accommodate. The semantical game rules for connectives and quantifiers, on the other hand, articulate how the evaluation of complex propositions may be traced to that of atomic propositions.

Of course, no matter how complex such constructions may become, this will not get us beyond a treatment of ability-based empirical logics residing at the bottom of the ladder of logical analysis. Such abilities and possible empirical outcomes are the basic elements determining the contents and meanings of our thought and linguistic expression, but they are by no means the whole of it. We need to make a rather different kind of constructive leap to get from ability-based empirical logics to kinds and objects and grammars of potential facts. Namely, the present hypothesis is that operational abilities and empirical outcomes are basic elements of ability-based empirical logics, whereas it will be classes of *models* defined on such logics which provide the basic semantic contents of linguistic expressions concerning existential facts. Potential facts may be analyzed in terms of objects and kinds as basic lexical units, where *kinds* (as object-types) are to be regarded as classes or families of models defined on such ability-based empirical logics. Rather than define kinds by means of collections of sentences in some dubiously privileged operationally grounded *language*, the strategy here is to build operational/empirical logics (ABELs) of various sorts solely on the basis of the notions of "abilities" and their resultant "outcomes," and then to define kinds as classes or families of models for such logics.

The emphasis here on classes or families of ABEL models allows us to accommodate Wittgenstein's notion of "family resemblance" (1953). There may be no single core model in such a class to serve as the prototype for a given kind, and yet that class may determine a definite kind. On the other hand, single prototype models may function as kernels around which such classes are determined. For that matter, such classes may be singleton sets.

Kinds in this sense may be as simple or as complex as one may like. The range of options here is enormous especially when we add the consideration that such classes of models may be fuzzy classes. Practically speaking, actual objects, at least initially, can and will supply prototype models that determine kinds (which is why Wittgenstein's observation about family resemblance is so interesting). The kind *apple* is largely determined for you by the actual objects with which you have been acquainted.

Note that standard accounts of constructivist and/or empirical logic (e.g., Dummett 1957, 1975a, 1975b, 1976; Hintikka 1996) have little affinity with what makes an ability-based empirical logic empirical and operational. This is not just a matter of grammatical recursion or of constraints on what constitutes an acceptable proof or demonstration of consequence relations. Here the empiricism is built into the contents of an ABEL's basic terms—taking abilities and qualitative outcomes as formal primitives, and attributing operational content to variables. The emphasis on classes of ABEL models also works against a classical *reductionist* operationalism (Bridgman 1927, 1936). The *existence* of kinds will more often than not precede and otherwise escape our capacity, even in principle, to entirely specify ability-based empirical logics in terms of which they might be analytically defined as possibly fuzzy classes of ABEL models. ABEL models constitute limits of logical analysis, not limits on what *is*. An ABEL is defined recursively, given some basic abilities (operations) and their possible outcomes. But specifying a class of ABEL models on a single ABEL (not to mention on a class of ABELs) is not part of this recursion. Generally speaking, a kind will be what it is by virtue of the way the world is, notwithstanding our inability to completely reduce it to a class of ABEL models, much less to a class of operations.

Nevertheless, this formal conception of kinds is a version of the idea that, in describing a concept or kind intensionally, we must specify some array or bundle of features or characteristics that objects must have in order to be in its extension. In our case these are bundles of phenomenal features only with reference to respective ways of acting that give rise to those phenomena. Such a bundle of features generally is not just an ordered list but a space of possibilities with a potentially complex logical structure. In this regard phenomenal events, as possible consequences of specific ways of acting, have the potential to serve as evidence—as evidential signs, as operationally accessible differential traits—of certain kinds of things. While avoiding operational reductionism, this conception of kinds nevertheless builds operational and empirical meaningfulness into the basic fabric of inquiry—linking systems of kinds and objects in an inquiry to the basic operational abilities and empirical sensitivities of the inquirer.

This last point is crucial. Kinds (and objects) are cast in such a way as to incorporate and integrate *both* operational and empirical factors. Hence they are at once compatible with both ideational and existential features of inquiry. Namely, their operational factors are directly related (or relatable) to ideational systems. Likewise, their empirical factors are directly existential in nature. It is our attunements to kinds, with all of the operational and empirical schemata they embody, that constitute the hub of inquiry through and by which initial order is brought to existential subject matters, and through and by which ideas are suggested and may be developed and refined in order to steer an inquirer toward better solutions to a given problem with the least existential cost.

Propositions and Judgments

In preceding sections we have introduced both existential and ideational propositional forms, each having both unarticulated and articulated features. In the case of ideational propositions, the unarticulated features are described formally in terms of ideology-types and their various elements. Articulated features of ideational propositions should respect the syntactic constraints of a natural language *L*, where the terms involved will specifically denote simple or complex ideas (universals) and relations among them.

In the case of existential propositions, the unarticulated features are described formally in terms of situation-types and their various elements. Articulated features of existential propositions should respect the syntactic constraints of the same language *L*, where the terms involved denote singular objects, qualitative traits of such objects, kinds (as general classification terms), and various relations among such terms.

Various appropriate combinations and permutations of any of these features, factors, elements, and terms will account for the array of propositional forms that Dewey outlines in chapter 15 of the *Logic*. One trained in mid- to late twentieth-century symbolic logic may easily conclude that Dewey's taxonomy of propositional forms is needlessly complicated. But the conclusion here would have to be that his taxonomy, while on the right track, is still too simple. We can easily conceive of other distinct types of propositional forms that Dewey's theory of inquiry should countenance but that Dewey did not include in his list. This is especially evident when we consider the potentially rich content of *kind* terms and their possible connections with existential *qualities* and ideational *universals*.

Consider, for instance, a subgrammar of the simple generative grammar outlined earlier. Namely, consider the various propositional forms we might construct whose articulated features respect the following compositional rules:

(A′) Sentence → NounPhrase VerbPhrase
(B′) XPhrase → (Determiner) X-bar
(C′) X-bar → X

Allow further that grammatical expression-types X, besides being nominal or verbal, may be instantiated by demonstratives, quality terms, universal terms, or kind terms. This will generate a sparse and stilted language, with sentences like *the tiger run, every tiger stripes, few tiger docile, this animal,* etc., with *run, stripes, docile,* and *animal* serving as verbs (in place of more complex verb phrases like *is running, is striped, are docile,* or *is an animal*). The fact that such sentences are poor English does not preclude the possibility that such simple dialects may exist and may be in use as sensible and legitimate natural dialects. But the important point here is rather how rich this simple dialect is in the range of propositional forms it is able to accommodate.

This sort of dialect will include sentences of the form $(D:X,X′)$, where D is an optional determiner used in the formation of noun phrases, $D:X$, and where terms X and $X′$ may be singular demonstratives, quality terms, universal terms, or kind terms. With this simple dialect, we can account for the basic propositional forms Dewey explicitly lists and discusses in chapter 15 of the *Logic*, plus others. Table 1 illustrates numerous possibilities sanctioned by this simple generative grammar. Here we use a single determiner *Only* for illustration purposes, allowing this one English word to have several interpretations. The absence of a determiner is denoted by a dash "–"; and a theta "θ" denotes a demonstrative (*this* or *these*). One should try to imagine circumstances in which each suggested English paraphrase in Table 1 would be not just meaningful but distinguishable in meaning from the others.

The more extensive grammar (A)–(C) will allow for more complex propositional forms, including the use of disjunctive or conjunctive terms (*lemon and lime, green or yellow,* etc.). This will accommodate Dewey's discussion of disjunctive generic and universal propositions. The limited grammar specified by (A′)–(C′) is enough, though, to indicate that the range of possible propositional forms goes beyond Dewey's initial list.

Determiners D may be defined *extensionally,* as discussed in detail by Barwise and Cooper (1981). Others will be defined *intensionally,* e.g., involving relations among sets of abilities and/or traits that constitute "kind" terms or compositional features of complex terms of any sort. For instance,

Table 1: Possible Propositional Forms (Articulated Features Only)

Form	Example	Possible English Paraphrase	Type
$(-{:}\theta,Q)$	*this yellow*	This has (or is) a yellow quality	Particular
$(D{:}\theta,Q)$	*only this yellow*	Only this is (these are) yellow in quality	Particular
$(D{:}Q,\theta)$	*only yellow this*	The only thing yellow in quality is this	Particular
$(-{:}\theta,K)$	*this yellow*	This is yellow in kind	Singular
$(D{:}\theta,K)$	*only this yellow*	Only this is yellow in kind	Singular
$(D{:}K,\theta)$	*only yellow this*	The only thing yellow in kind is this	Singular
$(-{:}\theta,W)$	*this yellow*	This exhibits yellowness	?
$(D{:}\theta,W)$	*only this yellow*	Only this exhibits yellowness	?
$(D{:}W,\theta)$	*only yellow this*	Only yellowness engenders this	?
$(D{:}K,K')$	*only lemon yellow*	Only things of the lemon kind are of the yellow kind	Generic
$(D{:}W,W')$	*only lemon yellow*	Only lemonhood entails yellowness	Universal
$(D{:}Q,K)$	*only lemon yellow*	Only a lemon quality is a trait of the yellow kind	?
$(D{:}K,Q)$	*only lemon yellow*	Only things of the lemon kind have a yellow quality	?
$(D{:}W,K)$	*only lemon yellow*	Only lemonhood characterizes the yellow kind	?
$(D{:}K,W)$	*only lemon yellow*	Only the lemon kind has the character of yellowness	?
$(D{:}W,Q)$	*only lemon yellow*	Only lemonhood engenders a yellow quality	?
$(D{:}Q,W)$	*only lemon yellow*	Only a lemon quality exhibits yellowness	?

that all humans are animals may mean that any extension of the kind *human* will be contained within a respective extension of the kind *animal*. Conversely, it may mean that any essential tests and traits embodied in the ABEL-contents of the kind *animal* will be embodied in those for the kind *human*. So, of these two kinds, *animal* is broader in extension, while *human* is broader (deeper, more specific) in intension. Of course, both extensions and operational/empirical intensions of kinds may be related in ways other than being narrower or broader. Determiners may also be used to denote relations among other sorts of terms besides kinds. A logical treatment of determiners would thus aim at delineating any such relations that are sufficiently regular and systematic to warrant expression by some term or phrase in a natural or artificial language.

The fact that intensional determiners may draw on both empirical and operational factors suggests a type of proposition that is both existential and ideational in character—a type of proposition that combines and synthesizes existential and ideational features of inquiry. We would thus have to recognize propositions with the basic form

Unarticulated features $\Vdash$ Articulated features

(where the "$\Vdash$" symbol may be read as "warrants"). Specifically, the articulated features of such propositions may run the whole gamut of possible linguistic expressions. The unarticulated contextual features would draw on elements of both situation-types and ideology-types. So it may be only with respect to a given situation in conjunction with a given ideology that, for example, *Only lemonhood characterizes the yellow kind.* Kind terms are multipurpose terms insofar as they have both operational and empirical contents. In other words, kinds are directly related to ideational subject matters by virtue of their operational contents, and they are directly related to existential subject matters due to their empirical contents.

It is, of course, a defining feature of *judgments* that they combine and synthesize existential and ideational features of inquiry. The culmination of an inquiry, insofar as warranted results are the aim, will come about only as potential facts and possible courses of action have been adequately squared away. A solution to the problem at hand will have been formulated and implemented in the course of or in conjunction with assertion of "final" judgment. Inquiry in this sense is a process of rectifying some existential situation. The subject of judgment (encompassing the facts of the matter) will be determined insofar as the situation at hand is identified with or likened to specific situation-types. A solution is at hand when we come to terms with what *type(s)* of situation the situation at hand is. As potential facts include classifications of things as instances of kinds, and of relations of kinds to one another, the predicate of judgment (encompassing what is to be done) is directly borne by the operational contents of these kind-terms.

Although the functional difference between propositions and judgments is obvious, it is not clear how to distinguish them as linguistic expressions, if judgments invite linguistic expression at all (versus direct assertion or implementation in one's response(s) to given situations). Unlike the rich variety of propositional forms, judgments allegedly have a simple subject-predicate form. Existential and ideational propositions articulate features of the subject and predicate of judgment, respectively, though the subject and predicate of judgment are best regarded as being contained in the *unarticulated* features of these propositions. The subject is best treated as denoting an individual situation—an individual *this*—determined to be of a certain type through processes of inquiry; while the predicate essentially denotes an ideology of a certain type (or a class of ideology-types), likewise determined through processes of inquiry. In responding to a given problem, one basically implements an ideology (not just a theory, much less a singular idea).

With this we have pretty much covered the full range of technical concerns built into Dewey's logical theory, from the overarching notions of inquiry and judgment to the ground-level logics of abilities and qualitative events. Each of the various levels and components of formal structure we have considered—associated respectively with empirical events, abstract symbols, kinds, facts, hypotheses, states of affairs, worldviews, situations, ideologies, or inquiry as a whole—has its own distinctive irreducible autonomy, such that potentially complex formal features at each level of analysis systematically dovetail with those of the next. From one level or component to the next, there is no reduction of one to the other. These various components correspond to different orders of detail typically arising in full-fledged inquiries, where each is subject to more or less distinct sorts of formal analysis. For instance, various objects or kinds of objects will have an immediate wholeness that is inexplicable otherwise, though we might analyze as far as we can the operational constitution of such objects. Likewise, we may acknowledge and determine that various states of affairs may be accessible to others by virtue of their structural differences (e.g., adding fact Q to state of affairs u yields state of affairs v, etc.); yet some accessibility relations may have to be acknowledged (impressed on us in the course of experience) in spite of our inability to find an internal structural explanation for this linkage. The structural details outlined above thus do not reduce inquiry to a mechanical or routine process but simply identify various distinguishable levels and components in terms of which formal resolutions and rectifications of a given subject matter are possible. At best this outline barely conforms to minimal requirements that must be met to accommodate the breadth and depth of Dewey's philosophy of logic.

Obviously this approach to logic involves a philosophical perspective that is unusual by present standards. The philosophical principles and constraints underlying Dewey's theory of inquiry are quite rich—almost unwieldy in their complexity. But clearly these principles and constraints are not at odds with the techniques of contemporary mathematical logic once we piece these techniques together in appropriate ways.

Works Cited

Arbib, Michael A., and Ernest G. Manes. 1975. *Arrows, Structures, and Functors: The Categorical Imperative.* New York: Academic Press.

Bandemer, Hans, and Siegfried Gottwald. 1995. *Fuzzy Sets, Fuzzy Logic, Fuzzy Methods, with Applications.* New York: John Wiley. Originally published in German by Akademie Verlag under the title *Einfühüng in die Fuzzy Methoden* (1993).

Barendregt, Hendrik Pieter. 1984. *The Lambda Calculus: Its Syntax and Semantics.* Rev. ed. Amsterdam: Elsevier.

Barr, Michael, and Charles Wells. 1990. *Category Theory for Computing Science.* New York: Prentice Hall.

Barwise, Jon. 1989. *The Situation in Logic.* Stanford: Center for the Study of Language and Information.

Barwise, Jon, and Robin Cooper. 1981. Generalized Quantifiers and Natural Language. *Linguistics and Philosophy* 4:159–219.

Barwise, Jon, and John Etchemendy. 1989. Model-Theoretic Semantics. In *Foundations of Cognitive Science,* ed. Michael I. Posner, 207–43. Cambridge: MIT Press.

Black, Max. 1937. Vagueness: An Exercise in Logical Analysis. *Philosophy of Science* 4:427–55.

Boydston, Jo Ann, ed. 1970. *Guide to the Works of John Dewey.* Carbondale: Southern Illinois University Press.

Brandom, Robert B. 1994. *Making It Explicit: Reasoning, Representing, and Discursive Commitment.* Cambridge: Harvard University Press.

Bridgman, Percy William. 1927. *The Logic of Modern Physics.* New York: Macmillan.

———. 1936. *The Nature of Physical Theory.* Princeton: Princeton University Press.

Brooks, Rodney A. 1990. Intelligence Without Reason. AI Memo 1293. (MIT AI Lab). Also in *Computers and Thought,* Proceedings of the International Joint Conference on Artificial Intelligence, Sydney (Los Altos, Calif.: Morgan Kauffman, 1990, 569–95).

Chomsky, Noam. 1981. *Lectures on Government and Binding.* Dordrecht: Foris.

———. 1995. *The Minimalist Program.* Cambridge: MIT Press.

Church, Alonzo. 1941. *The Calculi of Lambda-Conversion.* Annals of Mathematics Studies, vol. 6. Princeton: Princeton University Press.

Church, Alonzo, and J. B. Rosser. 1936. Some Properties of Conversion. *Transactions of the American Mathematical Society* 39:472–82.

Dewey, John. 1905. The Postulate of Immediate Empiricism. *Journal of Philosophy, Psychology, and Scientific Methods* 2:393–99. Reprinted in Dewey 1910, 226–41, and in MW3:158–67.

———. 1910. *The Influence of Darwin on Philosophy, and Other Essays in Contemporary Thought.* New York: Henry Holt. Essays reprinted separately in EW5, MW1, 3, 4, 6.

———. 1916. *Essays in Experimental Logic.* Chicago: University of Chicago Press. Essays reprinted separately in MW1, 2, 4, 6, 8, 10.

————. 1922. Types of Philosophic Thought. *Syllabus for course at Columbia University, 1922–1923.* Included in MW13:349–95.

————. 1925. *Experience and Nature.* Chicago: Open Court. Reprinted in LW1.

————. 1929. *The Quest for Certainty: A Study of the Relation of Knowledge and Action.* New York: Minton, Balch. Reprinted in LW4.

————. 1930. Qualitative Thought. *Symposium* 1:5–32. Reprinted in Dewey 1931c, 93–116, and in LW5:243–62.

————. 1931a. Context and Thought. *University of California Publications in Philosophy* 12:203–24. Reprinted in LW6:3–21.

————. 1931b. George Herbert Mead as I Knew Him. *Journal of Philosophy* 4:309–14. Dewey's eulogy at the memorial service for George Herbert Mead in Chicago on April 30, 1931. Reprinted in LW6:22–28.

————. 1931c. *Philosophy and Civilization.* New York: Minton, Balch.

————. 1931d. Prefatory Remarks in *The Philosophy of the Present.* First published in Mead 1932, xxvi–xl. Reprinted in LW6:307–10.

————. 1934. *Art as Experience.* New York: Henry Holt. Reprinted in LW10.

————. 1936. The Work of George Mead. *New Republic* 87:329–30. Reviews of Mead 1934, 1936. Reprinted in LW11:450–53.

————. 1938. *Logic: The Theory of Inquiry.* New York: Henry Holt. Reprinted in LW12.

————. 1942. Inquiry and the Indeterminateness of Situations. *Journal of Philosophy* 39 (11):290–96. Reprinted in Dewey 1946, 322–30, and in LW15:34–41.

————. 1946. *Problems of Men.* New York: Philosophical Library. Essays reprinted separately in LW.

Dubois, Didier, and Henri Prade. 1980. *Fuzzy Sets and Systems: Theory and Applications.* New York: Academic Press.

Dummett, Michael. 1957. Constructionalism. *Philosophical Review* 66:47–65. Reprinted in Dummett 1978, 50–65.

————. 1975a. The Philosophical Basis of Intuitionistic Logic. In *Logic Colloquium '73,* ed. H. E. Rose and J. C. Shepherdson, 5–40. New York: American Elsevier. Reprinted in Dummett 1978, 214–47.

————. 1975b. Wang's Paradox. *Synthese* 30:301–24. Reprinted in Dummett 1978, 248–68.

————. 1976. Is Logic Empirical? In *Contemporary British Philosophy,* 4th ed., ed. H. D. Lewis, 45–68. London: G. Allen and Unwin. Reprinted in Dummett 1978, 269–89.

————. 1978. *Truth and Other Enigmas.* Cambridge: Harvard University Press.

Eilenberg, Samuel, and Saunders MacLane. 1942. Group Extensions and Homology. *Annals of Mathematics* 43:757–831.

————. 1945. General Theory of Natural Equivalences. *Transactions of the American Mathematical Society* 58:231–44.

Fenstad, Jens Erik. 1996. Partiality. In *Handbook of Logic and Language,* ed. Johan van Benthem and Alice ter Meulen. Amsterdam: Elsevier.

Fenstad, Jens Erik, Per-Kristian Halvorsen, Tore Langholm, and Johan van Benthem. 1987. *Situations, Language, and Logic.* Dordrecht: D. Reidel.

Fischer, Michael J., and Richard E. Ladner. 1979. Propositional Dynamic Logic of Regular Programs. *Journal of Computer and Systems Sciences* 18 (2):194–211.

Fodor, Jerry A., and Zenon W. Pylyshyn. 1981. How Direct Is Visual Perception? Some Reflections on Gibson's 'Ecological Approach.'" *Cognition* 9:139–96.

Gabbay, Dov M., and Franz Guenthner, eds. 1984. *Extensions of Classical Logic.* Dordrecht: D. Reidel.

Gärdenfors, Peter. 1990. Induction, Conceptual Spaces, and AI. *Philosophy of Science* 57 (1):78–95.

———, ed. 1987. *Generalized Quantifiers.* Dordrecht: D. Reidel.

Gärdenfors, Peter, and Simon Winter. 1995. Linguistic Modality as Expressions of Social Power. *Nordic Journal of Linguistics* 18:137–66.

Gibson, James J. 1979. *The Ecological Approach to Visual Perception.* Boston: Houghton Mifflin.

Groenendijk, Jeroen, and Martin Stokhof. 1990. Dynamic Montague Grammar. In *Proceedings of the Second Symposium on Logic and Language*, ed. L. Kálmán et al. Budapest.

———. 1991. Dynamic Predicate Logic. *Linguistics and Philosophy* 14:39–100.

Harary, Frank, Robert Z. Norman, and Dorwin Cartwright. 1965. *Structural Models: An Introduction to the Theory of Directed Graphs.* New York: John Wiley.

Harel, David. 1984. Dynamic Logic. In Gabbay and Guenther 1984, 497–604.

Hickman, Larry A. 1990. *John Dewey's Pragmatic Technology.* Bloomington: Indiana University Press.

Hilpinen, Risto. 1983. On C. S. Peirce's Theory of the Proposition: Peirce as a Precursor of Game-Theoretic Semantics. In *The Relevance of Charles Peirce*, ed. Eugene Freeman, 264–70. La Salle, Ill.: Hegeler Institute.

Hindley, J. Roger, and Jonathan P. Seldin. 1986. *Introduction to Combinators and Lambda-Calculus.* Cambridge: Cambridge University Press.

Hintikka, Jaakko. 1996. *The Principles of Mathematics Revisited.* Cambridge: Cambridge University Press.

James, William. 1912. *Essays in Radical Empiricism.* New York: Longmans, Green. Reprint, Cambridge: Harvard University Press, 1976.

Kennedy, Gail. 1970. Dewey's Logic and Theory of Knowledge. In Boydston 1970, 61–98.

Klir, George J., and Tina A. Folger. 1988. *Fuzzy Sets, Uncertainty, and Information.* Englewood Cliffs, N.J.: Prentice Hall.

Klir, George J., and Bo Yuan. 1995. *Fuzzy Sets and Fuzzy Logic: Theory and Applications.* Upper Saddle River, N.J.: Prentice Hall.

Knoke, David, and James H. Kuklinksi. 1982. *Network Analysis.* Beverly Hills: Sage.

McClamrock, Ron. 1995. *Existential Cognition.* Chicago: University of Chicago Press.

Markovsky, Barry, Jon Skvoretz, David Willer, Michael J. Lovaglia, and Jeffrey Erger. 1993. The Seeds of Weak Power: An Extension of Network Exchange Theory. *American Sociological Review* 58:197–209.

Mead, George Herbert. 1932. *The Philosophy of the Present.* Edited by Arthur E. Murphy. La Salle, Ill.: Open Court.

———. 1934. *Mind, Self, and Society from the Standpoint of a Social Behavioris*. Edited by Charles W. Morris. Chicago: University of Chicago Press.

———. 1936. *Movements of Thought in the Nineteenth Century*. Edited by Merritt H. Moore. Chicago: University of Chicago Press.

———. 1956. *On Social Psychology*. Edited by Anselm Strauss. Chicago: University of Chicago Press.

Neisser, Ulric. 1976. *Cognition and Reality: Principles and Implications of Cognitive Psychology*. San Francisco: W. H. Freeman.

Pierce, Benjamin C. 1991. *Basic Category Theory for Computer Scientists*. Cambridge: MIT Press.

Putnam, Hilary. 1983. Computational Psychology and Interpretation Theory. In his *Realism and Reason: Philosophical Papers*, 3:139–54. Cambridge: Cambridge University Press.

Rydeheard, David E., and Rod M. Burstall. 1988. *Computational Category Theory*. New York: Prentice Hall.

Searle, John. 1980. Minds, Brains, and Programs. *Behavioral and Brain Sciences* 3:417–24.

Sleeper, Ralph William. 1986. *The Necessity of Pragmatism*. New Haven: Yale University Press. Reprinted with introduction by Tom Burke. Urbana: University of Illinois Press, 2001.

Stansifer, Ryan D. 1995. *The Study of Programming Languages*. Englewood Cliffs: Prentice Hall.

Taylor, Charles. 1995. *Philosophical Arguments*. Cambridge: Harvard University Press.

Turvey, Michael T., Robert E. Shaw, Edward S. Reed, and William M. Mace. 1981. Ecological Laws of Perceiving and Acting: In Reply to Fodor and Pylyshyn. *Cognition* 9:237–304. A reply to Fodor and Pylyshyn 1981.

Willer, David. 1987. *Theory and the Experimental Investigation of Social Structures*. New York: Gordon and Breach.

———, ed. 1999. *Network Exchange Theory*. Westport: Praeger.

Willer, David, and Bo Anderson, eds. 1981. *Networks, Exchange, and Coercion: The Elementary Theory and Its Applications*. New York: Elsevier.

Willer, David, Michael J. Lovaglia, and Barry Markovsky. 1997. Power and Influence: A Theoretical Bridge. *Social Forces* 76 (2):571–603.

Willer, David, and John Skvoretz. 1997a. Games and Structures. *Rationality and Society* 9 (1):5–35.

———. 1997b. Network Connection and Exchange Ratios: Theory, Predictions, and Experimental Tests. *Advances in Group Processes* 14:199–234.

Wittgenstein, Ludwig. 1953. *Philosophical Investigations*. Trans. G. E. M. Anscombe. New York: Macmillan.

Yager, Ronald R., and Dimitar P. Filev. 1994. *Essentials of Fuzzy Modeling and Control*. New York: John Wiley.

Zadeh, Lotfi A. 1965. Fuzzy Sets. *Information and Control* 8 (3):338–53.

7

Designation, Characterization, and Theory in Dewey's *Logic*

Douglas Browning

John Dewey's *Logic: The Theory of Inquiry* (1938) provides an elaboration of the theoretical outcome of a rather exhaustive inquiry into inquiry. More specifically, it provides a general theory of inquiry that is proposed as clarifying and justifying three hypotheses regarding logical form.[1] Given this aim of providing an exposition and defense of such a theory, it is hardly surprising that Dewey does not see it as essential to his task to take the reader through the course of the inquiry into inquiry which culminated in that theory or to set out its distinctive phases of the designation and characterization of the subject-matter.[2] He does not do this, but he does provide significant clues regarding the general pattern that such an inquiry into inquiry will follow, if carried through with proper care. Relying on such clues, I will attempt to distinguish the major phases of that pattern. I will then argue that confusion among these phases is logically disastrous.

The Phases of Inquiry into Inquiry

[I]nquiry occupies an intermediate and mediating place in the development of an experience. If this be granted, it follows at once that a philosophical discussion of the distinctions and relations which figure most largely in logical theories depends upon a proper placing of them in their temporal context; and that in default of such placing we are prone to transfer the traits of the subject-matter of one phase to that of another—with a confusing outcome. (Dewey 1916, MW10:320)

I begin by distinguishing (A) Dewey's developed theory of inquiry from (B) the inquiry into inquiry which culminated in that theory.

A. On Dewey's developed theory, any inquiry must follow *the general pattern of inquiry*. The pattern of inquiry is therefore exhibited by both first-order inquiries (or primary inquiries, as Dewey calls them), which are not inquiries into inquiries, and second-order inquiries, which are.[3] This applies as well to an inquiry into inquiry-into-inquiry.

The pattern of inquiry that Dewey proposes begins with a problematic situation that is evoked by an indeterminate situation. It moves through initial observational orientation within that situation to the institution and hypothetical formulation of the problem, follows through the phases of the observational and conceptual sort, enters into reasoning in the narrow sense, experimentally tests hypotheses, and culminates in a final judgment that marks the final transformation of the stream of problematic situations into a situation which is determinate relative to the indeterminacy that has been taken as problematic. It is important to emphasize that, on this theory, every inquiry is initiated by and within a specific situation with a unique and pervasive quality of indetermination. The specificity of this situation and of the problem taken to be appropriate to it, then, limits the scope of the resulting inquiry and the solution at which it aims. Thus there will be as many different inquiries into inquiry as there are distinctive problematic situations that initiate them and problems to be addressed by them. On the other hand, the consummation of a successful inquiry into inquiry will be limited to a "terminal sentence" that serves both as (a) the "asserting" of the hypothesis which has received final affirmation and (b) the final judgment instituting the determinate situation.[4] The hypothesis "asserted" by the terminal sentence in an inquiry into inquiry will be an *account* of that subject-matter, namely, the specific range of inquiries inquired into, in regard to just that limited and specific problem to which it provides a response.

Now, any such limited account may be said to be a logical account, at least if Dewey is correct in saying that inquiry into inquiry yields logical theory,[5] but it is not necessarily the same as a general theory of logic of the sort which Dewey proposes in the *Logic*. It would be the same only if the inquiry into inquiry were initiated by a problematic situation which was itself such as to yield a problem of such broad scope that only a general logical theory could answer to it. In fact, Dewey sets up the problem addressed in the *Logic* in just that way. It is identified as the main or focal concern of the logician, namely, that of determining the ground of logical forms, in other words, the forms involved as norms for arriving at conclusions. This means that the concern of the inquirer is to deal with logical forms by considering them in their variety and to propose and test hypotheses against them with the aim of coming to rest on one hypothesis that is judged to solve problems adequately. This final hypothesis, warrantably assertible, is, as Dewey contends, the general theory of inquiry that he presents and defends in the book. Of course, the conception of the logician's task as that of providing a systematic ordering of logical forms is itself limited by the fact that, as Dewey puts it, that subject-matter is only proximate. The ultimate subject-matter for the logician consists of the grounds of logical forms, for it is only on that basis that we are able to pick out what genuinely counts as a logical form. Dewey's logical theory addresses this issue. It is that "all logical forms (with their characteristic properties) arise within the operations of inquiry and are concerned with control of inquiry so that it may yield warranted assertions" (LW12: 11).

B. Now, it would be a mistake to read the above developed and theoretical picture back into that inquiry into inquiry which culminated in it. If Dewey's *Logic* is the outcome of an inquiry into inquiry, we cannot—and he would not—presuppose that very outcome in initiating that inquiry. This means that, in first engaging upon inquiry into inquiry, we cannot assume that our subject-matter for inquiry, i.e., inquiries, can be designated or initially characterized in terms of the determinate structure which theory offers. If our inquiry into inquiry is genuine, sincere, to be trusted, then we must begin more innocently. How, then, can inquiry into inquiry begin?

First of all, we must note that inquiry into inquiry already has a specific subject-matter, namely, inquiries wherever they may be found. Of course, if Dewey is correct in his account, there will be more to the initial problematic situation than just that subject-matter, for there must be something specifically problematic about it. Nonetheless, the fact remains that, for whatever limited reasons we may have, the concern of inquiry into inquiry is to examine inquiries. Thus, the inquirer must at the beginning *designate*, mark out, that subject-matter in such a way as to (a) make clear what is being inquired into (b) without presupposing one account or theory of inquiry rather than another. Item (a) is required in order that the inquirer be properly oriented throughout inquiry and in order that other inquirers, who may propose different accounts or theories of that subject-matter, be able to evaluate critically the adequacy to that subject-matter of whatever theories may be proposed. Item (b) is required in order that the inquiry not be prejudiced in favor of one theory rather than another. An inquiry into inquiry, then, must indicate *pretheoretically* what is to count as an inquiry.

Designation, however carried out, is a modest or, better, minimalist business. Nothing is needed for the purpose, save but enough to mark out a subject-matter in such a way as to allow other inquirers to recognize it and distinguish it from other subject-matters. Barely enough is sufficient; anything more is risky, since the threat of spoilage by the careless insertion of a theoretical presupposition is ever present.

But the inquirer cannot go forward on bare designation alone. The next phase, logically speaking, is one of surveying what has been circumscribed by designation, of looking around to see what else can be said about that subject-matter, and then attempting to characterize what is found. This phase of initial characterization is quite different from the sort of description that may be found in an account. It is, in fact, a pretheoretical collection of "the facts" against which the account and its theoretically regimented and sanitized terms of characterization must test its adequacy. Of course, these "initial facts of the case" are always provisional, subject to subsequent sharpening, revision, and even, perhaps, rejection. Moreover, once one has proposed an account, then that proposal may well serve as a guide for a resurveying of the subject-matter.

In light of these remarks, I offer the following listing of phases of inquiry into inquiry.

Pretheoretical phases
1. Designation of the subject-matter, namely, inquiries
2. Pretheoretical characterization of inquiries

Intermediate phases
3. Process of inquiring toward an account

Theoretical phases
4. Provision of a limited account of inquiry
5. Provision of a general theory of inquiry
6. Testing of the applicability of the account or theory to the range of inquiries
7. Provision of a background theory for a theory of inquiry

Let me make two general observations about this list. First, it is not proposed as complete. Speaking autobiographically, the account is limited by the problematic subject-matter that I confronted when I found myself confused by the apparent clash between what I had come to think I understood about Dewey's *Logic* and certain remarks made by several interpreters of it. Since the initiating problem did not concern the important work of inquiry that comes between (2) and (4) above, I have merely indicated the phases in (3), which develop in a decreasingly pretheoretical and increasingly theoretical manner, in a generously vague way.

A second point is this. Although the order of the items in the list are to be taken as logically (in Dewey's use of the term) necessary, each proposal offered at each phase is, by virtue of being hypothetical, subject to reconsideration at temporally later points in the course of inquiry. For example, though characterization of a subject-matter logically presupposes *some* understanding of what that subject-matter is, a more careful attempt at designation may come about only after confusions or disagreements about characterization have led to an impasse.

Regarding (6), I want to make two critically important observations. First, what is involved is the consideration *from a theoretical perspective* of a *pretheoretical subject-matter*, namely, inquiries as they are lived through and carried out *from the inquiring agent's perspective*. At this phase the inquirer brings logical theory up against immediately experienced subject-matter. Second, given this very limited concern, every metaphysical, psychological, scientific, historical, or otherwise external theoretical consideration is an irrelevance and, in the final analysis, a distracting and spoiling intrusion. Otherwise, the question of the applicability and adequacy of the *logical account*, considered in its own right, is avoided, if not actually begged.

It is in light of these considerations that we may consider (7), the provision of a background theory for a theory of inquiry. Its purpose would be to offer an *explanation* for the specific elements of a theory of inquiry by indicating why those elements would, given the broader context provided by the background theory, be expected to be as they are. It can only be introduced from the perspective of one who is concerned to fit things into a larger context, e.g., human culture, history, or the world, a perspective which, depending on its invoked context, we might call cultural, psychological, historical, epistemological, or metaphysical. A background theory that is invoked in order to explain a logical theory is not part of the logical theory it purportedly explains, however much its acceptance might add to the persuasiveness of that logic. We need to be clear about this. No background theory could provide an inquirer into inquiry with principles that could legitimately be invoked from the inquirer's perspective.

That this represents Dewey's own view is clear enough from what he says when he directly confronts the issue. Under the heading "Logic is autonomous," he makes the following remarks:

> Logic as inquiry into inquiry is, if you please, a circular process; it does not depend upon anything extraneous to inquiry. The force of this proposition may perhaps be most readily understood by noting what it precludes. It precludes the determination and selection of logical first principles by an *a priori* intuitional act. . . . It precludes resting logic upon metaphysical and epistemological assumptions and presuppositions. . . . The autonomy of logic also precludes the idea that its "foundations" are psychological. (Dewey 1938, LW12:28)

But in spite of these remarks, it nonetheless remains true that, in *presenting* his theory of inquiry in the *Logic*, Dewey often draws upon a background of theories which he argues for elsewhere. This, of itself, is not surprising. His vision is wide, and he finds it illuminating and supportive to show how his special concern fits into the larger picture. (The fact, well known to all serious readers of Dewey, that his philosophy as a whole is amazingly coherent becomes strikingly evident in the *Logic*.) His invocation of this background picture is sporadic and, unfortunately, only sporadically identified as such. It is unfortunate because, without such identification, it may appear to the reader that the background is part of the logical theory itself. Among the elements of a larger context which Dewey invokes in his presentation of his logic is his view of experience as an emergent from an organism/environment interaction. Another element that rests partially upon his view of experience and partially upon his metaphysical biology is his view of the experienced indeterminate situation as an emergent upon a disequilibrium arising from that interaction. (At a still deeper level, which Dewey does not often invoke in the *Logic*, there is a reading of this view of experience and of situations from the standpoint of his more general process-metaphysics. In this case what is involved is an emergent, not from interaction between two distinct entities but from a transaction within a context in which the distinctiveness of entities, e.g., organisms, is functional only.)

Now, of course, if the background theory provides an explanation of an item in the logical theory, such as experience, situations, or inquiry itself, then that explanation becomes part of Dewey's *theory* of that item. If we ask at large for his theory of situations, for example, we might well expect to be told about certain metaphysical matters which he takes to be relevant to a proper understanding of situations, unless, of course, we specified that we were interested only in the character and place of situations in his logical (or other more limited) theory. In arguing for his own logical theory against Russell, who gratuitously injected his own metaphysical assumptions into the discussion, Dewey responded in print by presenting, all too frequently, an opposing metaphysical picture as one which is not only different from Russell's but more adequate. Since the context of the controversy was Russell's criticism of "Dewey's new logic" and Dewey's view of warranted assertibility, such responses by Dewey have served, I suppose, to mislead a number of readers of the controversy into thinking that metaphysical claims are a legitimate part of logical theory.[6]

So much, then, for a general picture of the phases of inquiry into inquiry. What remains is to consider how Dewey himself attends to the phases of designation and characterization in his *Logic*.

The Designation and Characterization of Inquiries

> [T]he words "experience," "situation," etc., are used to *remind* the thinker of
> the need of reversion to precisely something which never can be one of the
> terms of his reflection but which nevertheless furnishes the existential mean-
> ing and status of them all. (Dewey 1916, MW10:324n1)

The rather wholesale inquiry into inquiry that culminated in the general
logical theory of Dewey's *Logic* raises special problems of designation which
may not be shared by more limited inquiries into inquiry. My interest is
less with these special problems in the *Logic* than with the specific designative task it does share with any inquiry into inquiries, namely, the task of
circumscribing the range of inquiries that constitutes its subject-matter by
identifying what is to count as a legitimate occupant of it. But since the
larger project of the *Logic* includes this more specific task, I will center upon
the latter by first rehearsing the designative problems of the former.

Dewey states his general theory at the beginning of the *Logic*.

> The theory, in summary form, is that all logical forms (with their character-
> istic properties) arise within the operation of inquiry and are concerned with
> control of inquiry so that it may yield warranted assertions. This conception
> implies much more than that logical forms are disclosed or come to light
> when we reflect upon processes of inquiry that are in use. Of course it means
> that; but it also means that the forms *originate* in operations of inquiry. To
> employ a convenient expression, it means that while inquiry into inquiry is
> the *causa cognoscendi* of logical forms, primary inquiry is itself *causa essendi*
> of the forms which inquiry into inquiry discloses. (LW12:11-12)

> [A]ll logical forms, such as are represented by what has been called *proxi-
> mate logical* subject-matter, are instances of a relation between means and
> consequences in properly controlled inquiry, the word "controlled" in this
> statement standing for the methods of inquiry that are developed and per-
> fected in the processes of continuous inquiry. (LW12:19)

We can read the first passage as proposing three distinguishable hypotheses, namely, that logical forms are disclosed in inquiry, originate in inquiry, and are concerned with control of inquiry toward warranted assertions. The second passage, it seems, carries forward the sense of "control of
inquiry" as involving the functioning of subject-matter in the means-consequences relation. These hypotheses may be set out a bit more fully as follows:

H1: All logical forms are disclosed in the course of inquiry into inquiry, that is, reflection upon what is involved in primary inquiries.
H2: All logical forms originate in the operations of primary inquiries.
H3: A logical form is an instance of a relation between means and consequences in properly controlled inquiry.

Now, it would seem that in order to avoid begging the issue in these hypotheses, that is, by reading them in such a way as to employ the systematic sense of the term *logical form* from the start (as Ernest Nagel unfortunately does in his introduction to the *Logic* [LW12:xi]), Dewey must begin by (a) providing some manner of indicating what is to count as a logical form which is such as to be agreed upon by the great majority of logical theorists, including those who hold rival epistemic and ontological views about logical forms. It may, of course, be allowed that on the assumption of one theory something may be accorded the status of a logical form which on another theory would not be; different theories may expand an initially accepted subject-matter in different directions.[7] The point is that there must be an initially acceptable body of designatable entities each of which are accorded the status of a logical form in order for different theories to be in contention about what determines each logical form to be such. Furthermore, since Dewey's task is to ground this "proximate subject-matter" of logic, as he calls it, in an "ultimate subject-matter," meaning inquiry itself, he must also (b) provide a designation or identification of the latter subject-matter as it is invoked in the three hypotheses, that is to say, as "primary inquiry," "inquiry into inquiry," and "properly controlled inquiry." These two initial *designative* conditions must be satisfied in order to get properly started on the defense of the hypotheses. Otherwise, one does not understand exactly what is being defended. Only when this is done can Dewey attempt to show the superiority of his hypotheses to any rival ones.

As to designative condition (a), Dewey has maddeningly little to say. He does not speak to the requirement directly in the *Logic*. What he does do throughout the work is to provide examples of logical forms, some of which are exemplified in, though almost always misunderstood by, the tradition. For example, there is the lengthy discussion of the square of opposition and A, E, I, and O propositions in chapters 10 and 11. We could say that, in general, Dewey conceives the received domain of logical forms, the proximate subject-matter, as more or less hierarchically ordered, so that under the genus *logical form* one subgenus is that which is often labeled as *propositions*. The reader must be careful here, as well as in regard to his use of many other terms, to keep his systematic and presystematic uses of terms separate, perhaps by mentally inserting full quotation marks around the presystematic uses. Adopting this device temporarily, we might begin by considering "propositions" as including the sorts "general propositions," "particular propositions," and "singular propositions." Of course, the "terms" of "propositions," understood as "logical" elements in them, also comprise a subgenus of "logical forms," as do the "relations" among "propositions" which serve to cover the further sorts of "logical principles," such as *modus ponens* and *Barbara*, and "canons," such as identity, excluded middle, and contradiction.

There is little point in going further with this, since we have yet to discern any general conditions that a form must satisfy in order to be accorded the status of being "logical." One response to this lack might be that none is needed, for the domain is only intuitively drawn to begin with and can receive precision of specification only in terms of a proposed theory of what a "logical form" is. But this will do only so long as our intuitions coincide to a very large extent and are not prejudiced by some theory that we happen to hold. In any case, the first difficulty in the way of Dewey's hypotheses is that he does not go beyond this intuitive appeal, so we cannot avoid feeling a bit adrift, unanchored in a shared reference to a problematic subject-matter.

We may now briefly consider designative condition (b), that of specifying what is to count as inquiry in its three varieties of primary inquiry, inquiry into inquiry, and properly controlled inquiry. Here it might seem that Dewey has been, if anything, overly helpful, especially in chapters 4 and 6 of the *Logic* where he gives examples (farming, art, science, common sense) and where (in chapter 6) he even provides us with a "definition." But there are a number of puzzlements. The oft-quoted definition is less a specification of inquiry in general than it is of *successful* inquiry, where success is marked by the *actual* termination of inquiry in the establishment of a determinate situation (LW12:108-9). What seems to be ruled out as inquiry are unsuccessful and truncated cases of attempting to settle a problematic situation, but also cases of successful settlement which do not involve "controlled or directed transformation." This suggests that the specification is not one of inquiry as such, but rather of properly controlled inquiry. But this is not obvious either, for it is not precluded by *this* "definition" or even by the explication of "controlled or directed'" on the following page (LW12:109) that the control which results in success will be such as to constitute a *proper* control. To exercise "proper" control would seem to involve not merely providing direction and performing operations but being schooled in past successful and unsuccessful inquiries and applying this funded intelligence with sensitivity and flexibility. This would *seem* to be the case, at least on the most straightforward reading of the *Logic*, but perhaps it is not. In any event, neither the "definition" nor its explication helps us to decide. There is an additional obscurity introduced in the definition itself by its reference to the conversion of an initial indeterminate situation into a "unified whole." This language is, I think, unfortunate, for in other places in the *Logic* it is clear that Dewey wishes to treat *any* situation as a unified whole, indeterminate as well as determinate ones (LW12:72, 125, 218). But the major problem for our designative purposes is that of determining whether the "definition" is proposed as introducing a systemic use of the term *inquiry* or as appealing to a presystematic use that is sharable by others. The language in which Dewey introduces the "definition" inclines me to the latter view, but it is not altogether compelling. So there are unclarities about what is to count either as an inquiry in general or as a properly controlled inquiry. And if these give us pause, then the determination of what is to count as a case of inquiry into inquiry must do so as well.

But again, as with Dewey's designative insufficiency regarding "logical forms," his designative unclarities regarding what is to count as an inquiry do not seem to me to be incorrigible. In fact, I think we can extricate from his discussions the beginning of a more charitable designation in terms of situations.

The notion of a situation is introduced by Dewey in the *Logic* without appeal to any theory, logical or otherwise, that is already in place. It is a primitive notion.

> I begin the discussion by introducing and explaining the denotative force of the word *situation*. Its import may perhaps be most readily indicated by means of a preliminary negative statement. What is designated by the word "situation" is *not* a single object or event or set of objects and events. For we never experience nor form judgments about objects and events in isolation, but only in connection with a contextual whole. (LW12:72)

Dewey adds to this a characterization of situations drawn from a descriptive survey of immediate experience.

> [A] situation is a whole in virtue of its immediately pervasive quality. When we describe it from the psychological side, we have to say that the situation as a qualitative whole is sensed or *felt*. Such an expression is, however, valuable only as it is taken negatively to indicate that it is *not*, as such, an object in *discourse*. Stating that it is *felt* is wholly misleading if it gives the impression that the situation *is* a feeling or an emotion or anything mentalistic. On the contrary, feeling, sensation and emotion have themselves to be identi-

fied and described in terms of the immediate presence of a total qualitative situation. (LW12:73-74)

These remarks clearly are taken by Dewey to apply to any situation, even in the consummation of inquiry. Dewey's concluding remarks in the *Logic* are very instructive here.

> [E]very resolved situation which is the terminal state of inquiry exists directly as it is experienced. It is a qualitative individual situation in which are directly incorporated and absorbed the results of the mediating processes of inquiry. As an existential situation it is had as the consummation and fulfilment of the operations of inquiry. . . . [T]he experienced situation as a qualitative situation is not an object or a set of objects. It is just the qualitative situation which it is. It can be referred to, taken and used in subsequent inquiries, and then it presents itself as an object or ordered set of objects. But to treat *it* as an object involves confusion of two things which are experientially different: viz., an object of cognition and a situation that is noncognitively had. (LW12: 525-26)

Also, by further characterization the initial problem-setting situation of inquiry can be distinguished.

> Thus, it is of the very nature of the indeterminate situation which evokes inquiry to be *questionable*; or, in terms of actuality instead of potentiality, to be uncertain, unsettled, disturbed. The peculiar quality of what pervades the given materials, constituting them a situation, is not just uncertainty at large; it is a unique doubtfulness which makes that situation to be just and only the situation it is. . . . It is the *situation* that has these traits. We are doubtful because the situation is inherently doubtful. (LW12:109)

The emphases in these passages on how we experience a situation, on the fact that its character is precisely and no more than how it appears in its immediate presence as a qualitative whole, would seem to indicate that Dewey is well aware that a situation cannot be designated or initially characterized by means of the importation of any "cognitive" or theoretical apparatus and certainly not by some externally introduced theory about it, whether psychological, biological, or whatever, without doing violence to its role before, in, or after inquiry.

Situations, so introduced, play a role in Dewey's logic by virtue of the fact that they and only they exhibit, in their differences and in a certain serial ordering, the pattern of inquiry. What Dewey provides us with at the beginning of his *logical* presentation is *a contextual framework of notions* that is intended to indicate the ambit within which all further logical notions, such as those of various logical forms, are to be logically placed and understood. The framework is itself designated under the title "inquiry."[8] It is then filled out by characterizing it as consisting of a changing succession or stream of situations, as they are experienced by an agent as wholes pervaded by a unique and relevance-guiding quality, which is evoked by an indeterminate situation, followed by a problematic situation, and involves phases of agentive input and control which serve to transform the succeeding situations toward the achievement of a determinate situation. This framework is *bedrock* in the carrying forward of any inquiry into inquiry that is directed to solving a problem of the general sort which Dewey assumes, that is, one which is concerned with the identification and ground of logical forms. Simply put, the framework of inquiry, including its general pattern, provides the context to which Dewey appeals in his functional characterization of logical forms.

Dewey rather consistently depicts inquiry as a succession of situations. But another way of talking about inquiry that also makes sense to Dewey would be to say that it consists of a continuous course or stream of ongoing and ever-changing experience. Dewey *could* have referred in the *Logic* to this entire course of experience, which constitutes an inquiry, in the countterm fashion in which he spoke of "an experience" in *Art as Experience* (1934), by stipulating a use of the term *situation* to indicate the whole. He did not take this path. The reason he did not is perhaps this. It was important for logical purposes to construe the framework of inquiry in a manner that preserved the view of the inquiring agent as being *en route*, concerned with work to be done, with engaging within an unfinished and only hopefully consummated project. To treat the whole of inquiry as an experience, as one situation, would be to treat it as though it were consummated, finished, rounded off, done. From the inquiring agent's perspective, however, it is always in process, in the making. And as such, from within the course of experience, it is lived through in such a way that, at whatever present place the agent stands, the scope of the experience had is temporally horizoned. No doubt the description of this ongoing process in terms of a *succession of situations* is misleading in its suggestion of discreteness or hard-and-fast boundaries between situations. Apart from some experienced gap between or obvious closure of situations, there is no way to understand this succession as a plurality other than on some such metaphor as that employed by George Herbert Mead: Each situation of a temporal succession of situations "slides into" the next.

The experientially had present of a situation is itself temporal, that is to say, it includes change. A situation is not an instantaneous, temporally dimensionless, slice or cut in the experiential flow. Internal to experience, the aptness of the notion of a single, qualitatively unified situation is nonetheless already decided by the manner in which the inquiring agent's immediately had experience is temporally and spatially horizoned. But since each situation "slides" into its successor without break, the agent's immediately had experience is continually shifting its horizon. It makes no sense to ask, then, how many situations made up this or that course of experience. There is a sense of plurality which does not yield to denumerability.

Two Mistakes

> To read back into the preliminary situation those distinctions of mere conjunction of material and of valid coherence which get existence, to say nothing of fixation, only within the process of inquiry is a fallacy. (Dewey 1903, MW2:328)

Given the pattern of inquiry into inquiry proposed, there are two sorts of mistakes which may easily be made by one who, without proper care, attempts to make sense of Dewey's general logical theory. Both are mistakes of reading back into an earlier phase of inquiry into inquiry items that have their proper place only in a later phase.[9]

(a) Items appropriate for the provision of a background theory for a theory of inquiry should not be imported into *either* the logical theory *or* the pretheoretical presentation (designation or characterization) of the subject-matter to which that theory is claimed to be adequate. This pertains to assumptions or concepts that are not explicitly part of the logical theory but that have their home in a background theory (whether metaphysical, epistemological, or whatever) which is or might be invoked in order to explain or otherwise support the logical theory. Also it hardly needs saying that no such assumptions or concepts can be allowed into the initial presentation of the logical subject-matter without spoiling its pretheoretical and incorrigibly perspectival character. An offense in either of these respects is what we may call *a mistake of improper importation*.

(b) Items appropriate for logical theory as such should not appear in the pretheoretical presentation (designation or characterization) of the subject-matter of logical theory. This precludes any reference to or use of assumptions or concepts which have their home in any logical account or theory that is being tested for applicability. The point is that the subject-matter that is presented and articulated at the pretheoretical level is a subject-matter against which, without begging the issue, some theory or element of a theory is to be considered and tested. An offense of this general sort is, we might say, *a mistake of improper characterization*. It follows from this, for example, that no description or characterization of any constituent of the subject-matter can contain any reference to a logical form which is so identified only at the level of theory. One cannot be allowed to build into *any* presentation of the subject-matter *any* content or form that invokes or presupposes *any* part of the theory that serves to identify such a content or form as a logical form.

Unfortunately, we find that these mistakes are fairly common. I will, however, limit my discussion to an example of each drawn from Tom Burke's *Dewey's New Logic* (1994), which is easily the best book-length work yet published on Dewey's logical theory. That Burke seems to fall into these mistakes indicates how very insidious they are.

In the second chapter of his book Burke begins an extended criticism of Russell's misunderstandings of Dewey's logic. Much of what he says in this chapter centers around Russell's contention that Dewey, in keeping with his strong Hegelian influence, is logically committed to the view that a situation must embrace the entire universe. Since, however, it is an essential and grounding claim of Dewey's logic of inquiry that each of the many different inquiries which we have undertaken in our lives is evoked by an indeterminate situation that is unique and distinct from any other situation and that, in the course of each successful inquiry, the evoking indeterminate situation is succeeded by a series of situations which, though problematic, are replaced eventually by a distinct but determinate situation, Burke finds it important to set out in detail Dewey's view of situations and to show how each situation is to be understood as limited and locally specific. Burke conceives this issue as one of "finding bounds" for situations, and about halfway through the chapter he indicates the direction in which a solution may be found.

> Note that one approach to a solution might be to appeal to certain cognitive notions, such as arguing that we can think of a situation "under a description" and thereby put boundaries of a sort on it. But this is contrary to what Dewey was trying to do with the notion of a situation. Dewey would relativize situations to organisms and environments, to particular dispositional perspectives, even concretely to particular instances of breakdown in organism/environment affairs. But it would beg the question to appeal to a cognitive notion of objects or situations "under this or that description" in the present context. The aim is to be able to make sense of cognitive intentionality, once we have recourse to the notion of situation, not the other way around. . . . What follows may seem like an odd path out of the problem of

finding bounds for situations because it is a "pre-cognitive" one—i.e., one which by design does not initially have cognitive notions to appeal to. The argument here will be that situations are bounded by the reach, scope, or content of a living creature's experience. (Burke 1994, 36-37)

Now this makes good sense of Dewey's own approach, especially if we understand Burke as saying that we cannot appeal to the description of a situation as "relativized . . . to instances of breakdown in organism/environment affairs." Unfortunately, Burke soon lapses back into an approach that he adopted earlier in the chapter, an approach that "defines" a situation in just this way. For example, some six pages later Burke writes, "[W]e have to address the question of what it is in Dewey's theory which can independently account for the boundedness of situations in the first place. It is in fact Dewey's definition of a situation as an instance of disequilibrium which guarantees this boundedness" (43). He continues in this vein in the next paragraph:

> Previous discussion has indicated how incredibly complex situations can be, but also how incredibly simple they can be. That is to say, Dewey's theory of inquiry has to be able to guarantee that inquiring into the tides, for instance, may directly involve the moon and stars, but dealing with a car which will not start or finding one's way to a grocery store probably will not. Simply put, such boundedness is entailed by Dewey's characterization of situations as concrete fields of organism/environment "life functions" subject to, and directed away from, breakdowns. (43-44)

Part of what is wrong with this approach is that it is not precognitive, for the characterization of situations to which Burke appeals derives from an explanatory theory of a highly cognitive sort. But the main problem is that this approach brings into the discussion considerations which are not part and cannot be part of Dewey's logical theory. In fact, that theory rests solidly and consistently upon that notion of a situation which, experientially had as limited and horizoned from the start, provides the bedrock structure of the contextual framework of inquiry into inquiry itself. It is not that Dewey would disagree with the "characterization" which Burke takes to "independently account" for the boundedness of situations; it is just that that characterization derives, not from Dewey's logic as theory of inquiry and not from a theory to be examined and tested from a logician's perspective, but from Dewey's background theory, which is invoked to explain the items that appear in his logic. And this is, as indicated earlier, to make the mistake of improper importation.

Let me now note briefly one manner in which Burke improperly introduces a genuinely logical notion from Dewey's logical theory into his characterization of the subject-matter of inquiry into inquiry, thereby making the mistake of improper characterization. This is involved in his use of the notion of causality in such passages as these:

> An organism/environment system may well be said to include everything that it is causally linked to (though we may safely remain neutral about that), but not so for a situation. A situation may be causally linked to but not contain those parts of the organism/environment system to which the respective disturbance (and its eventual rectification) does not extend. (Burke 1994, 48)

> The existence of causal connections between events is not enough to make them parts of a single whole, or at least not parts of a single situation. The question is not how far causal connections reach, since that is virtually boundless. It is rather a question of how far the breakdown in normal causal processes reaches. (52)

Now, it may make sense to talk of an organism/environmental system in causal terms, but if so that is because a notion of causality is devised to serve in making sense of the interconnection of "objects," in Dewey's sense of that term. That is, talking of causes in that context can only be a way of talking about objects that are introduced, identified, and described from the standpoint of some background theory. It may even make sense to talk of causal connections between events, so long, that is, as we mean to indicate by the term *events* objects of a sort that is theoretically sanctioned. But, be that as it may, causal talk is completely and thoroughly inappropriate in regard to situations as Dewey introduces them into inquiry and into the subject-matter with which inquiry is concerned. It's a mistake for the simple reason that the notion of causation is identified as a logical form in Dewey's logical theory and because no such item of logical status can be introduced back into the subject-matter against which it is to be tested, as though it were somehow, antecedently to inquiry, already there.

Now the claim that causality is a logical form is not a view "that will receive ready acceptance" (Dewey 1938, LW12:456). But it is Dewey's view, as the following passages make clear.

> [T]he category of causation accrues to existential subject-matter as a logical form when and because determinate problems about such subject-matter are present. . . . While the category is logical, not ontological, it is *not an arbitrary* logical postulate. (LW12:454)

The conclusion to be drawn is that the ontological interpretation is to be abandoned. Recognition of the value of the causal category as a leading principle of existential inquiry is in fact confirmed, and the theory of causation is brought into consonance with scientific practice. The institution of qualitative individual existential situations consisting of ordered sequences and coexistences is the goal of all existential inquiry. "Causation" is a category that directs the operations by which this goal is reached in the case of problematic situations. (LW12:457)

If we accept this, then situations as they are lived through—and as they form the bedrock framework of inquiry—cannot be legitimately characterized by assuming that they are, by their nature or by definition, subject to causal connections.

A final point: There is an ordinary and nontechnical way of talking of causes and effects. We can hardly get by without it. Dewey talks this way quite often. A rather humorous example of this is found in the very midst of an extended discussion in which he insists that causality, because it is a logical form, is not to be employed except functionally and in the context of inquiry. He says: "Already difficulties have arisen in actual scientific findings which have caused some persons to believe that the whole idea of causation must be thrown overboard" (1938, LW12:456-57). But the manner in which Burke brings causal connections into the above passages can hardly be of this kind. He is in those contexts attempting to answer the question of "boundedness" by being as careful and theoretically precise in his language as he can.

Concluding Remark

My concern has been limited to the issues of the designation and characterization of the subject-matter as they arise in inquiry into inquiry. They certainly arise there. The natural question is whether they also arise in cases of primary inquiry. I believe that they do. They arise in the context of that phase of inquiry which Dewey, in presenting his account of the pattern of inquiry, terms "the institution of a problem." Though not the initial *reflective* move of inquiry, which is the taking of an indeterminate situation to be problematic (Dewey 1938, LW12:111), this is the first move of a distinctively *theoretical* sort. Nonetheless, this move involves or presupposes a certain provisional *pretheoretical* circumscribing of a subject-matter which becomes, upon the institution of the problem, the relevant *content*, to use Dewey's term for reference to subject-matter considered in the course of inquiry "in the context of either observation or ideation" (LW12:122). In regard to what is involved in the institution of a problem, Dewey is disappointingly laconic, but he does say this: "The way in which the problem is conceived decides what specific suggestions are entertained and which are dismissed; what data are selected and which rejected; it is the criterion for relevancy and irrelevancy of hypotheses and conceptual structures" (LW12:112).

But this notion of a "criterion for relevancy" is misleading if taken out of context, for a few pages earlier he notes that "the peculiar quality" which "pervades" the indeterminate situation "not only evokes the particular inquiry engaged in but . . . exercises control over its special procedures" (LW12:109). Taking the two passages together, I can only assume that the *force* of the "criterion," its very instrumentality, derives from the qualitative character of a subject-matter which, though pretheoretically designated, is, in the same breath, so to speak, identified for the purpose of becoming a content.

Thus it is that designation and characterization may well be, at least in most cases of inquiry in which there is no appeal to a community of inquirers, merely implicit in the first crude conception of the problem. On the other hand, in such cases as those which we might call "philosophical" or "logical," the role of designation and characterization must, I think, be potentially dialogical and thus capable of being opened to other inquirers. For that purpose the initial and provisional designation and characterization, as well as any later revisions of either, must be carefully attended to in order that they be formulated in such a way as to be sharable. Surely there are many cases of that sort. And inquiry into inquiry is clearly one of them.

Notes

1. I will outline these three hypotheses below. For the present let me point out that it is the last of these hypotheses (H3) which Dewey wishes his entire book to "justify." The term is his. "It is not the task of this chapter to try to justify this hypothesis. . . . That is the business of the work as a whole" (Dewey 1938, LW12:12).

2. Dewey's method of discovery (i.e., inquiry) and the procedure that he adopts for presenting his position should be carefully distinguished. The latter, to which he faithfully adheres in the *Logic*—as well as in *The Quest for Certainty* (1929) and *Experience and Nature* (1925)—involves, first, the offering of a hypothesis and then, usually in the order listed, satisfying the three conditions of providing for that hypothesis a *vera causa*, ordering and accounting for the subject-matter to which the hypothesis is directed as that subject-matter has been (I would say) pretheoretically characterized, and accounting for the arguments presented for and the apparent

adequacy of rival hypotheses which have been or might have been advanced. Cf. Dewey 1938, LW12:11.

3. Dewey speaks of "inquiry into inquiry." I will sometimes speak of "inquiry into inquiries." I take the phrases to mean the same thing, and I use them interchangeably. Tom Burke has suggested that I may be mistaken in this, that Dewey's inquiry into inquiry may be an inquiry into *inquiry-in-general*. But surely Dewey would deny that there is such a subject-matter as inquiry-in-general or inquiry *überhaupt*. Indeed, the only *general* conception of inquiry is that which is arrived at in the process of developing a general *theory* of inquiry.

4. I adopt this terminology from a passage in the *Logic* where Dewey concludes a long analogy of judgment, in his technical sense, with judgment in a court of law. The relevant remarks are these: "The sentence is a proposition, differing, however, from the propositions formed during the trial, whether they concern matters of fact or legal conceptions, in that it takes overt effect in operations which construct a new qualitative situation. While prior propositions are means of instituting the sentence, the sentence is terminal as a means of instituting a definite existential situation" (LW12:125). We have, then, three distinguishable (though not separable) items: the proposition which constitutes the final hypothesis, the performatory sentence or "asserting" of that hypothesis (something like "So be it!"), and the sentence qua judgment, which is the actual instituting of "the resulting state of actual affairs" (LW12:124-25).

5. Logic as the *theory of inquiry* cannot be identified with inquiry into inquiry; it can only be, in some sense, the result of such inquiry. Unfortunately, Dewey is himself somewhat sloppy about this. He says, "Logic as inquiry into inquiry is, if you please, a circular process" (LW12:28). Of course, there is nothing wrong with using the term *logic* in this fashion; we do use it often to indicate something like a process of studying such and so. But the title of the book is more revealing of the central use of the term: Logic is the *theory* of inquiry.

6. Tom Burke is not so misled, perhaps, but he does devote considerable discussion (in his 1994 book *Dewey's New Logic*) to how the metaphysical picture of situations which Russell takes to be assumed by Dewey is not in fact representative of Dewey's own metaphysical assumptions. One effect of this, whether intended by Burke or not, is that such metaphysical disputes come to appear as issues which make some sort of sense from the logician's perspective. As we have seen, this cannot be so. From the logician's perspective, the proper reply to Russell would be not that his and Dewey's worldviews were different but that Russell's metaphysical assumptions (as well as Dewey's own) were simply irrelevant to the issue of the logic of inquiry. Burke may well want to deny that Dewey's metaphysics is a part of his logical theory, but he allows certain metaphysical views to intrude into his conception of the logical status of situations.

7. For example, Dewey argues that the category of causality is a logical form (1938, LW12:454), a view surely at variance with most traditional theories of causality or logical form. But this comes as a benefit of his theory, not as an initial assumption.

8. This is not quite sufficient, for the framework is one of a possible succession

of inquiries, such that the "relied upon" content of one inquiry may be carried forward into subsequent inquiries as provisionally "reliable" assumptions. It is this extension of the framework which allows the proposal of one of the foundational hypotheses regarding inquiry under the title "the continuum of inquiry."

9. In the final analysis, both of these mistakes are cases of what Dewey often calls the "philosophical fallacy," which he defines in *Experience and Nature* as "the conversion of eventual functions into antecedent existence" (1925, LW1:34) and to which he gives a more pointed reading in the *Logic* in regard to improper characterization as "the conversion of a function in inquiry into an independent structure" (1938, LW12:151) or the "hypostatization of a logical function into a supraempirical entity" (LW12:135).

Works Cited

Burke, Thomas. 1994. *Dewey's New Logic: A Reply to Russell*. Chicago: University of Chicago Press.

Dewey, John. 1916. *Essays in Experimental Logic*. Chicago: University of Chicago Press. Essays reprinted separately in MW1, 2, 4, 6, 8, 10.

———. 1925-53. *The Later Works*. 17 vols. Edited by Jo Ann Boydston. Carbondale: Southern Illinois University Press, 1981-90. Citations of items in this edition are indicated by LW followed by volume and page numbers.

———. 1925. *Experience and Nature*. Chicago: Open Court. Reprinted in LW1.

———. 1929: *The Quest for Certainty*. New York: Minton, Balch. Reprinted in LW4.

———. 1934. *Art as Experience*. New York: Henry Holt. Reprinted in LW10.

———. 1938. *Logic: The Theory of Inquiry*. New York: Henry Holt. Reprinted in LW12.

———, ed. 1903. *Studies in Logical Theory*. University of Chicago Decennial Publications, 2d ser., vol. 11. Chicago: University of Chicago Press. Dewey's contributions reprinted in Dewey 1916, 75-182, and in MW2:293-375.

8

Dewey's Logical Forms

Hans Seigfried

> Without systematic formulation of ruling ideas, inquiry is
> kept in the domain of opinion and action in the realm of
> conflict. (Dewey 1938, LW12:501)

With his 1938 *Logic*, Dewey presents a theory of directed and controlled
experimental inquiry. He claims that the control of inquiry depends on what
he calls logical forms. They are the conditions which all inquiry must satisfy. Only knowledge of these general, and as such formal, conditions can
furnish axioms, or guiding principles, required for the control of inquiry,
and criteria for recognizing patterns of successful inquiry.[1] And yet, in the
presentation of his theory there is no detailed account of the origin and
nature of these axioms and principles. What is said about them is said in
passing.

In the preface, Dewey (LW12:5) says that his treatise is introductory and
that he is well aware that in this form the presentation of his point of view
and method of approach "does not have and could not have the finish and
completeness that are theoretically possible." But he is convinced, he adds,
that his standpoint is "so thoroughly sound that those who are willing to
entertain it will in coming years develop a theory of logic that is in thorough accord with all the best authenticated methods of attaining knowledge." In this essay, I am willing to entertain his standpoint and try to
clarify some puzzling aspects of Dewey's idea of logical forms, and through
comparison-contrast of his theory with the theories of Plato and Kant, I will
bring out what is radically new and philosophically promising in his exceptional account of the forms and axioms of controlled inquiry.

Dewey (LW12:21, 24f.) agrees with Plato and Kant that these formal conditions are a priori conditions, that is, "demands, requirements, postulates,
to be fulfilled" by all inquiries, but he insists against them that these demands are only the empirically, temporally, and operationally a priori conditions of all inquiry. For understanding the possibility of controlled and

successful inquiry, it is not necessary to postulate that they are permanently and externally fixed, "fixed antecedently to inquiry and conditioning it *ab extra*" (LW12:19). Like Plato before him, Dewey (1929, LW4:231) contends, Kant was able to "assert the existence of his apparatus of forms and categories" only on the basis of "an elaborate process of dialectical inference"; his forms are "as inaccessible to observation as were the occult forms and essences whose rejection was a prerequisite of development of modern science." In contrast, Dewey sees in the logical forms of inquiry "formulations of conditions, discovered in the course of inquiry itself, which further inquiries must satisfy if they are to yield warranted assertibility as a consequence" (1938, LW12:24). Kant still believed, says Dewey, that the understanding has rules and principles in itself that are logically prior and external to experience and inquiry. Against Kant Dewey claims that all such rules or logical forms of inquiry "arise within the operation of inquiry and are concerned with control of inquiry so that it may yield warranted assertions" (LW12:11). Any such rule, Dewey argues, is only empirically, temporally, and operationally a priori in the sense that "while it is derived from what is involved in inquiries that have been successful in the past, it imposes a condition to be satisfied in future inquiries, until the results of such inquiries show reason for modifying it" (LW12:25).

I will try to answer three questions about Dewey's peculiar understanding of the axioms of controlled inquiry. First, how is it possible to "derive" from past investigations of concrete subject-matters directives for future inquiries into all subject-matters? Dewey claims that certain directives "must be employed if assertibility is to be obtained as an end" (LW12:21, 23f.). How then can we justify the "imposition" of formal conditions to be satisfied in all inquiries? Second, how can abstract logical forms fruitfully direct investigations into concrete subject-matters? And third, what criteria must we use for determining that warranted assertibility has been obtained in a given case?

The answer to the first question takes up the greater part of this essay; it makes replies to the other questions predictable, so they can be much briefer. In my development of the answers, I argue that Dewey's understanding of logical forms is based on an alternative to the received epistemological understanding of knowledge as accurate representation of the real. His axioms of inquiry cannot direct the search for knowledge in the received sense; they are meant to direct the search for propositions as promising proposals for the transformation of the real and for the resolution of existential conflict situations. I conclude with a brief review of the advantages and disadvantages of the two accounts of inquiry for the efficient management of human affairs.

The Experiential Continuum of Inquiry

At the very outset, Dewey claims that the application of the principle of the experiential continuum of inquiry makes it possible to give an empirical account of logical forms, "whose necessity traditional empiricism overlooked or denied" (LW12:3), and to prove that Plato's and Kant's interpretations of them as completely a priori are unnecessary.[2] Only Peirce, he claims, had previously noted the importance of this continuity. And yet, as Dewey points out,

> That earlier conclusions have the function of preparing the way for later inquiries and judgments, and that the later are dependent upon facts and conceptions instituted in earlier ones, are commonplaces in the intellectual development of individuals and the historic growth of any science. . . . It would even be too obvious to be worth mentioning were it not that this continuity is something more than an indispensable condition of intellectual growth. It is the only principle by which certain fundamentally important logical forms can be understood; namely, those of standardized general conceptions and of general propositions. (LW12:245f.)

In an effort to bar misunderstandings of his "fundamental 'doctrine of the continuum of inquiry,'" Dewey subsequently reemphasizes the claim he made in *Logic* that this continuum is a thoroughly "temporal existential continuum" (1942, LW15:37). No matter how general and abstract, Dewey argues in *Logic* (1938, LW12:480), all logical forms are relative to the temporal existential continuum of inquiry from which they derive and which they serve. The syllogistic form, for example,

> serves as a check in the case of specific judgments, holding up the logical conditions that are to be satisfied. It represents a limiting ideal. Even though no actual judgment really satisfies the ideal conditions, a perception of failure to do so occasions and directs further inquiry upon both the observational and the conceptual sides. It promotes and supports the continuum of inquiry. (LW12:326)

As Dewey points out, what gives a mere opportunity and possibility a definite logical form is "explicit formulation in propositional form of the expectation [of inquiry], together with active use of the formulation as a means of controlling and checking further operations in the continuum of inquiry" (LW12:250). Naturally, we cannot give such a formulation of the expectation of the whole experiential continuum; we would be able to give it only, as Peirce argued, at that "ideal limit towards which endless investigation would tend to bring scientific belief." In temporally restricted, well-planned investigations, some abstract statement may look like such a formulation only by virtue of its inaccuracy and one-sidedness.[3] Its continuity and temporal character, then, make total control of inquiry with logical forms and axioms impossible.

And yet Dewey makes it clear that it is the fundamental thesis of his theory of inquiry that "logical forms accrue to subject-matter when the latter is subjected to controlled inquiry" (LW12:105). What calls for the control of inquiry, Dewey argues, are not the abstractions of free-floating speculation but indeterminate existential conflict situations (LW12:108). In each case it is such a situation that calls for inquiry as a means for "the controlled or directed transformation" of the situation "into a unified whole." In an earlier discussion of "the new logic" that emerged from Galilean and Darwinian inquiries, Dewey contends that what is required for such a transformation of the concrete circumstances of indeterminate situations is the exploration of the specific, existent conditions that generate them. The search for absolute finalities and the efforts to formulate ultimate expectations in propositional form turn inquiry into unbridled analysis, remove our conclusions from subjection to experimental testing, and make impossible even minimally responsible control of inquiry (1910, MW4:11f.). Even if such final inclusive propositions were "a thousand times dialectically demonstrated," the management of human affairs would not thereby be one less step forwarded. And were it not for the inbred refusal to accept the temporality and malleability of human existence, such demonstrations "would be despised in comparison with the demonstrations of experience that knowable energies are daily generating about us precious [resources]."

Dewey's observation that the temporality and malleability of the human condition make the control of inquiry necessary is not particularly new, nor is Dewey's critique of the traditional belief that such control is possible *only* by an appeal to "a fixed structure of eternal and unchanging principles already in our possession to which everything else should be made to conform" (1944, LW15:273). In the past, Plato believed that we could take possession of such a fixed structure through dialectical reasoning about a supersensible realm of forms. More recently neo-Kantians believed it to be a set of a priori rules of operation inscribed in our minds that can be expressed and formalized in concepts. Presently philosophical realists believe it to be something that inference can extrapolate from the reality of experience and that is "real in the same sense (whatever that is) as rocks on the ground," just as are the laws of physics, as Steven Weinberg (1998, 52; 1996, 14) claims. Dewey explicitly mentions the distinctively American attitude and outlook that led Peirce to reject such views (LW15:273), but we could easily list the criticism many others leveled, before and since then, against the traditional belief in fixity that implies, as Dewey observes, "the dogmatism that historically has always exhibited itself in intolerance and brutal persecution of the dissenter and the inquirer." Yet traditional beliefs in "rock-bottom" reality and absolute fixity retain their seductive appeal despite such dark sides, due to fear of "anything goes," failure to recognize the profound difference between flux and change, and inability to see (as Dewey puts it in his 1934 discussion of "Criticism [Judgment] and Perception") that "nature and life manifest not flux but continuity, and continuity involves forces and structures that endure through change" (LW10:327). Against the counterproductive fear of change and flux, Dewey observes that "there is also the definite implication that change can mean continuous growth, development, liberation, and cooperation" in the conduct of human affairs (1944, LW15:273). This observation explains, perhaps, what originally led to the development of the new theory of inquiry, which substitutes the new "faith in endlessly pursued inquiry and in an undogmatic friendly attitude toward present possessions (which is the spur to continued persistent effort)" for the old belief in fixity.

For such reasons, then, two early chapters in *Logic* are devoted to the clarification of the endless continuum of inquiry. It is the framework, or existential matrix, within which inquiry actually operates. Dewey agrees that logic "does not depend upon anything extraneous to inquiry," and that the meaning of concepts and principles must be assigned to them exclusively "in terms of what is discovered by inquiry into inquiry" (1938, LW12:28f.). But the study of what actually occurs shows that such meanings cannot be determined apart from the context of inquiry and that the traditional assumption that context is extraneous to logical subject-matter is mistaken. The chapters on the existential matrix are occupied, says Dewey, "with the development of the statement that logic is naturalistic" (LW12:30). It is naturalistic in a twofold sense, says Dewey:

> As [the term *naturalistic*] is here employed it means, on one side, that there is no breach of continuity between operations of inquiry and biological operations and physical operations. "Continuity," on the other side, means that rational operations *grow out of* organic activities, without being identical with that from which they emerge. . . . The logic in question is also naturalistic in the sense of observability, in the ordinary sense of the word, of activities of inquiry. Conceptions derived from a mystical faculty of *intuition* or anything that is so occult as not to be open to public inspection and verification (such as the purely psychical for example) are excluded. (LW12:26)

The involvement of biological factors in inquiry does not indicate, says Dewey, that there is some deep metaphysical or epistemological problem, such as the mind-body problem (LW12:30). It means that we must "accept the undeniable fact that they are necessary factors in inquiry," and then consider how they operate. Of course, the environment in which we act and inquire, says Dewey, is "not simply physical. It is cultural as well." The situations that call for inquiry "grow out of the relations of fellow beings to one another, and the organs for dealing with these relations are not only the eye and ear, but the meanings which have developed in the course of living, together with the ways of forming and transmitting culture with all its constituents of tools, arts, institutions, traditions and customary beliefs" (LW12:48). The ways we respond "even to physical" conditions are to a large extent influenced by our cultural environment.[4]

The two matrix-chapters are supposed to show in some detail how these biological and cultural factors and influences prepare for deliberate controlled inquiry and how they suggest its pattern; or as Dewey restates their purpose at the end, they are supposed to give an analytical account of the "transformation of animal activities into intelligent behavior having the properties which, when formulated, are *logical* in nature" (LW12:62). The primary postulate of a naturalistic theory, Dewey says, is "continuity of the lower (less complex) and the higher (more complex) activities and forms" (LW12:30). The idea of continuity is not self-explanatory, but "it precludes reduction of the 'higher' to 'the lower' just as it precludes complete breaks and gaps." Its meaning is illustrated by the growth and development of any organism from seed to maturity. What course such development takes must be established by "a study of what actually occurs." The following remarks state what Dewey believes to be the main finding of such a study.

> Indeed, living may be regarded as a continual rhythm of disequilibrations and recoveries of equilibrium. The "higher" the organism, the more serious become the disturbances and the more energetic (and often more prolonged) are the efforts necessary for its reestablishment. The state of disturbed equilibration constitutes *need*. The movement towards its restoration is search and exploration. The recovery is fulfilment or satisfaction. (LW12:34)[5]

Satisfaction is accomplished through the integrated interaction of the organism and its environment (i.e., the natural world that exists independently of the organism as it directly or indirectly takes on life functions), and it represents equilibrium of energies in the organism and the existence of satisfying conditions in the natural world. The interaction of higher organisms with their environment, Dewey argues, does not simply restore the initial conditions before disintegration; it changes conditions on both sides (LW12: 38). The modification that occurs in the organism conditions further behavior; it constitutes what we call habits that are "the basis of organic learning." This modification especially characterizes human activities carried on for satisfying needs. They "so change the environment," Dewey finds, "that new needs arise which demand still further change in the activities of the organism by which they are satisfied; and so on in a potentially endless chain" (LW12:35).

From such considerations, Dewey draws two general conclusions in support of his claim that the pattern of inquiry is the development of certain aspects of the pattern of life activities: (1) "Environmental conditions and energies are inherent in inquiry as a special mode of organic behavior," and (2) "The structure and course of life-behavior has a definite pattern, spatial and temporal. This pattern definitely foreshadows the general pattern of inquiry" (LW12:39ff.). But it certainly does not exemplify or fulfill it. For controlled inquiry to be possible at all, more drastic modifications and transformations are necessary. His analysis of the cultural matrix shows how such modifications occur.

Cultural modifications, Dewey claims, transform purely organic behavior into behavior marked by "intellectual properties . . . that mark off the activities and achievements of human beings from those of other biological forms" (LW12:49). Since these extraordinary differences led to theories that trace them to some non-natural source, Dewey feels that it is necessary to demonstrate that "the development of language (in its widest sense) out of prior biological activities is, in its connection with wider cultural forces, the key to this transformation. The problem . . . is not the problem of the transition of organic behavior into something wholly discontinuous with it. . . . It is a special form of the general problem of continuity of change and the emergence of new modes of activity—the problem of development at any level" (LW12:49f.).

It is obvious that language occupies a peculiarly significant place in the cultural environment. Dewey lists three reasons for it: (1) "It is the agency by which other institutions and acquired habits are *transmitted,*" (2) "It *permeates* both the forms and the contents of all other cultural activities," and (3) Its own peculiar structure is "capable of abstraction as a *form*" (LW12:51). In the past, the last aspect had a decisive influence on the development of logical theory, and it remains peculiarly important for the theory of inquiry because these abstractions can be appropriately symbolized and instrumentalized. Dewey admits that he takes the influence of the wider cultural environment for granted and restricts his analysis to "the especial function of language in effecting the transformation of the biological into the intellectual and the potentially logical."

Dewey draws the following four conclusions from his analysis: First, "'culture' . . . , as distinguished from 'nature', is both a condition and a product of language." Second, "animal activities, such as eating and drinking, searching for food, copulation, etc., acquire new properties. Eating food becomes a group festival and celebration." Third, "apart from the existence of symbol-meanings the results of prior experience are retained only through strictly organic modifications. . . . The existence of symbols makes possible *deliberate* recollection and expectation, and thereby the institution of new combinations of selected elements of experiences having an intellectual dimension" (emphasis added). Fourth, "organic biological activities end in overt actions, whose consequences are irretrievable. When an activity and its consequences can be rehearsed by representation in symbolic terms, there is no such final commitment" (LW12:62f.). Activities can be reconsidered, replanned, or avoided altogether. Certainly, these grounds make control of life activities possible, but they do not show by what means we may accomplish it. Dewey therefore cautions:

> These [cultural] transformations and others which they suggest, are not of themselves equivalent to accrual of logical properties to behavior. But they provide requisite conditions for it. The use of meaning-symbols for institution of purposes or ends-in-view, for deliberation, as a rehearsal through such symbols of the activities by which the ends may be brought into being, is at least a rudimentary form of reasoning in connection with solution of problems. (LW12:63)

Logical theory has its origin, Dewey claims, in efforts to explicitly formulate with the help of symbols some of the conditions implicit in the connections that emerge in "the ordered development of meanings in their relation to one another." The theory of inquiry began with the reflection on language, on "*logos*, in its syntactical structure and wealth of meaning contents," and unfortunately it had as its first result "the hypostatization of *Logos*" that for centuries frustrated efforts to develop inquiries adequate for dealing with problems of the existent world.[6] The necessity of existential operations for "application of meaning to natural existence" was ignored, Dewey argues, and the hypostatized, supposedly immutable, forms of syntactical structures were assigned superior status and thereby "isolated from the operations by means of which meanings originate, function and are tested." The traditional petrification of the cultural conditions of inquiry made it impossible to make use of "the immense potentialities for attainment of knowledge that were resident in the activities of the arts—resident in them because they involve operations of active modification of existing conditions which contain the procedures constituting the experimental method when once they are employed for the sake of obtaining knowledge" (LW12:64).

Under the traditional setup, then, control of inquiry was an illusion because it was achieved by subordination and final commitment to given sociocultural conditions. Against such dogmatism, Dewey means to demonstrate that genuine control is possible only through the experimental operations of deliberation as a rehearsal through symbols of the activities by which solutions of problems and ends-in-view may be realized. He provides grounds for replacing the traditional static forms of inquiry in his account of the "accrual" of successful ways of inquiry, habits, and traditions that constitute the cumulative continuity of inquiry. Of themselves, however, such ways, habits, and traditions of inquiry are not equivalent to the strictly operational logical forms Dewey's theory is supposed to account for. For they could, and often do, amount to the abdication of control and surrender to what once was functional before changed existential conditions frustrated it.

Ways, Habits, and Traditions

Dewey states the obvious when he says that "any habit is a way or manner of action, not a particular act or deed" (LW12:21). In the past, philosophers failed in their efforts to explain the fact of habit. Peirce made the first promising move, Dewey claims, when he connected the fact, "as Hume and Mill did not, with basic organic or biological functions instead of leaving habit as an ultimate 'mysterious' tie" (LW12:20n3). In his own studies, such as *Human Nature and Conduct*, *Art as Experience*, and *Logic: The Theory of Inquiry*, Dewey traces these connections and examines in much detail the transformation of animal activities into intelligent behavior and cultivated habits.

He points out that the relations of organisms to their environment, the rhythms of struggle and consummation, are varied and prolonged, and he describes this ebb and flow as an organized and organizing process of acting upon the environment and being acted upon by it. In the course of this process, organism and environment become integral parts of a continuous transaction of doing and undergoing. Repeated failures lead to the destruction of organism and/or environment, and successful interactions are renewed in further transactions whereby something is retained as an integral part of the organism that organizes its behavior into specific ways of seeking fulfillment. As pointed out earlier, Dewey argues that such biological modifications constitute what is called "organic learning."

At least among the lower animals, biological activities end in overt actions whose consequences are final and irretrievable; in other words, the way they are realized is not explicitly planned, rehearsed, and eventually chosen from among alternative ways. Actions are taken blindly and automatically, as it were, in the same way they were taken before, until repeated failure to reach fulfillment in a given environment requires the reshaping of the ready-made organization of the abilities of the organism, that is, the sequencing of the organic operations for securing prompt and exact adjustment to the environment is shaped and reshaped by objective environmental conditions. What directs the organic process on the side of the organism is the inscribed organization of its abilities, i.e., instinct. Since this organization is a function of strictly reactive operations, acting by instinct is a form of undergoing that cannot be genuinely controlled; it is a happening, rather than doing. Still, in this process the organism gets enriched by the "accrual" of a reorganization of its abilities that secures an adequate adjustment to its changing environment.

Control of the "accrual" of the organization of the abilities of organisms becomes possible, however, through the development of instrumentalities for the rehearsing of activities that, as Dewey puts it, "lack the complex ready-made organization of the animals' original abilities" (1922, MW14:77), such as our native human activities, for example, processing information about and making sense of the world around us by connecting things and understanding situations and events in linear terms of cause and effect, and by making inferences from one to the other. By representing such activities in symbolic terms we can play and replay them, break them down into sequences of steps, calculate and plan a course of action, survey our resources, experimentally test the efficiency of an emerging strategy ahead of actual performance, and thereby warrant that the proposed course of action will produce the desired outcome in the existential situation that calls for inquiry. Successful strategic conceptions and directing ideas frequently become habitual, get cultivated and preserved in customs and traditions, and are embodied in institutions such as research laboratories and universities. But no matter how established and pervasive such forms of inquiry are, they still lack what is required for what Dewey describes as the logical forms that guarantee the control of inquiry and distinguish it from what Kant called "a merely random groping" (1787, 21).[7] As Dewey argues, by itself the habitual and traditional character of these forms easily defeats the control of inquiry:

Directing conceptions tend to be taken for granted after they have once come into general currency. In consequence they either remain implicit or unstated, or else are propositionally formulated in a way which is static instead of functional. Failure to examine the conceptual structures and frames of reference which are unconsciously implicated in even the seemingly most innocent factual inquiries is the greatest single defect that can be found in any field of inquiry. Even in physical matters, after a certain conceptual frame of reference has once become habitual, it tends to become finally obstructive with reference to new lines of investigation. (1938, LW12:501)

I will return to the discussion of the "legislation" required for turning "accrued" successful and habitual frames of inquiry into operational rules, axioms and principles of controlled inquiry after a brief review of what Dewey describes as a common pattern among the many forms of inquiry (LW12:105–22). This pattern makes it possible to keep the discussion of logical forms within manageable limits.

The Pattern of Inquiry

Dewey argues that we can distinguish five steps, phases, aspects, functions, or operations that are required for the completion of a thought, i.e., for establishing a proposition and "warrantably assertible conclusion," through controlled inquiry. He observes that their sequence is not fixed and that they may vary in expansion.

In his first analysis, Dewey lists five "logically distinct steps": (1) the felt difficulty, (2) its location and definition, (3) the suggestion of a possible solution, (4) the reasoning of the bearings of the suggestion, and (5) observation and experiment leading to the suggestion's acceptance or rejection (1910b, MW6:236–41; see also 1933, LW8:200–209).

In "The Pattern of Inquiry," his final account, Dewey expands and more precisely redescribes these five steps as the operations that are necessary for all successful inquiry, namely, (1) the description of the existential conflict situation that calls for inquiry, (2) the institution or formulation of the problem, (3) the determination or formulation of an idea of a solution, or end-in-view (via a review of "suggestions"), (4) reasoning, i.e., the review of the relevance of connected ideas (i.e., "suggestions") and the development of a "proposition" about what needs to be done, and (5) the review of available resources, i.e., the establishment of facts relevant to the proposed solution (1938, LW12:105–22). On Dewey's account, then, all these operations are required for a warranted assertion about what needs and can be done to resolve an existing conflict. In other words, it is only on the basis of these combined operations that we can meaningfully expect to acquire the confidence in ideas (suggestions, proposition-proposals) that is required for warranted assertions and the decision to act on them.

In his short catechism concerning truth Dewey says that "experience is a matter of functions and habits, of active adjustments and readjustments, of coordinations and activities, rather than of states of consciousness" that mysteriously represent the real (1910c, MW6:5ff.). As Dewey describes it, the same must be said about inquiry in its common form. It is the transformation of an uncertain, unsettled, disturbed existential situation by operations that modify existing conditions such that they get integrated into a harmonious situation. In the course of it we draft ideas of means and ends and of strategies for creating a settled situation in which people can realize their capacities. These ideas are not representations of existing conditions or states of affairs; rather, they are anticipations of consequences, forecasts, suggestions of what does not yet exist anywhere, and therefore embodied in symbols. The ideas are then examined for their *functional* fitness for resolving existential conflict situations and thereby, Dewey contends, they become *operational* "in that they instigate and direct further operations of observation; they are proposals and plans for acting upon existing conditions to bring new facts to light and to organize all the selected facts into a coherent whole" (1938, LW12:116).

The observed facts, Dewey argues, "which present themselves in consequences of the experimental observations the ideas call out and direct, are *trial* facts" that are as operational as are the ideas because they are selected and described and arranged for solving the conflict in a given situation and because they are such that they fit together with one another in ways adequate for that purpose (LW12:117). They are *provisional* facts because they have yet to be tested for evidence "of their power to exercise the function of resolution" in the case and it has yet to be demonstrated by experiment that they can be instrumental in the matter.

As long as the resolution remains a mere possibility, however, it can be worked out only in *symbolic* form, regardless of the actual status of the observed trial facts. For the resolution cannot be carried to term unless the trial facts are functionally connected with the conflict that calls for inquiry, and they can be so connected only with the help of ideas and symbols in propositions. Very unlike in traditional (representational) theories of inquiry, in Dewey's operational account, therefore, propositions are, strictly speaking, proposals in which what is "*pre*-sented" in observation is tentatively projected onto the conflict that calls for inquiry and taken as "*repre*-sentative" for its resolution. Without such symbolic propositional connection, Dewey claims, the observed facts would simply "relapse into the total qualitative situation" and lose their significance for the resolution of the conflict through inquiry. As Dewey points out in his final response to Russell's critique, propositions so understood "are [intermediate] means, instrumentalities, since they are operational agencies by which *beliefs* that have adequate grounds for acceptance [warranted assertions] are reached as *end* of inquiry" (1941, LW14:175).

Propositions, Rules, and Realities

The symbolic propositional connections of particular operations, meticulously described and discussed in Dewey's account of the common pattern of inquiry, cannot be what Dewey has in mind with logical forms of inquiry. Propositional forms of themselves are not logical forms. Such propositional connections are means for attaining judgments, or warranted assertions, concerning a given problem. They are "operational agencies" for initiating the action required for the desired reshaping of antecedent existential subject-matters or for the transformation of a given problematic into a resolved unified situation. Ordinarily we make such connections by following the tracks of successful past operations, cultivated habits, and established patterns. Dewey argues that we are able to derive from such operations, habits, and patterns what we call "logical forms" only if we can make out and experimentally establish what shapes, forms, and determines them, and then accept it as a rule, or set of rules, for further inquiry.

> Any habit is a way or manner of action, not a particular act or deed. When it is formulated it becomes, as far as it is accepted, a rule, or more generally, a principle or "law" of action. It can hardly be denied that there are habits of inference and they may be formulated as rules or principles. If there are such habits as are necessary to conduct every successful inferential inquiry, then the formulations that express them will be logical principles of all inquiries. (1938, LW12:21)

"Successful" in this context simply means, Dewey adds, that in its continuity inquiry produces results that are either confirmed or corrected in further inquiry "by use of the same procedures." It is this sameness (i.e., what is constant and invariant in them) that constitutes ways, habits, customs, and traditions of inquiry. But by themselves such invariants are not principles of direction and of testing, axioms, rules, and binding laws that can and must govern all inquiries. Only if they meet certain conditions capable of formal statement can we turn them into binding laws and recognize them as the logical forms of all inquiry, in other words, as demands that inquiry in order to be inquiry in the complete sense must satisfy. These conditions, and not the common traits of habits, customs, and traditions of inquiry, are therefore the proper subject-matter of logical analysis, as Dewey argues in the opening chapter of *Logic* (LW12:9–29). Since these conditions can be discovered in the course of inquiry itself, Dewey argues, it is not necessary to assume that they somehow "subsist prior to and independently of inquiry," either as Platonic forms or as Kantian structures of consciousness, and that they "are completely and inherently *a priori* and are disclosed to a faculty called *pure reason*" (LW12:23).

When we habitually use without formulation of a leading principle the same procedures that in the past yielded conclusions that were "stable and productive in further inquiry," our research efforts may be equally successful, in spite of differences of subject-matter. Although Dewey claims at one point that when in a set of procedures habitually performed something invariant is noticed and made explicit in propositional form, then this formulation, "being free from connection with any particular subject-matter," becomes a leading formal principle for further research (LW12:20), it is obvious that being noticed and given propositional form cannot be enough for claiming it to be a binding rule for all inquiries. The propositional formulation of an invariant in relation to a specified set of procedures as such is not a logical form. The formulation becomes a logical form only, Dewey argues, when it is "accepted" as a rule or, more generally, as a principle or law of operations (LW12:21). The decisive condition, then, that a propositional form must satisfy in order to become a logical form of inquiry is that it must be accepted and formally recognized as a necessary and thus binding rule for the operations of every successful inquiry, as defined above, i.e., logical legislation must impose on it the force of law.

In efforts to justify acts of logical legislation, it is tempting to misconstrue propositional forms that satisfy this condition as metaphysical presuppositions about experience or its existential material, or as premises of inference or argument, to anchor them in some existential order which logical legislation merely makes explicit and to which it must conform in order to be justified. Dewey argues that such representational interpretations are unnecessary because the rules of successful inquiry are to be understood as "directly operational" (LW12:9–29 passim). And as operational demands they obviously are

> conditions to be satisfied such that knowledge of them provides a principle
> of direction and of testing. They are ways of treating subject-matter that have

been found to be so determinative of sound conclusions in the past that they are taken to regulate further inquiry until definite grounds are found for questioning them. While they are derived from examination of methods previously used in their connection with the kind of conclusion they have produced, they are *operationally a priori* with respect to further inquiry. (LW12:21).

Against their metaphysical and epistemological interpretations, Dewey argues that as operational conditions imposed on future inquiries, logical forms must be "intrinsically postulates of and for inquiry" (LW12:23f.)—*intrinsically*, because they must not be imposed from without but discovered in the course of inquiry itself, and *postulates*, because they can and must be nothing but stipulations and responsibilities accepted for the conduct of inquiry by those committed to it. Dewey illustrates this point by comparing a law in the logical sense with a law in the legal sense as follows:

> One of the highly generalized demands to be met in inquiry is the following: "If anything has a certain property, and whatever has this property has a certain other property, then the thing in question has this certain other property." This logical "law" is a stipulation. If you are going to inquire in a way which meets the requirements of inquiry, you must proceed in a way which observes this rule, just as when you make a business contract there are certain conditions to be fulfilled. (LW12:24)

The same must be said about the principles of identity, noncontradiction, excluded middle, the law of causality, the syllogistic forms, etc.

According to the most notorious metaphysical and epistemological interpretations, on the other hand, the logical requirements of inquiry are "externally postulates" and "externally *a priori*" because they must be imposed from without, say, from some fixed Platonic form that exists καθ' αυτὸ or some fixed Kantian structure of consciousness, if inquiry is to yield warranted assertibility as a consequence. But external requirements unavoidably obscure the conduct of controlled inquiry because such fixed forms and structures are by definition inaccessible to empirical inquiry and at odds with its continuity. Ironically, in the effort to avoid all arbitrariness and to secure an unshakeable solidity of logical legislation, all is lost, because claims about such unchanging static external conditions can be maintained, Dewey argues, as pointed out earlier, only on the basis of "an elaborate process of dialectical inference" (1929, LW4:231). Kant's own efforts to secure "externally *a priori*" knowledge, so it seems, were as misled and unsuccessful as he scoldingly says Plato's were (1781/1787, A5f/B9f). They leave empirical inquiry without operational guidance and direction, and ignore the logical rules that continuously develop in inquiry itself.

But uneasiness with the very idea of logical forms that evolve and develop in the continuous course of inquiry have lately bred interpretations (Sleeper 1986; Boisvert 1988) that mean to show that Dewey's strictly operational a priori must be intrinsically connected with, or anchored in, some independent metaphysical or ontological reality after all, or that the necessity of logical forms must be different in kind from the experimental necessity generated in inquiry, or that all propositions, including propositional formulations of the rules of inquiry, must be interpreted in terms of classification or attribution, in other words, that they all are, or depend on, descriptions of generic traits of existence.

It would seem, however, that the interpretation of rules of controlled inquiry as descriptions of realities or of traits of realities is deeply flawed. Reliable descriptions can be secured only through the controlled operations of inquiry that bring out of "the total qualitative situation" facts about realities and traits of realities that matter in the resolution of existential conflicts that call for inquiry. In other words, propositions of classification and attribution are necessarily functions of the propositional formulations of the rules that guide and govern the controlled transactions of inquiry between environment, existential conflict situations, and their desired transformations. Without such controlled transactions (i.e., without explicit formulation and acceptance of the rules that govern them), we would be left either with the realities of as yet untested and thus haphazard transactions of our ancestors or with what William James notoriously called a "big blooming buzzing confusion" (1911, 32). The flaw, then, in the very idea of metaphysical or realist interpretations of logical forms is much more fatal than Dewey's observation that "the interpretation of all propositions in terms of classification or attribution (and of extension and intension) obscures their intermediary and functional nature" suggests (1938, LW12:298). In order to be able to claim that the propositional formulations of the rules of inquiry must be based on descriptive propositions of realities, one must be totally unaware of, or as Nietzsche argued, have completely forgotten about (1873, 86ff.), or deny altogether the "intermediary and functional nature" of such propositions.

But the uneasiness behind such metaphysical, ontological, or realist turns against the idea of a strictly operational a priori and the postulational theory of logical forms proposed in Dewey's *Logic* cannot be easily overcome by such reasoning nor by the sort of "compelling" arguments Dewey uses against Platonic and Kantian efforts to ground lawmaking in logic on some unshakeable realities that remain unaffected by the continuous operations of inquiry. In his 1910 discussion of the emergence of the new logic, Dewey demonstrates in some detail that it is precisely this removed reality with its remote causes and eventual goals that prevents "the classic type of logic" from furnishing guidance and direction that is useful for inquiry into specific conditions of existential conflict situations and into specific consequences of ideas. It is tempting to conclude with Dewey that if metaphysical and realist interpretations of logical forms will ever be displaced, it will not be "by sheer logical disproof, but rather by growing recognition of [their] futility" (1910a, MW4:12).

But the obvious source of the uneasiness with an operational and postulational theory of logical forms is the belief that such a theory is much less capable of furnishing the steady direction that is required for the control of inquiry in the management of human affairs than "the classical type of logic." Being strictly operational, logical forms are intrinsically limited postulates, and the more serious problems that occur in life, many believe, require universally applicable rules of inquiry that enable anyone to locate and to solve such problems wherever and whenever they occur. We learn, however, from experimental scientists that what enables anyone to do so, ironically, are precisely the explicitly stated limited conditions, as Dewey observes.[8]

> Postulates alter as methods of inquiry are perfected; the logical forms that express modern scientific inquiry are in many respects quite unlike those that formulated the procedures of Greek science. An experimenter in the laboratory who publishes his results states [1] the materials used, [2] the setup of apparatus, and [3] the procedures employed. These specifications are limited postulates, demands and stipulations, for any inquirer who wishes to test the conclusion reached. Generalize this performance for procedures of inquiry as such, that is, with respect to the form of every inquiry, and logical forms as postulates are the outcome. (1938, LW12:26)

Consider also, as does Dewey, the possibility "of carrying over the essential elements of the pattern of experimental knowing into the experience of man in its everyday traits" and of broadening it to insight into specific conditions of value and into specific consequences of ideas, and the belief that the logical forms of modern inquiry must in time develop into "a method for locating and interpreting the more serious of the conflicts that occur in life, and a method of projecting ways for dealing with them: a method of moral and political diagnosis and prognosis" is the outcome (1929, LW4:155). Dewey not only confidently expresses this hope (1910, MW4:13), but by using social inquiry "to test the general logical conceptions that have been reached," he demonstrates at length how it can become such a method (1938, LW12:481–505).[9]

Without explicit formulation of the limiting conditions imposed by the experimental setup, inquiry would be uncontrolled and irresponsible "random groping." Its results would have to remain matters of mere opinion, because without the specifications of the setup, inquirers in any field, including the subject-matter of human relations, would remain free to bring out and observe whatever they please. Information about the setup must tell them what to look for and how to observe it, and thus participate in concerted efforts to address existing problems. Publishing results without detailed information about the setup would irresponsibly send others on a wild goose chase.

Of course, we have learned from modern physics that what reliable experimental observations we are able to make depends on the setup of apparatus in the narrow sense, as Dewey shows in his review of Heisenberg's principle of indeterminacy (1929, LW4:160–64). But the lesson Dewey draws from this fact is much broader, namely, that "knowing is one kind of interaction which goes on within the world" and that "knowing marks the conversion of undirected changes into changes directed toward an intended conclusion" (LW4:163). And the intended conclusion depends largely, though not exclusively, on the setup of the institutional "apparatus" that regulates modern research, that is, on the logical forms that govern modern inquiry and explain the intricate organization of research programs with their specific fields, goals, commitments, assignments, tools, teams, and procedures.

With his operational and postulational theory of logical forms, Dewey gives an initial account which demonstrates that this whole setup is the result of human ingenuity, a construction devised in direct response to existential conflict situations that call for inquiry, i.e., a temporary construction that must be overhauled and revised, or abandoned altogether, as soon as it turns out to be inadequate for, or an obstacle to, the resolution of an existing problematic situation. Heisenberg (1930, 1934) argues that the concept of causality, for instance, must be revised simply because in its received—say, Kantian—form it has become meaningless in the situation created by the development of atomic physics. The control mechanism of logical forms in modern inquiry, then, is a complex transaction, not at all the sort of thing it used to be for the Greeks. Unlike Greek physicists, Heisenberg argues, modern physicists are no longer detached observers and spectators, nor prescriptive dictators, but participants in a transaction (*Wechselspiel*) between physicists and nature shrouded by indeterminacy and uncertainty (1954, 418). Commenting on the broader consequences of the situation in modern physics, Dewey argues that it is this existential situation which calls for a radical revision of the received concept of inquiry:

> If we persist in the traditional conception, according to which the thing to be known is something which exists prior to and wholly apart from the act of knowing, then discovery of the fact that the act of observation, necessary in existential knowing, modifies that preexistent something is proof that the act of knowing gets in its own way, frustrating its own intent. . . . Fundamentally, the issue is raised whether philosophy is willing to surrender a theory of mind and its organs of knowing which originated when the practice of knowing was in its infancy. (1929, LW4:164)

Dewey's revised account is designed to avoid such frustration through the setup of logical forms and laws of inquiry, devised for prompting nature to release the resources required for the desired transformation of existential conflict situations that prompted the setup. This multiply corresponding setup sustains and guarantees the continuous transaction of inquiry. In a word, it's all in the setup.

Notes

1. As Dewey observes at the beginning of the chapter on the pattern of inquiry (LW12:106f.), formalized conceptions are operational in the sense that "they formulate and define ways of operation" on the part of those engaged in them. They develop "in consequence of operations." Yet, without such definitions, we could not observe or identify any such ways or patterns of operation. Both forms and patterns, Dewey argues, "originate in operations of inquiry," but they are "disclosed or come to light when we reflect upon processes of inquiry that are in use" (LW12:11f.). This means, he adds, "that while inquiry into inquiry is the *causa cognoscendi* of logical forms, primary inquiry is itself *causa essendi* of the forms which inquiry into inquiry [i.e., such as in *Logic: The Theory of Inquiry*] discloses."

2. Kant stated his view of the matter perhaps nowhere more concisely than in the preface to his *Groundwork of the Metaphysic of Morals* (1785, 55): "Logic can have no empirical parts—that is, no part in which the universal and necessary laws of thinking are based on grounds taken from experience. Otherwise it would not be logic—that is, it would not be a canon for understanding and reason, valid for all thinking and capable of demonstration."

3. See Dewey's comments on Peirce's definition of truth (1938, LW12:343n) and the defense of it in his later essay, "Challenge to Liberal Thought" (1944, LW15:273).

4. Erica Goode (2000, D1) reports about more recent work on these influences. In a series of studies comparing European Americans with East Asians, Richard Nisbett and others "found that people who grow up in different cultures do not

just think about different things: they think differently." She quotes Nisbett: "We used to think that everybody uses categories in the same way, that logic plays the same kind of role for everyone in the understanding of everyday life, that memory, perception, rule application and so on are the same. But we're now arguing that cognitive processes themselves are just far more malleable than mainstream psychology assumed." For a summary of this research, see Nisbett 2001. I will discuss below whether such findings conflict with what Dewey argues about logical forms as requirements that must be fulfilled by *all* inquiries.

5. For Dewey's most vivid account of his findings on this matter, see his chapter "The Live Creature" (1934, LW10:9–25).

6. For a detailed account of these early developments of *Logos*, especially of its syntactical structure, in Plato's dialogues, see Prauss 1966.

7. For a comparison-contrast of Kant's and Dewey's accounts of controlled inquiry, see Seigfried 2001.

8. Kant makes similar observations about the philosophical significance of the experimental method. For a discussion of the influence of experimental science on his "treatise on method" see Seigfried 1993. In this essay I ignore this influence and go along with Dewey's neo-Kantian understanding of Kant's position.

9. Frequently these endeavors are seen as sufficient evidence for dismissing *Logic* as uncritical scientism, or physicalism, that is at odds with Dewey's other writings, such as *Human Nature and Conduct* (1922) and *Art as Experience* (1934). Dewey, however, emphatically rejects this view: "The question is not whether the subject-matter of human relations is or can ever become a science in the sense in which physics is now a science, but whether it is such as to permit of the development of methods which, as far as they go, satisfy the logical conditions that have to be satisfied in other branches of inquiry" (1938, LW12:480). It would be odd, indeed, if such conditions could be safely ignored where the conflict of leading ideas in inquiry seems to be worst and where we can least afford to trust uncontrolled intuition and unbridled conversation.

Works Cited

Boisvert, Raymond D. 1988. *Dewey's Metaphysics*. New York: Fordham University Press.

Dewey, John. 1910a. The Influence of Darwinism on Philosophy. In *The Influence of Darwin on Philosophy, and Other Essays in Contemporary Thought*. New York: Henry Holt. Revision of an article originally published in 1909 with the title "Darwin's Influence upon Philosophy" (*Popular Science Monthly* 75:90–98). Reprinted in MW4:3–14.

———. 1910b. *How We Think*. Boston: D. C. Heath. Reprinted in MW6:177–356.

———. 1910c. A Short Catechism Concerning Truth. In *The Influence of Darwin on Philosophy, and Other Essays in Contemporary Thought*. New York: Henry Holt. Reprinted in MW6:3–11.

——. 1922. *Human Nature and Conduct*. New York: Henry Holt. Reprinted in MW14.

——. 1929. *The Quest for Certainty: A Study of the Relation of Knowledge and Action*. New York: Minton, Balch. Reprinted in LW4.

——. 1933. *How We Think*. Rev. ed. Boston: D. C. Heath. Reprinted in LW8:105–354.

——. 1934. *Art as Experience*. New York: Henry Holt. Reprinted in LW10.

——. 1938. *Logic: The Theory of Inquiry*. New York: Henry Holt. Reprinted in LW12.

——. 1941. Propositions, Warranted Assertibility, and Truth. *Journal of Philosophy* 38 (7):169–86. Reprinted in LW14:168–88.

——. 1942. Inquiry and Indeterminateness of Situations. *Journal of Philosophy* 39 (11):290–96. Reprinted in LW15:34–41.

——. 1944. Challenge to Liberal Thought. *Fortune,* August:155–57, 180, 182, 184, 186, 188, 190. Reprinted in LW15:261–75.

Goode, Erica. 2000. How Culture Molds Habits of Thought. *New York Times*, August 8, D1, D4.

Heisenberg, Werner. 1930. Kausalitätsgesetz und Quantenmechanik. In *Werner Heisenberg, Gesammelte Werke*, Abteilung C: Allgemeinverständliche Schriften, Band 1: Physik und Erkenntnis, 1927–1955, ed. Walter Blum, Hans-Peter Dürr, and Helmut Rechenberg, 29–39. Munich: Piper, 1984.

——. 1934. Wandlungen der Grundlagen der Exakten Naturwissenschaften in jüngster Zeit. In *Werner Heisenberg, Gesammelte Werke*, Abteilung C: Allgemeinverständliche Schriften, Band 1: Physik und Erkenntnis, 1927–1955, ed. Walter Blum, Hans-Peter Dürr, and Helmut Rechenberg, 96–101. Munich: Piper, 1984.

——. 1954. Das Naturbild der heutigen Physik. In *Werner Heisenberg, Gesammelte Werke*, Abteilung C: Allgemeinverständliche Schriften, Band 1: Physik und Erkenntnis, 1927–1955, ed. Walter Blum, Hans-Peter Dürr, and Helmut Rechenberg, 398–420. Munich: Piper, 1984.

James, William. 1911. *Some Problems of Philosophy*. Cambridge: Harvard University Press, 1979.

Kant, Immanuel. 1781/1787. *The Critique of Pure Reason*. Translated by Norman Kemp Smith. New York: St Martin's Press, 1965.

——. 1785. *Groundwork of the Metaphysic of Morals*. Translated by H. J. Paton. New York: Harper Torchbooks, 1964.

——. 1787. Preface to the Second Edition. In *The Critique of Pure Reason*. Translated by Norman Kemp Smith. New York: St. Martin's Press, 1965.

Nietzsche, Friedrich. 1873. On Truth and Lies in a Nonmoral Sense. In *Philosophy and Truth: Selections from Nietzsche's Notebooks of the Early 1870s*, ed. Daniel Breazeale, 79–91. Atlantic Highlands, N.J.: Humanities Press, 1979.

Nisbett, Richard E., Kaiping Peng, Incheol Choi, and Ara Norenzayan. 2001. Culture and Systems of Thought: Holistic Versus Analytic Cognition. *Psychological Review* 108 (April): 291–310.

Prauss, Gerold. 1966. *Platon und der logische Eleatismus*. Berlin: Walter de Gruyter.

Seigfried, Hans. 1993. Dewey's Critique of Kant's Copernican Revolution Revisited. In *Kant-Studien* 83:356–68.

———. 2001. Truth and Use. *Synthese* July 1–2, 128:1–13.

Sleeper, R. W. 1986. *The Necessity of Pragmatism: John Dewey's Conception of Philosophy*. New Haven: Yale University Press.

Weinberg, Steven. 1996. Sokal's Hoax. *New York Review of Books*, August 8, 11–15.

———. 1998. The Revolution That Didn't Happen. *New York Review of Books*, October 8, 48–52.

9

The Role of Measurement in Inquiry

Jayne Tristan

Measurement, Dewey argues (1938, LW12:94), marks a fundamental difference between ancient Greek conceptions of science and scientific practices
today. In Aristotelian science, measurements hold the status of "accidents,"
a technical term that contrasts with "essence." The essence of an oak is its
fully functioning oakness; it is mere accident that it is of a particular height
and lives a particular number of years. Accidents cannot ground inferences,
because accidents are unstable occurrences. The quantity and measurement
of a thing contribute little to securing inference. The most secure inference
is ground by insight into essence, for only essences can guarantee inferences. Consequently, knowledge does not advance by making measurements.

Today measurement plays a significant role in securing inference and
producing scientific knowledge. The periodic table of the elements contrasts
in every detail with the ancient Greek conception of the elements: earth,
air, water, and fire. Each of the four elements is a qualitative whole and is,
in turn, constituted by comparisons of qualitative wholes: wet-dry, cold-
hot, heavy-light. By contrast, each element in the periodic table is defined
in terms of the measurement of qualities transformed by operations of various kinds and by comparing relations among abstract characters derived
from selected qualitative characteristics revealed by experimental operations.

In Aristotle's science, magnitude is separated from qualities of existence
by an ontological distinction. Numbers exist as stable realities, while qualities appear but are not stable. The resulting attitude is that propositions of
quantity are considered more stable—so, more scientific—than propositions
of quality. Measuring is contrast with, and sometimes considered indifferent to, the qualitative aspects of a situation. The ontological distinction is
misleading. For Dewey, quantity and quality are related as characteristic to
character. Quantity is a kind of quality; that is, quantity is a formulated

characteristic of a situation. A magnitude is a qualitative characteristic of each situation, which can be transformed into a determinate character of an individual situation. Operations transform a characteristic into an abstract character. It follows then that a proposition expressing magnitude, first, is formulated out of an underlying pervasive quality in the situation itself and, second, it depends upon an operational means of selection that relates the proposed magnitude to its expected consequences. A proposal of magnitude is thus of qualitative characteristics found within a situation. So measurement is not indifferent to qualities, but rather the contrary. An operation of measuring is indifferent only to differences within a quality measured; that is, measuring is indifferent only to such qualities within a pervasive quality of a situation that are irrelevant to the aims of an inquiry at hand. A quality is selected and formulated as a means to effecting changes to achieve anticipated consequences (Dewey 1938, LW12:207). In this way, operations of comparison disclose discrete relationships of generic traits of existence and create relations of characters that function to secure inference.

Dewey argues that such operations produce a kind of logical form which *originates* in operations of inquiry and *accrues* to subject matter. Logical formulations, by his definition, make inference secure. This essay examines how the securing of inference happens, for Dewey's account has significant implications for questions relating to the difference between the quantitative and qualitative sciences. To avoid confusion with traditional definitions of logical form, I discuss Dewey's logical forms not as grammatical forms but as formulations that secure inference.

Setting Standards for Measurement

Standards are necessary for measurements, and measuring is a definite means of comparison (Dewey 1938, LW12:205). Comparisons of qualities found in a subject matter cannot become more definite than shorter-longer, more-less, many-few, hotter-colder until a number of conditions are met in connection with establishing standards. There are perhaps three steps. First, selected qualities must be formulated out of a problematic subject matter that is homogeneous enough to permit a range of serial gradation to be instituted. This means that if the problem is a question such as "How tall is this tree?" the quality of length is selected, because "length" is homogeneous enough to permit institution of a range of serial gradation (Dewey 1938, LW12:203). Second, a standard range of serial gradation such as "meters" is invented in operations of comparison and adopted. Third, so that each measure is susceptible to comparison with others, standard reference points are established.

These three conditions often involve extensive operations of comparison and elimination of alternative possibilities. Fixing standard points, to facilitate correlation of measurements, might appear a matter of arbitrary selection, but it is not. The freezing point of water appears an obvious choice to calibrate temperature scales. Prior to the discovery by careful measurements of various kinds, however, its relationship to other conditions was unclear. Does the freezing point of water vary with the "height" above sea level, with the "time" of day or year, with the "distance" from the poles? The astronomer Edmund Halley insisted, for example, that the freezing point of water would not be the same in London as in Paris, and so should not be used as a fixed point for calibrating thermometers (Middleton 1966). Turning water to ice may vary in connection with other changes and conditions. How does the composition of water influence its freezing point? Does the freezing point of seawater differ from water drawn from a well? How does boiling water influence its freezing point? Answers to such questions depend upon calibrated equipment, standardized techniques, and the adoption and coordination of standards of many kinds.

Standards function to make inferences secure, because standards establish both the qualities to be compared and the means of comparing them. The general concern of inquiry is to discover the connections between differences and changes. The point of Aristotelian science, on the other hand, is to discover the cause of an effect, such as "cold." The problems involved in discovering causes are legendary. Aristotle required *phenomenon* to have no less than four kinds of cause. In his ontology, the cause of cold is *primum frigidum,* a qualitative whole and a constituent of water. Particular experiences such as water feeling cold and unchallenged biases with respect to connections (such as that water is a constituent of most things) tend to suggest and support his conclusions, but they leave plenty of room for controversy. The scholastics argued, for example, that air causes cold; Thomas Hobbes isolated wind as the cause. Plutarch argued for the earth; Pierre Gassendi favored nitre. With nothing but arguments to connect cold to its cause, controversy is endless.

Part of the problem is that *primum frigidum* and other formal causes cannot be observed by the senses. Nevertheless, the experimentalist, Robert Boyle, tried to rule out each guess by arguing from observations. He showed that substances with no water content could become quite cold and that many cold substances exist without nitre or its exhalations. Boyle argued that steaming springs and volcanic activity suggest the core of the earth is more likely hot than cold. Boyle rejected air, based on reports of ice that formed in the depths of the sea far from contact with air or wind. Boyle next began to test implications of the theoretical cause. *Primum frigidum* is an essence and so cannot change. Observations that water changes to ice might seem a decisive refutation, but any observation is easily refuted by scholastics with the ontological distinction between real essences and apparent changes. This distinction works against Boyle's next experimental observations, too. Yet Boyle tested another implication of the theoretical cause: that water cannot gain or lose weight and size.[1] To refute this, Boyle measured the expansion of water as it changed to ice. Observation alone is never enough to determine the cause of anything.[2] In practice, observation simply invites alternative explanations. Boyle's scholastic opponents suggested that what the expansion proved is only that *primum frigidum* exists and migrates into the water as it expands. Boyle had no more success locating causes by observation than Aristotle had forecast.

Boyle's observations and experiments only began to pay off when he introduced standards by which to judge the relations between things by measured correlations of changes. Without standard equipment and standard techniques, nothing existed on which to base a guarantee, nor anything to rule out alternative possibilities such as Rene Descartes's guess that the cold is nothing but a privation of heat. In centuries of discussion and in Boyle's initial trials, no one could measure temperatures or isolate qualities and determine the relationships existing between them. Observations, for example, that boiled water cools more rapidly than unboiled water add to the controversy and mystery, but they add nothing to settle the question about the cause of cold. Learning "what happens" to cause such a difference in cooling requires that finer attention be given to formulating and recording the qualities of the subject matter, and this requires instruments for standardizing observations and measurements. Boyle rejected Aristotle's formulation of cold as the substance of *primum frigidum* as an "unwarrantable conceit," but initially had nothing but speculation to put in its place (Shachtman 1999, 29).

Robert Hooke, an assistant in Boyle's laboratory, created the instruments Boyle used to conduct his experiments. Hooke invented a vacuum apparatus and modified a Florentine thermometer by substituting mercury for "spirit of wine" within the glass tubing. The more reliable thermometer avoided the variations in readings due to insurmountable difficulties in standardizing wine consistency. Measuring alone did not yield much useful information. Records of temperatures and vacuum air pressures are useful in securing inferences in repeatable ways only after fixed reference points and calibrated scales are established. Using instruments that revealed the relevant qualities, Boyle developed a hypothetical proposition that the volume of a specified amount of air at a specified temperature is inversely proportional to the pressure: the smaller the volume the greater the pressure. In this series of experiments, Boyle formulated what Dewey calls a "relation of characters" by calibrating his instruments and comparing experimental results with one another. Scientists are still exploring the implications of more finely standardized versions of this hypothetical proposition.

Before the possibility of conducting operations of weighing and freezing, standard conceptual operations must also exist. To become a standard point of reference, the freezing point of water relies on previously established conceptual systems that can function as conceptual standards, such as numerical, algebraic, and geometric systems. A Cartesian coordinate system functions as a means for displaying relations derived from numerical records of operations of comparison. Such systems are frameworks in which implications of records can be evolved independently from the subject matter.

Fixing standard points of reference involves many kinds of operations that function, first, to uncover relationships among qualitative characteristics which, in turn, are used as standards for further measurement and comparison. Second, the interrelation of measuring systems functions to standardize further inferences and makes inference more secure. Consider size, a commonly measured quantity: Size is defined in three ways. Distance between tree rings is measured by length, and the surface of the cut can be measured by area, while a forest of trees is measured by board feet (volume). Length, area, and volume are interrelated and are easily represented on a coordinate system. Area is related to length by a mathematical technique of squaring. Squaring is a technique developed in purely conceptual terms and functions in inquiry as a fundamental standard by which to secure inferences in the following way. Squaring is coupled with SI units, which is a system of measure developed to provide fixed standard units of measure that are easily translated into one another. A basic unit of size is the meter, so because a meter is the dimension of length, area is m^2 and volume is m^3. Such convenient transformations facilitate comparison of results of one series of operations with another, and they facilitate the establishment of results that are repeatable from one inquiry to another.

Standards are only partly arbitrary, for standards are established by operations in which means used to effect a change and the change itself are established to be in strict correspondence. Fixing the length of the meter, for example, involves a number of standard operations and depends upon previously established fixed points such as the location of the poles and equator. Knowing the location of the Poles and the equator results from operations of measuring, which, in turn, relies on other fixed points of reference, in this case, relative locations of stars; and it uses standard geometric theorems dealing with spheres and triangulation. Thus when the meter was originally defined by techniques used to measure the distance from the North Pole to the equator, the sole arbitrary decision involved the adoption of one ten-millionth of this distance for the actual length of a meter. The standard unit of length fixed in 1791 was replaced in the twentieth century by a figure 1,650,763.73 times the wavelength of a frequency of orange-red light in a vacuum (specifically, the transition between the level $2p_{10}$ and $5d_5$ of the atom of Krypton 86; see Weast 1977). The intricate operations and refined measurements involved in obtaining this last measurement suggest that establishing interrelated systems of standards and establishing fixed points of reference is not trivial. Rather it relies on successive refinements of operations of measurement and draws on increasingly complex conceptual relations.

The selection of qualities for comparison is preparatory to measuring. Selecting one quality over another requires that a definition be established in terms of comparative operations. Dewey writes, "To compare is to pair, and things that are paired are thereby made commensurate with respect to carrying out some operation in view" (Dewey 1938, LW12:203). In purely conceptual matters, a definition in terms of standards adopted earlier may suffice. Instead of adding up numbers from, say, 1 to 100, one at a time, one might use the short cut of summing an arithmetic progression (Erdos 1973). Adding numbers is an operation. But other operations are possible here. The short cut reformulates the subject matter so that comparisons are more easily made: 1 and 100 add up to 101; 2 and 99 also add up to 101. Such pairing ends with 50 and 51, which also add up to 101. This reformulation operation makes a kind of comparison possible that the simpler adding operation obscures. The new comparison facilitates the inference that the sum of the numbers from 1 to 100 is $50 \times 101 = 5,050$. In this case, the standard notation for numbers and operations of addition and multiplication secure the inference. The pairwise summing operation reorganizes the subject matter so that relations hidden by the simpler adding operation are revealed. Qualities relevant to the solution of the problem are more easily noticed and appropriated.

Thus a subject matter (in the above case, a mathematical one) may accrue new formulations by means of novel operations that secure inference within the process of inquiry itself. This is unremarkable for a subject matter such as mathematics, for no one doubts that a mathematical operation secures its own inference. The assurance that one plus one equals two appears so strong that from Aristotle on most have considered the equation

self-evident. The self-evidence of "one plus one equals two," Dewey argues, however, is its meaning "in the meaning system of which it is a member" (Dewey 1938, LW12:158). The security of mathematical judgments
stems from, first, the institution of standards such as axioms and theorems
and, second, the performance of operations in accordance with the standards adopted.

Measurement in Existential Inquiry

The techniques for selection of qualities differs in each kind of existential
subject matter, but standards are always defined in terms of operations to
be performed. In this section, I will attempt to indicate the ways in which
standards that secure inference are constructed out of the materials of a
situation of both conceptual and existential kinds in order to build reliable
structures for the purpose of securing warranted judgments. Operations of
measurement are involved at every step and are used as standards to direct and control inferences in systematic ways. Dewey notes in his discussion of this point that "it would require several pages in a treatise on chemistry to set forth the experiments, with the apparatus and techniques that
are involved" (1938, LW12:449). Even this is not enough. Dewey writes, "It
would require a chapter or chapters in a chemical treatise to set forth explicitly the conceptions and interrelations of conceptions that are directly
and indirectly involved in the conduct of the experiments by which the law
or generalization in question is warrantably arrived at" (LW12:449). The
relations of conceptions that secure inference are formulated out of individual subject matters, and the comparative operations involved would no
doubt be difficult to explain to nonspecialists.

The main features to look for in such explanations include the following: First, interrelated standards are imported from other inquiries and used
to measure qualities. Second, the qualitative characteristics selected for measurement are transformed in specific ways. Third, the qualities selected are
generated in experimental operations and often go unnoticed or are impossible to notice without the transformations wrought by operations. Fourth,
research design is guided both by implications of the formulations of subject matter resulting from transformative operations that yield generic traits
of existence, and by implications evolved in abstract systems of conceptual
relations which can be both transformed to make further comparisons and
correlated with other conceptual systems. Fifth, interactions are correlated
with conceptual relations and so function to secure individual warranted
judgments.

Dewey (1938, LW12:123) argues that a judgment has "direct existential import" and designates "a subject matter which has been prepared to be final" in that it settles a problematic situation. In Dewey's terminology, judgments are not the same as propositions. The latter propose operations to be executed and suggest novel occurrences that might result. Such proposals formulate selected qualities of a subject matter for purposes of finding out how each changes under controlled conditions. "The scientific object, *par excellence*, is a correlation of functional correspondence of changes. There is no way to determine the presence or absence of such correlations save by measurements whose results are numerically stated" (Dewey 1938, LW12:202). Propositions propose activities and do not merely represent a state of affairs. Propositions are intermediate means for securing conclusive judgments, whereas a judgment is a conclusive end. Propositions schedule transformations of qualities using standard equipment and techniques. A judgment purports to address and answer a problem that arises within a situation so that the problem no longer exists. A successful course of inquiry using propositions as intermediate means may result in a judgment warranted for an individual situation.

An important distinction relevant to securing inferences is one between abstract *relations* and formulations of existential *relationships*. Relations are terms "used to designate abstract terms whose meaning is exhaustively contained in the terms" (Dewey 1938, LW12:329). For instance, the term *meter* designates each measured interval and, in pointing out this relation between marks, exhausts the meaning of *meter*. On the other hand, meanings continue to be revealed by operations of transformative inquiry for terms that designate formulations of relationships. Relationships point to concealed involvements and hidden entailments. The relationships revealed by measuring, say, a beam of light are not exhausted in measuring its length from the window to the floor. Light is susceptible to many different kinds of quantitative relationships, each of which can be designated by relations among abstract variables, or conceptual categories, or what Dewey calls "characters" (as opposed to characteristic "traits"). One measured relationship, for instance, is designated by the speed of light, while another is designated by measured wavelengths. The subject matter (in this case, light) accrues novel formulations by means of novel operations and secures inference by sets of interactions that correlate results from operations of inquiry directed by relations of abstract characters (Dewey 1938, LW12:11–14, 19, 29, 105–8, 130–41).

Specifically, in comparative operations that discover such quantitative relationships, alternative possibilities are ruled out when a change fails to fulfill expectations set by the propositions directing the inquiry. The "discrepancies between experimental measurements and predictions based on Maxwell's theory concerning the spectral content of light," for example, forced Max Planck "to reject the classical theory in which energy exchanges can take place in continuous amounts. Instead, he had to postulate that matter emits radiant energy only in discrete chunks that are integral multiples of a fundamental quantity" (Pullman 1998, 261). The experiments in question were designed to show how a heated object changes color in relation to its temperature. As a result of inconsistencies between expectations set by Maxwell's propositions and experimental results, Planck postulated that matter emits energy only in discrete chunks which are integral multiples of a fundamental quantity hv. The proportionality factor h has a numerical value of 6.6251×10^{-27} (if masses are expressed in grams, distances in centimeters, and time in seconds), which is multiplied by another measurement, v, the frequency of the radiation.[3] This means that the higher the frequency, v, of emitted radiation, the greater the amount of energy a quantum of light possesses. Planck's quantity, hv, and quantities like it, such as the mass of an electron, the speed of light, and the magnitude of the electric charge of a proton, share a special status physicists designate as fundamental constants. Such constant quantities state what Dewey (1938, LW 12:448) calls a relation of characters.

A relation of characters is discovered in operations of inquiry in which "gross qualitative events and immediately observed qualities (such as how heated objects change color and how temperature varies) . . . are transformed into a determinate set of *interactions*" (Dewey 1938, LW 12:447). Experiments upon existential materials reveal the determinate interactions that exist between characters and upon which the relation of characters is based. A character is itself the result of a determinate set of interactions discovered in prior inquiries. Characters can be numerical values of the quantities for things like momentum, $\mathbf{p}$; energy, E; wavelength, λ; and characters can be instituted by serial gradations such as degrees of temperature, or levels of viscosity, density, and inertial force, or any set of interactions that can be expressed numerically.

A fundamental constant, as a relation of characters, designates or is otherwise closely connected with a specific kind of relationship between generic traits of existence. The relationship involved is revealed in operations that transform materials of *both* existential and conceptual kinds. This is important for a theory of inquiry because controlled existential transformations always involve conceptual transformations. Conceptual transformations in mathematics can remain free of existential reference, but the reverse is not possible for a *proposition* used to direct inquiry. This is because propositions formulate a subject matter in specific ways. Such formulations, in subsequent inquiry, may be modified or changed altogether. A prominent example is Joseph Priestley's definition of newly discovered "airs" in terms of varying amounts of phlogiston given off during combustion (see Holmes 1985). Dephlogisticated air burns more readily than phlogisticated air that results from combustion. While oxygen and dephlogisticated air are both "eminently respirable," each formulation—which results from different measured operations of comparison—has different implications. Implications of the formulation, dephlogisticated air, which is produced by reducing mercury calx without charcoal, is limited to what might be suggested by the observation that the new air burns more readily than airs with more phlogiston. On the other hand, the oxygen element presented in the nested measurements symbolized on the periodic table carries implications far beyond the imagination and symbols of the experimentalists who isolated dephlogisticated air from common air. The measurements used to evidence dephlogisticated air could not be used to predict that oxygen has orbital shells, electric charge, magnetic moment, or that the elements taken together display a periodicity in atomic weight. Such discoveries await novel equipment and novel techniques that formulate subject matter in novel and fruitful ways.

I have introduced concepts and distinctions needed to understand how inference is secured. In the distinction between "relations of characters" and "relationships among generic traits of existence," it is important to remember that the former are discovered in controlled experimental operations upon the latter. Characters are the related contents of abstract universal propositions (Dewey 1938, LW12:259); that is, characters are subject to abstract symbolic formulation even as they are operationally extracted from generic traits of existence.

Another distinction important to Dewey's theory of inquiry is the difference between abstract universal propositions and generic propositions. The difference is not captured, respectively, by the distinction between conceptual and existential matters, nor is this important distinction indicated adequately by the difference between mathematics and physics. Rather, the distinction is marked best by that of a recipe to its ingredients, with important asymmetries. The distinction is asymmetric because even though physicists operationally extract relations of characters (universal propositions) from generic traits of existence, terms denoting these generic traits have existential reference while a relation of characters, even though operationally extracted from existential materials, do not. Relations of characters are instrumental and intermediate abstract propositions useful in directing operations that elicit *determinate kinds of interactions*, while generic propositions are instrumental and intermediate existential propositions that *formu-*

late selected qualities for definite purposes which are operationally extracted by means of determinate kinds of interactions.

There are a number of notions inherited from the Aristotelian traditional ways of thinking that inhibit understanding Dewey's way of viewing propositions. First, the notion of induction suggests that a fundamental constant is a generalization that is inferred from uniform sequences of observations. Dewey argues that this interpretation neglects the "radical transformation wrought by the scientific formulation" (Dewey 1938, LW12:447). A uniform sequence of observations does not adequately analyze how relations of characters are established. Instead, the route from "changes in color and temperature" to Planck's constant involves a nested series of correlated changes, where each abstract formulation of related characters correlates changes that comport with other correlated changes. Correlations are determined in a series of comparative inquiries using a variety of equipment and techniques used to measure existential interactions involving both existential and abstract transformations. Standards developed in one inquiry are imported to initiate and advance another by providing means to transform and discover qualities relevant to establishing relations of characters.

Second, a determination of the interactions which yield traits that are extracted and then abstracted to constitute a nontemporal relation of characters is constant in respect to its evidential function, not constant in respect to existential recurrence (Dewey 1938, LW12:449n1). The classical notion that experimental operations are relevant for the most part to inductive inference and that induction draws on sequences of observations from which universal generalizations may be inferred goes against and even obscures Dewey's point. From a perspective removed from the work involved in establishing relations of characters, Dewey's insistence on this point appears contrary to actual practices. Sequences of repeatable experiments appear to be the only route to confirming or disconfirming 'the probability' of a scientific theory. But we should look at this more carefully.

A fundamental constant, such as Planck's constant, is not a theory, nor (as a relation of characters) is it a matter of probability. Planck's constant is a relation of characters that have been determined to be sets of interactions in operations of inquiry and can be used to direct operations that elicit a determinate set of interactions. Namely,[4] the momentum, **p**, of an electron (or proton, or light wave) is equal to its wave vector, **k**, multiplied by Planck's constant, *h*, *and* the total energy, *E*, is given by the frequency, *v*, multiplied by Planck's constant, *h*:

$$\mathbf{p} = h\mathbf{k} \quad \text{and} \quad E = hv$$

Viewed together, the consistency among so many relations of characters operationally extracted and symbolically represented is remarkable. That one set of relations of characters should be consistent with another set of relations of characters demonstrates at least that Dewey's view of abstract propositions is plausible. Consistency between these relations of characters marks a kind of guarantee that is hard to ignore. Of course, the set of interactions in question are, here, assumed rather than detailed.

The significance of this comparison of two interrelated relations of characters will remain opaque unless the functional meaning of Dewey's terminological distinctions that result in "relations of characters" is kept in mind. Likewise, the complexity of relations that the institution of various kinds of measurement makes possible must be sufficiently understood. The claims that support the interpretation of Planck's constant as a functional relation of characters, again, in summary are, first, standards secure inference of both conceptual and existential kinds; second, standards are constructed out of qualities of the subject matter itself; third, this construction occurs in operations upon materials of both conceptual and existential kinds; fourth, the propositions constructed establish relations of characters and determine relationships among generic kinds; fifth, such propositions yield reliable structures consisting of standard equipment and techniques because propositions direct transformation (promote interactions) of materials of both conceptual and existential kinds; sixth, such interactions function to secure individual warranted judgments; and finally, seventh, comparative operations of measurement are involved at every step and are used as standards to direct and control inferences in systematic ways.

The differences between the Aristotelian approach to securing inferences and Dewey's could hardly be more stark. Yet Ernest Nagel, in the introduction to the critical edition of Dewey's *Logic: The Theory of Inquiry*, remarks that Dewey's ideas "are much behind the times" (Nagel 1986, LW12:xxii). Mathematical logic advanced beyond Aristotle, well before Dewey began to worry about measurement and logical form. It was already being stressed, by Frege in particular, that "everyday language proves to be insufficient to preserve thinking from errors" (Frege quoted in Dumitriu 1977, 52). On the basis of such observations, Frege developed an abstract formal calculus that was to stand in place of everyday language as the medium of clear and precise deductive inference. Frege's quantification theory advanced the discipline, while Dewey's theory slipped into obscurity. Yet Dewey's multifaceted critique of Aristotle's science has not yet been appreciated, nor has its relevance to unresolved questions in the philosophy of science and philosophy of logic been adequately evaluated.

Measurement: The Essence That Secures Inference

Aristotle said that "in pursuing the truth one must start from things that are always in the same state and never change" (Ross trans. quoted in Dewey 1938, LW12:133). Aristotle may be right about this, but the stable entity is not unchanging Being. The basic understanding of the general nature of things has shifted from Parmenides' postulate of an unchanging and timeless Being governing apparent phenomena to the initial assumption of Galileo and Newton that motion and time rule.

Aristotle starts from what is self-evident and moves by means of inference alone to new knowledge. His theory of the "cause" of the success of mathematics differs from that of today, which institutes different axioms and definitions to suit various purposes. Even so, mathematical operations appear to support Aristotle's contention that it is possible to secure inference by means of sanctioned transformations from self-evident knowledge (adopted axioms) to new knowledge (consequences of the adopted axioms). Given the "self-evident" concept of number and the "self-evident" concept of addition, inference moves securely to new and conclusive knowledge.

For Aristotle the relation between concepts and knowledge is direct. Insight grounds self-evidence. From a self-evident subject matter, say, a circle, its attributes can be guaranteed by deductive inference. Deductive inference alone determines logical forms (Dewey 1938, LW12:160). On the other hand, because the object of induction is changing appearance, inductive inference is unstable. Securing inductive inferences involves confirmation by observation and is possible only for particular objects in their particularity. The copula represents unchanging and timeless Being, so a single judgment is enough to draw a conclusion. For inductive inference, a single judgment about particular matters gives rise to the problem of induction, which is a problem only partly resolved by the rise of probability and statistics.

Scientific practices today do not treat single judgments as final. The direct, immediate evaluation of the qualities of a subject matter are not constant enough to be of evidential value. Direct judgments of weight by the eye, for instance, are replaced by a *series* of estimates, and direct judgment of color is replaced by a spectral display that measures a color by its wavelength. Moreover, judgments are often built into instruments calibrated on the basis of qualitative continuities not explicitly present. Even a simple visual judgment of a temperature by looking at mercury levels in a glass tube is more than a single judgment, for the instrument itself embodies and depends upon the adoption of standards. The correlation of selected qualities to instituted conceptual standards depends on many kinds of interaction. Measuring discloses relations of characters and generic traits of existence in its operations, which function as standards that regulate inference. Only after standard techniques and equipment are adopted do the characters of things begin to appear.

The stable "essence" that does not change and upon which science is based is not Being. Rather, it is the relations of characters disclosed by developing and using standards which, once adopted, function as sources of stability. Inference is secured by the development of stable characters and kinds correlated with interactions and with standard equipment, measures, and techniques. Standards are the functional essence of repeatable experiments. Scientists do not rely only on testing and confirming particular objects in their particularity. They correlate changes with abstract systems of relations that designate the relationships between qualitative characteristics of a situation. New kinds of things and new kinds of relations are determined to be constituents of a systematic set of changes that are related to one another not by inference but by a tested functional correspondence of interactions (Dewey 1938, LW12:133).

The Aristotelian distinction between deduction and induction is traditionally used to mark off the domain of formal logic and mathematics from the domain of other scientific disciplines. "Logical forms" function to secure deductive inferences, and scientific methods, broadly conceived, function to secure inductive inferences. Aristotle distinguished kinds of inference on the basis of their source of knowledge. From the "formal" essences of things one deduces; from the "accidental" individuating matter one induces. Such forms "cause" and secure knowledge of truth. In the absence of an Aristotelian metaphysics the distinction is oversimplified and misleading. Dewey tackles the problem of securing inferences quite differently. Deduction is marked off from induction not so much by the kind of subject matter each acts upon but by the functional role each plays in inquiry. The concept of inductive inference ranges in functional meaning from an inference reporting a mere observation to the more precise concepts of "statistical inference." One function of the distinction between inductive and deductive inference is to mark two distinct ways of securing inferences.

The thesis, again, is that it is operationally instituted standards, not the kind of inference, that are responsible for securing warranted judgments and that the subject matter itself suggests possibilities used to direct operations. Consider the spectrograph, which functions not only as a standard but as a heuristic for discovering and making novel correlations of changes. In addition to rainbow colors, a spectrograph exhibits dark lines.[5] Direct observation of dark lines does not constitute knowledge; rather, it constitutes a problem. Initially, dark lines were attributed to imperfections of the prism used to transform the light beam. In the early 1800s, when techniques for standardizing lenses were perfected and the dark lines still persisted, inquiry into their nature began. Independent inquiry discovered chemical elements that radiate characteristic energy. The correlation of periodic functions with radiant energy could now be correlated with the functioning of a spectrograph, introducing a means of correlating wavelengths with colors of visible radiation. The dark lines also function as a heuristic. The dark lines persisting in the color spectrum suggests "missing" elements. Comparative operations correlated relations of characters with interactions. A dark line appears where a color would appear, if the related radiant energy had not been absorbed. Inquiry into these dark lines resulted in the discovery of characters (wavelengths of light) and relations of characters (wavelengths to trigonometric functions), which, in turn, are correlated with interactions that direct light through a prism and so produce generic traits (colors and dark lines). Not only did the spectrograph intervene in this process to help establish characters and generic kinds in the study of optics, but the correlations of relations of characters, in independent inquiries, further help to secure inferences about, for example, the chemical composition of the sun. For instance, the judgment that the sun is composed of a specific percentage of hydrogen is constructed by a series of intermediate partial judgments (Dewey 1938, LW12:143). In this case, it is that hydrogen is correlated with certain frequencies of light, which are correlated with complex trigonometric functions and then correlated with equipment that transforms the qualitative whole (sunlight) into its generic traits: specific series of colors and dark lines.

Scientific status is accorded to disciplines such as mathematics and physics that feature deductive inference. The praise of deductive systems and procedures is well earned. But it is a mistake to suppose that *deductive inference* is responsible for making inferences secure. Deductive inference only suggests possibilities. Deduction alone cannot be what makes an inference secure. Dewey locates "the cause" of secure inferences in the adoption of formulations of subject matter such as axioms, theorems, and proof rules. He also finds it in calibrated measuring devices and techniques that equally function as standards to direct and control inference. Such standards allow reformulations of qualities, refinements of measurements, and reconfigurations of models of quantities and qualities of subject matter that function in their own way to regulate further inference. The conceptual subject matters illustrated by mathematics and the various so-called "concrete" subject matters of other scientific disciplines are all made secure in the same general way, namely, by hypothetical universal propositions and existential generic propositions working together in appropriate ways according to principles whose discovery and formulation is the objective of logic as the theory of inquiry.

The Function of Logical Form: To Secure Inference

In his introduction to the critical edition of Dewey's *Logic: The Theory of Inquiry*, Nagel (1986) finds that Dewey's definition of logical form "makes no sense." Nagel's negative evaluation of Dewey's logical theory stems from his expectations about the nature of logical form. To help explicate Dewey's conception of logical form, the present section contrasts their respective views on the issue of logical form. Dewey treats logical form in its functional capacity to secure inferences. Nagel does not.

Nagel's disapproving tone is odd in light of his own work on "Measurement" published in 1932. In this work, Nagel delineates, in a manner consistent with Dewey's account, the role of measurement in inquiry. Nagel writes that "measurement as practiced in the developed sciences" includes "acts of identification, delimitation," and "comparison" (Nagel 1932). He clarifies that measurement is connected with predication, because "measurement can be regarded as the delimitation and fixation of our ideas of things, so that the determination of what it is to be a man or to be a circle is a case of measurement" (Nagel 1932). Measurement is not primarily numerical, Nagel points out, although enumeration is a most versatile and fruitful kind of formulation. Measurements can transform qualities of things into numerical form which is susceptible to mathematical treatment, and this transformation discloses characters of existence in its operations. Nagel discusses how the character of density, for instance, is formulated out of subject matters in much the same terms that Dewey uses. He emphasizes the necessity of correlating characters with operations that elicit interactions. Nagel writes that the character of density

> which liquids manifest in relation to one another [can be defined] as the capacity of a liquid to float upon other liquids. Liquid **a** will be said to be more dense than **b** if **b** can float on **a** but **a** cannot float on **b**. And it can and *must* be shown experimentally, that, for a set of liquids distinguishable from each other by all sorts of physical and chemical properties, the relation > (more dense) is a transitive asymmetrical relation: if liquid **a** is more dense than **b** (i. e., **b** floats on **a**) and if **b** is more dense than **c**, then **a** is more dense than **c** (i. e., **c** floats on **a**). (Nagel 1932)

There are many more types of characters than at first appear likely. Nagel notes that only after standard measures are adopted do the characters of things begin to appear. And the subject matter from which density is abstracted "is some discovered qualitative domain which is sufficiently homogeneous to allow identification as a well-defined range of a single quality. Within this domain the character studied must be capable of such a serial gradation that a transitive asymmetrical relation can be discovered to hold between discriminated elements" (Nagel 1932). Nagel also explains how the character of equality functions to regulate measurements. Equality, to be measured, must be transformed into operationally defined terms that are built into equipment and employed in routine techniques. The diversity of equipment for performing such operations reflects "the diversity of qualities homogeneous enough to permit a range of serial gradation to be instituted" (Nagel 1932).

Nagel's interest in writing this article on measurement is also compatible with Dewey's. His main point, he says, is to shift the interpretation of the scientific subject matter from that of an opposition between "concrete actuality" and "a realm of essences having a necessary reference to existences" to an interpretation in which selected qualities are transformed through comparative-eliminative operations into ordered relationships between existences. Nagel argues, as Dewey does, that the hypostatization of relations such as space and time "may be construed more simply as pervasive relations between events, rather than as containers extrinsic and outside the changing qualities" (Nagel 1932). If this approach is generalized, Nagel argues, in accord with Dewey, the dichotomy between primary and secondary qualities, instead of instituting a distinction between objective and subjective, indicates rather a distinction between those qualities which are already transformed and so capable of fundamental measurement and those not yet transformed by operations designed to elicit measurable interactions.

Nagel elsewhere explains: "For we require to know only the most general characters of a subject matter (that which it has in common with everything else) in order to reason upon its validity" (Nagel and Cohen 1993, 185–86). One is tempted to suppose that Nagel refers to characters such as density (extracted operationally from existential subject matter) and equality (extracted operationally from conceptual subject matter). This quoted passage, however, comes from Nagel's introduction to formal logic and has nothing to do with measurement.

Nagel and Dewey agree on the functional role of measurement in inquiry. Nagel even elaborates on the way in which qualities of subject matter are transformed into measured serial relationships in the way Dewey (1938, LW12:212–19; 379–90) does. They part company at the point where

Dewey argues that such transformations of selected qualities of a subject matter are instituted to regulate inference for the *logical* purpose of securing warranted judgments. Nagel does not allow, where Dewey does, that the standards adopted and instituted for the purpose of measurement are examples of *logical form*. Dewey argues that the function of logical form is to secure inferences, and standards once adopted anchor inferences. Dewey views logical form as a formulation of subject matter that becomes logical by virtue of its capacity to regulate inferences and to secure warranted judgments. Dewey's definition of logical form encompasses instruments designed to measure, weigh, and inspect (e.g., x-ray, MRI, cat-scan), conceptual systems such as calculus or statistics, instituted standards such as soil-texture-and-color schemes used to reconstruct historical environments, or even computer programs.

However, Nagel rejects Dewey's definition. Nagel uses Aristotle's statements to clarify the nature of logical form. Nagel writes, "Logic may be regarded as the study of the most general, the most pervasive characters of both whatever is and whatever may be" (Nagel and Cohen 1993, 186). It is not surprising that Nagel traces this metaphysical insight to Aristotle, who was the first to clearly recognize "that since the general nature of things is the ground for the correctness or incorrectness of reasoning, that general nature is also expressed in the principles of logic or inference" (Nagel and Cohen 1993, 186). Yet Nagel's endorsement of Aristotle's claim is puzzling. The general nature of things, for Aristotle, is a thing's universal formal essence. Essence is the fully realized functioning of a being. That is, when the active formal principle is in *ousia*, an individual (thing) can be said to be. *Ousia* is an individual being (thing) in one sense and a species (kind of thing) in another. The formal essence can be expressed in *logos* and realized in cognition. Aristotle can say that the general nature of things is also expressed in the principles of logic, because his metaphysics allows that universal formal essences exist (and in some sense participate both in the being and in the word). Nagel would never endorse the metaphysics of securing logical forms solely through cognition.[6] So how does he understand Aristotle's account of how the correctness of reasoning is guaranteed?

To understand how Nagel interprets Aristotle's statement, I turn to what Nagel takes to be a shortcoming of traditional logical theory. Traditional logic is basically sound, Nagel argues, because it has made clear the formal factors upon which validity depends. Nagel locates the basis of the validity of logical relations and logical principles in "the generic traits of all things whatsoever" (Nagel and Cohen 1993, 185). He explains that the main function of formal logic is to guide and test inferences. Yet he writes that "traditional logic has been remiss in not studying systematically those logical relations which are the basis for the complicated inferences in the mathematical and natural sciences" (Nagel and Cohen 1993, 111). The key must lie in what Nagel means by "the generic traits of all things whatsoever." Dewey also argues that generic traits of existence are the subject matter of logical theory. But Nagel cannot mean what Dewey means, nor does he mean what Aristotle meant. So, what does Nagel mean? "Most propositions are about objects like the sun and the stars, the earth and its contents, our fellow-creatures and their affairs, and the like; and the implications between propositions, which is the subject matter of logic, has to do with the possible relations between all such objects" (Nagel and Cohen 1993, 18).

Therefore, the subject matter of logic involves the forms of implication between propositions that have "to do with the possible relations" between objects. Nagel believes that actual relations between objects are discovered by experimental procedures and statistical inference. But what are the "possible relations" that have to do with all such objects, where such objects range from human affairs to astronomy?

Mathematics systematically treats of "possible relations," and mathematical relations have to do with everything from economics to astronomy. Perhaps mathematical logic is the key to grasping the "general nature of things," given the view that "logical relations" are the "basis for the complicated inferences" found in various sciences. Nagel, after all, applauds mathematical logic as an improvement upon traditional logic; and mathematical logic supports the idea that "logical form alone" is enough to secure validity. Along such lines Nagel is able to conceive of logical forms as self-validating relations (between propositions) that are entirely independent of subject matter. In particular, such a theory of logical form is not bound to give, much less address, an account of measurement practices and techniques.

Dewey and Nagel both agree about the nature and importance of measurement, and while this appears a reasonable way to avoid Nagel's apparent endorsement of Aristotle's metaphysical way of securing inference, measurement techniques are not included in what Nagel means by logical form. For Nagel also says, "As principles of being, logical principles are universally applicable . . . when we draw a conclusion from the premises correctly we are tacitly recognizing the truth of the proposition, which is grounded in the general nature of things" (Nagel and Cohen 1993, 186). The simplest way to understand this claim is to suppose that Nagel requires logical form to meet criteria of an architectonic scholastic realism. Yet what he says in his article on measurement rules this interpretation out. Nagel does not believe a proposition *is* true in the way scholastics believed. He interprets the passages from Aristotle in a manner more consistent with empirical science but not so compatible that it reduces to methods and procedures of measurement adopted in such sciences. The logical relations he has in mind are not measurable. Rather, in his introduction to mathematical logic, Nagel moves immediately into a discussion of the relations between language and grammar overlooked by traditional logic. He writes that traditional logic "overlooked the logical properties of the copula upon which the validity of an inference rests. It was therefore hindered from developing a more general theory of inference and more satisfactory calculus of reasoning than the syllogism. The theory of compound propositions was neglected by it, and the important topic of the existential import of propositions was not explicitly considered" (Nagel and Cohen 1993, 111). Nagel also mentions that "implications like the following: *If* A *is taller than* B, *and* B *is taller than* C, *then* A *is taller than* C do not fall into any of the types . . . discussed" in the older logic (Nagel and Cohen 1993, 111). Nevertheless, even with the substantial expansion of recognized logical forms in contemporary mathematical logic, the techniques of formulating qualities of a subject matter itself and of correlating relations of characters with interactions discovered in operations that transform the qualities in question still lie outside of the domain of what Nagel is prepared to acknowledge as logical relations, namely, the grammatical relations found in language.[7] Following Aristotle, he interprets logical form as relations between propositions in an argument form. Ignoring techniques of measurement and of extracting characters correlated with interactions used by the natural sciences to secure inference, Nagel instead focuses exclusively on language and grammar.

Though he would protest such a claim, Nagel appears to harbor a hypostatized "realm of essences" in his expectations for logical form. Nagel quotes the metaphysical statements of Aristotle with approval: Logical inquiry "investigates being as being." His interpretation of this statement, though, is simply that "logical principles must be formal—they represent the common characters of any subject matter, and they cannot be employed to differentiate one subject matter from another" (Nagel and Cohen 1993, 186). Yet Nagel, in his article on measurement, shows precisely how logical operations do function to differentiate one subject matter from another and how each can be made susceptible to measurement. Nevertheless, "logical" does not mean to Nagel what it means to Dewey. "Logical" to Dewey means a formulation of subject matter that can be instituted and used to regulate inferences. To Nagel, a logical form "must be formal," not in Dewey's sense of being capable of regulating inference but in the hypostatized sense of being valid-in-itself. Nagel adopts part of the scholastic understanding of the function of logical form (that logical form alone guarantees . . .) and substitutes for the scholastic claim that it "guarantees the truth of a proposition" the relational claim that it "guarantees the validity of an argument form."

If Dewey had stayed away from the term *logical form*, perhaps what he had to say about securing inference might have gained an earlier and more favorable hearing.

Conclusion

Propositions do not primarily "represent." They function as intermediate means that promote interactions so that the qualities involved in correlations of changes are discovered and related by measurements to one another. New qualities, in turn, modify prior formulations and function to regulate and secure inferences.

Regulating inference involves several related factors. Qualitative characteristics of a subject matter itself suggest formulations for its own regulation, while characters that designate relationships between generic traits of existence may also be formulated on their own terms. These formulations occur in operations directed by relations of characters imported from prior inquiries, and they promote interactions of materials of both conceptual and existential kinds. Techniques of measuring promote the construction of equipment and procedures, which, in turn, function to regulate interactions and direct transformations of materials of both conceptual and existential kinds. Resulting propositions function to establish relations of characters and determine relationships among generic kinds. Comparative operations of measurement are involved at every step along the way and are used as standards to direct and control inferences in systematic ways. The operations used to transform qualities are often controlled by nested standardized transformations of subject matter, each of which institute a series of principled judgments.

For instance, the felt effects of an earthquake are transformed by a mechanical recording device into a visual line on a graph, and this is eventually interpreted in terms of an instituted scale of exponential intensity. The transformation of subject matter and intercalibrated measurements, in this case, records the qualitative movement felt during an earthquake as a line on a graph. Such records may eventually suggest the construction of new equipment or techniques to promote and record interactions in novel ways.

Relevant abstract relations of characters are likewise devised and employed (adapted from other inquiries) to make sense of banks of such data. Inferences become secure only by means of reliable correlations of interactions of formulations of selected generic traits of existence (involved in individual situations in which doubt is a pervasive quality) with formulations of relations of characters. Relations of characters result from the strict correlation of interactions with prior formulations of standards of various kinds. In this case, the magnitudes of earthquakes have been defined in terms of a scale instituted in terms of sound wave amplitudes of kinds S and Π, and these are coordinated with velocities that calibrate a spatial measure with a temporal measure. The resulting figure is calibrated with a numerical scale, which is further correlated with characteristic types and levels of damage sustained by buildings built to specific codes. Standards imposed on the subject matter, both conceptual and existential, are calibrated to each other with each reformulation of the subject matter.

Of course, occurrences of earthquakes cannot be reliably predicted. This inability to secure reliable predictions of earthquakes reflects the limits of techniques of measuring and instituting standards. But it also suggests that limits of techniques of measuring and instituting standards have not yet been reached in an inquiry into the nature of earthquakes. More to the point, what this example as a whole illustrates is that practices and techniques of measurement are indispensable to a careful regulation of inference and are an integral part of a theory of inquiry. As such, measurement lies at the heart of logical theory.

Notes

1. In Boyle's ontology, weight and size are primary qualities that function as essences do in Aristotle's ontology. In Aristotle's, weight and size are accidents that function as secondary qualities do in Boyle's.

2. If you can point to a cause of something, you are thinking of its efficient cause, not its formal cause.

3. "The proportionality factor has the dimensions of an action (energy multiplied by time)" (Pullman 1998, 261).

4. Note the following convention is important to understanding this point. "Instead of saying that the wavelength is l centimeters, it is customary to count the number of crests per centimeter of the wave (which is equal to $1/l$), and call it the wave number, k. Thus $k = 1/l$ per cm. Such a wave is traveling in some direction and its wave vector, $\mathbf{k}$, whose size is given by k." Adapted from Chandrasekhar 1998, 51.

5. I am indebted for this example to Dorres 1994.

6. Kant 1787 can be read as a critique of the power of *intellectus agens*: The nature of the thing in-itself is not available to us.

7. Nagel is mistaken when he claims such topics were not covered by scholastic logicians. See Hickman 1980 for references.

Works Cited

Chandrasekhar, B. S. 1998. *Why Things Are the Way They Are*. Cambridge: Cambridge University Press.

Dewey, John. 1938. *Logic: The Theory of Inquiry*. New York: Henry Holt. Reprinted in LW12.

Dorres, Mattias. 1994. Balances, Spectroscopes, and the Reflexive Nature of Experiment. *Studies in History and Philosophy of Science* 25 (1):1–36.

Dumitriu, Anton. 1977. *History of Logic*, vol. 4. Tunbridge Wells: Abacus Press.

Erdos, Paul. 1973. *The Art of Counting: Selected Writings*. Edited by Joel Spencer. Cambridge: MIT Press.

Hickman, Larry. 1980. *Modern Theories of Higher Level Predicates: Second Intentions in the Neuzeit*. Munich: Philosophia.

Holmes, Frederic Lawrence. 1985. *Lavoisier and the Chemistry of Life: An Exploration of Scientific Creativity*. Madison: University of Wisconsin Press.

Kant, Immanuel. 1787. *Critique of Pure Reason*. Translated by Norman Kent Smith. New York: St. Martin's Press, 1929, 1933, 1961.

Middleton, W. E. Knowles. 1966. *A History of the Thermometer and Its Use in Meteorology*. Baltimore: Johns Hopkins University Press.

Nagel, Ernest. 1932. Measurement. In *Erkenntnis*, vol. 2, book 5:313–33.

———. 1986. Introduction to LW12:ix–xxvii.

Nagel, Ernest, and Morris Cohen. 1993. *An Introduction to Logic*. 2d ed. Indianapolis: Hackett.

Pullman, Bernard. 1998. *The Atom in the History of Human Thought*. Oxford: Oxford University Press.

Shachtman, Tom. 1999. *Absolute Zero and the Conquest of the Cold*. New York: Houghton Mifflin.

Weast, R. C., ed. 1977. *CRC Handbook of Chemistry and Physics*. Cleveland: CRC Press.

10

Qualities, Universals, Kinds, and the New Riddle of Induction

Tom Burke

In *Fact, Fiction, and Forecast* (1954), Nelson Goodman presented his "new riddle of induction," illustrated by the famous *grue* predicate. The traditional problem of induction, viewed as a problem of *justifying* induction, may be disposed of easily enough, Goodman asserts, by noting that induction is no more justifiable without recourse to inductive arguments than deduction is justifiable without recourse to deduction itself. The justification in either case is circular, and we need not look for anything better; that is, we should not require what is not possible. Whether we accept this dissolution of the traditional justification problem or not, there is still a problem with induction, not to justify it once and for all but to formulate reliable principles that allow us to distinguish good and bad inductive inferences. Extant theories of inductive generalization and confirmation are apparently not adequate in this regard.

Goodman presents his *grue* example to demonstrate this problem. The *grue* predicate applies to any blue thing not observed before a certain fixed time *and* to anything examined before that time and found to be green. If the given time is, say, January 1, 2000, then our current observations of a thousand (so far unobserved) emeralds would disconfirm the generalization that emeralds are *grue*, whereas observations of those same thousand emeralds prior to that date would have confirmed the claim that emeralds are *grue* as much as that they are green. Thus inductive generalizations at different times could lead us to opposite results. How can we decide when this is or is not happening in particular stages of an inquiry?

An understandable first reaction to this example is that the *grue* predicate is simply too strange to warrant serious concern. We need not be bothered by such arbitrary and artificial predicates. The example may even be thought to have some force against Goodman's own nominalism because of its obvious nonsensical results. It may be more to the purposes of sci-

ence to presume that continuity, projectability, and other such "generals"
have a kind of reality as much as do individual emeralds. But this kind of
reaction moves us in the wrong direction (for the present essay anyway).
Goodman's example does apparently illustrate an interesting logical problem. The *grue* predicate is odd because its time dependence is unusual when
applied to things like emeralds. But how can we be sure that the sciences
and our commonsense beliefs are not peppered with more subtle *grue*-like
predicates? The predicates *whale, fish,* and *mammal* were misconstrued
(ill-defined, insufficiently specified) for some time by many who believed
on the basis of selected evidence that whales are fish. The problem in this
case is not time dependent but is due to reliance on a too-limited range of
observable features of things. The idea of restricting and not restricting observations to a given set of features can play much the same role here that
observing before and after a given time plays in the *grue* example. Similarly, in medieval astronomy, evidence garnered, examined, and analyzed
over a long period confirmed a system of generalizations involving odd
predicates like *celestial sphere* and *epicycle*. Again the problem is not time
dependent but involves hypothesis formation that goes way beyond what
is directly observable. If we rule out the use of telescopes and other new
observational technologies, or if such technologies had not emerged on the
scene when they did, there might not be any reliable way to dispel a medieval cosmology. Again, the notion of observing the heavens with and without telescopes plays a similar role that observing before and after a given
time plays in the *grue* example.

Could a more carefully formulated theory of confirmation serve to identify such mistakes in a reliable way? How and when do we decide such
matters? What are the principles by which we distinguish acceptable from
unacceptable predicates that are constitutive of hypotheses confirmed by
our experience? How do we deal with potential restrictions on sources of
evidence or methods of observation if we have no grounds for realizing
that such restrictions are now coloring our view of the world? Is it just a
matter of luck and happenstance?

This essay will not address these larger questions to any great extent.
Rather, the limited aim here is to explain what Dewey might say in particular about the formulation of the *grue* example. Goodman's problem of
distinguishing good and bad inductive inferences (and their constituent
predicates) is an important one, but the *grue* example misconstrues this
complex problem for certain technical reasons, due to ambiguities that contemporary logical theory has not yet come to terms with.

Goodman's problem is a problem for the theory of induction and thus
for logical theory in general. We may safely assume that behind the whole

discussion of these issues over the last five decades is a certain view of logic hammered out by Russell, Carnap, Tarski, Quine, and many others. Goodman's nominalism hinges in essential ways on a certain view of formal logic with an extensional quantification theory at its core. This raises any number of issues, but the one issue most germane to the present discussion is the conception of predicates ensconced in this view of logic. The problem here is the implicit assumption that there is just one type of first-order predicate. Predicate symbols stand for properties and relations that hold for given individuals. The ontological status of these properties and relations, as general terms, is problematic, raising questions such as whether we need to be able to quantify over such things and thus acknowledge them as higher-order individuals in themselves. Several such problems could occupy us here. But underlying all of them is an unquestioned assumption that properties and relations constitute one logical category (symbolized by some indexed collection of capital letters, say, in a recursive first-order grammar). Questioning this assumption is essential, Dewey would say, to dissolving if not solving many of these problems. Before we get locked into any particular formalism like first-order or higher-order quantification theory, and putting aside for now the whole nominalism/realism issue, we first need to acknowledge several distinct types of properties and relations (and respective predicates). Goodman's *grue* example seems confusing just because we have not done this. The force of the argument based on such examples rides on an unfortunate ambiguity in how we regard properties and relations of things.

Dewey casts logic broadly as a theory of inquiry. It is not just a study of formal languages even if this is an integral part of its subject matter. Dewey's notion that inquiry is a clarification and transformation of some concrete problematic situation (1938, chap. 6) is well known. This pattern of inquiry is essentially the basic pattern of experience—a redirection of life activities against disturbances or imbalances (1916, chap. 11; 1925, chap. 1; 1930; 1934, chap. 3)—except that it also involves deliberate observation and experimentation guided by theoretical reflection. In short, inquiry is a type of concrete experience that involves experimentally applied thinking. Of special interest here is the notion that inquiry involves the correlative development and manipulation of both existential and ideational contents:

> Inquiry is progressive and cumulative. Propositions are the instruments by which provisional conclusions of preparatory inquiries are summed up, recorded, and retained for subsequent uses. In this way they function as effective means, material and procedural, in the conduct of inquiry, till the latter

institutes subject-matter so unified in significance as to be warrantably assertible. It follows (1) that there is no such thing as an isolated proposition; or, positively stated, that propositions stand in ordered relations to one another; and (2) that there are two main types of such order, one referring to the factual or existential material which determines the final subject of judgment, the other referring to the ideational material, the conceptual meanings, which determine the predicate of final judgment. In the words of ordinary use, there are the propositions having the relation which constitutes *inference*, and the propositions having the serial relation which constitutes reasoning or *discourse*. (LW12:310; also see Dewey 1942, LW15:37–38)

This passage ranges widely over matters we need not delve into here. Of particular importance, though, is the identification of two types of ordered relations among propositions, namely, existential and ideational. In his 1938 *Logic* (and in several papers written at roughly the same time: 1935, 1936a, 1936b, 1936c) this distinction serves as the basis for a rather elaborate scheme for classifying different sorts of propositions and their constituent terms. In particular, it supports acknowledgment of three distinct sorts of predicates.

In the first place, we use predicates like *green, blue, sweet,* or *soft* to denote *qualities* of things. Qualities are not limited to simple or atomic sense data, but they are the most immediate results of exploiting various operational capabilities and observational sensitivities. A so-called particular proposition is one in which a quality is attributed to some discernible *this* or *that*: This is green; that is soft. Things like voter preferences or salary levels as recorded by means of some properly administered survey instrument may just as well be regarded as qualities of individuals in a given population. Presumably there may be qualities of various arities, not just unary qualities. Hence, *this is between that and the other* may be as much a qualitative proposition as any color attribution. A spatial *between* quality may be seen to hold among three or more individuals as immediately as are the color qualities of those individuals. Generally speaking, observational results—data—are constituted by particular propositions in this sense.

Second, some predicates function in inquiry to denote abstract ideas, or what Dewey sometimes prefers to call *universals*. By themselves, universals and the abstract propositions they constitute are not directly subject to inductive methods. They are subject rather to standards of comprehensive systematic coherence. It must be said though that Dewey does not embrace any traditional notion of universals. Dewey identifies ideas as plans of action and thus espouses a kind of operationalism in which ideas designate possible ways of acting, possible modes of being, abilities to act or be in specific ways, etc. (LW12:289, 350, 516): "Ideas are operational in that they instigate and direct further operations of observation; they are proposals and plans for acting upon existing conditions to bring new facts to light and to organize all the selected facts into a coherent whole" (LW12:116). As denoting possible modes of action, ideas are termed *universals* by Dewey in virtue of their abstract function in inquiry. Possible ways of acting or modes of being, as terms which are functionally universal, are rooted in basic animal abilities tempered by distinctly human cultural forces. Dewey's characterization of universals as abilities or possible modes of action is rooted in a natural history of biological and sociocultural developments. He discusses such genetic matters in the opening chapters of his 1938 *Logic* as necessary background for his logical theory. While genetic considerations are crucial to understanding the functional nature of universals in inquiry, our primary concern here is specifically with that function. Engrained abilities may function as universals insofar as they are possibly relevant and thus available for use in virtually any situation that comes about. Such abilities embody ideational aspects of inquiry insofar as a specimen inquirer has the capacity to consider different options regarding how to act under given conditions, rather than simply being driven mechanically by established habits. Existential conditions will support certain suggestions as to possible options, and these suggestions take on the status of "ideas" when developed symbolically in relation with other ideas (LW12:58, 113, 275, 300, 350). Reflection upon ideational aspects of a problem constitutes a significant portion of our abstract discourse in a given inquiry, including (but not limited to) mathematical discourse (1938, chap. 20). Of particular note here is Dewey's point that universal propositions, stating relations among universals, will be *definitional* in character, ideal, and very likely contrary to fact, as opposed to existentially descriptive (LW12:259–60, 270–71, 300–303, 404–5).

Third, we use predicates in inquiry to denote what Dewey refers to as *kinds*. Classifying an individual emerald as being of the kind *green* (a singular proposition) or subsuming a kind *emerald* under a kind *green* (a generic proposition) differs in important ways both from subsuming a universal *emerald* under a universal *green* and from attributing a quality *green* to some individual emerald. Nevertheless, a kind constitutes a systematic synthesis of such qualitative and universal contents, that is, an integration of existential and ideational contents. If anything is basic in Dewey's philosophy of logic, it is the claim that we cannot rectify an agent's grasp of things in the world except in terms of that agent's operational abilities and possible qualitative outcomes of exercising such abilities. Quality predicates and universal predicates serve to denote each of these aspects of human experience, respectively. But attunements to kinds, as well-behaved systematic associations of such abilities and the qualitative events to which these abilities provide access, are the primary means by which an inquirer finds structure and meaning in the world. Actual objects serve as actual or potential instantiations of kinds insofar as they are capable of evidencing an array of characteristic qualitative traits resulting from prescribed systematic activities. This sort of classification is obviously subject to inductive methods. Qualitative propositions express supporting (confirming or disconfirming) data for such classifications, while universal propositions should convey whatever systematicity there is in the activities that yield such data. This view of kinds incorporates and integrates operational and empirical meaningfulness into the basic fabric of inquiry, where the operational contents of kinds are directly relatable to ideational matters while the empirical contents of kinds are directly existential in nature.

To illustrate these three distinct sorts of predicates, consider the notion of temperature. (1) Our bodily sense of cold and warmth is a sense of heat-differential qualities. Temperatures, as degrees of heat, are rather what we determine primarily with thermometers. Thermometer readings indicate *qualities* attributable to objects to which thermometers are applied. (2) The *abstract idea* of temperature is grounded in such measurement capabilities, but these remain mere possibilities when the idea of temperature is employed abstractly in relation to other ideas, for instance, in the theory of ideal gases or in thermodynamics more generally. The idea of temperature is meaningful because of its grounding in operational measurement activities, though its full meaning is expanded greatly by explicating its relations to other ideas. Ideas which are not so simply grounded, such as the idea of *energy*, are rendered (more) meaningful by their abstract linkage with ideas like that of temperature. In turn, by virtue of such linkages, temperature qualities (e.g., of objects to which thermometers cannot be applied) may be determined indirectly by means other than thermometers (by registering colors, pressures, electrical potential differences, and so forth). (3) A temperature *kind* may be specified with respect to one or more classes of thermometers and methods for their use and is thus articulated in terms of specifications for the proper use of these instruments and the range of readings possible as results of their employment. *Temperature* as a kind term is inherently a general term applicable in certain existential conditions—integrating the *idea* of temperature (and its abstract links to other ideas) with a respective range of registrable temperature *qualities*. Another kind that we might call *water in a fluid state* would incorporate, among many things, specifications referring to the kind *temperature* with allowable thermometer readings falling anywhere between zero and a hundred degrees centigrade, excluding readings outside of this range (in a simplest characterization anyway, applicable under usual terrestrial conditions). The point of this example is that we need to distinguish the abstract idea embodied in possible uses of thermometers, the potential readings we get from mercury levels or digital displays, and systematic pairings of these possible uses and their results. This distinguishes three sorts of temperature predicates—a universal, respective qualities, and one or more kinds—all of which function rather differently, though in an understandably coordinated way, in the language of physics. Failing to distinguish these predicates can easily lead to nonsense because predicates are not simply intersubstitutable as we move between existential and ideational considerations in physical inquiries.

So where does Goodman's *grue* example stand in this kind of framework? On one reading, one could essentially treat the *grue* example as an abstract construction, incorporating relevant universals like *green* and *blue*. It would also incorporate abstract conceptions of *time* and *observation*. There is nothing illegitimate here so long as we realize that we are dealing with a system of abstractions. An abstract notion of observation in such definitions must be handled with care, though, insofar as it is a notion employed generally in logical theory and cannot be constrained so easily by its use in specific cases like the *grue* definition. To define a universal *grue* that puts temporal limits on observation processes is not unlike defining *fish* in such a way that one is explicitly limited once and for all to considering only specific features of things to the exclusion of anything else that may later seem to gain relevance, and not unlike condoning only currently used instruments and methods of observation in astronomy to the exclusion of others as they arrive on the scene. Such restrictions may be legitimate for purposes of analytical simplicity (say) or for historical analysis, but it runs contrary to the sorts of concerns we should have when it comes to justifying inductive inferences about fish or planets in light of full-blown contemporary scientific methods. In general terms, proper applications of systems of abstract ideas in concrete inquiries are bound by principles whose incremental development and standing trumps any one abstract definition taken singularly. Over the centuries we have developed a body of guiding principles of good experimental design, of proper methods of testing and confirmation, and so forth. Any abstract predicate whose definition restricts the use of these principles requires that one should not use the techniques of induction properly. It is hardly surprising then that methods of induction are at best difficult to evaluate when considering such a predicate, because these methods are hamstrung from the start by the predicate's definition. One is inclined to say that the problem lies with the abstract predicate rather than with principles of induction.

On Dewey's account, abstract definitions in and of themselves are not immediately subject to inductive methods. Goodman is mistaken if he thinks that his *grue* predicate is already subject to inductive methods just because it speaks of observations at or before or after a given time. Applying the *grue* definition in concrete situations in such a way as to inductively distinguish grue things is not just an abstract procedure. On another reading of the *grue* example, one could treat it as a concretely applicable system of specifications for a certain kind of thing (as opposed to an abstract universal). Or we could construct such specifications for a certain kind of thing from the definition of a *grue* universal. In either case, one identifies certain appropriate methods of interaction applicable to candidate objects, along with a range of qualities that should result from applying these methods under which conditions. Because Goodman was not sensitive to the distinctions we are working with here, there are several ways to translate his definition into Dewey's terminology. The predicates *green* and *blue* may be taken to denote either qualities or kinds. Similarly, phrases like *after January 1, 2000* and *at or before January 1, 2000* may be regarded as denoting kinds or else as specifying intervals of temporal qualities in a wholesale fashion. The possible combinations of these options make for several ways to characterize the kind *grue*, though they all lead pretty much to the same conclusion here given the simplicity and straightforward correspondence of these particular kinds and respective qualities. Indeed, it is such simplicity and straightforward correspondence that makes it difficult not to run these logical categories together as if they were indistinguishable. The distinction is more salient with kinds like *fish* or *heavenly body*. But we are concerned now with the predicate *grue*. It is safe to read Goodman as if he were wanting to compare and contrast kinds like *green*, *blue*, and *grue*, ultimately to make a point about how their relations to each other and to kinds like *emerald* may be inductively ascertained. The role of the term *observation* here is also flexible, depending on whether we want to read it as a kind term in the language of gemology or as a more general term used in the language of (inductive) logic. One would think that Goodman intends to use this term in the latter sense, and that is how we will take it here. It is a meta-term widely employed in the specifications for any kind term where observational methods applied under certain conditions are linked with expected qualitative results.

On this reading one has to admit the oddity of the kind term *grue* in contrast with kind terms like *blue*, *green*, or *emerald*. Only a simplistic conception of inductive generalization would move us to say that observations of a thousand emeralds at or before January 1, 2000, support the claim that emeralds are *grue* as much as that they are green. This blatantly ignores too much else that is relevant to rational inductive inference. There is more at work here than laws of probability applied to a single sample of a thousand emeralds. If emeralds are grue, then one would predict from the specifications of the kind *grue* that emeralds examined only after the key date would be observed to be blue. Indeed, the very same thousand emeralds observed before the key date, if they had instead been hidden away from all observation until after the key date, would later have been observed to be blue. But why would one expect any such thing of emeralds? Is this a problem for induction, or just a matter of trying to run with an unusual and unreasonable predicate? We can define universals with few constraints other than systematic abstract coherence (which may seem to give Goodman's definition some initial credence), but kinds employed in conjunction with other kinds require systematic *existential* compatibility as well. A thousand observations of emerald colors carry some weight, but the specifications for the kind *emerald* (supported by centuries of observations at or before the key date) also strongly suggest that they do not change colors. Our thousand observations by themselves do not disconfirm their being grue, but everything else we believe about emeralds suggests that other emeralds observed only after the key date will not be blue (and hence that they are not grue). There is nothing particularly reasonable about such a possibility in light of other existential factors of which we are well aware, even if it may seem possible in the abstract. If the possibility of their being grue were to seem pertinent to us, then principles of good inductive method would suggest that we continue to observe new emeralds beyond the key date and to forego judgment until then—no other test is possible except to wait and see. On the other hand, if emeralds are in fact *grue* (relative to some unknown future key date), then we will eventually discover it. Until then, the claim that they are green is far more likely in light of current principles of induction than is the claim that they are grue.

This bit of plain and unsophisticated common sense may not solve the new riddle of induction, but it does bring into question whether the *grue* example is an appropriate illustration of the problem. Note that the unreasonableness of the *grue* predicate is not due to the time dependence in itself but only because this time dependence is imposed within a system of kinds where it is out of place and unmotivated by any sort of existential functionality. What should move us to give any weight to a merely abstract possibility? Instead, consider voter preferences, where timing is crucial. A large enough poll must be taken quickly to obtain a trustworthy snapshot of voter preferences. Results may change within a short time, so mixing up results from polls taken at different times is not acceptable. That would be as bad as visually ascertaining the color of one emerald against some standard color scheme by applying the color scheme to a second emerald, or calling the flip of a fair coin on the basis of the result of a different independent flip. Suppose we are interested in classifying each of the fifty states as a Bush state or a Gore state, if there are such states at all. This classification would be based on polls taken at different times before and after the 2000 presidential election. Polls in a Bush state would consistently show a preference for Bush before and after the November 7 election. Similarly for a Gore state. For good reasons, we might also be interested in knowing which states are Gush and Bore states. Namely, the kind *Gush* applies to a state if polls there after the November 7 election consistently indicate a preference for Bush, while polls prior to the election consistently indicate a preference for Gore. A Bore state would be just the converse. This example has very much in common with the *grue* example except that timing and a key date are relevant to a meaningful classification scheme. Of course, a state may fall under none of these four predicates, and the idea that voter preferences may be hidden away and not observed until after the key date is feasible but not particularly relevant since voter preferences, fickle as they are, are commonly tied to specific times anyway. In any case, observations of preferences before and after the key date make all the difference, and identical results over any significant time span cannot generally be assumed on the basis of past experience. Before the election, a state may be showing signs (from a thousand different surveys) of being a Gore state, and hence a potential Gush state, but we are not inclined by any principles of good inductive inference to infer that the state is both. In fact, as levels of support for the one conclusion rise, levels of support for the other decline (though any such conclusion would have to be offered rather tentatively given what we know about voter preferences and the contingencies of election politics). The point is that in a domain like this where time dependence does make a meaningful difference, the principles of good inductive inference seem to function well enough with a grue-like predicate.

Of course, it does little good to counter a counterexample with an example. But the point here is to illustrate how the ideas employed in the *grue* example are applied in a domain where they have no obvious existential relevance. When applied to domains where they do have such relevance (such as with the *Gush* predicate), the alleged problems for inductive inference would seem to evaporate. Thus it is not clear that the *grue* example has any significance for the general problem of distinguishing better and worse inductive inferences.

Nevertheless, the new riddle of induction remains an important concern. In fact, one might argue that it will always be an important concern as new tools, methods, and principles of better and worse inquiry continue to emerge in the ongoing cumulative development of human experience. Such developments potentially bring results of past experience into question, including existing principles of logic itself. But this is and always has been *the* problem of logic in general as an open and unfinished science. It is hardly a new problem at all.

Works Cited

Dewey, John. 1916. *Democracy and Education*. New York: Macmillan. Reprinted in MW9.

———. 1925. *Experience and Nature*. Chicago: Open Court. Reprinted in LW1.

———. 1930. Qualitative Thought. *Symposium* 1:5–32. Reprinted in LW5:243–62.

———. 1934. *Art as Experience*. New York: Henry Holt. Reprinted in LW10.

———. 1935. Peirce's Theory of Quality. *Journal of Philosophy* 32:701–8. Reprinted in LW11:86–94.

———. 1936a. Characteristics and Characters: Kinds and Classes. *Journal of Philosophy* 33:253–61. Reprinted in LW11:95–104.

———. 1936b. General Propositions, Kinds, and Classes. *Journal of Philosophy* 33:673–80. Reprinted in LW11:118–26.

———. 1936c. What Are Universals? *Journal of Philosophy* 33:281–88. Reprinted in LW11:105–14.

———. 1938. *Logic: The Theory of Inquiry*. New York: Henry Holt. Reprinted in LW12.

———. 1942. Inquiry and the Indeterminateness of Situations. *Journal of Philosophy* 39 (11):290–96. Reprinted in LW15:34–41.

Goodman, Nelson. 1954. *Fact, Fiction, and Forecast*. 4th ed. London: University of London; Cambridge: Harvard University Press, 1983.

Part III

Values and Social Inquiry

11

Achieving Pluralism: Why AIDS Activists Differ from Creationists

John Capps

I will begin where Dewey ended, with the concluding words of *Logic: The Theory of Inquiry*:

> Failure to institute a logic based inclusively and exclusively upon the operations of inquiry has enormous cultural consequences. . . . Since scientific methods simply exhibit free intelligence operating in the best manner available at a given time, the cultural waste, confusion and distortion that results from the failure to use these methods, in all fields in connection with all problems, is incalculable. These considerations reinforce the claim of logical theory, as the theory of inquiry, to assume and to hold a position of primary human importance. (1938, LW12:527)

Dewey intends "logic" (or the theory of inquiry) to have practical implications, to help solve social problems. Here I will focus on the features of Dewey's *Logic* that make it a valuable resource for "social inquiry." In particular I will stress the *pluralistic* nature of inquiry: that inquiry involves a diverse range of methods and goals and entails the inclusion of those who pursue and hold these methods and goals.[1] In practice, Dewey's theory of inquiry is sensitive to the needs of marginalized groups: It realizes the importance of recognizing different points of view. To illustrate this point, I will present a case example discussing the role of AIDS activists in shaping the clinical trials for experimental AIDS treatments. I will use this example to show the importance of pluralism as well as the empirical adequacy of Dewey's logical theory.

However, I hope to go further than that. A common criticism of Dewey (and of pragmatism in general) is that he is difficult to pin down. For example, Matthew Festenstein argues that Dewey's undeniably good intentions provide little support for an otherwise underdeveloped political theory (1997, 99). I think this criticism points to a deeper underlying concern: Pragmatists are unjustified in attempting to bypass many of the traditional philosophical problems, such as the problem of skepticism.[2] While I think part of this concern is misplaced—Dewey preferred the uncertainty of real inquiry to the artificial security of broad, all-encompassing theories— part of it needs to be taken seriously. Thus, even sympathetic readers of Dewey can note where he pulled his punches or failed to develop the radical implications of his pragmatism (see Eldridge 1998 and Seigfried 1996). For present purposes, it is important that he had little to say about attitudes that are incompatible with inquiry—those methods and goals, in short, that cannot and should not be included in the normal course of inquiry. This leads me to a second case example where I will suggest that objective inquiry is compatible with excluding certain points of view. This example will look at "intelligent design" creationism and its attitude toward science and Darwinism. I will argue that creationism, unlike AIDS activism, has no place in scientific inquiry. In addition, this case example will show how Dewey's logical theory responds to a real problematic situation. The debate between evolutionism and creationism is a persistent one, and I will conclude that Dewey's theory of inquiry offers one plausible way to resolve this debate. The example will also illustrate the limits of pluralism. It will show that inquiry should sometimes be exclusive, not inclusive. This example will suggest a response to the concern raised above: Even though pragmatists are not always forthcoming in their reasons for bypassing many of the usual philosophical problems, this avoidance can be justified for many of the same reasons that biologists and educators bypass creationism.

Logic, Society, and Politics

As my opening quote makes clear, Dewey was well aware that his *Logic* had social and political consequences. For one thing, insofar as it leads to improved methods of inquiry, logic should cast light on the experiences and concerns of traditionally marginalized groups: women, racial and ethnic minorities, lesbians and gay men, the disabled, the mentally ill, and so on. Second, the process of inquiry should be consistent with its product. Thus, if inquiry shows that marginalized groups deserve recognition and inclusion, then the process of inquiry should itself be inclusive and pluralistic. This follows from Dewey's observation that subject matters and forms of inquiry are interrelated: "[F]orms regularly accrue to matter in virtue of the adaptation of materials and operations to one another in the service of specified ends. . . . [F]orm and matter are instituted, develop and function in strict correspondence with each other" (LW12:383).

Four features of Dewey's logical theory are especially important. These are (1) its emphasis on *"warrantably assertible"* results; (2) its view of inquiry as *operational*, having *existential* consequences; (3) its dependence on particular concrete *situations*; and (4) its *pluralism*, that is, its inclusion of a broad range of methods, goals, theoretical perspectives, and practical points of view. Although these features are internal to inquiry, helping it function properly, they also have external implications. These, in turn, are the following:

1. Because the goal of inquiry is not exclusively epistemic, inquiry may lead to conclusions that are primarily normative.
2. Because inquiry is operational and transformative, the objects of inquiry do not possess essential characteristics (at least not in the classical sense of the term).
3. Because it is situational, social inquiry requires awareness of contextual social factors. Moreover, these factors are instrumental in achieving warrantably assertible conclusions.
4. Because successful inquiry encourages a plurality of methods and goals, it also encourages the recognition of the marginalized political and social groups that employ these methods and goals.

Warranted Assertibility and the Goals of Inquiry

Dewey, of course, described the goal of inquiry in terms of "warrantably assertible" results. Thus, warranted assertibility supersedes both knowledge and truth as goals of inquiry. He prefers warranted assertibility to "knowledge," since knowledge, properly understood, simply *is* "the appropriate close of inquiry" (LW12:15)—and thus comes to the same thing as warranted assertibility. From Dewey's standpoint, this conception of warranted assertibility highlights the sense in which knowledge is procedural, thereby avoiding the metaphysical difficulties of a more substantive conception of knowledge. In particular, his conception avoids the implication that knowledge is primarily an abstract transcendental relation between one's mental representations and an external physical reality where it does not matter how this relation is achieved. Likewise, warranted assertibility is preferable to truth not because it replaces the *concept* of truth (Dewey instead—at LW12:343n—endorses Peirce's theory of truth) but because it can better serve the traditional *function* of "truth" as the primary goal of inquiry. To identify this goal with truth (or with *the* truth) suggests that inquiry is primarily a matter of discovery: of uncovering antecedent and preexisting facts. Instead, according to Dewey, inquiry *shapes* its subject matter: In reaching a conclusion, inquiry makes modifications to the material under investigation. This is a crucial stage in the general "pattern" of inquiry: While the exact *method* of modification will differ depending on what is being studied, the *pattern* that inquiry takes remains the same.

Dewey's discussion of warranted assertibility highlights, among other things, the instrumental as opposed to the epistemic character of inquiry. Instrumental success, of course, is not opposed to truth. The conclusions of many inquiries are both useful *and* true. However, truth is not the goal of every inquiry. More generally, inquiry also aims at "judgments of practice" stating what should be done in a particular situation. Such judgments are primarily evaluative, not just descriptive:

> [E]valuative judgments are clearly an instance of judgments of practice; or, more strictly, all judgments of practice are evaluations, being occupied with judging what to do on the basis of estimated consequences of conditions. . . . A point still more important for logical theory is that these evaluative judgments . . . enter into the formation of all final judgments. (LW12:175–76)

Because judgments of practice are essential both in the process and as the product of inquiry, they play a crucial role as we inquire into both how the world is and how it ought to be. Indeed, from Dewey's standpoint, all inquiries have normative and descriptive aspects; the latter cannot be reduced to calculation or cost-benefit analysis. (In this Dewey distances himself from both emotivism and, he would argue, Mill's utilitarianism.) Dewey's theory of inquiry is thus more general than theories that focus exclusively on truth or knowledge. It does not rank epistemic or scientific problems over moral, political, or social issues. Thus, for Dewey, scientific disciplines differ from other forms of inquiry in degree, not in kind:

They, too, develop "out of the direct problems and methods of common sense" (LW12:71). As a result, all inquiry involves a normative dimension, and this makes it capable not just of describing but also of addressing the conditions of traditionally marginalized groups.

Existential Consequences vs. Essential Traits

According to Dewey, judgments of practice are "constructed." This leads to a more general point: Inquiry is *operational* and has *existential* consequences. In short, inquiry transforms the physical and conceptual resources at hand in order to construct a "final" judgment. This final judgment will, ideally, resolve a problematic situation. Not only do these judgments have existential consequences. They also are the direct result of modifications to the original problematic situation:

> The pre-cognitive unsettled situation can be settled only by modification of its constituents. Experimental operations change existing conditions. . . . Only execution of existential operations . . . can bring about the re-ordering of environing conditions required to produce a settled and definite situation. (LW12:121)

In practice this leads to the conclusion that objects of inquiry do not have *essential* traits in the classical sense. Objects of inquiry do not fall into categories naturally or by themselves; rather, they are modified so as to bring certain traits to the fore. Specific traits emerge over the course of inquiry as investigators select particular qualities as means to their end: "The traits which descriptively determine kinds are selected and ordered with reference to their *function* in promoting and controlling extensive inference" (LW12:269). When inquiry turns to problems of particular groups, this means that neither these groups nor their problems can be assumed to have essential traits or fall into natural kinds. For instance, the solution to one problem might give rise or shift attention to another: Women and racial minorities may go from being underrepresented in certain professions to being the target of a backlash against affirmative action. Similarly, the identifying characteristics of certain groups—as well as the self-image of particular members of those groups—can change: from "black" to "African American" or from "Indian" to "Native American" or "indigenous." Each of these terms emphasizes certain features at the expense of others: skin color as opposed to geographical origin, for example. Furthermore, because these different groupings are not necessarily co-extensive (not all blacks consider themselves African American, for example, and vice versa), it would be wrong to conclude that they constitute natural kinds. Finally, membership in a particular group does not mean that one necessarily shares the concerns and goals of other members. Feminists, for example, have long recognized that not all women share the same concerns: lesbians as opposed to heterosexual women; middle-class as opposed to poor women; Hispanic as opposed to Anglo women. Failing to admit these differences can lead to one-sided solutions that also have oppressive (and better camouflaged) consequences. This is especially true for marginalized groups, who are also among the most easily stereotyped.[3]

Dewey avoids stereotypes by stressing the operational aspect of so-called natural kinds.[4] Successful social inquiry must recognize that groups are internally heterogeneous, defined by an evolving set of features, and faced with a changing set of problems. Without this recognition, proposed solutions risk inflexibility: an inability to anticipate and adapt to changing circumstances or differences among affected parties.

A Contextual Logic

"Situations" play a central role in Dewey's logical theory. These "contextual wholes" (LW12:72) are the basis of inquiry: When problematic, they provide both the impetus as well as resources for inquiry; and when settled, they function as its end. As we have seen, inquiry involves modifications to the original problematic situation. When successful, this leads to a "warrantably assertible" judgment that is a blueprint for reconstructing a new, unproblematic situation. Inquiry, therefore, is context-sensitive. Namely, first, it always begins from a *specific* problem, not just a vague or abstract uncertainty. Second, inquiry depends on resources that are *contextually*, not intrinsically, basic. These resources may be appropriate only for certain situations; at other times they may themselves be open to doubt and possible inquiry. And third, the problematic situation will be partly determined by social factors: "[E]very inquiry grows out of a background of culture and takes effect in greater or less modification of the conditions out of which it arises. . . . [I]n every interaction that involves intelligent direction, the physical environment is part of a more inclusive social or cultural environment" (LW12:27).

These social factors may include the linguistic and conceptual resources of investigators, the institutional structures within which inquiry takes place, and the contingent historical and political setting of that inquiry. They direct (but do not necessarily determine) the course of inquiry. These factors do influence the recognition and description of problematic situations, the formulation of possible courses of action, and the acceptance of particular solutions. In contrast with positivist theories of justification, then, Dewey does not treat these factors as inherently deceptive or logically irrelevant. As a result, he does not encourage their elimination. Under the heading "Determination of Facts in Social Inquiry," he writes, "Since transformation of a problematic situation . . . is effected by interaction of specially discriminated existential conditions, *facts have to be determined in their dual function as obstacles and as resources*" (LW12:494; emphasis added). Importantly, while these factors can act as impediments to inquiry, they are also a necessary condition for inquiry in the first place.

In *social* inquiry, however, social factors provide not just the conditions for inquiry to take place; they also serve as the subject matter of that inquiry. In this case we need to distinguish those features which are not problematic from those which are: that is, those features which facilitate inquiry (for example, because they allow for division of labor) from those which serve as impediments (because they exclude some points of view unjustifiably). Inquiry into the problematic features will, of course, depend partly on those which are not concurrently in question. It will also depend, as many feminist theorists have argued, on paying close attention to the concrete lived experiences of the parties affected. More theoretical starting points can distort these experiences. As Charlene Haddock Seigfried writes, "By taking the integrated unity of what is experienced and the concretely embodied way of experiencing as the starting point of philosophic thought Dewey . . . provided a means of legitimating women's special angles of vision and tendency to theorize on the basis of our experiences" (1993, 115).

Similarly, when liberal political theory separates the public from the private sphere, it can marginalize the domestic context in which many women work. Social inquiry into the systemic discrimination of women must then focus both on the social factors that banish women to the "private" sphere as well as the theoretical presuppositions that treat the analytic distinction between public and private spheres as the natural framework for discussing these questions. This latter presupposition can distort the nature of women's social role and conceal the range of forces preventing greater participation in the public sphere (see Fraser 1989). Thus, becoming aware of the experiences and social situation of women—as well as the ways we have of conceptualizing these experiences—becomes an important condition for addressing women's issues. More generally, these contextual and social features are valuable resources (and potential obstacles) for understanding and responding to marginalized groups.

Pluralism

Finally, Dewey's logical theory is pluralistic in encouraging multiple methods and goals and with these the participation of a range of inquirers. This is evident when Dewey describes the superior qualities of physical science (which he takes to include "physics, chemistry, biology, and medicine"):

As these sciences have advanced in genuine scientific quality, doubt and inquiry have centered upon the efficacy of different *methods* of procedure. The result has been that . . . a plurality of hypotheses is positively welcome. For the plurality of alternatives is the effective means of rendering inquiry

more extensive (sufficient) and more flexible, more capable of taking cogni-
zance of all facts that are discovered. (LW12:500)

Dewey's first point is that physical science differs from social science (circa
1938) by its focus on methods and their instrumental success, as opposed
to the purported "intrinsic truth or falsity of certain conceptions." His second point is that successful inquiry—of which physical science is a paradigm—demands receptiveness to a variety of methods and goals (at least
so long as these methods are compatible with the general "pattern of inquiry"). Since science is an extension of common sense, this point holds for
more routine inquiry as well.

    We find traces of pluralism in the three features already discussed. This
pluralism may take the form of either including a range of different methods and goals or (what may amount to the same thing) including a number
of different investigators, interested parties, and points of view. First, because the goal of inquiry is not exclusively epistemic but can result in normative judgments of practice, it is likely that different investigators will
approach the same situation with different methods and goals. Resolving a
problematic situation may then involve weighing both the effectiveness of
different approaches as well as the merits of these different goals. Second,
the operational character of inquiry virtually guarantees that objects of inquiry will be modified in the process of inquiry (see LW12:121). As a result, different methods and goals are relevant at different stages of inquiry.
As the problematic situation develops—as inquiry shifts from determining
the facts of the case, to weighing and testing alternative courses of action,
to implementing a final judgment—the range of appropriate methods and
goals will likewise evolve. Finally, because inquiry is contextual, it must
respond to the experiences and felt needs of those involved in problematic
situations. Since a situation affects different groups (and subgroups) in different ways, inquiry must consider a range of possible solutions and means
of achieving those solutions.

    In Dewey's logical theory, as a result, we find that pluralism is compat-
ible with—and will even contribute to—successful inquiry. By considering
a range of methods and goals, investigators are better able to respond effectively to different features of a problematic situation. This openness to
alternatives can take several forms: It may involve recognizing and weighing various options, or it may mean that different research programs are
combined or pursued simultaneously. Moreover, pluralism with respect to
methods and practices invites a plurality of participants. Including a range
of viewpoints entails including those who hold those views.

    Pluralism also comes in degrees. In some cases the problematic situation will be so routine as to generate a nearly unanimous consensus among investigators and interested parties. In that case, weighing different methods and goals would be an unnecessary and academic exercise. In other cases, a satisfactory solution to a problematic situation could require application of different methods and even the development of new methods altogether. The goals of inquiry may also change as the character of the problematic situation becomes clearer. Thus, as Dewey noted, the purpose of pluralism is to encourage flexibility and responsiveness. Neither the route nor the destination of inquiry, nor the appropriateness of certain methods over others, are predetermined once and for all.

In conclusion, Dewey's logical theory is committed to methodological pluralism. Because the process of inquiry shapes its product, this theory is also committed to pluralistic solutions to problematic situations. As a result, even though it does not guarantee progressive political results, his theory of inquiry is a potential resource for those who have such goals. My point is not that activists should read Dewey's *Logic*. Rather, I want to stress its capacity for accurately describing particular episodes of inquiry, whether these be scientific or political. To illustrate this I will now introduce a case example where science and politics merge. This example will provide empirical support for Dewey's logical theory while illustrating the four features discussed above.

AIDS Activism and Clinical Research

In the past fifteen years, AIDS research has become highly politicized, with much attention focused on the protocols for clinical trials.[5] At the outset of the AIDS epidemic, clinical trials were conducted using a placebo control group. AIDS activists raised ethical and political objections to this practice. They argued that an experimental treatment's effectiveness was being measured in terms of the deaths of those in the placebo group. In addition, patients were marginalized in that there were no recognized avenues for lodging their concerns about this process. However, over time, the design of clinical trials changed dramatically in response to activists' objections. Trials became streamlined (thus speeding the approval process), but, significantly, their guiding assumptions and methodology also changed. In particular, biostatisticians showed that relevant results could be achieved without the use of traditional placebo (i.e., untreated) control groups. Thus, ethical and political concerns gave rise to new yet valid ways of testing experimental treatments. This example will show how Dewey's logical theory can shed light on actual episodes of inquiry and on how new logical principles emerge in inquiry. Moreover, it points to the importance of methodological pluralism and an inclusive tolerance for multiple points of view.

By the mid-1980s, by raising their objections in a very public and dramatic fashion, AIDS activists had succeeded in identifying if not creating a problematic situation. Clinicians had argued that clinical trials, including the use of double-blind placebo controls, played an invaluable role in determining the effectiveness of experimental treatments. Activists instead saw clinical trials as a way of gaining early access to potentially beneficial drugs: of "getting drugs into bodies." At the same time they publicized the human cost of placebo controls. Typically half the participants in a clinical trial received an experimental treatment and half received a placebo. An experimental treatment's effectiveness was measured against the placebo group's mortality rate. Thus, if one purpose of clinical trials was to provide early access to experimental treatments, the use of placebo groups ensured that half the participants received no benefit at all. Worse, these untreated participants may have received less benefit than if they had remained out of the study and had received the best available, approved treatment option. Therefore, a problematic situation arose from a tension between the requirements of good science and the undeniable medical needs of patients. While such tensions were not new to medical research, the situation became unarguably problematic only in the context of the AIDS epidemic. Because this fatal disease struck a predominately young, politically active community of homosexual men, activists soon emerged who had the political, social, educational, and financial resources to bring their moral reservations to the attention of both clinical researchers and the general public.

The situation was resolved with the recognition that the researchers' scientific requirements were not necessarily in conflict with the political and ethical concerns of patients and activists. Thus, while clinicians originally defended their methods on both epistemic and ethical grounds (the standard protocols were designed to ensure safe and reliable treatments), biostatisticians showed that these methods could be adapted to meet the activists' concerns. For example, entrance requirements were loosened to include women of childbearing age, those with atypical test results, and those who had already participated in earlier clinical trials.[6] An important change was also made to the protocols for placebo control groups: The end point of the trials (i.e., the point at which treatment is judged effective) was changed from measuring mortality rates to measuring "surrogate markers" such as CD4 cell counts and time-to-progression of full-blown AIDS. This shortened the running time of clinical trials, allowing participants in the placebo group earlier access to promising treatments. By the early 1990s, then, the protocols of clinical trials had changed in two important ways: (1) less demanding entrance requirements and (2) use of intermediate end points. These solutions preserved the goal of reliable science while largely satisfying the treatment activists' concerns. In addition, clinicians and activists were able to appreciate—if not always completely accept—the methods and goals of the other.[7] The original problematic situation was resolved.

This example points to several lessons. First, it illustrates a central theme of Dewey's logical theory: Principles of inquiry emerge in the course of making inquiries. Dewey gives the following overview:

> The theory, in summary form, is that all logical forms (with their characteristic properties) arise within the operation of inquiry and are concerned with control of inquiry so that it may yield warranted assertions. . . . [F]orms *originate* in operations of inquiry. To employ a convenient expression, it means that while inquiry into inquiry is the *causa cognoscendi* of logical forms, primary inquiry is itself *causa essendi* of the forms which inquiry into inquiry discloses. (LW12:11–12)

As "logical forms," the protocols of clinical trials and related principles of statistical analysis are neither a priori nor merely conventional. Instead, as this case example shows, they evolve in response to a particular problematic situation. They are then justified insofar as they help achieve warrantably assertible results—in this case, findings that satisfy clinicians, activists, and patients. However, satisfying the clinicians, activists, and patients was not a matter of meeting arbitrary requirements set by each group. In each case these requirements can be traced to a specific measurable desideratum: increasing the life span of persons with AIDS. If the revised protocols had not achieved this goal—and promised to be similarly effective in other contexts—they would not have been accepted by the different parties.

Turning to the four features discussed earlier, this example first illustrates how inquiry can involve *nonepistemic goals*. The resolution of this inquiry amounted to a judgment of *practice*, a statement of what *should* be done to meet the goals of the interested parties. While clinicians stressed the importance of achieving scientifically valid conclusions, their concerns were also partly ethical. Unreliable results could endanger the health of patients in the long run. The goals of treatment activists were *primarily* ethical and political; however, while they wished to ensure access to experimental treatments, they were also aware of the need for reliable, safe medications. By respecting these different goals, the final judgment of practice was *instrumentally* effective in resolving the problematic situation.

Second, this example also illustrates the *operational* and *existential* character of inquiry. To begin with, significant changes were made in the protocols of clinical trials. These changes obviously had direct existential implications for the trial participants. In addition, this example shows that particular groups should not be treated as having a single, unified agenda. Thus, as the problematic situation unfolded, the different sides achieved a broad consensus as to what could constitute an acceptable resolution. In addition, with regard to the third feature discussed earlier, this case study indicates the importance of *contextual* and especially *social* factors—not just the biological factors governing the response of HIV to particular treatments. An accurate description of this episode must include the fact that inquiry originated from the concrete experiences and particular objections of patients and activists. Significantly, these social and political influences were not impediments to inquiry; instead, they provided the impetus and necessary resources for revising clinical trials.

Finally, this example also shows the importance of *pluralism* in the sense that a range of different methods and goals contributed to the resolution of this problematic situation. In this case, the problematic situation was resolved through the actions of at least three distinct groups: clinicians, biostatisticians, and activists/patients. Inquiry was pluralistic in that each group's goals were recognized and new protocols developed, and it is unlikely that this outcome could have been achieved without interaction among these groups. Even though the new protocols were subsequently applied to other diseases, it took the AIDS epidemic—not to mention AIDS activists—for the necessary changes to occur. Pluralism was in this case crucial for successful inquiry.

These points suggest two additional conclusions. First, it should be clear that this example sheds light on the theory described in Dewey's *Logic:* It shows how principles of inquiry (here, principles that constrain the design of clinical protocols) can develop over the course of resolving problematic situations. In short, it is not necessary to explain these principles either as a priori or as simply social constructions. Second, Dewey's *Logic* provides a theoretical basis for the treatment activists' success. Since accurate descriptions of successful inquiry also perform a normative function, this points again to Dewey's theory as a possible resource for marginalized groups.[8]

Objectivity and Pluralism

We have seen that Dewey's *Logic* can explain a particular episode of successful inquiry. However, this example also poses the question of how pluralism—openness to a range of methods and goals—is related to objectivity. That is, there is an apparent tension between encouraging multiple theoretical and practical perspectives and ensuring the objectivity of inquiry. Unfortunately, Dewey's scattered references to objectivity are not very helpful. For example, in an early passage of the *Logic*, Dewey refers to "objectivity" as marking the transition from merely biological behavior to more "intellectual" interactions with the environment:

> To be intellectually "objective" is to discount and eliminate merely personal factors in the operations by which a conclusion is reached. . . . Transformation from organic behavior to intellectual behavior, marked by logical properties, is a product of the fact that individuals live in a cultural environment. Such living compels them to assume in their behavior the standpoint of customs, beliefs, institutions, meanings and projects which are at least relatively general and objective. (LW12:50–51)

It would seem, in other words, that objective inquiry first requires the elimination of strictly personal points of view in favor of a more general perspective—one that is at least "relatively" general. For inquiry to be completely scientific, however, this perspective should be even broader than that of any particular group. It must be not just practically but also *intellectually* "disinterested."

> [U]ntil the rise of science, there were no problems of common sense that called for such inquiry. Disinterestedness existed practically in the demand that group interests and concerns be put above private needs and interests. But there was no intellectual disinterestedness beyond the activities, interests and concerns of the group. In other words, there was no science as such. (LW12:119)

Dewey then continues: "In scientific inquiry, then, meanings are related to one another on the ground of their character *as* meanings, freed from direct reference to the concerns of a limited group" (LW12:119). Thus, according to Dewey, objectivity requires "intellectual disinterestedness" on the part of inquirers.

This raises a problem. The difficulty with equating objectivity with intellectual disinterestedness is that this might appear to conflict with the earlier claim that inquiry begins from, and depends on, the *particular* experiences of affected parties. As we saw earlier, this claim has strong reasons in its support: More abstract starting points can ignore or distort the experiences of marginalized groups. Not only may "disinterested" starting points actually reflect the goals of dominant groups, but the preceding case example shows that successful inquiry is compatible with recognizing the particular goals of different groups. My concern, then, is that taking objectivity in terms of intellectual disinterestedness requires these groups to discount their particular perspectives in favor of some yet more general point of view. Not only is it unclear whether this is psychologically possible, but it would also eliminate vital resources for resolving problematic situations. If intellectual disinterestedness means taking the perspective of no interested parties, then we seem very close to a sort of nonperspectival conception of objectivity: the idea of a view from nowhere (see Nagel 1986 and Fine 1998). One problem with this view is that it neglects the importance of pluralism. This conception of objectivity would suggest that pluralism (receptivity to a range of methods, goals, and the interested parties who hold these) serves as a substitute for objectivity when true disinterestedness cannot be achieved. But the question is whether objectivity in that sense *can* be achieved, and if not, whether pluralism is nothing more than a pale substitute for the objectivity we cannot attain.[9] First of all, I do not think objectivity in that sense can be achieved, but second, I do not think pluralism is just a poor substitute for it. Finally, it is not clear how the concept of intellectual disinterestedness is compatible with Dewey's well-known objections to "apart thought," "spectator theories of knowledge," and the "intellectualist fallacy" of instantiating "a definite separation between the world in which man thinks and knows and the world in which he lives and acts" (LW4:233).

To shed light on this problem, it is worth considering Helen Longino's claim that scientific objectivity is actually best conceived as "the critically achieved consensus of the scientific community" (Longino 1990, 79). Longino arrives at this conclusion by considering the shortcomings of both logical positivism (represented by Hempel, Carnap, and Popper) and constructivist "wholism" (represented by Hanson, Kuhn, and Feyerabend). While the former fails to recognize the necessary role of contextual background assumptions, she argues that the latter amounts to an internally inconsistent relativism. In their place Longino proposes a "contextual empiricism" that treats "experience as the basis of knowledge claims" while simultaneously recognizing "the relevance of context . . . to the construction of knowledge" (219). Objectivity, as a result, cannot require a supposedly context-free view from nowhere. Instead, because objectivity is opposed to subjective personal or idiosyncratic perspectives, it encourages the expression of multiple points of view. Inquiry reaches an objective conclusion when it allows criticism and comparison of background assumptions: "Thus understood, objectivity is dependent upon the depth and scope of the transformative interrogation that occurs in any given scientific community" (79).

Longino's theory of objectivity as critically achieved consensus is compatible with both pluralism and the requirement that inquiry start from concrete problems and experiences. It also suggests a plausible response to the earlier problem: If objectivity *implies* a plurality of methods and goals—and not disinterestedness—then the results of Deweyan inquiry *can* be objective. This is because objectivity, in this sense, does not require that inquiry somehow get at the "really Real" (see Lloyd 1995, 353) or be an accurate indicator of literal truth. Since Dewey's logical theory emphasizes the instrumental and nonepistemic aspects of inquiry, this is a concession pragmatists should be willing to make. Understood pragmatically, then, objectivity is a measure of confidence (specifically, confidence that the result of inquiry is not *simply* the result that a particular interested party desires). In other words, the result of *objective* inquiry cannot be merely what we—or any other group—want them to be. (When the result of inquiry happens also to be the result that an interested party desires, objectivity ensures that the desire was not decisive in reaching that result.) This confidence, moreover, can be understood in terms of two familiar features of Deweyan inquiry. First, the fact that inquiry is *pluralistic* helps ensure that results do not reflect the biases of any particular group. By requiring acknowledgment of different goals and methods, pluralism serves to limit the influence of a particular group with respect to the direction and outcome of inquiry. Second, the fact that inquiry is operational and existential helps ensure that the results of inquiry do not reflect the biases of any group in general. Thus, even when groups are unanimous in their wishes, the existential consequences of inquiry serve as a restraint on unchecked wishful thinking.

We can recognize the role of both features in the preceding case example. First, because inquiry was pluralistic in allowing a range of different methods and goals, no one group's biases took priority over another's. Instead, the concerns and goals of each group evolved until a resolution emerged. Second, this particular resolution would not have been successful *if clinical trials had not actually improved*. The trials' improvement depended both on the biostatistical data and on the actual behavior of the HIV virus. If either had been different (and they well could have been had the nature of HIV been different), and if the revised protocols had not actually generated acceptable data while actually improving the participants' condition, then the revised protocols would not have constituted an objective solution to the problem.

Despite ambiguities in its letter, then, the spirit of Dewey's *Logic* is clear. As Seigfried writes, referring to political deliberation:

[Dewey] makes inclusiveness of others in decision-making processes a condition of objectivity. It is not just morally wrong to refuse to include in deliberations that affect their lives those members of society that are believed to be inferior. It is also an intellectual fallacy to suppose that limiting points of view to those of an intellectual elite would more adequately achieve the objectivity expressed in the resolution of problematic situations. (1998, 194)

Pluralism, then, is not opposed to objectivity—at least so long as objectivity does not imply a view from nowhere. In fact, not only is pluralism compatible with objectivity (as Longino argues) but it can actually serve as one of its preconditions. Thus, from the perspective of Dewey's logical theory, pluralism is an important feature of *objective* inquiry. This pluralism leads to the inclusion of a range of methods and goals as well as to the inclusion of those who hold them.

Of course, pluralism also has its limits. While Deweyan inquiry encourages multiple points of view, this cannot mean that anything goes: Inquiry cannot possibly include every perspective. In some cases there are pragmatic reasons for excluding viewpoints: for example, limitations on time, money, and interest. In other cases inquiry simply refuses to accept a particular point of view as a viable option. For example, objective moral inquiry need not include the views of racists, Nazis, sadomasochists, or any other denizen of our usual rogues' gallery. However, this poses an interesting question: If, as I have argued, Dewey's logical theory is a valuable resource for marginalized groups, how are the worthy groups separated from the unworthy? When should the interests, methods, and goals of a marginalized group be excluded from inquiry?

To shed light on this question I will introduce a second case example which, I hope, will indicate the limits of pluralism. This example will involve the current debate among scientists, philosophers, and "intelligent design" creationists. While the latter are more sophisticated than the proponents of "creation science," I will argue that their position is at odds with central presuppositions of inquiry. For that reason their perspective may be justifiably excluded. Even pluralism has its limits.

Intelligent Design vs. Evolution

Creationists, like any group, are not all of a kind.[10] While they share the belief that the origin of human beings is inexplicable in entirely natural terms, they disagree over specifics. Some ("young Earth") creationists believe that the Earth is only a few thousand years old; other ("old Earth") creationists entertain much greater ages. In addition, while some creationists base their beliefs entirely on the Bible, others cite empirical evidence supposedly supporting the Genesis account. In the 1970s, this led to "creation science" and proposals for its inclusion in public school science curriculums. This strategy failed, largely for two reasons. First, the evidence in support of creationism was too weak to withstand scientific scrutiny, and second, it became clear that creation science was primarily a *religious* belief, making its teaching unconstitutional in public schools.[11]

Creationism has became more sophisticated, however, with proponents drawing the apparently more modest conclusion that evolutionary biology is unable to explain very complex biological structures (see, e.g., Behe 1996). These creationists then argue that an equally (or even more) plausible explanation is that these structures are the work of an "intelligent designer." Scientists have not explored this possibility, they claim, because of a dogmatic (and thus unscientific) attachment to *natural* explanations. Therefore, these creationists still hope to level the difference between creationism and evolutionary biology: If creationism is not a science, then perhaps biology isn't either. Scientists would then not be as objective or as scientific as they appear. In contrast, intelligent design creationists can present themselves as objective and open-minded: They are committed neither to naturalism (like scientists) nor to a literal interpretation of the Bible (like other creationists). They can also plead their marginal status: The fact that intelligent design has not received scientific attention is due, apparently, to the institutional power of naturalistic scientists.

Phillip E. Johnson, a law professor at the University of California, has led the charge: His book *Darwin on Trial* (1991) is a rallying point of intelligent design creationism. He argues there that scientists have unfairly stacked the deck against creationists:

Theistic or "guided" evolution has to be excluded as a possibility because Darwinists identify science with a philosophical doctrine known as naturalism. Naturalism assumes the entire realm of nature to be a closed system of material causes and effects, which cannot be influenced by anything "outside." (114)

Naturalism, Johnson subsequently claims, is a "metaphysical doctrine, which means simply that it states a particular view of what is ultimately real and unreal" (Johnson 1995, 37). In its place he proposes a "theistic realism" based on the claim that "I am convinced that God is objectively real, not merely a concept or fantasy in my own mind" (1995, 49). Theistic realism would encourage a creationist "theory of knowledge" (1995, 107) that, presumably, is capable of acknowledging empirical evidence of an intelligent designer. Thus, it is "the right and duty of theologians to point out that there is another way of looking at the evidence" (1995, 109).

But is it also the duty of scientists, philosophers, and educators to recognize Johnson's claims? It would appear not: For one thing, Johnson's argument depends on a misleading and tendentious conception of naturalism. As Robert Pennock and others argue, there is an important distinction between *metaphysical* and *methodological* naturalism. The former, as Pennock puts it, is a "substantive claim about what exists in nature" (1999, 190), and the latter is a commitment "to a set of methods as a reliable way to find out about the world—typically the methods of the natural sciences, and perhaps extensions that are continuous with them" (191). While metaphysical naturalism is committed to stating what—and just what—can exist, methodological naturalism limits itself to stating what exists *given the current evidence*. Beyond this it does not speculate. Johnson's target is clearly *metaphysical* naturalism; thus, he proposes theistic realism as an alternative account of *what* really exists. However, metaphysical and methodological naturalism are not the same, and the methodological naturalist is not necessarily committed to metaphysical naturalism. It is equally clear that *methodological* naturalism is most central to the kind of inquiry discussed here. To return to the *Logic*, recall Dewey's claim:

> *Logic is a naturalistic theory.* . . . [I]t means, on one side, that there is no breach of continuity between operations of inquiry and biological and physical operations. . . . The logic in question is also naturalistic in the sense of observability, in the ordinary sense of the word, of activities of inquiry. (LW12:26)

There are good reasons, furthermore, for being a methodological naturalist. Not only does methodological naturalism account for the importance of observability and hence empirical testing, but it is itself a testable and revisable hypothesis.[12] That is, if the methods of inquiry *fail* to achieve warrantably assertible results, this would be grounds for revising those methods. Conversely, to the extent that inquiry *does* achieve warrantably assertible results, this is evidence in favor of methodological naturalism.

The flaw in Johnson's "theistic realism" is that by failing to distinguish metaphysical from methodological naturalism, he offers no alternative to the methodological naturalism that is central to inquiry.[13] Nor is it clear what this alternative might be. If Johnson's intention is to question any scientific result that does not directly *support* the existence of God, then he is proposing the overthrow of science as we know it: a radical proposal indeed.[14] If instead he intends only to question those results that (apparently)[15] *oppose* the existence of God—for example, evidence that life could have an entirely natural origin—then he must account for the success of methodological naturalism in other areas. He cannot accept naturalistic explanations in some areas yet deny these in others, at least not without providing a principled basis for distinguishing the two. As it stands, however, the only reason for denying naturalistic explanations where they (apparently) oppose the existence of God is the fact that they would also undermine his "theistic realism." But this is not a *principled* basis, since "theistic realism" is only the postulated basis of an as yet unspecified "creationist theory of knowledge." As such, Johnson's position seems to amount to the claim that he can question any scientific result that (apparently) opposes the existence of God for the simple reason that it (apparently) opposes the existence of God. But this is not principled. It is viciously question-begging. In either case, his proposal for a creationist theory of knowledge amounts to nothing more than the assumption that God exists, which as it stands is an insufficient basis for a theory of inquiry. At the very least, this hypothesis is unable to make a useful contribution to inquiry; at worst, it is diametrically opposed to inquiry in the first place. In either case, these are justifiable, nondogmatic grounds for excluding "theistic realism" from scientific inquiry.[16]

Besides the obvious differences, then, intelligent design creationists differ from AIDS activists in their attitude toward inquiry. The activists had well-defined methods and goals that permitted interaction with their clinical counterparts. Despite their disagreements, there was also a common understanding of how inquiry could proceed and how the problematic situations could be resolved. There was implicit agreement over the general "pattern" of inquiry if not always over the specific methods and goals of that inquiry. These features are missing from the present example. The creationist's proposal is either entirely without merit, because it simply ignores the results of scientific inquiry, or it is sterile because it fails to suggest an alternative line of inquiry.

To conclude, the purpose of this case is to illustrate the limits of pluralism. While, all things being equal, Deweyan inquiry is committed to recognizing a range of theoretical points of view, this does not mean that all perspectives, all methods, and all goals have equal merit. In particular, as we have seen, some perspectives, methods, and goals are opposed to the spirit of inquiry, either by arbitrarily rejecting the results of earlier investigations or by failing to enter into meaningful dialogue with other positions. This latter shortcoming takes the form, in general, of an inability to present a viable research program—where this may mean a failure to make falsifiable predictions, account for the success of rival theories, offer explanations that are well integrated with established facts, or propose experiments with verifiable, existential consequences.[17] This case also shows that Deweyan inquiry has some teeth. While it is a valuable resource for marginalized groups, it also comes with conditions. When these conditions are not met, this suggests that some groups are marginal for good reason.

Conclusion

I began this essay by quoting Dewey's claim that logic has "enormous cultural consequences." These consequences are due, in no small part, to the fact that inquiry is *pluralistic* in its methods and goals. I have argued here that pluralism is a central feature of inquiry conceived along Deweyan lines: Inquiry functions best (all things being equal) when it recognizes a *range* of methods and goals. Moreover, I have argued that pluralism is also closely connected with objectivity, so long as objectivity is distinguished from nonperspectival disinterestedness. For these reasons Dewey's logical theory is well suited to recognize and appreciate the perspectives of marginalized groups, whether these be women, ethnic minorities, AIDS activists, or others. Their points of view can be included in inquiry, with the hope that their concerns will be addressed and hopefully resolved. In addition, fortunately, his logical theory is also capable of *excluding* the perspectives of groups whose goals and methods are incompatible with the pattern that Deweyan inquiry must follow. This latter point is especially important because it suggests limits to an otherwise open-minded pluralism.

Philosophically, this point is also important because it suggests a possible response to an earlier complaint: viz., that pragmatists fail to justify their avoidance of traditional philosophical problems. While this complaint is a bit too dramatic—it downplays the overlap and dialogue between pragmatism and other philosophical traditions—it also raises the question of what to do when faced with a range of philosophical questions, methods, and goals. For example, Dewey's *Logic* is noteworthy for its near total silence on many standard epistemological topics, such as the problem of skepticism and the correct analysis of knowledge. The proper response, I think, is that these are issues which arise only when pursuing a peculiar sort of investigation—one that may well lack the relevant features of "inquiry" in Dewey's sense. While it is not possible to defend this response in detail here, it is worth noting that there is something odd about philosophical investigations when these show too little concern for avoiding "cultural waste, confusion and distortion" (LW12:527)—when these are too far removed from the practical considerations that provide the impetus for philosophical inquiry.

Philosophy, on Dewey's view, should not be understood as that special area where it is appropriate to pose abstract questions with little concrete importance. (It is for this reason, also, that I have used real-life case examples, not artificial thought-experiments, to make my general point.) Instead, philosophy—like science, logic, and common sense—is a reflection of the culture in which it is practiced.[18] The pragmatist's lack of interest in other philosophical approaches should then be viewed as a commitment to philosophical *inquiry* (in the sense used here), justifiably excluding those approaches too distant from the concrete problems of living. To return to where I began, we should not ignore the centrality of logic and its cultural significance. Quoting Dewey, "These considerations reinforce the claim of logical theory . . . to assume and to hold a position of primary human importance" (LW12:527). Thus not only is logic an important part of human experience but human experience constitutes an indispensable part of logic.

Notes

1. It is important to note that I am distinguishing between the general pattern of inquiry (a term of art for Dewey) and the different methods that may exemplify that pattern. While I will argue for pluralism with respect to the latter, I will follow Dewey in arguing that there is only one pattern that all good methods of inquiry follow.

2. For another perspective, see West 1989.

3. For a discussion of this point, see Capps 1996.

4. Dewey writes, "One only has to consider the traits that describe a kind in scientific inquiry to note that their institution is an arduous process. . . . For scientific kinds, say that of metals, are instituted by operations that disclose traits that are not present to ordinary observation but are produced by operations of experimentation, as a manifestation of interactions that are taking place" (LW12:268). The same point holds for kinds in general, whether we think of these as natural or otherwise.

5. The material in this section depends on Epstein 1996.

6. An analogous point is familiar from the feminist philosophy of science literature: The exclusion of female subjects from studies (on the grounds that the female reproductive cycle adds a complicating variable to the trial) begs the question of what is variable as opposed to constant, "normal" as opposed to "abnormal."

7. Epstein quotes biostatistician Susan Ellenberg, describing her reaction to the activists' concerns: "I found myself saying, 'You mean, we're not doing this?' or 'We're not doing it this way?'" (1996, 247). Similarly, the activists began to shift their attention away from "getting drugs into bodies" and toward basic research. While this shift was partly due to the realization that a cure was not imminent, it was also the result of activists working more closely with researchers in designing the protocols (see 251; also 334–37).

8. For example, Eldridge 1998 shows how a Deweyan "pragmatic political democracy" was formed in response to the gentrification of San Francisco's Tenderloin District (117–23).

9. For a similar discussion of this theme from the direction of feminist naturalized epistemology, see Antony 1992.

10. In this section I draw on Pennock 1999.

11. For discussion of creation science and the relevant court cases, see Ruse 1988; for discussion of specific claims of creation science, see Kitcher 1982, esp. chaps. 3–5.

12. Pennock also points out that methodological naturalism "is essential for the basic standards of empirical evidence" (1999, 196), and is thus partly constitutive of "scientific evidence" in any meaningful sense.

13. For Johnson's attempt to blur this distinction, see Pennock 1999, 201–3.

14. However, such radical proposals are implied in earlier versions of creation science. Kitcher (1982, 44) points to one such line of argument.

15. A further question, of course, is whether these results do, in fact, oppose the existence of God—and exactly what sort of God if they do.

16. In addition, it should be added that philosophers and scientists are acting objectively in excluding the creationists' perspective. A commitment to methodological naturalism does not predetermine the results of inquiry; in fact, this charge applies more to the proponents of "theistic realism."

17. These concerns touch on the demarcation problem of distinguishing science from nonscience (or pseudoscience). While I am willing to accept a fairly broad conception of what is science, this does not mean that meaningful albeit contextual distinctions cannot be drawn. This would also suggest that the meaning of science is somewhat flexible, so it is even possible that "creation science" need not be an oxymoron. However, as I have argued here, current versions of creationism are unscientific even by pragmatic standards.

18. This is also Dewey's point. See esp. LW12:86–102.

Works Cited

Antony, Louise. 1992. Quine as Feminist: The Radical Import of Naturalized Epistemology. In *A Mind of One's Own: Feminist Essays on Reason and Objectivity*, ed.
Louise Antony and Charlotte Witt, 185–225. Boulder: Westview Press.

Behe, Michael. 1996. *Darwin's Black Box: The Biochemical Challenge to Evolution*. New
York: Free Press.

Capps, John. 1996. Pragmatism, Feminism, and the Sameness-Difference Debate.
Transactions of the Charles S. Peirce Society 32:65–105.

Dewey, John. 1938. *Logic: The Theory of Inquiry*. New York: Henry Holt. Reprinted in
LW12.

Eldridge, Michael. 1998. *Transforming Experience: John Dewey's Cultural Instrumentalism*. Nashville: Vanderbilt University Press.

Epstein, Steven. 1996. *Impure Science: AIDS, Activism, and the Politics of Knowledge*.
Berkeley: University of California Press.

Festenstein, Matthew. 1997. *Pragmatism and Political Theory*. Chicago: University of
Chicago Press.

Fine, Arthur. 1998. The Viewpoint of No-One in Particular. *Proceedings and Addresses
of the American Philosophical Association* 72 (November): 9–20.

Fraser, Nancy. 1989. What's Critical about Critical Theory? The Case of Habermas
and Gender. In *Unruly Practices: Power, Discourse, and Gender in Contemporary Social Theory*. Minneapolis: University of Minnesota Press.

Johnson, Phillip E. 1991. *Darwin on Trial*. Washington, D.C.: Regnery Gateway.

———. 1995. *Reason in the Balance: The Case Against Naturalism in Science, Law, and
Education*. Downers Grove, Ill.: InterVarsity Press.

Kitcher, Philip. 1982. *Abusing Science: The Case Against Creationism*. Cambridge: MIT
Press.

Lloyd, Elisabeth. 1995. Objectivity and the Double Standard for Feminist Episte-
mologies. *Synthese* 104: 351–81.

Longino, Helen. 1990. *Science as Social Knowledge*. Princeton: Princeton University
Press.

Nagel, Thomas. 1986. *The View from Nowhere*. Oxford: Oxford University Press.

Pennock, Robert. 1999. *Tower of Babel*. Cambridge: MIT Press.

Ruse, Michael. 1988. *But Is It Science? The Philosophical Question in the Creation/Evo-
lution Controversy*. Buffalo, N.Y.: Prometheus Books.

Seigfried, Charlene Haddock. 1993. Validating Women's Experiences Pragmatically.
In *Philosophy and the Reconstruction of Culture: Pragmatic Essays after Dewey*, ed.
John J. Stuhr. Albany: SUNY Press.

———. 1996. *Pragmatism and Feminism: Reweaving the Social Fabric*. Chicago: University of Chicago Press.

———. 1998. John Dewey's Pragmatist Feminism. In *Reading Dewey: Interpretations
for a Postmodern Generation*, ed. Larry Hickman. Bloomington: Indiana University Press.

West, Cornel. 1989. *The American Evasion of Philosophy: A Genealogy of Pragmatism*.
Madison: University of Wisconsin Press.

12

The Teachers Union Fight
and the Scope of Dewey's Logic

Michael Eldridge

During an internal dispute in the New York Teachers Union in 1932–33, John Dewey chaired a grievance committee. The committee's initial report on the dispute was well received by the general membership. But their recommendation to suspend radical union members was not accepted, in part because of a mistake made by the union president. Dewey's failure to be more political also played a role in the course of these events. Although his committee's recommendation was sound, consistent with Dewey's philosophy, and possibly workable, Dewey did not take steps before the general meeting that could have prevented the president's error.

This case, examined in terms of Dewey's definition of inquiry and the chapter on social inquiry in his 1938 *Logic: The Theory of Inquiry*, enables us to grasp that inquiry understood simply as an intellectual activity is insufficiently Deweyan. Deweyan inquiry is a transformation of experience, a remaking of actual situations. In this situation, Dewey's actions did not measure up to his own standards of effective inquiry despite its intellectual coherence and attractiveness. But rather than merely fault Dewey, we can see—by examining this unsuccessful effort—what an effective Deweyan social inquiry would be. For anyone who has some experience in getting things done, this suggested scenario will seem commonplace. We have come a long way in terms of day-to-day democratic action since the 1930s, an achievement in workplace democracy that would be very satisfying to Dewey. But where we still fall short is in our thinking about informed social change. We lack an adequate democratic political technology, one that will guide the action.

I dealt with the need for a better formed political technology in my *Transforming Experience: John Dewey's Cultural Instrumentalism* (1998). Here I want to discuss the logic of such a technology. Does the logic presented in the 1938 volume enable us to understand and evaluate a democratic political technology? Specifically, does Dewey's discussion in the chapter on social inquiry (LW12:481–505) provide agents of democratic change with the needed logic?

A Deweyan Social Inquiry

The Teachers Union case provides an example of an actual effort by Dewey to effect democratic social change. By looking at what he did and did not do, we will have before us an instance of attempted social inquiry.

What Happened: Dewey and the Local 5 Conflict

Dewey became a charter member of the New York Teachers Union in 1916 and served for three years as its first vice president (Dykhuizen 1973, 171). In 1927 he characterized himself as a "somewhat nominal" dues-paying member rather than an "active working" one (1928, LW3:275). His role was not as slight as his self-characterization indicated, however, for the address in which it occurs, "Why I Am a Member of the Teachers Union," was still being used in American Federation of Teachers recruitment brochures in 1984 (see the textual commentary on Dewey 1928, LW3:441). He became increasingly active politically after retiring from teaching in 1929. For these and other reasons, he was asked to resolve the conflict occasioned by the challenge of two radical factions in the New York Teachers Union, Local 5, of the American Federation of Teachers.

The two factions, the Progressives and the Rank and File, opposed one another as well as the union's leadership, Henry Linville and Abraham Lefkowitz. In 1932 Lefkowitz, the union's legislative representative, moved to expel the leaders of these two factions for disruptive behavior and for repeated misrepresentations of the leadership's actions. At a meeting of the general membership in October, a five-person grievance committee was elected. This committee then elected Dewey as its chair. Over the next several months the committee met extensively, hearing more than a hundred witnesses on both sides, as well as the six members against whom specific charges had been made. Dewey wrote the report submitted to the general membership before the next general meeting. The report recommended that a delegate assembly be created and that a provision for suspending members from meetings be adopted. A separate report, which was not submitted until the meeting occurred, dealt with the specific charges. At the meeting, the recommendation to suspend one of the six failed to gain the necessary two-thirds majority. The cases against the other five were then dropped (Dewey 1933, LW9:320f, 342f, 476–78).

The crucial two-thirds requirement was actually a mistake on Linville's part. As president, Linville chaired the meeting. According to Robert W. Iversen, Linville "had calmly announced that a two-thirds vote would be required on any disciplinary action recommended." This, however, was a more stringent requirement than the union's constitution specified. The constitution stipulated a two-thirds vote for *expulsion*, but a suspension needed only a majority of those voting. Linville had expected Dewey's committee to recommend expulsion, and so he was caught by his own ruling when the committee recommended the less extreme penalty. Lefkowitz, Linville's ally, sought to correct the error by appealing Linville's ruling, but the mistake was compounded by the failure of their supporters to be similarly alert. Iversen explains, "At this critical point in the proceedings, the administration forces, which were in the majority, should have seen that a vote against Linville's ruling would have been a vote *for* him, because Lefkowitz was obviously voicing the Linville position. Instead, the meeting upheld Linville's ruling of the two-thirds requirement" (1959, 43). Thus Dewey's moderating committee report was less effective than it might have been. Thanks to the mistakes of the chair, his supporters, and Dewey himself, the radicals were able to avoid being disciplined. Dewey's effort to find sufficient common ground for the union to proceed was compromised.[1]

What Could Have Happened: Better Communication

If inquiry were nothing more than an intellectual process resulting in the sort of product that was the recommendation of Dewey's committee, then Dewey's committee report could be considered a success. But a Deweyan inquiry requires more.

Dewey's committee report was in two parts. The report distributed to the general membership before the crucial meeting is what is reprinted in the critical edition of Dewey's work (LW9:320–45). It outlines the committee's procedures, analyzes the conflict, and proposes remedies. It does not say what action should be taken regarding the individual members who were being challenged by the leadership. But it promises that such a report will be forthcoming: "The report of the Committee on specific charges against individuals will be presented at the general meeting called for April 29, 1933. Copies of that report will be sent to the defendants and their counsel in season to allow plenty of time for their consideration and for preparation of such defense as they may wish to make" (LW9:345).

We do not know what Linville knew at the beginning of the April meeting. He had presided over the union since 1916, so I suppose he was both knowledgeable and shrewd. Perhaps he knew that Dewey's committee was recommending suspension rather than expulsion, but I doubt it. Instead, I suspect that Dewey's committee had communicated their recommendation only to the defendants and their counsel as the committee's published report indicated they would. Then, during the meeting, Dewey announced the committee's recommendation to suspend. Perhaps he did so out of a sense of fair play. His committee did not telegraph its recommendation to the union leadership, choosing to be and appear impartial. The committee, before the meeting, apparently reported its recommendations regarding the defendants only to the defendants and their counsel.

The failure here resulted from poor communication between Dewey's committee and Linville. If Linville had known that Dewey's committee was recommending suspension, then he could have known that only a majority vote would have been required. If Dewey did not brief Linville because, as union president, he was also involved in the dispute, then the functions should have been separated. The president should have yielded the gavel on this issue. The will of the majority was frustrated because of this failure to communicate. The issue and the future of the union would have been very different if Dewey had briefed Linville on the recommendation and the necessary parliamentary procedure. But, for whatever reason, he did not. The committee's recommendation to suspend was defeated, and the Teachers Union experienced several more years of turmoil.

What Should Have Happened: The Requirement of a Successful Deweyan Inquiry

Dewey's committee report met the needs of the situation in that it was a well-written and politically astute accounting of matters that provided a democratic way out of a difficult situation. But it was not enough to solve the conflict, and more to the point, it was not sufficient on a Deweyan understanding of inquiry as existential transformation of experience.

In the 1938 *Logic*, in the chapter entitled "The Pattern of Inquiry," Dewey defined inquiry as "the controlled or directed transformation of an indeterminate situation into one that is so determinate in its constituent distinctions and relations as to convert the elements of the original situation into a unified whole" (LW12:108, emphasis removed). In a summary of the chapter in which this definition is stated, Dewey notes, "Experimental operations change existing conditions. Reasoning, as such, can provide means for effecting the change of conditions but by itself cannot effect it. Only

execution of existential operations directed by an idea in which ratiocination terminates can bring about the re-ordering of environing conditions
required to produce a settled and unified situation" (LW12:121).

The work of Dewey's committee was flawed in that the committee did
not initiate cooperation with the chair of the general meeting to ensure that
the committee's recommendation would be acted on in a way to enable its
passage. This is something that an experienced, effective committee chair
would do. Dewey could have worked out with the parties involved a procedure for bringing the proposal to suspend to an appropriate (and successful) vote. It is just this sort of cooperation and determination of procedures which constitute existential operations in a social arena like this and
which should have been implemented in order to complete the work of the
committee. I emphasize that it is the procedure (and not the outcome) which
should have been worked out in advance. The outcome must be left to the
general members themselves. They should have had the opportunity to review and revise the procedure. But large groups are cumbersome decision
makers. They should not be asked to resolve complex issues. Democracy in
this case would have been better served by procedures that squared with
the union's rules and that did not forestall the intent of the committee. Thus
the means Dewey chose were, in fact, undemocratic in this respect. By not
alerting Linville of his committee's exact recommendation, Dewey caught
him by surprise. Hence the members were not able to do what they wanted
to do—suspend the defendants. Dewey, the advocate of openness and communication, acted inconsistently with his own beliefs by failing to execute
appropriate existential operations directed by the ideas in which the deliberations of his committee terminated. In short, Dewey did not adequately
follow through on the committee's means-ends analysis in the way that his
logic requires.

Dewey on Social Inquiry

My question is not so much what happened or did not happen in 1933, nor
what one could be expected to do today. My question has to do with the
scope of a Deweyan logic of social transformation. Should such a logic include techniques for getting one's recommendations passed? Dewey believed that logic is the theory of inquiry. The sort of inquiry he had in mind,
moreover, was not just a cognitive enterprise; it was, to use his term, an
"existential" process. So what should such a theory include? Specifically,
should a theory of how we transform situations include a political technology? It seems a bit much to expect a philosopher to detail a set of opera-

tions for getting things done, yet a theory of existential transformation seems to require such details.

Fortunately, Dewey included a chapter on social inquiry in the 1938 *Logic*. Unfortunately, the situation in social inquiry was such that he felt obliged to begin the chapter with an observation concerning its "backwardness" in comparison with "physical and biological inquiry" and with mathematics (LW12:480, 487). These fields had reached a point "where problems are mainly set by subject-matter already prepared by the results of prior inquiries, so that further inquiries have a store of scientific data, conceptions and method already at hand. This is not the case with material of social inquiry. This material exists chiefly in a crude qualitative state" (LW12:487). In Dewey's view, since theory reflects practice, we should not expect a well worked out theory of social inquiry. Over time, the move from practice to theory can enhance practice, leading in turn to improved theory; but Dewey in the late 1930s did not think we were as far along in the social inquiry as in other types of inquiry.

Social inquiry, in particular, lacks methods whereby "the materials of existential situations may be converted into the prepared materials which facilitate and control inquiry" (LW12:487). So Dewey focused his attention on needed "modes of procedure" and observed that the existing means of social inquiry all involved taking some aspect of social inquiry—problems, facts, or ends—as being fixed. In the field of politics and public administration, the mistake made is one of taking the *problem* as being known, and thus making the mistake of not examining carefully that which originates the inquiry. Additionally, those not being guided by scientific method often attempt to understand the problem not just as being already known but also as moral. This prevents the use of scientific methods where they are most needed, on the basis of a false dichotomy between scientific and moral affairs (see Welchman, this volume). Emphasis is put instead on a search for "moral blame and moral approbation," understanding the matter in terms of "wickedness or righteousness." This, he observes, "is probably the greatest single obstacle now existing to development of competent method in the field of social subject-matter" (LW12:489).

In social science, the tendency is to assume that the *facts* are just out there, waiting to be discovered and then assembled into appropriate generalizations. In an attempt to avoid the error just noted of treating social problems as primarily moral problems that are immune to scientific methods, social scientists sometimes go to the other extreme and try to avoid all evaluations, remaining value-neutral. Thus they take *ends* as fixed. Their job is to determine not ends but only facts and the means to those ends. For if the "correct solution is already given," then one only has "to find the facts" to prove it, reducing "inquiry at its very best to the truncated and distorted business of finding out means for realizing objectives already settled upon" (LW12:490). Dewey contended that successful inquiry requires that all three elements—problems, facts, and ends—must be open to examination and allowed to influence each other. None are privileged; all are conjugately related to one another.

In the midst of this discussion of the errors associated with fixing on one of these three aspects of social inquiry, Dewey concisely stated the controlling idea of his instrumentalist logic of inquiry. "Judgment which is actually judgment (that satisfies the logical conditions of judgment) institutes means-consequences (ends) in *strict conjugate relation* to each other. Ends have to be adjudged (evaluated) on the basis of the available means by which they can be attained just as much as existential materials have to be adjudged (evaluated) with respect to their function as material means of effecting a resolved situation." He closed the paragraph with an observation he often made: "For an end-in-view is itself a means, namely, a procedural means" (LW12:490). There is no sharp separation between ends and means, hence his condemnation in the next paragraph of the familiar dictum "The end justifies the means."

The problem with the crude understanding of instrumentalism that this maxim reflects is that it places one's ends outside the scope of inquiry, as if one already knows what one is trying to do and is simply trying to figure out a way to get there. But Dewey exempted no part of the process from judgment. Each aspect—problem, means, and ends—of the inquirential process is subject to judgment and must be correlated with the others.

If I am right in my speculation that Dewey did not alert Linville that his committee was recommending suspension rather than expulsion out of concern that the committee both be and appear impartial, then Dewey's error was one of taking a procedural norm as a fixed operative end. He did not call into question an operative principle that turned out to obstruct what could have otherwise been a successful inquiry.

This mistake could have been prevented if Dewey had implemented the democratic value of interpersonal deliberation. By conferring with the parties involved, Dewey could have negotiated a procedure whereby the committee's recommendation could have been more favorably considered. This value would have been an instantiation of the principle that Dewey formulated in the following year—namely, that democratic ends require democratic means. In 1939, when Dewey was eighty, he wrote a message, "Democratic Ends Need Democratic Methods for Their Realization," which was read to the first public meeting of the Committee for Cultural Freedom. The title, adapted from a line in the speech, conveyed his message succinctly (LW14:367–68).

To understand Dewey's insight about the necessity of democratic means, we need to consider his notion of "genuine instrumentality."[2] A valuable discussion of "genuine instrumentality" is found in a consideration of art in *Experience and Nature* (1929). After noting that "the prevailing conception of instrumentality" fastened only on the temporal succession of events, observing that the first event was a means to the second, he turned to his own view of the matter. Means are causes and thus temporally prior, and ends are effects and thus temporally posterior. But, he argued, what distinguishes them as means and ends is "an added qualification": Means become so by "being freely used, because of perceived connection with chosen consequences" (LW1:275). Dewey's instrumentalism required a concentration not just on evaluation of means but also of ends. Moreover, this attention to causes and effects should be sufficiently well informed and imaginative that one could trace out a variety of causal relationships and choose the best route to the most desirable end (all things considered). The best route, of course, would be one in which means and ends were compatible. This compatibility would be attained when the means were *constitutive* of the end. He offered several examples: "Paints and skill in manipulative arrangement are means of a picture as end, because the picture is *their* assemblage and organization. Tones and susceptibility of the ear when properly interacting are the means of music, because they constitute, make, are, music. . . . A good political constitution, honest police-system, and competent judiciary, are means of the prosperous life of the community because they are integrated portions of that life." In summing up his own view, he recapitulated the point about the limitation of temporal succession as the defining feature and made his positive point: "The connection of means-consequences is never one of bare succession in time, such that the element that is means is past and gone when the end is instituted. An active process is strung out temporally, but there is a deposit at each stage and point entering cumulatively and constitutively into the outcome. A genuine instrumentality *for* is always an organ *of* an end. It confers continued efficacy upon the object in which it is embodied" (LW1:275–76).[3]

Dewey's instrumentalism, then, was not an exclusive concern with means. It was an advocacy of a constitutive instrumentality in which the means were integral to the ends sought. Moreover, it required—indeed, it constituted—intelligence as he understood it. To be intelligent was to be able to choose from among alternative causal scenarios one that best achieved a desirable end. This choice, he contended, would be one in which the means were constitutive of the end.

Some of the methods he identified in "Democratic Ends Need Democratic Methods" were the "methods of consultation, persuasion, negotiation, cooperative intelligence" and were to be practiced in "politics, industry, education—our culture generally." Moreover, democracy could "be served only by the slow day by day adoption and contagious diffusion in every phase of our common life of methods that are identical with the ends to be reached" (1939, LW14:367–68). This reflects Dewey's view that democracy is more than procedures. One cannot just rely on a checklist of so-called democratic activities to determine whether a group or society is democratic. A truly democratic society will embed these procedures in a shared way of life. Its democratic politics will reflect the democratic values of the society, and vice versa. A group's democratic values must find expression in democratic procedures.

Democracy, then, for Dewey is political machinery—frequent elections, universal suffrage, majority rule, protection of minorities—but it is more than these. It is also, and more fundamentally, the day-to-day practice of "consultation, persuasion, negotiation, cooperative intelligence." These activities define democracy and are both ends and means in their own right. Democracy itself as an end comes about by engaging in "consultation, persuasion, negotiation, cooperative intelligence." These democratic activities are the "genuine instrumentalities" of democracy. They are both means and ends.

The Logic of Democratic Social Change

I have criticized Dewey for possibly employing a fixed norm—to be and to appear impartial—and for failing to employ the democratic norms of interpersonal deliberation as an instantiation of the principle that "democratic ends require democratic means." Now we need to sort out what is logical and what is political technology. Otherwise, we run the risk of having merely pulled together some Deweyan values, juxtaposed them with a discussion of some points he makes in his chapter on social inquiry, and used those values to criticize Dewey's actual practice. We need to be more precise than we have been.

As one tries to make sense of this case in relation to Dewey's logical theory, it is hard to sort out what is logic and what is not. It is difficult to tell the difference between the various values and principles that Dewey employed or did not employ in the inquiry. This is especially the case if one tries to understand such values and principles in a non-Deweyan way— namely, as categorical rather than as functional in nature. The correct reading of these matters can be found in Larry Hickman's essay "Dewey's Theory of Inquiry" (1998). Hickman writes of Dewey: "He undermined the customary ontological approach to the problem of logical objects (which relied on sorting them into pre-existing categories) and then he argued that they should be treated in functional terms. . . . To treat them as having existence apart from . . . purposes and processes is to fall back into the older practice of giving them a spurious ontological status" (172–73).

The problem with the norm of being and appearing impartial is not that it is a bad idea in and of itself. Rather, in the situation in which Dewey found himself, it was misapplied in the sense that it did not meet the *logical* test of the reciprocity of means and ends; it did not have genuine instrumentality. This is the overriding positive recommendation that is present but not always center stage in the social inquiry chapter of the 1938 *Logic*: One's means must actually lead to the end-in-view, given the facts of the case. The principle that democratic ends require democratic means appears to be, and in some sense is, a substantive political directive. It substantiates Dewey's democratic social and political values. But it is also capable of logical analysis insofar as it articulates a means-ends test that I am suggesting is a distinguishing characteristic of Dewey's instrumentalist logic. The democratic-ends-require-democratic-means principle is not something that can be exclusively categorized as either political or logical. To try to do so is to address the wrong question. Rather, one needs to ask *in what respect* it is one or the other. The answer is that it is logical insofar as it articulates a means-ends relationship characteristic of the proper conduct of social inquiry, and it is political insofar as it expresses Dewey's values of ordered richness or sustainable development in human affairs (see Eldridge 1998, 97–108).

We set out to determine the scope of Dewey's logical theory: What is logic, and what is political technology? His definition of logic as the theory of inquiry and his understanding of inquiry as an existential transformation prevent him from limiting logic to the formal. Yet his opening the door to the material of actual social change seems to set no limits to the scope of logic. One would have to constantly be expanding one's logic to include more and more substantive principles as they were discovered to be effective in democratic social change (as well as in other areas of inquiry). Dewey's logic risks being hegemonic, taking over his whole philosophy.

But in making the functional move, one is able to recognize a limit to his logic, preserving the distinction between inquiry and reflection on inquiry. The answer to our original question is that social inquiry is formal, but it is formal in Dewey's sense. Forms are always "forms of matter." They are not pure, isolated, fixed. In social inquiry, a chief principle that one wants to apply is one that stresses the *reciprocal* interdependence of means and ends. If a particular norm does not lead to an end-in-view, then it is not a suitable means in this situation. It is not an appropriate tool in this situation. Likewise, if an end-in-view can be achieved only by certain means, then that end is not achievable without effectively implementing those means. What gets expanded in Dewey's logic of social inquiry is an emphasis on the material, the existential processes and results required of various inquiries if they are to be effective.

Conclusion

An important problem that Dewey addressed in the 1938 *Logic* was that one might think that any means to a given end was justified only by its effectiveness. But if one follows the practice of making sure that one's democratic means and ends are reciprocally evaluated, then one will tend not to be selecting means that may ultimately turn out to be counterproductive. One must use a democratic ideal to shape particular ends as well as to determine which available means to deploy. Thus there would be the reciprocity of ends and means that Dewey prized.

Dewey could have expanded his theory of inquiry as developed in the already voluminous 1938 *Logic* by incorporating ideas that he had worked out elsewhere but did not specifically include in his systematic expression of his theory of inquiry. The chapter on social inquiry does not directly discuss means of interpersonal social transformation. But it does provide the needed logical tools. One must critically relate one's problems, facts, and ends to one another, not allowing any aspect of the inquiry to be isolated and emphasized to the exclusion of the others. Thus, in principle, his logical theory covers all of the essential features that a theory of social inquiry should address. But the theory of social inquiry itself must be expanded by further developing and refining the social equivalent of experimental methods and procedures of exploratory application that one finds in more mature sciences (LW12:487).

One is inclined to say then that in terms of scope Dewey's logical theory is sufficiently broad yet not unconstrained. There is no unfilled need for a separate logic of political technology. In particular, the principle that democratic ends require democratic means is not a principle that needs to be incorporated into an imagined political logic. Rather, it functions as a political principle that is subject to logical analysis. In a social inquiry, such as in Dewey's involvement in the Teachers Union fight, one should be guided by this principle. But one can also evaluate this principle more generally, determining how well it functions instrumentally as a logical principle. One is then concerned with its capacity to help distinguish better and worse methods of inquiry in general terms. At this secondary level of inquiry, one is nevertheless working with a principle informed by distinct primary levels of inquiry. Dewey's complaint in the chapter on social inquiry in the 1938 *Logic* concerned not the logic to be employed but the relative lack of development of primary inquiries in this area.

Acknowledgments

This has been a difficult essay for me to write because of certain difficulties in understanding the 1938 *Logic*. For a long time I was asking the wrong question, on the basis of mistaken expectations. Fortunately, the Center for Dewey Studies awarded me a Democracy and Education Fellowship, enabling me to spend time at the Center in June 1999, reading the *Logic* with the assistance of their relevant primary and secondary resources. The results of this research are reflected in this essay.

Notes

1. This section is taken, with some minor modifications, from Eldridge 1998, 91–92. There the focus is on the nature of Dewey's proposal and his willingness to propose a representative form of democracy. Here I am paying attention to the politics of the matter. Political technology is also a concern of the book, but it is dealt with elsewhere in the book.
2. The following four paragraphs are taken from Eldridge 1998, 67–69.
3. James Tiles, whose discussion of this section of *Experience and Nature* can be usefully consulted, says, "Dewey indulges here in a piece of hyperbole which does not serve to clarify his position; he says 'external and accidental antecedents' 'are not means at all'" (1988, 192, referring to LW1:277).

Works Cited

Dewey, John. 1925. *Experience and Nature*. Chicago: Open Court. Reprinted in LW1.
———. 1925–53. *The Later Works (LW)*. 17 vols. Carbondale: Southern Illinois University Press (1981–90). Edited by Jo Ann Boydston. Citations of items in this edition are indicated by LW followed by volume and page numbers.
———. 1928. Why I Am a Member of the Teachers Union. *American Teacher* 12:3–6. Address delivered at the membership meeting of the Teachers Union of the City

of New York, Local 5, American Federation of Teachers, on November 18, 1927. Reprinted in LW3:269–75 with textual commentary 441.

———. 1933. Report of the Special Grievance Committee of the Teachers Union. First published as an eight-page report by the Teachers Union, Local 5, American Federation of Teachers (New York: Meadowbrook Press). Reprinted in LW9:320–45 with textual commentary 476–78.

———. 1938. *Logic: The Theory of Inquiry.* New York: Henry Holt. Reprinted in LW12.

———. 1939. Democratic Ends Need Democratic Methods. *New Leader* 22:3. From a message read at the first public meeting of the Committee for Cultural Freedom on October 13, 1939, at Town Hall in New York City. Reprinted in LW14:367–68.

Dykhuizen, George. 1973. *The Life and Mind of John Dewey.* Carbondale: Southern Illinois University Press.

Eldridge, Michael. 1998. *Transforming Experience: John Dewey's Cultural Instrumentalism.* Nashville: Vanderbilt University Press.

Hickman, Larry A. 1998. Dewey's Theory of Inquiry. In *Reading Dewey: Interpretations for a Postmodern Generation,* ed. Larry A. Hickman, 166–86. Bloomington: Indiana University Press.

Iversen, Robert W. 1959. *The Communists and the Schools.* New York: Harcourt, Brace.

Tiles, James E. 1988. *Dewey. Arguments of the Philosophers series.* New York: Routledge.

13

Power/Inquiry:
The Logic of Pragmatism

John J. Stuhr

> Since inquiries and methods are better and worse, logic
> involves a standard for criticizing and evaluating them. How,
> it will be asked, can inquiry which has to be evaluated by
> reference to a standard be itself the source of the standard?
> How can inquiry originate logical forms (as it has been stated
> that it does) and yet be subject to the requirements of these
> forms? The question is one that must be met. (Dewey 1938,
> LW12:13)

> My problem is rather this: what rules of right are implemented
> by the relations of power in the production of discourses of
> truth? Or alternately, what type of power is susceptible of
> producing discourses of truth that in a society such as ours are
> endowed with such potent effects? . . . There can be no possible
> exercise of power without a certain economy of discourses of
> truth which operates through and on the basis of this associa-
> tion. We are subjected to the production of truth through
> power and we cannot exercise power except through the
> production of truth. (Foucault 1976, 93)

I

Charles Peirce wrote that few people care to study logic. This still seems
true today. Peirce explained that the reason for this lack of interest is that
people already, if mistakenly, consider themselves proficient in logic. This
explanation now seems false. People today do not refrain from the study of
logic because they believe they already are good at logic. Instead, they don't
study logic because they don't care whether or not they are good at logic.
Logic appears to have no relevance to them. Understanding logic does not

seem necessary or even very helpful for success in real inquiries in agricul-
ture, aeronautics, basketball, business, chemistry, communications, economics, engineering, painting, psychology, law, literature, music, medicine, or any
other field. In short, the study of logic does not appear to be pragmatic.

There is no gap between appearance and reality here. Logic not only
almost always appears irrelevant; it almost always is irrelevant. This judgment may be distressing to logicians, but it should not be surprising. Any
field of study, after all, that tells us that "if 'p' is false, then 'if p, then q' is
true" is a field of study that substantially has parted company with real
investigations that aim at real amelioration of real problems.

In this context, Dewey was right to observe, in the concluding lines of
his *Logic: The Theory of Inquiry,* that the separation of logic from a general
account of the processes for attaining and testing sound beliefs in any field
is a recipe for the intellectual crippling and irrelevance of logic, for inatten-
tion to the cultural consequences of this irrelevance, and for incalculable
cultural waste, confusion, and distortion that result from beliefs supported
by logics independent of the most intelligent methods of inquiry available
at any given present time (1938, LW12:526–27). Dewey had made this same
point more than thirty years earlier in the introduction to his *Essays in Experimental Logic* (1916). Logical theory, he wrote, "is an account of the processes and tools which have actually been found effective in inquiry, com-
prising in the term 'inquiry' both deliberate discovery and deliberate
invention." This view, he added, should eliminate "a lot of epistemological
hangers-on to logic" (MW10:332, 334).

II

Dewey's account of logic as the theory of inquiry and his account of the
nature and pattern of inquiry signaled a far-reaching revolution in logic,
even if this signal has been missed by most professional "logicians" and
epistemological hangers-on preoccupied with truth tables and formal systems, Polish notation, modalities, and possible worlds. While the full ben-
efits of Dewey's revolution may be incalculable, the strengths of this approach are many. They include the following ten points, briefly summarized
below.

First, Dewey's account of logic as the theory of inquiry is *antidualistic.*
Dewey clearly and steadfastly rejected any split or separation between logic
and the actual methods of the currently most intelligent inquiries. He
claimed that ongoing inquiry can develop the logical standards and forms
for further inquiry (1938, LW12:13).

Second, Dewey's view of logic is *antifoundational*. The methodology of Dewey's inquiry has no theoretical foundation or justification independent of inquiry itself. Inquiry, in and over time, is its own justification—a justification that is circular (historically but not viciously), autonomous, self-reconstructing. The only justifications for the methods of a given inquiry are the results of other inquiry. As Dewey argued, as the theory of controlled inquiry, logic is autonomous and does not rest on metaphysical and epistemological assumptions or perspectives.

Third, this account of logic is *antiabstractionist*. Knowledge, Dewey held, is just the general name of, and for, the results of particular inquiries. These inquiries always arise within particular contexts, times, and places. This is true for the knowledges that are the results of these inquiries. Moreover, there is no other knowledge, no knowledge unmediated by inquiry (1938, LW12:14).

Fourth, Dewey's view of logic is *antistatic*. It is, Dewey said, a progressive discipline. Logic is not fixed or final because inquiry is unfinished, ongoing, progressive, open to modification and abandonment. It is no more closed than the open universe that constitutes its subject. There is no guarantee, Dewey wrote, that the conclusion of an inquiry will remain settled: "The attainment of settled beliefs is a progressive matter; there is no belief so settled as not to be exposed to further inquiry" (1938, LW12:16).

Fifth, logic is *operational*. The subject matter of logic is determined operationally. Facts are not fixed or merely given; they are always in the process of being determined and becoming determinate. Fact finding is fact fixing. It takes place or operates from, and with, a goal or purpose. Accordingly, logical forms, Dewey claimed, are postulational. Similarly, essences and accidents have only functional, not ontological, status. To be essential is simply to be indispensable in a particular inquiry; to be accidental is to be unimportant relative to that inquiry (1938, LW12:141). Inquiry arises from within, and in turn establishes, the continuity of experience and nature: "There is no breach of continuity between operations of inquiry and biological operations and physical operations" and "Rational operations grow out of organic activities, without being identical with that from which they emerge" (LW12:26).

Sixth, logic is the theory of inquiry understood as *reconstructive*. Inquiry is *existentially transformative*. It remakes the material with which it deals. Accordingly, objects of knowledge are results, not antecedents, of inquiries—just as William James recognized truth (verity) to be the result or consequence of a process of verification. Truth, knowledge, and justification thus are mediated rather than immediate, consequences rather than starting points, effects. Logical forms thus originate in, and are produced by, inquiry. And in turn, inquiry is a power: "There is no inquiry that does not involve the making of *some* change in environing conditions" (1938, LW12:41). This view of inquiry as power to reconstruct or as control of transformation lies at the heart of Dewey's famous definition: "Inquiry is the controlled or directed transformation of an indeterminate situation into one that is so determinate in its constituent distinctions and relations as to convert the elements of the original situation into a unified whole" (LW12:108). This focus on control and power parallels Dewey's earlier thesis that "thinking is instrumental to a control of the environment, a control effected through acts which would not be undertaken without the prior resolution of a complex situation into assured elements and an accompanying projection of possibilities—without, that is to say, thinking" (1916, MW10:338).

Seventh, as the theory of inquiry, logic is *temporal*. As Dewey noted, inquiry and judgment are temporal not only in the external sense of taking time but also in an internal sense: "Its subject matter undergoes reconstruction in attaining the final state of determinate resolution and unification" (1938, LW12:137). This subject matter is thus irreducibly relative to time—and to a span of time rather than a single moment, since inquiry cannot be instantaneous (LW12:136).

Eighth, this temporality of inquiry replaces concern for truth with *concern for warrant*, just as, in another context, taking time seriously replaces concern for the good with concern for particular ends in view (Stuhr 1997, 181–204). Taken in the abstract, knowledge simply is "warranted assertibility," and "logical forms accrue in and because of control that yields conclusions which are warrantably asssertible" (Dewey 1938, LW12:16, 29). While this understanding may highlight the contingency of the results of any given inquiry, this contingency is not mere arbitrariness. (When this point is missed, "we pragmatists" may turn to illusions of pure self-creation and open choices of vocabularies and descriptions. In contrast, Dewey noted that real confusions and real conflicts, like the real selves involved in them, exist prior to a given inquiry and are not simply created or chosen.)

Ninth, this theory of logic is *interdisciplinary* in its orientation. As such, it stands in sharp contrast to the familiar compartmentalized, departmentalized, supposedly mutually independent disciplines and areas of investigation. Dewey observed that there is "an urgent need for breaking down these conceptual barriers so as to promote cross-fertilization of ideas, and greater scope, variety, and flexibility of hypotheses" (1938, LW12:501–2). This is a point that pragmatist philosophers would do well to acknowledge—and acknowledge in practice as well as theory. It may be lost, for example, when they contribute essays (by and principally for philosophers) about a phi-

losopher who urged philosophers to turn away from the problems of philosophers and instead turn toward the real problems and real inquiries of
persons.

The subject matter of logic is determined operationally. These operations
constitute existential reconstructions or transformations. When these transformations produce control, they yield warranted conclusions. And these
conclusions are irreducibly temporal. This perspective allows, even leads
to, a tenth point about inquiry and its origins, operations, products, and
formalizations. Logic, as the theory of inquiry, is *contextual*. This context,
Dewey stressed in early chapters of his *Logic*, is biological and cultural (and
it is in this cultural context, and in his account of the role of reasoning in
his "pattern of inquiry," that Dewey detailed the special significance of language). In other words, inquiry is not an exercise in pure reason. It is impure, intrinsically and irreducibly situated. It always arises from, empow-
ers, and constitutes selective interests: "Neither inquiry nor the most
abstractly formal set of symbols can escape from the cultural matrix in
which they live, move, and have their being" (1938, LW12:28). "All inquiry,"
Dewey wrote, "proceeds within a cultural matrix which is ultimately determined by the nature of social relations" (LW12:481).

III

At the beginning of "Social Inquiry," the twenty-fourth and penultimate
chapter of his 1938 *Logic*, Dewey stressed again this contextual character of
logic. He put it succinctly: "The impact of cultural conditions upon social
inquiry is obvious" (LW12:482). This is both true and false. It is true in the
sense that it is obvious that cultural conditions impact all social inquiry.
Indeed, Dewey claimed that cultural conditions constitute the existential
matrix of all inquiry. However, it is false to view as obvious the role of
culture on inquiry in the sense that it is not at all obvious *what or how* particular cultural conditions impact particular social inquiries.

To inquire, for Dewey, is to control and direct. To inquire is to exercise
power. So what, then, is the impact of cultural conditions on the exercise of
power that is inquiry?

Do cultural conditions distort, stall, or prevent inquiry? At times, Dewey
appears to have set forth this view. For example, the last chapter of the
Logic surveys the ways in which previous philosophies (i.e., philosophies
prior to Dewey's own philosophy) distort the nature of inquiry by "one-
sided emphasis" and "selective extraction of some conditions and some factors from the actual pattern of controlled inquiry" (1938, LW12:507). The

history of epistemology is a history of this distortion, a history of the fallacy of selective emphasis (1925, LW1:34), a history of theory having parted company with practice. Dewey wrote: "Because they [epistemologies] are not constructed upon the ground of operations and conceived in terms of their actual procedures and consequences, they are necessarily formed in terms of preconceptions derived from various sources, mainly cosmological in ancient and mainly psychological (directly or indirectly) in modern theory" (1938, LW12:526–27).

This criticism of earlier philosophers is troubling. Dewey did not advance it as a prelude to a critical examination of his own selective emphases, his own special interests, or his own side of the story. Indeed, he does not identify his own selective emphasis or even admit its existence, recognized or unrecognized. Instead, he suggests that his *Logic* is a theory set forth without selective emphasis, a theory based "inclusively and exclusively upon the operations of inquiry" (LW12:527). This realistic view of the operations of inquiry as facts waiting to be found, rather than facts fixed by the operations of still other, earlier inquiries, is at odds with the operational account of inquiry central to the *Logic*. It is also at odds with Dewey's view in *Experience and Nature* that selective emphasis is inevitable whenever reflection takes place and is an evil only when its presence is concealed or denied.

Dewey expressed at length this same view with specific reference to logic. In *Essays in Experimental Logic*, he wrote:

Now, it is an old story that philosophers, in common with theologians and social theorists, are as sure that personal habits and interests shape their opponents' doctrines as they are that their own beliefs are "absolutely" universal and objective in quality. Hence arises that dishonesty, that insincerity characteristic of philosophic discussion. . . . Now the moment the complicity of the personal factor in our philosophic valuations is recognized, is recognized fully, frankly, and generally, that moment a new era in philosophy will begin. We shall have to discover the personal factors that now influence us unconsciously, and begin to accept a new and moral responsibility for them, a responsibility for judging and testing them by their consequences. So long as we ignore this factor, its deeds will be largely evil, not because *it* is evil, but because, flourishing in the dark, it is without responsibility and without check. The only way to control it is by recognizing it. (1916, MW4:113–14)

The "personal factor," ignored and unchecked in the *Logic* and still in need of recognition, is the belief that personal factors are not at work in the revolutionary theory of inquiry set forth. Dewey's inquiry into inquiry is neither impersonal nor disinterested.

Dewey's discussion of prejudice is a second example of viewing cultural conditions as distortions or blocks to inquiry. He noted that "prejudices of race, nationality, class and sect play such an important role [on social inquiry] that their influence is seen by any observer of the field" (1938, LW12:482). The impact of these prejudices on inquiry is surely immense, and we might add additional prejudices to the list: gender, sexual orientation, age, disability, ethnicity, and species. However, all this begs the question: When is a difference in believing or a difference in living a "prejudice"? The point is this: The impact of prejudice on inquiry is no doubt massive, but this impact may well not be seen by those observers who share the prejudice in question and who thus may view the prejudice as warranted. As Dewey noted, if we don't see that the conditioning of prejudice exists in our own cases, this failure is "due to an illusion of perspective" (1938, LW12:482). For example, are scientism or positivism or realism prejudices? Are operationalism or instrumentalism or empiricism prejudices? Is social inquiry, inquiry into human relations, as "backward" as Dewey lamented, or is this judgment of backwardness conditioned by prejudices about the nature of advance and success? Dewey's on-target recognition of the general impact of prejudice on inquiry is not followed by a needed first step toward a hermeneutic rehabilitation of prejudice and the circularity of inquiry. Rather, it is a misstep in the general direction of the illusion of the possibility of inquiry free of all prejudice. And it is a missed opportunity for reflection on the power of practices of inquiry, prejudice, and warrant to constitute our selves.

These problems are avoided if one sees the impact of cultural conditions on inquiry in a different way—not as distorting or blocking inquiry, but as constituting and determining it in specific and different ways in specific and different contexts. In much of the *Logic*, Dewey appears to champion this view. Dewey repeatedly stressed that inquiry is neither abstract nor static; it is operational and contextual. And Dewey set forth this same view in his earlier work on logic: Inquiry always has a particular purpose, and its success always is a function of particular conditions (1916, MW10:327).

However, this view is in considerable tension with Dewey's well-known and central account of the common "pattern of inquiry." Dewey wrote that all "inquiry has a common structure or pattern," despite the diversity of its subject matters and diversity of techniques for dealing with these subjects (1938, LW12:105). According to this pattern, an original indeterminate situation is transformed into a problem by means of reasoning that controls

the operation of facts and meanings so as to generate and assess a solution
to the problem that produces a new, determinate, unified situation.

This general account of inquiry, this account of the general or common
pattern of inquiry, readily appears to de-contextualize inquiry and thus appears counter to much of the rest of the *Logic*. This was not, I think, Dewey's
intent. And it need not necessarily be the result. However, because of what
Dewey does not say, it frequently is the result. Dewey characterizes the
cultural matrix of inquiry in terms of shared meanings, common purposes,
and conjoint activities. As a result, differences (sometimes to the point of
oppositions and conflict) in problems, goals, strategies, meanings, operations, and resolutions are omitted from the matrix of inquiry. Dewey simply does not pay any sustained attention to them, though he could have
done so. Instead, he characterizes inquiry as "objective" only to the extent
that subjectivity, difference, and plurality are eliminated. (It is interesting
to note that Dewey here, unlike most of his work, employs a standard, traditional philosophical dualism—subjectivity versus objectivity—without
undercutting it.)

This apparent de-contextualization of logic is everywhere evident in
Dewey's account of this general pattern of inquiry. For example, he claimed:

> We know that some methods of inquiry are better than others in just the
> same way we know that some methods of surgery, farming, road-making,
> navigating, or what-not are better than others. (1938, LW12:108)

> *We* are doubtful because the situation is inherently doubtful. (LW12:109)

> To mistake the problem involved is to cause subsequent inquiry to be irrel-
> evant or to go astray. . . . The way in which the problem is conceived de-
> cides what specific suggestions are entertained and which are dismissed.
> (LW12:112)

> If we assume, prematurely, that the problem involved is definite and clear,
> subsequent inquiry proceeds on the wrong track. (LW12:112)

> In many familiar situations, the meaning that is most relevant has been
> settled because of the eventuations of experiments in prior cases so that it is
> applicable almost immediately upon its occurrence. (LW12:116)

> In regulated inquiry facts are selected and arranged with the express intent
> of fulfilling this office [of resolving a difficulty]. (LW12:116)

For things exist *as* objects for us only as they have been previously determined as outcomes of inquiries. (LW12:122)

Compare Foucault: "In the end, we are judged, condemned, classified, determined in our undertakings, destined to a certain mode of living or dying, as a function of the true discourses which are the bearers of the specific effects of power" (Foucault 1976, 93). The *Logic* readily can seem to plaster a big yellow and black happy face on Foucault's genealogies of power. It does this by means of mere stipulation. Anything that does not exhibit the prescribed pattern of inquiry thus is not defined or classified as inquiry—and by means of unexamined circularity, it is a summary generalization of features found in particular inquiries that, in turn, are identified as such by presupposing the pattern of inquiry. As a result, inquiry is de-politicized and de-pluralized—and, so, de-contextualized.

The pattern of inquiry, abstract and universal, appears to presuppose abstract, universal subjects ("we," "us") who do not stand to one another in relations of difference, opposition, or power, but instead experience common indeterminacies, institute shared problems on the basis of shared past inquiries, and approach the present with shared purposes and selectivities. Thus Dewey talked confidently about the indeterminate situation that *we* experience, but he never asks the relevant political questions: Who is "we"? Whose situation is indeterminate? How was this indeterminate situation produced? By whom? In the service of what interests? What are the consequences of this indeterminate situation's arising? For whom are these consequences? What happens when some persons experience a situation as indeterminate and others do not? Through what cultural institutions, practices, and relations is a situation defined as indeterminate for some but not others, and what interests, values, truths are produced by this?

Similar questions and omissions confront the pattern of inquiry account of the institution of a problem. A problem may be instituted, but who is empowered to define the nature of the problem, to determine the way a problem is conceived, to decide whether a problem is posed with sufficient clarity? What happens when different persons or different groups or different cultures define different problems? How does the control of the formulation of problems produce, or reproduce, certain subjects, truths, meanings, and values?

Who gets to "operationally institute" the consequences of action? What is presupposed, created, and excluded in this process?

These questions and concerns are not just theoretical. Is a military group a bunch of criminals and terrorists or a band of freedom fighters? Is a new world order really an order at all? Is a conversation at work harmless flirting or sexual harassment? Is a fetus a person or not? Does the execution of a murderer establish a newly unified and determinate situation? What methods of farming are better than others?

These kinds of questions point to real flaws in Dewey's *Logic*. As omissions, these flaws need not be fatal—that is, they need not be fatal if it is possible to effect a genuine transformation of the *Logic*. This transformation would begin not with the claim that the social inquiries are branches of natural science because their subject matters are existential (1938, LW12:481). Instead, it would begin with the recognition that all inquiries, including those of natural and social sciences, are branches of criticism because their operations involve value judgments. In turn, this recognition would require an account not of a single, abstract pattern of inquiry. Instead, it would require multiple genealogies of particular inquiries, genealogies that focus on the productions of economies of warranted assertions.

Of course, disciples of Dewey's *Logic* will be quick to rise to its defense, claiming either that a logic need not address these issues or that Dewey already did so. This itself is a problem for further inquiry (and here I share Dewey's meliorism). The point here, of course, is not that Dewey's general account of logic cannot address these issues or that its ten basic strengths are incompatible with doing so. Instead, the point is that Dewey did not sufficiently acknowledge or address these issues. Doing so effects a reconstruction, a transformation, of his logic.

Along the way, these genealogies would pause at two important points. First, if the *Logic* is a recipe for thinking in shared, warranted ways, is it also a recipe for living in shared, approved ways? Is the practical (if unintentional) effect of a pattern of inquiry the production of shared indeterminate situations, shared instituted problems, and shared operations toward their resolution? If inquiry just simply shows us that some methods of farming are better than others, does it show us that some methods of living are better than others? Does it lead to agreement about what kinds of living count as being "better"? Second, is the most important task for any logic today the production of determinate, unified situations, or is it the multiplication of indeterminate situations and problems, the creation of a more fully pluralistic universe? These pauses are opportunities for epistemological and logical hangers-on finally to let go.

Works Cited

Dewey, John. 1916. *Essays in Experimental Logic.* Chicago: University of Chicago Press. Essays reprinted separately in MW1, 2, 4, 6, 8, 10.

———. 1925. *Experience and Nature*. Chicago: Open Court. Reprinted in LW1.

———. 1938. *Logic: The Theory of Inquiry*. New York: Henry Holt. Reprinted in LW12.

Foucault, Michel. 1976. Two Lectures. In *Power/Knowledge*. New York: Pantheon Books.

Stuhr, John J. 1997. *Genealogical Pragmatism: Philosophy, Experience, and Community*. Albany: State University of New York Press.

About the Authors

Thomas Alexander is professor at Southern Illinois University at Carbondale. He is the author of *John Dewey's Theory of Art, Experience, and Nature: The Horizons of Feeling* and coeditor with Larry Hickman of *The Essential Dewey*. In addition to articles on Dewey, he has published work on Native American philosophy, Santayana, aesthetics, and classical philosophy. He is currently exploring the possibility of an ecological ontology, making use of Madhyamaka as well as pragmatic-naturalist thought, which he is integrating with his previous philosophical anthropology of the Human Eros.

Douglas Browning, professor emeritus of philosophy at the University of Texas at Austin, is the author of *Act and Agent* and *Ontology and the Practical Arena* and the coeditor (with William Myers) of *Philosophers of Process*. Recent projects regarding Dewey's philosophy include the introduction to the new critical edition of *The Influence of Darwin on Philosophy and Other Essays in Contemporary Thought* and research (initiated at the Center for Dewey Studies as the Democracy and Education Fellow for 2000) into the significant shift in emphasis around 1930 in Dewey's philosophy.

Tom Burke is assistant professor of philosophy at the University of South Carolina. He is the author of *Dewey's New Logic: A Reply to Russell*. He continues to pursue interests in Dewey's philosophy of logic, recently writing introductions to new editions of Ralph Sleeper's *The Necessity of Pragmatism* and Dewey's *Essays in Experimental Logic*.

John Capps is assistant professor of philosophy at the Rochester Institute of Technology. He has published articles on naturalism, Dewey's epistemology, and feminism. He is currently working on the connection between contextualist theories of justification and naturalized epistemology.

Vincent Colapietro is professor of philosophy at Pennsylvania State University. His principal area of historical expertise is classical American pragmatism. He is a coeditor of the *Journal of Speculative Philosophy*. In addition, he is the author of *Peirce's Approach to the Self* , *A Glossary of Semiotics*, and *The Fateful Shapes of Human Freedom: An Introduction to John William Miller*. He edited *Peirce's Doctrine of Signs,* Vincent Potter's essays in *Peirce's Philosophical Perspectives*, and *Reason, Experience, and God: John E. Smith in Dialogue*. His present work, growing out of earlier explorations of subjectivity, is exploring the possible intersection between pragmatism and psychoanalysis.

Michael Eldridge, who teaches at the University of North Carolina at Charlotte, is the author of *Transforming Experience: John Dewey's Cultural Instru mentalism*. In 1999 Eldridge was selected as the first Democracy and Education Fellow of the Center for Dewey Studies. Eldridge is currently expanding his interest in Dewey's social and political philosophy into research in American philosophical naturalism, one product of which is a chapter on naturalism in the forthcoming *Blackwell's Guide to American Philosophy*.

D. Micah Hester is assistant professor of biomedical ethics and humanities at Mercer University's School of Medicine. The current volume marks Hester's second collaboration with Robert Talisse, a team whose first effort resulted in a scholarly edition of John Dewey's *Essays in Experimental Logic*. Hester is also the author of *Community as Healing: Pragmatist Ethics in Medical Encounters* and coeditor of *Computer and Ethics in the Cyberage* as well as *William Ernest Hocking: A Reader*.

Sandra B. Rosenthal, Provost Distinguished Professor of Philosophy at Loyola University, New Orleans, has published eleven books and approximately 175 articles on various aspects of American pragmatism, and she has lectured on pragmatism in China, Poland, and Germany. She is on the editorial boards of numerous journals and book series, and has served as president of several philosophical societies, including the Society for the Advancement of American Philosophy, the Metaphysical Society of America, and the Charles Peirce Society.

Hans Seigfried is professor of philosophy at Loyola University. His recent research and publications focus on systematic connections between German philosophy and American pragmatism.

John R. Shook is assistant professor of philosophy at Oklahoma State University, where he teaches American philosophy, philosophy of mind, and epistemology. His most recent book is *Dewey's Empirical Theory of Knowledge and Reality*, and he edits two book series, Studies in Pragmatism and Values and Pragmatism and American Thought. Shook is also director of the Pragmatism Archive at OSU and webmaster of the Pragmatism Cybrary.

John J. Stuhr heads the philosophy department at Penn State University. His publications include *Genealogical Pragmatism: Philosophy, Experience, and Community*; *John Dewey*; *Pragmatism and Classical American Philosophy*; and *Philosophy and the Reconstruction of Culture: Pragmatic Essays after Dewey*. He is the coeditor of the book series Studies in American and European Philosophy and the *Journal of Speculative Philosophy*, and he is completing a book on Dewey's view of experience and another on pragmatism and postmodernism.

Robert Talisse is assistant professor of philosophy at Vanderbilt University. He is the editor (with D. Micah Hester) of a scholarly reprint of Dewey's *Essays in Experimental Logic* and the author of *On Dewey: The Reconstruction of Philosophy*. His current work is focused on contemporary liberalism and deliberativist theories of democracy.

Jayne Tristan is a lecturer in philosophy at University of North Carolina at Charlotte. She is writing and classroom testing a logic text based on Dewey's 1938 *Logic*.

Jennifer Welchman is an associate professor of philosophy at the University of Alberta. She is the author of *Dewey's Ethical Thought* and has published articles in the history of moral philosophy and environmental ethics. Her current research is focused on development of pragmatic approaches to virtue ethics.

Name Index

Subject Index

147, 171, 191, 195, 209, 213, 215, 218, 229, 270–71, 277
future, 13, 21, 37, 39, 46, 66, 68, 105
fuzzy: assignment, 131; class, 126, 137, 150; function, 137; ideology, 141; logic, 121, 131, 141; ontology, 141; relation, 126; set theory, 121, 126, 131, 141; situation, 126; world-view, 141

game: rule, 148–49; semantic, 148–49; -theoretical semantics, 121, 148–49
general: conception, 182; fact, 127–28; perspective, 251–52; proposition, 107, 110, 128, 152–53, 168, 182; schema, 83; term, 230
generalization, 44, 53, 55, 208, 212, 219, 226, 267, 283; empirical, 86, 88; inductive, xiii, 225, 233; universal, 212
generic: kind, 213, 216, 222; proposition, 107, 110, 128, 152–53, 211, 216, 229; trait, 195, 203, 208–11, 215–16, 219–22
genetic: continuity, 102; fallacy, 7; form, 62; logic, 52, 56, 61, 63; method, 7, 15, 51–52, 61, 63, 134–35, 229; process, 7
geometry, 206–7
given, 34, 81, 124, 170, 277; emergence of, 77; evidence, 33, 256; facts, 271, 277; immediate, xvi
goal, 197, 252–53, 277; -directed interaction, 105; epistemic, 241–42, 246; ethical, 249; instrumental, 242; non-epistemic, 249, 253; normative, 246; of inquiry, 28, 58, 131, 176, 239–50, 254, 258, 268; political, 249; practical, 247–49; shared, 243; unrealizable, 34, 196
God, 11–12, 23, 255–57, 260
good, 23, 30, 278; definition of, 30, 36; experience of, 36; thing, 30
gradation, serial, 203–4
grammar, 221; formal, 108; generative, 121, 129–31, 140, 151–53; mathematical, 128; of facts, 125–31, 146–49; of hypotheses, 137–38; X-bar, 129–30, 151–52

growth, 47, 67, 184–85, 277; intellectual, 182; of abilities, 134–35; of inquiry, 244; of knowledge, 97, 101; of science, 182; process, 14
grue, 225, 231–34
guiding: assumption, 247; methodology, 247; principle, xvi, 175–76, 180, 193, 231

habit, xi, 68, 82–87, 90, 134–35, 186, 188–93, 280; as tool, 95; cultivated, 188, 192; of inference, 192; social, 134; transmission, 186
hermeneutic, 281
heuristic, 66, 215–16; function, 47; practice, 47–48, 57, 63; tool, 47, 58–59
history, 52, 60, 164; natural, xix, 7, 13–16, 21, 43, 45, 48, 53, 56–57, 63, 68, 134–35, 229; of epistemology, 280; of experience, 63; of forms, 57; of logic, vii, 53–54; of philosophy, 5, 8–9, 19, 198; of science, xvii, xviii, 182
holism, 96, 124; constructivist, 252
horizon: of experience, 172, 174; temporal, 171–172
humanism, 4, 14
hypostatized: being, 23; essence, 221; form, 187, 221; function, 179; relation, 218
hypothesis, xix, 33–35, 39, 96, 107–8, 155, 161, 177–78, 205–6, 216, 226, 278; abstract, 137–43; empirical, 87; formation, xvii; grammar of, 137–38; plurality of, 245
hypothetico-deductive method, 96

idea, 15, 68, 133–35, 151, 155, 190–91, 217, 229, 266; abstract, 228–31; instrumental, 136; Lockean, 14; ruling, 180; system of, 136, 141
ideal, 11, 22, 51, 65–68; democratic, 272; form, 22; knower, 21–22; self, 11; unrealizable, 34
idealism, xiii, xix, 4–5, 9, 12, 15–16, 20–21, 28–33, 78–79, 99–100, 104; absolute, 6–7, 100–1; American, 3; critical, 78; dynamic, 3, 9; experimental, 6, 8; metaphysical, 6; psychological, 10; rationalistic, 101;

Subject Index

idealism, *continued*
  scientific, 3, 98; subjective, 101;
  theological, 3; transcendental, 14
ideational: content, 121–23, 227, 231;
  material, 121–24, 133–55, 228–29;
  proposition, 82, 151
identity, xix, 21, 139–40, 168, 194; fixed,
  22
ideology, 67, 135–38, 140, 143, 154–55;
  crisp, 141; fuzzy, 141; rigid, 141;
  structure of, 141; -type, 136–37, 140,
  143, 151, 154
illative: process, 60; relation, 61
illusion, 61, 64, 102, 105, 278, 281
imagination, 10, 21, 61, 98, 107, 113, 211;
  mathematical, 62
immediate: actuality, 60; apparency, 20;
  cognition, 31; empiricism, xvi, 9–18,
  101–5, 112, 115; existence, 60;
  experience, 20, 73, 124, 169, 172;
  given, xvi; insight, 32; judgment, 32;
  knowledge, 79, 277; outcome, 228;
  quality, 169, 210; reference, 142;
  situation, 143; truth, 277; whole, 154,
  169
impartiality, 66, 265, 268–71
imperative: hypothetical, 29; pragmatic,
  76–77
implication, 28, 35, 39, 76–77, 80, 82,
  137, 139, 208, 211, 220; material, 75;
  relation, 87; strict, 75
improper: assumption, 172; characterization, 173, 175, 179; designation,
  172; importation, 170–74
indeterminacy, xv, xxi, 68, 88–89, 125–
  26, 131, 165, 169–73, 176–77, 183,
  197, 265, 278, 281, 284; common, 283;
  of translation, 114; principle of, 197;
  quality of, 161
individual, 132, 135, 147, 182, 251;
  action, 122; agent, 132; consciousness, 10–11; development, 182, 185;
  judgment, 208, 213; mind, 102, 133;
  object, 22, 85, 128, 219, 226–29;
  proposition, 107; self, 133; sensation,
  117; situation, xvi, 124, 154, 170, 176,
  203, 209, 222–23; subject-matter, 208
individualism, 147

induction, xiii, xvii, xx, 33, 35, 85, 87,
  122, 212–15, 226; justified, 225, 231;
  methods of, 228–33; principles of,
  232–33; problem of, xii, 214, 225–35
inductive: argument, 225; confirmation,
  225; generalization, xiii, 225, 233;
  inference, xvii, 35, 122, 212, 215, 225–
  26, 231–34; logic, 232; methods, 228–
  33; reasoning, 33, 35; stability, 214;
  technique, 231
inference, xiv, xix, 28, 33, 35, 39, 45, 48,
  59, 61, 64–65, 68, 75–76, 84–85, 124,
  183, 189, 193, 220, 228; abductive,
  xvii; act of, 60, 62; anchored, 219; as
  doing, 62; controlled, 216, 243;
  deductive, xvii, xix, 76, 213–16;
  dialectical, 181, 194; directed, 216;
  good vs. bad, 225; habits of, 95, 192;
  inductive, xvii, 35, 122, 212, 215,
  225–26, 231–34; instruments of, 60;
  justified, 37, 193, 231; patterns of, 43;
  practical, 29; pragmatic, 40; process,
  53, 60–61, 181, 194; rational, 233;
  regulated, 221–23; secure, 40, 51, 63,
  202–23; statistical, 215, 220; valid,
  221
infinity, 11, 16–17
information, 125–26, 189, 197, 205;
  management, 131
inquiry, xv–xvi, 17, 20, 46, 49, 73, 81, 95,
  110, 112, 115, 123–24, 127, 129, 136,
  141, 144, 154–55, 169, 171, 191, 197–
  98, 206–7, 218, 229, 235, 239, 244,
  275, 280; abstract, 281; actual, xvi,
  xviii–xix; as aesthetic, 22; as
  analysis, 183; as experience, 171; as
  power, 275–84; backward, 281;
  circular, 164, 178, 281; closure of, 17,
  241, 277; common-sense, 242;
  community of, 246; conditions for,
  180, 182; contextual, 281, 283;
  continuity of, xviii, 166, 179, 182–88,
  192, 195, 198; control of, 249;
  controlled, xvi, xx, 162, 166–69, 180–
  85, 188–89, 194, 199, 267, 277, 279,
  282; cooperative, 66, 132; definition
  of, 262; development of, 74, 123,
  134–38, 141–42, 151, 163, 166, 186,